David Rubin was until his recent retirement Deputy General Counsel of the National Education Association and also served as counsel to NEA's Kate Frank/DuShane Unified Legal Services Program—a fund established for the protection of the rights of teachers. He has appeared in and argued cases involving the constitutional rights of teachers before the federal appellate courts, including the Supreme Court. Before his association with the NEA, Rubin was on the staff of the Civil Rights Division of the U.S. Justice Department and later became Deputy General Counsel and Acting General Counsel of the U.S. Commission on Civil Rights.

Steven Greenhouse is a reporter for *The New York Times*. He is a graduate of the New York University School of Law and the Columbia University Graduate School of Journalism and has clerked for a federal judge in New York City. His father is a high-school teacher.

Other Bantam Books in the series
Ask your bookseller for the books you have missed

QUANTITY PURCHASES

AN AMERICAN CIVIL LIBERTIES UNION HANDBOOK

THE RIGHTS OF TEACHERS

THE BASIC ACLU GUIDE TO A TEACHER'S CONSTITUTIONAL RIGHTS

REVISED EDITION

DAVID RUBIN
WITH
STEVEN GREENHOUSE

General Editor of this series:
~~Norman Dorsen, President, ACLU~~

BANTAM BOOKS
TORONTO · NEW YORK · LONDON · SYDNEY

THE RIGHTS OF TEACHERS
*A Bantam Book / published by arrangement with
the American Civil Liberties Union*

Bantam edition / January 1984

ISBN 0-553-23655-5

Published simultaneously in the United States and Canada

*Bantam Books are published by Bantam Books, Inc. Its trademark, consisting
of the words "Bantam Books" and the portrayal of a rooster, is Registered in
U.S. Patent and Trademark Office and in other countries. Marca Registrada.
Bantam Books, Inc., 666 Fifth Avenue, New York, New York 10103.*

PRINTED IN THE UNITED STATES OF AMERICA

O O 9 8 7 6 5 4 3 2 1

Dedication

To Julie, Suzie, and Emmy

Acknowledgments
for the Second Edition

We are indebted to Michael H. Gottesman, Robert Weinberg, Julia Penny Clark, David Silberman, Gary Sasso, Jerry D. Anker, Stephen J. Pollak, and Richard Sharp for many of the ideas and much of the analysis contained in this book. We would also like to thank Matthew Horowitz, Faith Hanna, Lawrence Dessem, and Joy Koletsky for making helpful comments and suggestions.

Contents

Preface

This guide sets forth your rights under the present law, and offers suggestions on how they can be protected. It is one of a continuing series of handbooks published in cooperation with the American Civil Liberties Union (ACLU).

Surrounding these publications is the hope that Americans, informed of their rights, will be encouraged to exercise them. Through their exercise, rights are given life. If they are rarely used, they may be forgotten and violations may become routine.

This guide offers no assurances that your rights will be respected. The laws may change and, in some of the subjects covered in these pages, they change quite rapidly. An effort has been made to note those parts of the law where movement is taking place, but it is not always possible to predict accurately when the law *will* change.

Even if the laws remain the same, their interpretations by courts and administrative officials often vary. In a federal system such as ours, there is a built-in problem of state and federal law, not to speak of the confusion between states. In addition, there are wide variations in the ways in which particular courts and administrative officials will interpret the same law at any given moment.

If you encounter what you consider to be a specific abuse of your rights, you should seek legal assistance. There are a number of agencies that may help you, among them, ACLU affiliate offices, but bear in mind that the ACLU is a limited-purpose organization. In many communities, there are federally funded legal service offices which provide assistance to persons who cannot afford the costs of legal representation. In general, the rights that the ACLU defends are freedom of inquiry and expression; due process of law; equal protection of the laws; and privacy. The authors in this series have discussed other rights (even though they sometimes fall outside the ACLU's usual concern) in order to provide as much guidance as possible.

These books have been planned as guides for the people directly affected; therefore, the question and answer format.

(In some areas there are more detailed works available for "experts.") These guides seek to raise the major issues and inform the nonspecialist of the basic law on the subject. The authors of these books are themselves specialists who understand the need for information at "street level."

If you encounter a specific legal problem in an area discussed in one of these handbooks, show the book to your attorney. Of course, he or she will not be able to rely exclusively on the handbook to provide you with adequate representation. But if your attorney hasn't had a great deal of experience in the specific area, the handbook can provide helpful suggestions on how to proceed.

Norman Dorsen, President
American Civil Liberties Union

Introduction

This book deals with those rights which the Constitution of the United States confers upon teachers in their relationships with the public educational institutions which employ them. The book also attempts, in Chapter VI, to sketch the principal federal statutes protecting teachers in these relationships— statutes which, like Title VII of the Civil Rights Act of 1964, may afford protections to teachers at private as well as public institutions. Many excellent books and articles—some of which are cited in the Selected Bibliography—have been written concerning these statutes, the regulations implementing them, and the voluminous case law interpreting the statutes and regulations.

In addition to federal constitutional and federal statutory sources, a teacher's rights are defined by his individual contract, any relevant collective agreement, state constitutional and statutory provisions, and policies of his state and local boards of education; also, at the college and university levels institutional policies may provide a faculty member with implied contract and other rights.

Since a teacher's rights may vary according to state laws, local rules, and contractual provisions involved, as well as the interpretations which the courts in his jurisdiction have placed on federal constitutional or statutory provisions, the legal principles applicable to a teacher's problem may differ depending on the school district or institution which employs him. In addition, virtually every case is unique in its facts. Furthermore, there are many cases pending in the courts involving the subject matter of this book, and the law is rapidly changing. Accordingly, this book is not designed to provide the answer to specific difficulties that a teacher may face, but rather as a general guide to developments in the law.

I

General Principles

May a teacher be dismissed, or otherwise penalized by school authorities, because he has exercised a right protected by the United States Constitution?

No. The Supreme Court's decisions make clear that the government may act to protect substantial governmental interests by imposing reasonable restrictions on employee activities that in other contexts might be constitutionally protected.[1] Nevertheless, there are many areas of protected conduct by a teacher for which he may not be fired.[2] Nor may any other penalty—including revocation of a teaching certificate, suspension (with[3] or without[4] loss of pay), reduction in rank or compensation,[5] involuntary transfer to an unwanted position,[6] reprimand,[7] or negative evaluation[8]—be imposed upon a teacher for engaging in such protected conduct. In short, the principle that government may not condition the exercise of a constitutional right "by the exaction of a 'price' "[9] applies to the constitutional rights of public employees. The government may not place such an employee in a worse position than he would have been in if he had not engaged in the constitutionally protected conduct.[10] Independently of this principle, moreover, a sanction imposed by a public employer on one of its employees may be vulnerable to constitutional attack where it has a chilling effect on speech or association.[11]

The same principle that a government employer may not require its employee to pay a price for exercising a constitutional right applies to the withdrawal of a privilege or the denial of a benefit. In 1972 the Supreme Court, in *Perry v. Sindermann*,[12] expressly held in a unanimous opinion that a school system cannot refuse to re-employ a teacher because he has exercised a First Amendment right. The Court said:

> [I]f the government could deny a benefit to a person because of his constitutionally protected speech or associations, his exercise of those freedoms would in effect be penalized and inhibited. This would allow the government to "produce a result which it could not command directly." . . . Such interference with constitutional rights is impermissible.[13]

In addition to re-employment, among the benefits or privileges which school authorities are forbidden to withhold as a price for a teacher's exercise of a constitutional right are tenure,[14] promotion,[15] a discretionary salary raise,[16] teaching summer school,[17] and leave to attend professional meetings.[18]

May a school system refuse to hire a teacher-applicant because he has engaged in constitutionally protected activity?

No. The principle stated in the quotation from *Perry v. Sindermann* cited in the answer to the previous question would bar such a refusal. As Justice Jackson once observed in a concurring opinion: "The fact that one may not have a legal right to get . . . a government post does not mean that he can be adjudged ineligible illegally."[19] Thus the Tenth Circuit has recognized that a board of regents of a public university "could not refuse to hire" an applicant for a faculty position "for a constitutionally impermissible reason."[20]

Can school officials forbid a teacher to engage in conduct which is constitutionally protected, or order him to engage in conduct in which he has a constitutional right not to engage, and then punish him for insubordination if he disobeys?

No. If school authorities cannot constitutionally penalize a teacher for doing or omitting a particular act, they cannot do so indirectly by ordering him to do or omit the act and punishing him for "insubordination" if he refuses to comply.[21]

Where, because a teacher has exercised a constitutional right, school authorities threaten to terminate his employ-

ment and the threat induces him to resign, can he repudiate
the resignation?

Yes. Generally a resignation procured by duress or fraud is
voidable and may be repudiated.[22] This doctrine applies to a
resignation induced by the threat of an unconstitutional
discharge.[23] A coerced resignation also may be treated as a
"constructive" discharge, and accordingly may be subject to
discharge procedures mandated by statute or policy.[24]

**Does a teacher whose employment has been terminated
or who has been disciplined in violation of his constitutional
rights have a right to sue for appropriate relief?**

Yes. The teacher may bring suit under the Civil Rights Act
of 1871 (42 U.S.C. § 1983), which makes the responsible
"person" liable in a suit "at law or in equity," that is to say, in
a suit for monetary or injunctive relief.[25] Teachers need not
exhaust their state administrative remedies before filing a
section 1983 suit in federal court.[26] Section 1983 suits are
most often brought in federal court, but may also be brought
in state court.[27]

**In what circumstances, if any, is a school board consid-
ered a "person" within the meaning of section 1983 so as to
make it amenable to suit?**

In *Monell v. Department of Social Services*,[28] the U.S.
Supreme Court held that the governing body of a school
district, and the members of that body in their official capacities,
are "persons" subject to suit under section 1983, even when
sued for monetary relief payable from the school district's
treasury, where "the action that is alleged to be unconstitutional implements or executes a policy statement, ordinance,
regulation or *decision* officially adopted and promulgated by
the body's officers." School district personnel decisions by
the body entrusted with such decisions (the school board) are
"officially adopted and promulgated."[29] A school board,
moreover, "may be sued for constitutional deprivations visited pursuant to governmental 'custom' even though such a
custom has not received formal approval through the body's
official decisionmaking channels."[30]

A school board, on the other hand, may not be sued under
section 1983 "for an injury inflicted solely by its employees or
agents."[31] While it has been argued that a cause of action

embracing such "vicarious" liability lies directly under the 14th Amendment, the courts in post-*Monell* decisions have not been receptive to this theory.[32]

Is a school board liable under section 1983 where it innocently terminates the employment of a teacher based on an impermissibly motivated recommendation of an administrator such as a principal or superintendent?

In order to establish a claim under section 1983, a plaintiff whose employment has been terminated must prove that constitutionally impermissible considerations "motivated" the termination decision.[33] But where decision-making responsibility is divided, it is possible for such considerations to play a decisive role even if the ultimate decision maker is not aware of them.[34]

Section 1983 provides in pertinent part that—

Every person who, under color of any statute, ordinance, regulation, custom or usage, of any State or Territory, *subjects or causes to be subjected* any citizen of the United States . . . *to the deprivation of any rights* . . . secured by the Constitution . . . *shall be liable* to the party injured in an action at law, suit in equity, or other proper proceeding for redress.[35]

By its terms section 1983 imposes liability on any person who "causes" a U.S. citizen "to be subjected" to a constitutional deprivation. Where, but for the board's act in terminating the plaintiff's employment, the violation, i.e., the termination, would not have occurred, it can be argued that the board, as well as the recommending official, has caused the plaintiff to be subjected to the constitutional deprivation.

In a Sixth Circuit decision a principal recommended that a teacher's contract not be renewed. The recommendation, although based on an admitted "personality conflict" and declining evaluations, was found by the trial court to be a response to, or linked with, the teacher's union activity, in which the teacher had a constitutional right to engage. The court ruled:

The Board members decided not to renew Hickman's contract on the basis of Young's recommendation, who in turn relied on Chestnut. The evidence does not demonstrate that the Board was insulated from the principal's or superintendent's reasoning or that the Board reached its decision on the basis of independent, intervening factors. Where this line of causation exists, and the principal or superintendent predicated their recommendations on constitutionally impermissible reasons, these reasons become the bases of the decision by the Board members.[36]

Several other decisions of U.S. courts of appeals are consistent with this Sixth Circuit ruling.[37] The Fifth Circuit has stated, however, that "to impose liability on a supervisory official, [such as a board or City Council member] section 1983 requires more than a simple ratification of an impermissible act when the ratification is based on legitimate independent reasons."[38]

Does liability under section 1983 extend to an official who recommends an unconstitutional action, as well as to the officials who directly inflict it?

The Act appears to contemplate such liability. Section 1983 imposes liability on any person who "causes to be subjected" any citizen of the United States to a deprivation of a constitutional right.[39] The statutory standard is met by showing "that the official charged acted personally in the deprivation of the plaintiff's rights."[40] The Ninth Circuit has ruled that "[t]he requisite causal connection can be established not only by some kind of direct personal participation in the deprivation, but also by setting in motion a series of acts by others which the actor knows or reasonably should know would cause others to inflict the constitutional injury."[41] Under this standard, and in light of the statutory language, an official with a constitutionally impermissible motive who recommends a course of action which is implemented would appear to be liable under the statute. Thus the Sixth Circuit has ruled that because a superintendent "recommended nonrenewal to the Board and the majority of the Board members acted on the basis of his recommendation, there [was] a sufficient causal connection between [the superintendent's] actions and [the plaintiff's] injury to warrant [the superintendent's] liability."[42] The decisions, however, are in conflict on this issue.[43]

Is a school official liable under section 1983 for his failure to perform a duty if that failure causes the deprivation of a protected right?

Yes. Several decisions have recognized that the section 1983 language "subjects, or causes to be subjected" embraces such a case.[44] A state or local official may be liable under section 1983, for example, where he causes a constitutional deprivation by breaching a duty to train or supervise a subordinate.[45] And several courts have determined that there is a cause of action under section 1983 where the defendant official was in a position of responsibility, knew or should have known of the unconstitutional misconduct of a subordinate, and failed to act to prevent future harm.[46]

Where a teacher, in a suit under section 1983, demonstrates that his exercise of a constitutional right was a substantial factor in the termination of his employment, is he entitled to relief?

In *Mount Healthy Board of Education v. Doyle*,[47] the U.S. Supreme Court ruled that the fact that protected conduct played a "substantial part" in the actual decision not to renew a teacher's contract would not necessarily "amount to a constitutional violation justifying remedial action." The Court held that the burden initially is on the teacher to show that his conduct was constitutionally protected and was a "substantial" or "motivating" factor in the board's decision not to rehire him. Once the teacher carries this burden, the Court ruled, the burden shifts to the board to show by a preponderance of the evidence that it would have reached the same decision on the teacher's re-employment even in the absence of the protected conduct.[48] The Court reasoned:

A rule of causation which focuses solely on whether protected conduct played a part, "substantial" or otherwise, in a decision not to rehire, could place an employee in a better position as a result of the exercise of constitutionally protected conduct than he would have occupied had he done nothing. The difficulty with the rule enunciated by the District Court is that it would require reinstatement in cases where a dramatic and perhaps abrasive incident is inevitably in the minds of those responsible for the decision to rehire, and does indeed play a part in that decision—even if the same decision would have been reached had the incident not occurred. The constitutional principle at stake is sufficiently vindicated if such an employee is placed in no worse a position than if he had not engaged in the conduct. A borderline or marginal candidate should not have the employment question resolved against him because of constitutionally protected conduct. But that same candidate ought not to be able, by engaging in such conduct, to prevent his employer from assessing his performance record and reaching a decision not to rehire on the basis of that record, simply because the protected conduct makes the employer more certain of the correctness of its decision.[49]

Factors that may make it difficult for the board to meet its burden of showing by a preponderance of the evidence that it would have reached the same decision even in the absence of the protected conduct may include evidence that other teachers had engaged in the type of conduct relied upon by the board and had not been similarly treated. Evidence that the conduct relied upon by the board in contending that it would have made the "same decision anyway" was not initially offered as a reason for its decision may also lead a court to reject the board's contention.[50] If the board relies upon alleged misfeasance for its "same decision anyway" contention, its failure to have conducted a thorough investigation may leave the court unconvinced.[51] And where the board's reasons for asserting that it would have reached the "same decision anyway" are "closely linked with, and colored by," its reactions to the teacher's protected activity, the board's proof also may fall short.[52] Where the board relied upon a "personality conflict" and decline in evaluations, both of which "started, grew and resulted from the [principal's and superintendent's] disapproval of some of a teacher's union activities," the Sixth Circuit held that the facts compelled the conclusion that the teacher "would not have been dismissed but for" those activities.[53]

Where a teacher proves that his conduct was both constitutionally protected and a "substantial" or "motivating" factor in the termination of his employment, and the employer fails to carry its burden of proving that the teacher's employment

would have been terminated even in the absence of the protected conduct, is the teacher entitled to reinstatement and back pay?

Since the Constitution bars governmental authorities from exacting a price for the exercise of constitutional rights,[54] it follows logically that where they have attempted to exact such a price—for example, by terminating the employment of a public employee because he has engaged in activity protected by the First Amendment—the victim must be made whole for all losses and restored to the position he would have occupied but for the constitutional violation. The Supreme Court in *Mount Healthy* recognized that the "constitutional principle at stake" requires that a public employee whose employment has been terminated because of protected conduct be "placed in no worse a position than if he had not engaged in the conduct."[55]

Reinstatement with back pay seems generally necessary to ensure that a public employee whose employment has been terminated because he exercised a constitutional right is "placed in no worse a position than if he had not engaged in the protected conduct." Additionally, as the U.S. Court of Appeals for the Fourth Circuit has noted, unless this remedy is afforded, "similar [unconstitutionally motivated terminations] would be encouraged."[56] In cases involving the termination of a public employee's employment because of protected speech, a further rationale for this remedy is that it is necessary to "thaw" the chilling effect of the termination upon free expression by employees fearful that speaking out will endanger their livelihoods. Since courts have stressed the particular importance of free speech among teachers,[57] this rationale seems especially compelling in teacher termination cases.

Most courts have awarded reinstatement with back pay routinely as a remedy for the termination of a public employee's employment in reprisal for exercising a constitutional right. As the Fourth Circuit has stated:

> [W]here there is no lawful basis for the discharge, the plaintiff is entitled to be restored to the position he occupied when he attempted to exercise this constitutionally protected right that led to that discharge. Thus the remedy for constitutionally impermissible discharge from public employment is backpay and reinstatement.[58]

Teacher cases are prominent among the cases in which public employees whose employment has been unconstitutionally terminated have been awarded reinstatement and back pay.[59]

Are there any circumstances in which a court may be justified in withholding the remedy of reinstatement?

Yes, but there is a good basis for arguing that such circumstances should be narrowly limited.

In confronting a stated ground for denying reinstatement, the Supreme Court's decision in *Albemarle Paper Co. v. Moody*[60] may provide guidance. *Albemarle* presented the question whether a district court could deny back pay as a remedy for employment discrimination in violation ot Title VII of the Civil Rights Act of 1964. In addressing this question, the Court identified two central purposes of Title VII: (1) to make persons whole for injuries suffered in violation of the Act, i.e., to restore victims insofar as possible to the positions they would have occupied but for the discrimination; and (2) to deter further violations by employers.[61] The Court concluded that "given a finding of unlawful discrimination, backpay should be denied only for reasons which, if applied generally, would not frustrate the central statutory purposes. . . ."[62] If an analogous rule were applied to First Amendment cases, reinstatement could not be denied for reasons which, if applied generally, would frustrate the purposes which courts have identified as those which should guide relief in cases involving termination of a teacher's employment for exercising First Amendment rights—making the victim whole, deterring future violations of First Amendment rights, and ensuring that other teachers will not be deterred from exercising those rights. Indeed, the Third Circuit has held that there is "no distinction in the law of equitable remedies [including back pay] between suits brought under Title VII and suits brought in reliance on . . . § 1983 . . ."[63]

Under such a rule, where a teacher's speech has been held protected, reinstatement could not be denied because of its nature or tone. Nor could reinstatement be withheld on the ground of anticipated disharmony resulting from the lawsuit. The Fifth Circuit considered the latter issue in *Sterzing v. Fort Bend Independent School District.*[64] In *Sterzing* the district court ruled that a teacher's First Amendment rights had been violated by his discharge. The court awarded damages but denied reinstatement on the ground that reinstatement "would only revive antagonisms." Reversing the denial of reinstatement, the Fifth Circuit stated:

> In declining to grant reinstatement on the basis that it would be too antagonistic, the Court used an impermissible ground. . . . Enforcement of constitutional rights frequently has disturbing consequences. Relief is not restricted to that which will be pleasing and free of irritation.[65]

In an important case following *Sterzing*, the Eleventh Circuit overturned a district court's refusal to reinstate a teacher who was not rehired because he had sent a petition to the state superintendent questioning the board's earmarking of funds. Rejecting the district court's conclusion that reinstatement was inappropriate on the grounds that it would "breed difficult working conditions" and that there was "a lack of mutual trust between" the principal and discharged teacher, the Eleventh Circuit wrote:

> Th[e] rule of presumptive reinstatement is justified by reason as well as precedent. When a person loses his job, it is at best disingenuous to say that money damages can suffice to make that person whole. The psychological benefits of work are intangible, yet they are real and cannot be ignored. Yet at the same time, there is a high probability that reinstatement will engender personal friction of one sort or another in almost every case in which a public employee is discharged for a constitutionally infirm reason. Unless we are willing to withhold full relief from all or most successful plaintiffs in discharge cases, and we are not, we cannot allow actual or expected ill-feeling alone to justify nonreinstatement. We also note that reinstatement is an effective deterrent in preventing employer retaliation against employees who exercise their constitutional rights. If an employer's best efforts to remove an employee for unconstitutional reasons are presumptively unlikely to succeed, there is, of course, less incentive to use employment decisions to chill the exercise of constitutional rights.[66]

Denial of reinstatement based on anticipated disharmony arising from the lawsuit cannot meet the *Albemarle* test. If such a rule were applied generally, reinstatement would be withheld in virtually every case, since litigation is an adversary process which tends to stir up emotions. In addition, it can be argued, it would be unjust to allow school officials to defeat the remedy of reinstatement on the ground that litigation made necessary by their own wrongful action had aroused strong feelings that might cause disharmony upon the plaintiff's return to work.

It has also been held that if authorities fill the position from which the plaintiff was terminated, that is not sufficient reason to deny reinstatement.[67] This conclusion seems consistent with the *Albemarle* test.

Extraordinary cases can arise in which denial of reinstatement because of events occurring after the termination of the teacher's employment may be justified, e.g., the bona fide elimination of the teacher's department for economic reasons or a physical disability rendering him unfit to teach.[68] In such a case denial of reinstatement would not penalize the teacher's pre-termination exercise of First Amendment rights, chill the exercise of First Amendment rights by other teachers, or leave the teacher in a position worse than the position he would have occupied but for the violation.

Presumably, however, reinstatement could not be denied because of post-termination conduct which is protected by the First Amendment. And any rule that would deny reinstatement based on post-termination misconduct arguably must be consistent with the principle that an employee cannot be placed in a worse position because he exercised First Amendment rights than he otherwise would have occupied. If an employee's post-termination conduct, standing alone, would not have caused his employer to fire him, then the failure to reinstate him because of that conduct would penalize him for the fact that he was wrongfully terminated in the first place for exercising his First Amendment rights. It would seem to follow that only where a court can be confident that the post-termination conduct would have led in any case to termination can reinstatement be denied consistently with the First Amendment. And it can be argued that the burden is on the employer to prove that the post-termination conduct would have led to termination in any case.[69]

Finally, even if the post-termination conduct was not protected by the First Amendment, and the employer proves that such conduct would have led to termination in any case, it can be argued that denial of reinstatement is improper where the conduct in question consists of otherwise unprotected expression prompted by a justified sense of indignation stemming from the wrongful termination.[70]

Is a teacher whose employment has been unconstitutionally terminated and who is entitled to reinstatement also entitled to recover his lost wages, i.e., to back pay?

Back pay generally has been awarded as an integral part of the equitable remedy of reinstatement,[71] and the back-pay period fixed as the period between wrongful termination and effective reinstatement.[72] There may be circumstances, however, in which a back-pay award is precluded by the 11th Amendment, which bars any claim for retrospective monetary relief against a state.[73] In its *Mount Healthy* decision the Supreme Court, in holding that a local school board in Ohio was not entitled to such immunity, relied upon the conclusion that "[o]n balance" the record in the case indicated that the school board was "more like a county or city [to which the 11th Amendment does not apply] than . . . like an arm of the state."[74] Since *Mount Healthy*, local school boards and school districts in many states have argued that in light of relevant state law they were entitled to the immunity from retrospective monetary relief provided by the 11th Amendment. The courts have uniformly rejected such arguments.[75]

In the case of public institutions of higher learning, the usual approach of the courts in attempting to determine the status of the institution for 11th Amendment purposes has been to look for indicia of fiscal and academic autonomy. The results have been mixed in light of the differences in such autonomy among public institutions of higher learning.[76]

In its *Monell* decision the Supreme Court held that local government bodies were "persons" suable under section 1983 for injuries inflicted by decisions "officially adopted and promulgated."[77] The Court also held that a school board was not entitled to absolute immunity lest its decision be "drained of meaning." The Court left open, however, and expressed no views upon whether a local government body such as a

school board enjoys "some form of official immunity" shield-
ing it from monetary liability under section 1983.[78]

Subsequently, in *Owen v. City of Independence*,[79] the
Supreme Court, in a 5–4 decision, ruled that a local government body—in that case, a municipality—has no immunity
from liability under section 1983 in connection with its constitutional violations and may not assert the good faith of its
officers as a defense to such liability. The Court rejected the
immunity claim even though the action taken was valid under
then current law and only later determined to be unconstitutional. The principle of the *Owen* decision applies to both
suits for damages and suits for back pay.

**If a teacher would have acquired tenure but for his exer-
cise of a constitutional right, is he entitled to an order of the
court requiring the school authorities to award him tenure
or having the effect of affording such relief?**

Yes. In *Mount Healthy Board of Education v. Doyle*[80] the
Supreme Court recognized that a teacher whose contract was
not renewed because he had exercised his First Amendment
rights would be entitled to be placed in no worse a position
than he would have occupied had he not exercised those
rights. Thus if his contract would have been renewed but for the
constitutional violation, he would be entitled to an award of
reinstatement even though, under state law, reinstatement
would carry with it the status of tenure. Subsequently the
Sixth Circuit concluded that a teacher's contract would have
been renewed but for her protected conduct (union activity),
in circumstances where renewal of her contract would have
given her tenure under Ohio law. The court ordered the
defendant school officials to offer her "reinstatement with a
continuing contract,"[81] i.e., tenure. Similarly, a Virginia federal district court held that a teacher whose contract was not
renewed in violation of her First Amendment free speech
rights, and who otherwise would have attained tenure, was
entitled to reinstatement with tenure, as well as back pay.[82]

However, where an award of tenure would place the plaintiff in a better position than he would have occupied in the
absence of the constitutional violation, a court will deny that
remedy. Thus the Third Circuit has held that an award of
tenure was inappropriate to remedy an unconstitutional refusal to hire, since the court would be granting tenure

without giving the school district any opportunity to evaluate the plaintiff's qualifications and performance as a teacher.[83]

If the teacher has found other employment in the interim, will the earnings from such employment be deducted from any back-pay award?

Yes, unless the interim job could have been held simultaneously with the position from which the teacher was terminated. For example, no deduction would be made for income earned during the summer, or from an evening job that could have been held along with the teaching position.[84]

After being unconstitutionally terminated a teacher may initially find no work or work at a lesser salary, and later obtain employment paying more than the job from which he was terminated. A Texas federal district court, in a case involving multiple teacher plaintiffs, concluded that "had there been no wrongful termination, some of the plaintiffs would, over the years, have obtained positions in which they would have earned more money . . . and would have left [that school district] for better paying jobs." Therefore, the court determined that back-pay should be awarded for the years immediately following termination during which the plaintiff earned less than he earned at the school district which discharged him, and that back-pay would stop running when he obtained a job in which he "consistently" earned more than he did at the school district which terminated his employment. The court also ruled that the back-pay award would not be offset by the incremental earnings from the better-paying job.[85]

Is a teacher whose employment has been unconstitutionally terminated required to seek or accept other employment in order to mitigate his damages?

Yes. One must use reasonable efforts to avoid the consequences of injury caused by another's illegal act.[86]

The burden of proof is on the school authorities to show that (1) suitable alternative employment was available and (2) the teacher failed to make reasonable efforts to obtain it.[87]

Alternative employment is not "suitable" if it is not consistent with the teacher's qualifications and training.[88] For example, a teacher need not accept a job as a short order cook in order to mitigate her damages. Nor is a teacher

bound by the mitigation rule to seek or accept other employment in a locality distant from her place of residence. At least
two courts have ruled that a teacher's duty to mitigate damages does not include an obligation to live away from her
spouse, and that the burden is on the board to prove that the
teacher could have found a teaching position in or near the
community where the teacher's family lived.[89]

A teacher is under no duty to accept an offer of employment from the school district that wrongfully terminated
her employment if acceptance would compromise her claim
involving the termination. For example, a teacher is not
required to accept the wrongdoing school board's offer of
employment if it is contingent upon settlement of the teacher's
pending lawsuit against the board.[90] The Supreme Court has
ruled, however, that an employer charged with discrimination in hiring can stop the continued accrual of back pay by
unconditionally offering the claimant the job previously denied,
even without offering retroactive seniority.[91]

The U.S. Court of Appeals for the Fourth Circuit has ruled
that a principal demoted because of his race is not required
by the mitigation rule to accept the demotion, since acceptance would constitute submission to illegal discrimination.[92]
The First Circuit, however, has held that where a public
employee has been punitively transferred in violation of his
First Amendment rights, he has the right to quit and obtain
the same damages he would have received had he actually
been discharged only if the transfer constitutes a "constructive
discharge." Before such a constructive discharge may be found,
the court ruled, "the trier of fact must be satisfied that the
new working conditions would have been so difficult or unpleasant that a reasonable person in the employee's shoes
would have felt compelled to resign."[93]

Where a teacher is entitled to institute appellate administrative proceedings to obtain review of a termination decision,
he may argue that the adverse action does not become final at
the administrative level until the conclusion of the appellate
administrative process, and that accordingly the obligation to
seek other employment does not arise until then. Such a rule
would reflect recognition that during this period the quest for
reinstatement inevitably will consume much of the teacher's
time, effort, and thought.[94] Because the teacher's argument

may be rejected, however, the risks of withholding the quest for other employment pending administrative review proceedings must be carefully weighed.

Is a teacher entitled to compensation from the treasury of his employer for losses, other than lost salary, incurred as a result of the unconstitutional termination of his employment?

Where the employer is subject to suit and monetary relief is not barred by the 11th Amendment or other immunity defense, the teacher is entitled to be "made whole"[95] and thus to recover his "net pecuniary loss by reason of the premature termination."[96] This "make whole" remedy should include seniority and experience credit for the academic years since the termination of his employment,[97] and should also include compensation for costs, expenses, and losses such as the following:

- expenses reasonably incurred in seeking other employment, including the cost of postage, photocopying, long-distance telephone calls, transcripts, transportation, newspaper subscriptions, required additional education courses, and updating of credentials;[98]
- the cost of locating and moving the family to a new home in the vicinity of the teacher's new employment,[99] including the cost of selling the teacher's old residence;
- losses resulting from inability to sell the teacher's old residence;[100]
- a finder's fee on the new house;[101]
- the cost of additional transportation necessitated by working in a school system more distant from the teacher's residence;[102]
- the cost of moving the family back to the vicinity of the teacher's old district upon reinstatement;[103]
- the loss of retirement benefits;[104]
- the cost of obtaining medical insurance coverage equivalent to that supplied by the defendant school system to its employees;[105]
- medical expenses incurred which would have been paid by the defendant school system's medical insurance coverage had the teacher's employment not been terminated;[106]
- medical expenses incurred in treating physical illness (such as an ulcer) or emotional problems (such as anxiety neurosis) resulting from the unconstitutional termination.[107]

• losses to a music teacher from diminished opportunity to give private piano lessons in the teacher's new location.[108]

Compensatory damages in a section 1983 case may also be awarded for injury to professional reputation and inability of the teacher to pursue his chosen profession.[109] Section 1983 compensatory damages, moreover, "are not limited to out-of-pocket pecuniary loss. They can be awarded for emotional and mental distress even though no actual monetary loss is proved.[110] As the Supreme Court stated in *Carey v. Piphus*,[111] a student suspension case, "[d]istress is a personal injury familiar to the law, customarily proved by showing the nature and circumstances of the wrong and its effect on the plaintiff." The Court noted that it was using the term "distress" to include mental suffering or emotional anguish, and that "genuine injury in this respect may be evidenced by one's conduct and observed by others."[112]

To what extent, if any, can a school official responsible for the unconstitutional termination of a teacher's employment be made to compensate the teacher out of the official's own pocket for resulting losses?

In *Wood v. Strickland*,[113] the Supreme Court confronted the question whether a school board member was immune from personal liability for damages where he had acted unconstitutionally in the suspension of a student. The Court held that—

[I]n the specific context of school discipline . . . a school board member is not immune from liability for damages under § 1983 if he knew or reasonably should have known that the action he took within his sphere of official responsibility would violate the constitutional rights of the student affected, or if he took the action with the malicious intention to cause a deprivation of constitutional rights or other injury to the student.[114]

In *Procunier v. Navarette*,[115] the Supreme Court elaborated on the first part of this rule:

Under the first part of the *Wood v. Strickland* rule, the immunity defense would be unavailing to petitioners if the constitutional right allegedly infringed by them was clearly established at the time of their challenged conduct, if they knew or should have known of that right, and if they knew or should have known that their conduct violated the constitutional norm.[116]

The courts have applied the *Wood v. Strickland* rule to teacher termination cases, since functionally school officials adjudicating a student discharge case and school officials adjudicating a teacher termination case are identically situated.[117]

In a recent decision, the Supreme Court abandoned the "subjective" aspect of the *Wood v. Strickland* rule and ruled that government officials performing discretionary functions are shielded from personal liability for civil damages "insofar as their conduct does not violate 'clearly established' statutory or constitutional rights of which a reasonable person would have known."[118]

The Supreme Court also has ruled that in an action under section 1983 against a public official whose position might entitle him to qualified immunity, the plaintiff is not required to allege that the defendant acted in bad faith in order to state a claim for relief, but the burden is on the defendant to plead good faith as an affirmative defense.[119] The Third Circuit has held that "in § 1983 actions the burden is on the defendant official claiming official immunity to come forward and to convince the trier of fact by a preponderance of the evidence that, under the standards of *Wood v. Strickland*, official immunity should attach."[120] The great bulk of authority in the federal courts supports this view.[121] The Supreme Court has characterized official immunity as a defense available to the official in question,[122] although the issue of who has the burden of persuasion, as distinguished from the burden of pleading, may still be open.[123]

A school official may have no immunity where he knew that the appropriateness of terminating a teacher's employment depended on questions of fact which he made no effort to resolve. Where a school official is not aware that his action would violate a teacher's constitutional rights, but fails to seek legal advice before acting, the reasonableness of the official's lack of knowledge may turn, not just on the relative certainty of the legal issue, but also on the extent to which counsel was available to him.[124] Holding that a university president was not immune from personal liability in connection with an unconstitutional refusal to renew a teacher's contract, a Delaware federal court concluded that "[w]here a public official who is aware of uncertainties surrounding the propriety of a particular course of conduct pursues that course of conduct without first attempting to resolve factual and legal doubts, . . . the public official has shed his cloak of official immunity and acts at his peril."[125] Where board members, in terminating a teacher's employment, relied on his written and spoken expressions of opinion but First Amendment considerations did not enter into their deliberative process—even after the teacher's post-hearing brief brought to the board's attention the relevance of those considerations—the board members were held not immune from personal liability.[126]

At least one court has held that "it is not enough that [the school official] sought the advice of counsel. He must establish that his actions did not violate a clearly established constitutional right. Such a right can be so clearly established that it is unreasonable for a defendant to rely upon contrary advice from legal counsel."[127] If a board member seeks to wrap himself in a cloak of official immunity by pointing to the advice of counsel, he may not be successful if he had no reasonable basis for trusting that advice or did not in fact view counsel as having offered advice concerning the teacher's constitutional rights upon which he could rely.[128] A school official may not be immunized where he did not understand the basis for his attorney's advice and the general reliability of the authority on which the attorney's conclusions were based.[129] It is still not entirely clear whether the plaintiff or the defendant has the burden of proof on these various immunity issues.[130]

Can a teacher who successfully challenges the constitutionality of his termination recover punitive damages?

In appropriate cases, yes. Even without proof of actual injury, a court may award a teacher punitive damages against a defendant school official in his personal capacity when the official acted with malice or in reckless disregard of the teacher's constitutional rights.[131] The courts have indicated that a district court's discretion should be guided in part by whether actual damages would suffice to deter a defendant's wrongdoing.[132] The Supreme Court has held, however, that in section 1983 suits punitive damages may not be awarded against municipalities for the bad-faith actions of their officials.[133]

Can a teacher who prevails in attacking the constitutionality of his employment termination under section 1983 recover attorneys' fees?

Yes. In *Alyeska Pipeline Service Co. v. Wilderness Society*,[134] the Supreme Court held that, absent statutory authorization, federal courts are without authority to award attorneys' fees to prevailing parties except in special circumstances. In response to that decision, Congress enacted the Civil Rights Attorneys' Fees Awards Act of 1976 (codified as the last sentence of 42 U.S.C. § 1988), which provides that "[i]n any action or proceeding [section 1983, among other statutes], the court, in its discretion, may allow the prevailing party . . . a reasonable attorney's fee as part of the costs."[135] It is clear from the legislative history that Congress intended that a prevailing plaintiff "should ordinarily recover an attorney's fee unless special circumstances would render such an award unjust,"[136] but that "[s]uch a party, if unsuccessful, could be assessed his opponent's fee only where it is shown that his suit was clearly frivolous, vexatious, or brought for harassment purposes."[137] In *Christianburg Garment Co. v. Equal Employment Opportunity Commission*,[138] the Supreme Court, considering similar language in Title VII of the Civil Rights Act of 1964,[139] held that the plaintiff should not be assessed his opponent's attorneys' fees unless the court finds that his claim was brought or continued in bad faith or was frivolous, unreasonable, or groundless, and that the plaintiff continued to litigate after it clearly became so.

In order to be a "prevailing party" who is entitled to an award of attorneys' fees under section 1983, the Supreme Court has ruled, a plaintiff must establish his entitlement to some relief on the merits of his claims, either in the trial court or on appeal.[140] But the fact that the plaintiff prevails through a settlement rather than through litigation, the Court has held, does not preclude him from receiving attorneys' fees as the "prevailing party" within the meaning of section 1983.[141] The Court also has determined that the statute allows the award of fees where (1) the plaintiff prevails on a wholly statutory, non-civil-rights claim "pendent" to a substantial constitutional claim, i.e., "arising out of a common nucleus of operative fact," or (2) both a statutory and a substantial constitutional claim are settled favorably to the plaintiff without adjudication.[142] The Court has ruled further that even though the statute allows attorneys' fees against a state, the 11th Amendment is no bar when a substantial constitutional claim is involved, since Congress was acting within its enforcement power under the 14th Amendment in providing for such ancillary relief.[143]

Lower-court decisions have held that fees may not be denied simply because only nominal damages are awarded,[144] and that while this is a factor that may be considered on the amount of the fee award,[145] "[t]his does not mean that the fee award may also be nominal."[146]

In recent years federal trial courts have awarded substantial fees in teacher termination cases, and in several instances federal appellate courts have overturned trial court fee awards as inadequate.[147]

Does appropriate relief for a teacher whose employment has been unconstitutionally terminated include an order directing school officials to expunge from the school district's records any reference to the fact of, or the reasons for, the termination?

Yes. This relief commonly is granted in such cases.[148] In addition, some courts have directed the defendant school officials to make no reference to the incident forming the basis for termination when prospective employers make inquiries.[149]

In one case a court directed that the records of a teacher whose employment had been unconstitutionally terminated be made to reflect, for the purpose of reference to potential employers, continuous service in good standing throughout the period of her wrongful exclusion from the school system. The court further ordered the defendants to ensure that any inquiries about the plaintiff from potential employers be processed, insofar as possible, by one identified responsible person within the school system, who was to be instructed to keep an exact record of the names and addresses of the employers who inquired for references on the plaintiff, the date of the inquiry, and the name of the person inquiring. The order also required that (1) the defendants make a summary of the reference in fact made; (2) such information and summary be retained in the plaintiff's personnel file; (3) should the prospective employer initiate inquiry about the teacher's lawsuit, the person responsible for the reference be instructed to send a copy of the court's opinion and judgment to the prospective employer, noting that fact on the summary made of the inquiry and reference, and (4) in responding to any inquiry from any prospective employer with respect to whether she had been dismissed from previous employment, the plaintiff could be allowed to lawfully respond as though she had continuously served in good standing throughout the period of her wrongful exclusion from the school system.[150]

Can a teacher who works for a private school that receives most of its funds from the state and is closely regulated by the state bring a section 1983 suit against the school and its officials if he is penalized by them for exercising his constitutional rights?

No. In a 1982 Supreme Court case several teachers brought a section 1983 suit against the director of a privately owned school who had fired them. The school, which was for troubled youths, had a private board of directors, received more than 90 percent of its funding from the state and nearby cities, had its students referred to it by those cities, and was closely regulated by those cities. The school's director fired one of the teachers after she had suggested that the director give more responsibility to the student-staff council. Five other teachers were discharged after writing a protest letter to a local newspaper and stating that they would form a union.

To sue under section 1983, the plaintiff must show that the defendant was acting under color of state law, and in rejecting the teachers' claims, the Supreme Court held that the requisite level of state action was not present.[151] The Court stated that "the school's receipt of public funds does not make the discharge decisions acts of the state,"[152] and added that the level of government "regulation [was] not sufficient to make a decision to discharge, made by private management, state action."[153] Similarly, the Court wrote "[t]hat a private entity that serves the public does not make its acts state action."[154]

Nevertheless, the Court intimated that if a private school's dismissals, which suppressed the teachers' speech, were pursuant to some state policy, then the requisite level of state action might be present.[155] Likewise, if the state, to circumvent its constitutional obligations, created private schools that carried out the functions of public schools, then the school officials arguably could be held liable under section 1983 because "[a] state may not deliberately delegate a task to a private entity in order to avoid its constitutional obligations."[156]

NOTES

1. *See Snepp v. United States*, 444 U.S. 507, 509 n.3 (1980), and cases cited.
2. *Perry v. Sindermann*, 408 U.S. 593 (1972).
3. *Puentes v. Board of Education*, 24 N.Y.S.2d 996, 250 N.E.2d 232, 302 N.Y.S.2d 824 (1969).
4. *Lafferty v. Carter*, 310 F.Supp. 465 (W.D. Wis. 1970).
5. *Trotman v. Board of Trustees of Lincoln University*, 635 F.2d 216 (3d Cir. 1980), *cert. denied*, 451 U.S. 986 (1981) (demotion of department head); *Soto v. Chardon*, 514 F.Supp. 339 (D.P.R. 1981) (demotion of school administrators); *Finot v. Pasadena City Board of Education*, 250 Cal. App.2d 189, 58 Cal. Rptr. 520 (1968).
6. *Childers v. Independent School District No. 1*, 676 F.2d 1338, 1342 (10th Cir. 1982) (when teacher transferred from desirable position of teaching vocational agriculture to teaching regular subjects, court writes: "Retaliation that takes the form of altered employment conditions instead of termination may nonetheless be an unconstitutional infringement of protected activity"); *Lemons v. Morgan*, 629 F.2d 1389 (8th Cir. 1980) (after making controversial statements on school radio, plaintiff transferred from teaching broadcasting to teaching electronics); *McGill v. Board of Education*, 602 F.2d 774 (7th Cir. 1979) (union activist transferred from one school to another); *Bernasconi v. Tempe Elementary School District No. 3*, 548 F.2d 857, 860 (9th Cir.), *cert. denied*, 434 U.S. 825 (1977) (transfer of teacher and counselor "from a position uniquely suited to her talents and desires" in retaliation for protected speech unconstitutional); *Acanfora v. Board of Education of Montgomery County*, 491 F.2d 498 (4th Cir.), *cert. denied*, 419 U.S. 836 (1974) (classroom teacher's public statements regarding his homosexual status could not constitutionally form basis for transfer from teaching to administrative work, even though without loss of pay). *See also Rosado v. Santiago*, 562 F.2d 114, 118 (1st Cir. 1977).
7. *Swilley v. Alexander*, 629 F.2d 1018 (5th Cir. 1980); *Muller v. Conlisk*, 429 F.2d 901 (7th Cir. 1970).

8. *Simpson v. Weeks,* 570 F.2d 240 (8th Cir. 1978), *cert. denied,* 443 U.S. 911 (1979).

9. *Garrity v. New Jersey,* 385 U.S. 493, 500 (1967) and cases cited.

10. *See Mount Healthy Board of Education v. Doyle,* 429 U.S. 274, 285–86 (1977) (recognizing that the constitutional principle at stake would not be sufficiently vindicated if a public employee who had engaged in constitutionally protected conduct were placed in a worse position than if he had not engaged in such conduct).

11. *Trotman v. Board of Trustees of Lincoln University,* 635 F.2d 216, 227–29 (3d Cir. 1980), *cert. denied,* 451 U.S. 986 (1981) (threats, demotions, and decisions not to rehire may have chilling effect); *Aebisher v. Ryan,* 622 F.2d 651 (2d Cir. 1980) (in action by school teachers charging school officials with violating their First Amendment rights by reprimanding them for speaking to newspaper reporters concerning student assault incident, trial court erred in granting summary judgment for defendants without considering practical effects of reprimand letters and whether such letters had chilling effect sufficient to trigger First Amendment inquiry); *Columbus Education Association v. Columbus City School District,* 623 F.2d 1155 (6th Cir. 1980) (reprimand to retaliate against building representative of local education association for zealous representation, as "designated union spokesperson," of fellow teacher at grievance meeting with supervising principal had chilling effect on exercise by the building representative and education association of First Amendment rights of free speech and association and impermissibly infringed upon those rights); *McGill v. Board of Education,* 602 F.2d 774, 780 (7th Cir. 1979) ("The test is whether the adverse action taken by the defendants is likely to chill the exercise of constitutionally protected speech. . . . This chilling effect can be accomplished through an unwanted transfer as well as through outright discharge"); *Bernasconi v. Tempe Elementary School District No. 3,* 548 F.2d 857, 860 (9th Cir.), *cert. denied,* 434 U.S. 825 (1977); *Riechert V. Draud,* 511 F.Supp. 679, 686 (E.D. Ky. 1981) (assigning union activist less desirable courses may have chilling effect); *Adcock v. Board of Education,* 10 Cal.3d 60, 66, 513 P.2d 900, 904, 109 Cal. Rptr. 676, 680 (1973) (*en banc*) ("Lesser penalties than dismissal can effectively silence teachers and compel them to forego exercise of the rights guaranteed them by our Constitution"). *See also NAACP v. Button,* 371 U.S. 415, 433 (1963) (exercise of First Amendment freedoms may be deterred almost as potently by the threat of sanctions as by their actual application); *Reporters Committee for Freedom of Press v. American Tel. & Tel. Co.,* 593 F.2d 1030, 1052 (D.C. Cir. 1978), *cert. denied,* 440 U.S. 949 (1979); *Simpson v. Weeks,* 570 F.2d 240 (8th Cir. 1978), *cert. denied,* 443 U.S. 911 (1979).

12. 408 U.S. 593 (1972).

13. *Id.* at 597.

14. *Pred v. Board of Public Instruction*, 415 F.2d 851 (5th Cir. 1969); *Tischler v. Board of Education*, 37 A.D.2d 261, 323 N.Y.S.2d 508 (1971).

15. *Lake Park Education Association v. Board of Education*, 526 F.Supp. 710 (N.D. Ill. 1981); *Orr v. Thorpe*, 427 F.2d 1129, 1131 (5th Cir. 1970).

16. *Allaire v. Rogers*, 658 F.2d 1055 (5th Cir. 1981), *cert. denied*, —— U.S. ——, 102 S.Ct. 1975 (1982); *Jervey v. Martin*, 336 F.Supp. 1350, 1354 (W.D. Va. 1972).

17. *Lake Park Education Association, supra* note 15.

18. *Orr v. Thorpe, supra* note 15.

19. *Joint Anti-Fascist Refugee Committee v. McGrath*, 341 U.S. 123, 185 (1951).

20. *Franklin v. Atkins*, 562 F.2d 1188, 1190 (10th Cir. 1977), *cert. denied*, 435 U.S. 994 (1978). *See also Rainey v. Jackson State College*, 435 F.2d 1031 (5th Cir. 1970).

21. *Bertot v. School District No. 1*, 522 F.2d 1171, 1182–83 (10th Cir. 1975); *Sindermann v. Perry*, 430 F.2d 939, 943 (5th Cir. 1970), *aff'd on other grounds*, 408 U.S. 593 (1972); *Parducci v. Rutland*, 316 F.Supp. 352, 358 (M.D. Ala. 1970); *Ramsey v. Hopkins*, 320 F.Supp. 477, 481 (M.D. Ala. 1970).

22. *See Atcherson v. Siebenmann*, 458 F.Supp. 526, 535 (S.D. Iowa 1978), *rev'd in part on other grounds*, 605 F.2d 1058 (8th Cir. 1979) and cases cited.

23. *See id.* at 534–35.

24. *See, e.g., Himmelbrand v. Harrison*, 484 F.Supp. 803, 812 (W.D. Va. 1980). *See also Welch v. University of Texas and Its Marine Science Institute*, 659 F.2d 531, 533 (5th Cir. 1981) ("A constructive discharge will be found where 'working conditions would have been so difficult that a reasonable person in the employee's shoes would have felt compelled to resign' "). *Cf. McDonald v. United Air Lines*, 587 F.2d 357, 359–60 (7th Cir. 1978), *cert. denied*, 442 U.S. 934 (1979) (stewardesses who resigned because of no-marriage rule held constructively discharged) with *Mitchell v. Visser*, 529 F.Supp. 1034 (D. Kan. 1981) (professor not constructively discharged although he was denied raises and not allowed to teach summer school, select the courses he taught, or vote in departmental meetings) and *English v. Powell*, 592 F.2d 727, 731 n.4 (4th Cir. 1979) (single statement that employee would be fired next morning is "simply not the type of systematic harassment which would support finding of constructive discharge").

25. 42 U.S.C. § 1983.

26. *Patsy v. Board of Regents of State of Florida*, —— U.S. ——, ——; 102 S.Ct. 2557, 2568 (1982). *See also Monroe v. Pape*, 365 U.S. 167, 183 (1961) ("The federal remedy is supplementary to the state remedy, and the latter need not be first sought and refused before the federal one is invoked").

27. *See Maine v. Thiboutot*, 448 U.S. 1, 3 n.1 (1980); *Martinez v. California*, 444 U.S. 277, 283–84 n.7 (1980).

28. 436 U.S. 658, 690 (1978) (emphasis added).

29. *Kingsville Independent School District v. Cooper*, 611 F.2d 1109, 1112 (5th Cir. 1980); *Moore v. Tangipahoa Parish School Board*, 594 F.2d 489, 493 (5th Cir. 1979). *See also Himmelbrand v. Harrison*, 484 F.Supp. 803, 810 (W.D. Va. 1980).

30. *Monell v. Department of Social Services*, 436 U.S. 658, 690–91 (1978).

31. *Id.* at 694.

32. *See, e.g., Molina v. Richardson*, 578 F.2d 846 (9th Cir. 1978), *cert. denied*, 439 U.S. 1048 (1979); *Jones v. City of Memphis*, 586 F.2d 622 (6th Cir. 1978), *cert. denied*, 440 U.S. 914 (1979). *See generally Davis v. Passman*, 442 U.S. 228 (1979). *Cf. Turpin v. Mailet*, 579 F.2d 152 (2d Cir. 1978) (*en banc*), *vacated*, 439 U.S. 974 (1978), *on remand*, 591 F.2d 426, *cert. denied*, 449 U.S. 1016 (1980) (decision rendered day before *Monell* decision of Supreme Court, rejecting vicarious liability under 14th Amendment).

33. *Mount Healthy Board of Education v. Doyle*, 429 U.S. 274 (1977); *Perry v. Sindermann*, 408 U.S. 593 (1972).

34. *Cf. Allegheny Pepsi-Cola Bottling Co. v. NLRB*, 312 F.2d 529, 531 (3d Cir. 1962) (employer guilty of statutory violation where supervisor, for discriminatory reasons, recommended employee's discharge and employer, without any illicit motivation, accepted recommendation: "To rule otherwise would provide a simple means for evading the Act by a division of corporate functions").

35. 42 U.S.C. § 1983 (emphasis added).

36. *Hickman v. Valley Board of Education*, 619 F.2d 606, 610 (6th Cir. 1980).

37. *Adams v. Campbell County Board of Education*, 511 F.2d 1242, 1245–46 (10th Cir. 1975); *Rampey v. Allen*, 501 F.2d 1090 (10th Cir. 1974), *cert. denied*, 420 U.S. 908 (1975); *Cook County College Teachers Union v. Byrd*, 456 F.2d 882, 889 (7th Cir.), *cert. denied*, 409 U.S. 848 (1972); *London v. Florida Department of Health & Rehabilitative Services*, 448 F.2d 655 (5th Cir. 1971), *cert. denied*, 406 U.S. 929 (1972). *See also Rowland v. Mad River Local School District*, No. C-3-75–125, slip. op. (Oct. 22, 1981 S.D. Ohio).

38. *Bowen v. Watkins*, 669 F.2d 979, 988 (5th Cir. 1982).

39. 42 U.S.C. § 1983.

40. *E.g., Vinnedge v. Gibbs*, 550 F.2d 926, 928 (4th Cir. 1977).

41. *Johnson v. Duffy*, 588 F.2d 740, 743–44 (9th Cir. 1978).

42. *Hickman v. Valley Board of Education*, 619 F.2d 606, 610 (6th Cir. 1980).

43. *See Berry v. Arthur*, 474 F.Supp. 427, 435 (D. S.D. 1979) and cases cited therein.

44. *McClelland v. Facteau*, 610 F.2d 693, 696 (10th Cir. 1979); *Johnson v. Duffy*, 588 F.2d 740, 743 (9th Cir. 1978); *Sims v. Adams*, 537 F.2d 829 (5th Cir. 1976).

45. *McClelland v. Facteau, supra* and cases cited; *Bowen v. Watkins*, 669 F.2d 979, 988 (5th Cir. 1982), *DiGiovanni v. City of Philadelphia*, 531 F.Supp. 141, 145 (E.D. Pa. 1982).

46. *McClelland v. Facteau, supra*, 610 F.2d at 697; *Sims v. Adams*, 537 F.2d 829 (5th Cir. 1976); *Wright v. McMann*, 460 F.2d 126 (2d Cir.), *cert. denied*, 409 U.S. 885 (1972). *But see Himmelbrand v. Harrison*, 484 F.Supp. 803, 811 (W.D. Va. 1980).

47. 429 U.S. 274, 285–86 (1977).

48. *Id*. at 287.

49. *Id*. at 286–87.

50. *Clark v. Mann*, 562 F.2d 1104, 1121 (8th Cir. 1977).

51. *Id*.

52. *Hickman v. Valley Board of Education*, 619 F.2d 606, 609 (6th Cir. 1980).

53. *Id. See also Daulton v. Affeldt*, 678 F.2d 487 (4th Cir. 1982) (teacher's evaluations decline after she makes controversial statements and court overturns dismissal).

54. *Garrity v. New Jersey*, 385 U.S. 493, 500 (1967) and cases cited.

55. 429 U.S. 274, 285–86 (1977).

56. *Smith v. Hampton Training School for Nurses*, 360 F.2d 577, 581 (4th Cir. 1966).

57. *Keyishian v. Board of Regents*, 385 U.S. 589, 603 (1967); *Shelton v. Tucker*, 364 U.S. 479, 487 (1960) ("The vigilant protection of constitutional freedoms is nowhere more vital than in the community of American schools").

58. *Jannetta v. Cole*, 493 F.2d 1334, 1338 (4th Cir. 1974).

59. *E.g., Greminger v. Seaborne*, 584 F.2d 275, 279 (8th Cir. 1978); *Clark v. Mann*, 562 F.2d 1104, 1128 (9th Cir. 1977); *Wagle v. Murray*, 546 F.2d 1329, 1336 (9th Cir. 1976), *cert. denied*, 434 U.S. 1014 (1978); *Sterzing v. Fort Bend Independent School District*, 496 F.2d 92 (5th Cir. 1974); *Gieringer v. Center School District No. 58*, 477 F.2d 1164, 1167 (8th Cir.), *cert. denied*, 414 U.S. 832 (1973); *Hanover Federation of Teachers v. Hanover Community School Corp.*, 457 F.2d 456 (7th Cir. 1972), *aff'g* 318 F.Supp. 757 (N.D. Ind. 1970); *Johnson v. Branch*, 364 F.2d 177 (4th Cir. 1966) *(en banc)*, *cert. denied*, 385 U.S. 1003 (1967); *Schreffler v. Board of Education*, 506 F.Supp. 1300 (D. Del. 1981).

60. 422 U.S. 405 (1975).

61. *Id*. at 417–21.

62. *Id*. at 421.

63. *Gurmankin v. Costanzo*, 556 F.2d 184, 188 (3d Cir. 1977).

64. 496 F.2d 92 (5th Cir. 1974).

65. *Id*. at 93. *See also Atcherson v. Siebenmann*, 458 F.Supp. 526, 537 (S.D. Iowa 1978), *rev'd in part on other grounds*, 605 F.2d 1058 (8th Cir. 1979).

66. *Allen v. Autauga County Board of Education*, 685 F.2d 1302, 1306 (11th Cir. 1982).

67. *McMullan v. Thornburgh*, 508 F.Supp. 1044, 1054 (E.D. Pa. 1981).

68. Cf. *Edwards v. School Board*, 658 F.2d 951, 956 (4th Cir. 1981) ("Edwards's entitlement to back pay and reinstatement [may not] survive every change of circumstance. For example, if the Board abolished the position of teacher's aide for either educational or financial reasons, Edwards's right to relief would be terminated at the time this change took effect").

69. See *Bigelow v. RKO Radio Pictures*, 327 U.S. 251, 265 (1946) ("The most elementary conceptions of justice and public policy require that the wrongdoer shall bear the risk of the uncertainty which his own wrong has created . . ."). In the words of Judge Learned Hand, speaking for the court in *NLRB v. Remington Rand, Inc.*, 94 F.2d 862, 872 (2d Cir. 1938), "it rest[s] upon the [wrongdoer] to disentangle the consequences for which it [is] chargeable from those from which it [is] immune." See also *Baxter v. Savannah Sugar Refining Corp.*, 495 F.2d 437, 445 (5th Cir. 1974), *cert. denied*, 419 U.S. 1033 (1974).

70. See *NLRB v. M&B Headwear Co.*, 349 F.2d 170, 174 (4th Cir. 1965).

71. See, e.g., *Harmon v. May Broadcasting Co.*, 583 F.2d 410, 411 (8th Cir. 1978); *Wagle v. Murray*, 546 F.2d 1329, 1336 (9th Cir. 1976), *cert. denied*, 434 U.S. 1014 (1978); *McFerren v. County Board of Education*, 455 F.2d 199 (6th Cir.), *cert. denied*, 407 U.S. 934 (1972); *Harkless v. Sweeny Independent School District*, 427 F.2d 319 (5th Cir. 1970), *cert. denied*, 400 U.S. 991 (1971); *Smith v. Hampton Training School for Nurses*, 360 F.2d 577, 581 (4th Cir. 1966) (*en banc*).

72. *Kingsville Independent School District v. Cooper*, 611 F.2d 1109, 1114 (5th Cir. 1980) and cases cited; *Cooley v. Board of Education of Forrest City School District*, 453 F.2d 282, 287 (8th Cir. 1972).

73. See *Edelman v. Jordan*, 415 U.S. 651 (1974).

74. *Mount Healthy Board of Education v. Doyle*, 429 U.S. 274, 281 (1977).

75. *Moore v. Tangipahoa Parish School Board*, 594 F.2d 489 (5th Cir. 1979) (Louisiana); *Unified School District No. 480 v. Epperson*, 551 F.2d 254 (10th Cir. 1977), *vacated and remanded on other grounds*, 435 U.S. 948 (1978) (Kansas); *Stoddard v. School District No. 1*, 590 F.2d 829 (10th Cir. 1979) (Wyoming); *Cline v. School District*, 476 F.Supp. 868 (D. Neb. 1979) (Nebraska); *Eckerd v. Indian River School District*, 475 F.Supp. 1350 (D. Del. 1979) (Delaware) and cases cited. For pre-*Mount Healthy* rulings to similar effect, *see*, e.g., *Miller v. Board of Education*, 450 F.Supp. 106 (S.D. W. Va. 1978) (West Virginia); *U.S. v. South Carolina*, 445 F.Supp. 1094, 1099 n.5 (D. S.C. 1977) (three-judge court), *aff'd mem.*, 434 U.S. 1026 (1978) (South Carolina); *Campbell v. Gadsden County District*

School Board, 534 F.2d 650, 655–56 (5th Cir. 1976) (Florida); *Monell v. Department of Social Services*, 532 F.2d 259 (2d Cir. 1976), *rev'd on other grounds*, 436 U.S. 658 (1978); (New York); *Adams v. Rankin County Board of Education*, 524 F.2d 928 (5th Cir. 1975), *cert. denied*, 438 U.S. 904 (1976) (Mississippi); *Burt v. Board of Trustees*, 521 F.2d 1201 (4th Cir. 1975) (South Carolina); *Hutchinson v. Lake Oswego School District*, 519 F.2d 961 (9th Cir. 1975), *cert. denied*, 429 U.S. 1037 (1977) (Oregon); *Handler v. San Jacinto Junior College*, 519 F.2d 273 (5th Cir.), *on rehearing*, 522 F.2d 204 (1975) (Texas); *Patterson v. Ramsey*, 413 F.Supp. 523, 529–30 (D. Md. 1976), *aff'd*, 552 F.2d 117 (4th Cir. 1977) (Maryland); *Morris v. Board of Education*, 401 F.Supp. 188, 203–05 (D. Del. 1975) (Delaware). *See also* Note, *Damages Remedies for Constitutional Violations*, 89 Harv. L.Rev. 922, 931–32 (1976).

76. For examples of post-*Mount Healthy* decisions in this area, *compare Bailey v. Ohio State University*, 487 F.Supp. 601, 605 (S.D. Ohio 1980) and *Henry v. Texas Tech University*, 466 F.Supp. 141 (N.D. Tex. 1979) *with Skehan v. Board of Trustees of Bloomsburg State College*, 669 F.2d 142 (3d Cir. 1982); *United Carolina Bank v. Board of Regents*, 665 F.2d 553, 556–59 (5th Cir. 1982), *and Goss v. San Jacinto Junior College*, 588 F.2d 96, *modified*, 595 F.2d at 1119 (5th Cir. 1979). Decisions rendered before *Mount Healthy* also may be instructive. For examples of pre-*Mount Healthy* decisions rejecting 11th Amendment immunity, see *Handler v. San Jacinto Junior College*, 519 F.2d 273 (5th Cir.), *on rehearing*, 522 F.2d 204 (1975); *Dyson v. Lavery*, 417 F.Supp. 103, 107–09 (E.D. Va. 1976); *Keller v. University of Michigan*, 411 F.Supp. 1055 (E.D. Mich. 1974); and *Gordenstein v. University of Delaware*, 381 F.Supp. 718, 722 (D. Del. 1974).

77. 436 U.S. 658, 690 (1978). School district personnel decisions by a school board are "officially adopted and promulgated" within the meaning of *Monell*. *Kingsville Independent School District v. Cooper*, 611 F.2d 1109 (5th Cir. 1980); *Moore v. Tangipahoa Parish School Board*, 594 F.2d 489, 493 (5th Cir. 1979). *Cf. Owen v. City of Independence*, 445 U.S. 622, 655 n.39 (1980) (where personnel decision alleged to be unconstitutional implemented decision officially promulgated by City Council, municipality liable under § 1983).

78. 436 U.S. 658, 701 (1978).

79. 445 U.S. 622 (1980).

80. 429 U.S. 274, 286 (1977).

81. *Hickman v. Valley Board of Education*, 619 F.2d 606, 610 (6th Cir. 1980).

82. *Johnson v. Butler*, 433 F.Supp. 531, 537 (W.D. Va. 1977).

83. *Gurmankin v. Costanzo*, 626 F.2d 1115, 1125–26 (3d Cir. 1980). *See also Kunda v. Muhlenberg College*, 621 F.2d 532 (3d Cir. 1980).

84. *Horton v. Lawrence County Board of Education*, 449 F.2d 793, 795 (5th Cir. 1971). *See also Smith v. Concordia Parish School Board*, 387 F.Supp. 887, 891 (W.D. La. 1975); *Lucia v. Duggan*, 303 F.Supp. 112, 119 (D. Mass. 1969). *Cf. Redman v. Department of Education*, 519 P.2d 760, 771 (Alaska 1974).

85. *Harkless v. Sweeny Independent School District*, 466 F.Supp. 457, 469 (S.D. Tex. 1978), *aff'd*, 608 F.2d 594 (5th Cir. 1979).

86. *University of Alaska v. Chauvin*, 521 P.2d 1234, 1239 (Alaska 1974).

87. *Edwards v. School Board*, 658 F.2d 951, 956 (4th Cir. 1981) (illegal dismissal under Title VII); *Hegler v. Board of Education*, 447 F.2d 1078, 1081 (8th Cir. 1971); *Rolfe v. County Board of Education*, 391 F.2d 77, 81 (6th Cir. 1968); *Eckerd v. Indian River School District*, 475 F.Supp. 1350, 1365 (D. Del. 1979). *See also University of Alaska v. Chauvin*, 521 P.2d 1234, 1240 (Alaska 1974); 11 S. WILLISTON, A TREATISE ON THE LAW OF CONTRACTS § 1360 (3d ed. 1968).

88. *Id.* at 1239. *Redman v. Department of Education*, 519 P.2d 760, 769 (Alaska 1974) (teacher had duty to use reasonable efforts to secure employment of "substantially similar nature" in mitigation of her damages); 11 S. WILLISTON, A TREATISE ON THE LAW OF CONTRACTS § 1360 (3d ed. 1968).

89. *Jackson v. Wheatley School District*, 464 F.2d 411, 413–14 (8th Cir. 1972); *Smith v. Concordia Parish School Board*, 387 F.Supp. 887, 890–91 (W.D. La. 1975).

90. *Redman v. Department of Education*, 519 P.2d 760, 769–70 (Alaska 1974).

91. *Ford Motor Co. v. E.E.O.C.*, —— U.S. ——, ——, 102 S.Ct. 3057, 1066 (1982).

92. *Williams v. Albemarle City Board of Education*, 508 F.2d 1242, 1244 (4th Cir. 1974).

93. *Rosado v. Santiago*, 562 F.2d 114, 119 (1st Cir. 1977). On the "constructive discharge" rule, *see English v. Powell*, 592 F.2d 727, 731 n.4 (4th Cir. 1979); *McDonald v. United Air Lines, Inc.*, 587 F.2d 357, 359–60 (7th Cir. 1978), *cert. denied*, 442 U.S. 934 (1979).

94. *See Power v. United States*, 597 F.2d 258, 264–65 (Ct.Cl. 1979), *cert. denied*, 444 U.S. 1044 (1980).

95. *Smith v. Hampton Training School for Nurses*, 360 F.2d 577, 581 (4th Cir. 1966).

96. *Horton v. Orange County Board of Education*, 464 F.2d 536, 538 (4th Cir. 1972).

97. *Eckerd v. Indian River School District*, 475 F.Supp. 1350, 1365 (D. Del. 1979). For an example of how substantial a "make whole" award can be, *see Stachura v. Memphis Community School District*, No. 79–30022 (E. D. Mich. Jan. 20, 1982), *appeal docketed* No. 82–1578 (6th Cir. Aug. 6, 1982), in which the plaintiff was terminated by the school board because of rumors it had heard about what he

had said in his life-science class. Stachura was awarded $303,000 in damages, including $233,000 in compensatory damages.

98. *Boyle v. Renton School District*, No. 740848 (Super. Ct. Wash., King County, July 10, 1972), *judgment vacated on other grounds*, 10 Wash. App. 523, 518 P.2d 221 (1972). *See generally* 11 S. WILLISTON, A TREATISE ON THE LAW OF CONTRACTS, §§ 1338, 1358, 1361 (3d ed. 1968).

99. *Id.; Wall v. Stanly County Board of Education*, 378 F.2d 275, 278 (4th Cir. 1967).

100. *Boyle v. Renton School District, supra* n.98.

101. *Id.*

102. *Id. See also Harkless v. Sweeny Independent School District*, 466 F.Supp. 457, 458 (S.D. Tex. 1978), *aff'd*, 608 F.2d 594 (5th Cir. 1979).

103. *Wall v. Stanly County Board of Education*, 378 F.2d 275, 278 (4th Cir. 1967).

104. *Burt v. Board of Trustees of Edgefield County School District*, 521 F.2d 1201, 1208 (4th Cir. 1975) (Winter, J., concurring and dissenting) and cases cited; *Morton v. Charles County Board of Education*, 520 F.2d 871, 873 n.4, 876 n.9 (4th Cir.), *cert. denied*, 423 U.S. 1034 (1975) (affirming order of trial court directing school board, which had discriminatorily denied plaintiff a promotion to principal, to compensate plaintiff "on the basis of a principal's salary until her retirement and . . . make such additional contributions to the Maryland Teachers Retirement System on her behalf as would have been made had she held the position of principal since 1969"). *See also Davis v. Griffin-Spaulding County Board of Education*, 445 F.Supp. 1048, 1056 (N.D. Ga. 1976) (teacher forced to retire before age 70 in violation of state law entitled to present value of additional retirement benefits she would have received had contributions been made until age 70); 5 A. Corbin, CONTRACTS § 1095 (1951).

105. *Boyle v. Renton School District No. 403, supra* n.98.

106. *Id.*

107. *Lucia v. Duggan*, 303 F.Supp. 112, 119 (D. Mass. 1969); *Aumiller v. University of Delaware*, 434 F.Supp. 1273 (D. Del. 1977).

108. *Eckerd v. Indian River School District*, 475 F.Supp. 1350, 1366 (D. Del. 1979).

109. *Sterzing v. Fort Bend Independent School District*, 496 F.2d 9 (5th Cir. 1974).

110. *Guzman v. Western State Bank of Devil's Lake*, 540 F.2d 948, 953 (8th Cir. 1976). *See, e.g., Glasson v. City of Louisville*, 518 F.2d 899, 912 (6th Cir.), *cert. denied*, 423 U.S. 930 (1975); *Eckerd v. Indian River School District*, 475 F.Supp. 1350 (D. Del. 1979), *Ruhlman v. Hankinson*, 461 F.Supp. 145, 151 (W.D. Pa. 1978), *aff'd mem.*, 605 F.2d 1195 (3d Cir. 1979), *cert. denied*, 445 U.S.

911 (1980); *Aumiller v. University of Delaware*, 434 F.Supp. 1273, 1310 (D. Del. 1977); *Endress v. Brookdale Community College*, 144 N.J. Super. 109, 364 A.2d 1080, 1097–98 (1976) and cases cited.

111. 435 U.S. 247 (1978).
112. 435 U.S. at 262–63.
113. 420 U.S. 308 (1975).
114. *Id.* at 322.
115. 434 U.S. 555 (1978).
116. *Id.* at 562.
117. *E.g.*, *Skehan v. Board of Trustees*, 538 F.2d 53, 60 (3d Cir.), *cert. denied*, 429 U.S. 979 (1976). *See also Soto v. Chardon*, 514 F.Supp. 339, 348–50 (D. P.R. 1981).
118. *Harlow v. Fitzgerald*, —— U.S. ——, ——, 102 S.Ct. 2727, 2730 (1982).
119. *Gomez v. Toledo*, 446 U.S. 635 (1980). *Cf. Harlow v. Fitzgerald*, —— U.S. ——, ——, 102 S.Ct. 2727, 2737 (1982) ("qualified or 'good faith' immunity is an affirmative defense that must be pleaded by a government official").
120. *Skehan v. Board of Trustees*, *supra* n. 112, at 61–62.
121. *See Reimber v. Short*, 578 F.2d 621, 626 (5th Cir. 1978), *cert. denied*, 440 U.S. 947 (1979); *Landrum v. Moats*, 576 F.2d 1320, 1329 (8th Cir.), *cert. denied*, 439 U.S. 912 (1978); *Gilker v. Baker*, 576 F.2d 245, 247 (9th Cir. 1978); *Dellums v. Powell*, 566 F.2d 167, 189 (D.C. Cir. 1977), *cert. denied*, 438 U.S. 916 (1978); *Thompson v. Burke*, 556 F.2d 231, 239 (3d Cir. 1977); *Bryan v. Jones*, 530 F.2d 1210, 1213 (5th Cir.) *(en banc)*, *cert. denied*, 429 U.S. 865 (1976); *Laverne v. Corning*, 522 F.2d 1144, 1147 (2d Cir. 1975); *Glasson v. City of Louisville*, 518 F.2d 899, 907–910 (6th Cir. 1975), *cert. denied*, 423 U.S. 930 (1975); *Boscarino v. Nelson*, 518 F.2d 879, 882 (7th Cir. 1975).
122. *Gomez v. Toledo*, 446 U.S. 635, 640 (1980); *Procunier v. Navarette*, 434 U.S. 555, 562 (1978); *Pierson v. Ray*, 386 U.S. 547, 556–57 (1976).
123. *Gomez v. Toledo supra* n. 122, at 642 (opinion of Rehnquist, J.).
124. *Skehan v. Board of Trustees*, 538 F.2d 53, 62 (3d Cir.), *cert. denied*, 429 U.S. 979 (1976).
125. *Aumiller v. University of Delaware*, 434 F.Supp. 1273, 1307 (D. Del. 1977).
126. *Eckerd v. Indian River School District*, 475 F.Supp. 1350, 1367 (D. Del. 1979).
127. *MacMurray v. Board of Trustees*, 428 F.Supp. 1171, 1177 (E.D. Pa. 1978).
128. *Eckerd v. Indian River School District*, 475 F.Supp. 1350, 1370 (D. Del. 1979). *Cf. Huebschen v. Department of Health and Social Services*, 547 F.Supp. 1168, 1177–78 (W.D. Wis. 1982).
129. *Eckerd v. Indian River School District*, *supra*.

130. *See Gomez v. Toledo*, 446 U.S. 635, 642 (1980) (opinion of Rehnquist, J.).

131. *Aumiller v. University of Delaware*, 434 F.Supp. 1273, 1311 (D. Del. 1977). *See Rosado v. Santiago*, 562 F.2d 114, 121 (1st Cir. 1977); *Guzman v. Western State Bank of Devil's Lake*, 540 F.2d 948, 953 (8th Cir. 1976); *Fisher v. Volz*, 496 F.2d 333, 347 (3d Cir. 1974); *Gill v. Manuel*, 488 F.2d 799, 801 (9th Cir. 1973); *Smith v. Losee*, 485 F.2d 334, 345 (10th Cir. 1973) (*en banc*), *cert. denied*, 414 U.S. 829 (1974); *Lee v. Southern Home Sites Corp.*, 429 F.2d 290, 294 (5th Cir. 1970); *Caperci v. Huntoon*, 397 F.2d 799, 801 (1st Cir.), *cert. denied*, 393 U.S. 940 (1968); *Mansell v. Saunders*, 372 F.2d 573, 576 (5th Cir. 1967); *Basista v. Weir*, 340 F.2d 74, 86–88 (3d Cir. 1965); *Endicott v. Van Petten*, 330 F.Supp. 878 (D. Kan. 1971); *Davis v. Board of Trustees*, 270 F.Supp. 528 (E.D. Ark. 1967), *aff'd*, 396 F.2d 730 (8th Cir.), *cert. denied*, 393 U.S. 962 (1968).

132. *Rosado v. Santiago, supra*.

133. *City of Newport v. Fact Concerts, Inc.*, 453 U.S. 247, 271 (1981).

134. 421 U.S. 240 (1975).

135. 42 U.S.C. § 1988.

136. S.Rep. No. 94–1011 (94th Cong., 2d Sess. 1976) at 5–6; H.Rep. No. 94–1558 (94th Cong., 2d Sess. 1976) at 6–7. *See Newman v. Piggie Park Enterprises, Inc.*, 390 U.S. 400, 402 (1968).

137. S.Rep. No. 94–1011, *supra;* H.Rep. No. 94–1558, *supra; Hughes v. Rowe*, 449 U.S. 5 (1980).

138. 434 U.S. 412, 422 (1978).

139. 42 U.S.C. § 2000e-5(k). The Supreme Court has held that Title VII of the Civil Rights Act of 1964 authorizes an award of attorneys' fees for work done for the prevailing complainant in state administrative and judicial proceedings to which the complainant was referred pursuant to the provisions of Title VII. *New York Gaslight Club v. Carey*, 447 U.S. 54 (1980). Among other statutory provisions authorizing attorneys' fee awards and having implications for teachers are 20 U.S.C. § 1617 (Emergency School Aid Act) and 29 U.S.C. § 794a (Rehabilitation Act Amendments of 1978).

140. *Hanrahan v. Hampton*, 446 U.S. 754, 757 (1980).

141. *Maher v. Gagne*, 448 U.S. 122, 129 (1980).

142. *Id.* at 132.

143. *Id.* at 132–33.

144. *E.g., Perez v. University of Puerto Rico*, 600 F.2d 1, 2 (1st Cir. 1979); *Burt v. Abel*, 585 F.2d 613, 618 (4th Cir. 1978).

145. *Perez v. University of Puerto Rico, supra; Burt v. Abel, supra*.

146. *Perez v. University of Puerto Rico, supra*, 600 F.2d at 2 n.2.

147. *See, e.g., Zoll v. Eastern Allamakee Community School District*, 588 F.2d 246, 252 (8th Cir. 1978); *Greminger v. Seaborne*, 584 F.2d 275, 279 (8th Cir. 1978); *Brown v. Bullard Independent School District*, 640 F.2d 651, 654 (5th Cir. 1981).

148. *Schreffler v. Board of Education*, 506 F.Supp. 1300, 1302 (D. Del. 1981); *Eckerd v. Indian River School District*, 475 F.Supp. 1350 (D. Del. 1979); *Aumiller v. University of Delaware*, 434 F.Supp. 1273, 1312–13 (D. Del. 1977); *Sterzing v. Fort Bend Independent School District*, 376 F.Supp. 657, 664 (S.D. Tex. 1972), *modified on other grounds*, 496 F.2d 92 (5th Cir. 1974); *Parducci v. Rutland*, 316 F.Supp. 352, 358 (M.D. Ala. 1970).

149. *E.g.*, *Aumiller v. University of Delaware*, 434 F.Supp. 1273, 1309 (D. Del. 1977).

150. *Phillips v. Amos*, No. 76–0077-R (W.D. Va. May 27, 1977).

151. *Rendell-Baker v. Kohn*, ——— U.S. ———, ———, 102 S.Ct. 2764, 2772 (1982).

152. *Id.* at 2771.

153. *Id.* at 2772.

154. *Id.*

155. *Id.* at 2770 n.6, 2771, *quoting Blum v. Yaretsky*, ——— U.S. ———, ———, 102 S.Ct. 2777, 2785 (1982) ("A State normally can be held responsible for a private decision only when it has exercised coercive power or has provided such significant encouragement, either overt or covert, that the choice must in law be deemed to be that of the State").

156. *Id.* at 2776 n.3 (Marshall, J., dissenting), *citing Terry v. Adams*, 345 U.S. 461 (1953).

II

First Amendment Rights in Private Capacity

Schools serve the vital function of teaching successive generations of citizens the habits of openmindedness and critical inquiry which are essential to the development of disciplined and responsible public opinion.[1] Teachers can perform that function—and thus contribute to the effective exercise of First Amendment rights by citizens generally—only if their freedom of thought and inquiry is fully protected.[2] An "unwarranted inhibition" on a teacher's exercise of First Amendment rights "affects not only those . . . who . . . are immediately before the court. It has an unmistakable tendency to chill that free play of the spirit which all teachers ought especially to cultivate and practice."[3]

For these reasons courts have been particularly alert to protect the First Amendment rights of teachers.

Speech and Beliefs

Can a teacher constitutionally be dismissed or disciplined for public out-of-class statements critical of school officials?

No categorical answer can be given. Although the Supreme Court has recognized that such criticism may be constitutionally protected, it has also warned that protection may not exist where the criticism would seriously undermine close employment relationships or certain other conditions necessary to the effective operation of the school system.

The leading case is *Pickering v. Board of Education*,[4] where a school board dismissed a teacher who wrote a letter to a newspaper editor which (1) attacked the board's handling of proposals to raise new school revenues and its allocation of resources between educational and athletic programs and (2) charged the district superintendent with attempting to prevent teachers from criticizing a proposed bond issue. Although the letter was factually incorrect in several respects, the U.S. Supreme Court held that the teacher's dismissal violated his First Amendment right of free speech.

The Court first "unequivocally" rejected any suggestion that "comments on matters of public concern that are *substantially correct* . . . may furnish grounds for dismissal if they are sufficiently critical in tone . . ." at least where "[t]he statements are in no way directed towards any person with whom . . . [the teacher] would normally be in contact in the course of his daily work . . ." and where "no question of maintaining either discipline by immediate superiors or harmony among coworkers is presented . . . ."[5] The Court hedged its ruling further in a footnote:

> It is possible to conceive of some positions in public employment in which the need for confidentiality is so great that even completely correct public statements might furnish a permissible ground for dismissal. Likewise, positions in public employment in which the relationship between superior and subordinate is of such a personal and intimate nature that certain forms of public criticism of the superior by the subordinate would seriously undermine the effectiveness of the working relationship between them can also be imagined.[6]

The Court intimated "no views" as to how it would resolve any such cases, but concluded that Pickering's "employment relationships with the Board and, to a somewhat lesser extent, with the superintendent are not the kind of close working relationships for which it can persuasively be claimed that personal loyalty and confidence are necessary for their proper functioning."[7]

With respect to the false statements, the Court concluded, the defendants had not shown that such statements had impeded the teacher's proper performance of his daily classroom duties or the regular operation of the schools. The

Court ruled that such interference is not to be presumed, and in such circumstances, "absent proof of false statements *knowingly or recklessly* made by him, a teacher's exercise of his right to speak on issues of public importance may not furnish the basis for his dismissal from public employment."[8] The Court stressed that—

> [T]he question whether a school system requires additional funds is a matter of legitimate public concern on which the judgment of the school administration, including the School Board, cannot, in a society that leaves such questions to popular vote, be taken as conclusive. On such a question free and open debate is vital to informed decision-making by the electorate. Teachers are, as a class, the members of a community most likely to have informed and definite opinions as to how funds allotted to the operation of the schools should be spent. Accordingly, it is essential that they be able to speak out freely on such questions without fear of retaliatory dismissal.[9]

Because the Court concluded that Pickering's statements were not knowingly or recklessly false it had "no occasion" to pass upon the additional question whether false statements knowingly or recklessly made by a teacher, if they could be neither shown nor reasonably presumed to have had any harmful effects, would still be protected by the First Amendment.[10] The Court also noted that the *Pickering* case did "not present a situation in which the teacher's public statements are so without foundation as to call into question his fitness to perform his duties in the classroom."[11]

To what extent does the First Amendment protect a teacher's public out-of-class criticism of his principal or department chairman?

The Supreme Court's opinion in *Pickering* cited certain factual contexts in which sufficient disruption might be found to override a public employee's interest in free speech. The Court declined to hold that the presence of any one of these factual contexts, taken alone, would require a finding that particular speech was unprotected.[12] Recently, the Court made clear that there is no per *se* rule that a public employee's

criticism directed at an immediate superior or any other
person in daily contact with the speaker is unprotected. In
Givhan v. Western Line Consolidated School District,[13] a
teacher criticized her principal in a private conversation with
him. The Supreme Court did not hold the speech unprotected as a matter of law because she had criticized her
principal, but remanded the case for a determination of the
Pickering issue on the record.[14] However, in *Connick v.
Myers*,[14a] in which an assistant district attorney who was
disgruntled over a job transfer circulated a questionnaire
soliciting the views of office members on office transfer policy,
office morale, the desirability of a grievance committee, and
the level of confidence in superiors, the Supreme Court, in
a 5–4 vote, found her speech unprotected. Emphasizing that
each case requires individualized balancing, the Court stated:
"Whether an employee's speech addresses a matter of public
concern must be determined by the content, form, and context
of a given statement."[14b] The federal appeals courts similarly
have treated the question as one to be decided on the facts
of each case.[15] Where such a court has relied upon the
fact of immediate supervision or close daily contact in
concluding that a public employee's criticism was unprotected,
that circumstance was merely one factor, which when taken
together with others, was held to establish disruption or
interference.[16]

Even where disruption or interference occurs in whole or
in part because a teacher's speech is targeted at his principal
or department chairman, it can be argued in many cases that
the teacher's free-speech interest, and the correlative interest
of the public in receiving information concerning the operation of the schools, outweighs such disruption or interference.
For example, a teacher who publicly and accurately exposes
corruption by his principal—for example, his principal's em-
bezzlement of school funds—might well "interfere" with or
"disrupt" the relationship, but it is likely that the strong
public interest in knowing the facts would lead a court to find
the teacher's speech protected.[17]

This point is illustrated by a Fifth Circuit case in which
an Alabama teacher sent a press release to the media in
which he stated that an unnamed principal had exposed children to the risk of serious physical harm by making them go
outside for a tornado drill during a thunderstorm. After the

school board placed a letter in the teacher's file labeling his actions "unethical" and "unprofessional," the teacher sued. Holding that the teacher's statement was constitutionally protected, the court wrote:

> Swilley's press release involved matters of public concern and was not merely a petty personal attack. In our view, the Supreme Court's language regarding the need for superior-subordinate discipline and harmony was intended to prevent public airing of obnoxious personal vendettas which are almost always detrimental to any working relationship. But, the Supreme Court did not intend to stifle discussion on matters of legitimate public importance concerning the professional conduct of school employees. Surely, the physical safety and well-being of our school-children is as important an issue for public scrutiny as is the allocation of school funds between athletic and educational programs. Indeed, our experience tells us that the more important the subject matter is to the public, the sharper the reaction will be by those whose conduct may be called into question. It is precisely the probability of oppressive over-reaction by the powers that be which requires our constant vigilance of the First Amendment protections accorded all public employees.[18]

Similarly, in a Texas case in which a teacher charged in appearances before the city council and school board that robberies and assaults were being committed in his school, the court found the teacher's speech protected. Concluding that the school board's decision to terminate his employment was based in substantial part on his remarks, the court held the termination unconstitutional, stating that although it could "understand the principal's reaction [to the charge] that there was crime in the corridors of [the school]," society's "interest in information concerning the operation of its schools far outweighs any strain on the teacher-principal relationship which existed."[19]

Some types of superior-subordinate relationships, as *Pickering* recognized, are so clearly the type of relationship requiring "personal loyalty and confidence"[20] as to justify a presumption that the relationship would be seriously disrupted by the subordinate's criticism of the superior. Examples are working relationships between a judge and his law clerk[21] or chief probation officer,[22] or between a district attorney and his first assistant serving as his "alter ego."[23] It cannot, however, be presumed that the relationship between a teacher and his principal, or between a faculty member and his department chairman, would be similarly disrupted by such criticism.[24] The facts may show that the specific relationship between a principal and a teacher is not one requiring the maintenance of "personal loyalty and confidence." A Delaware federal district court so held where the teacher's duties "were performed in the context of a large and diversified senior high school, and his job required him to apply his own specialized expertise to the direction of a music program over which the principal could and did exercise only a limited amount of day-to-day control."[25]

In particular, the relationship between a faculty member and his department chairman exists in a setting in which educational and administrative decisions traditionally are made by democratic vote of the faculty, and where such decisions are accompanied by robust debate and sometimes heated controversy within the faculty. These traditions of academic freedom and self-government belie the notion that the working relationship between a department chairman and a faculty member necessarily would be destroyed by criticism. As a Texas federal district court concluded, the idea "that a Department chair and an Associate Professor must enjoy a close, personal or confidential relationship . . ." is refuted by "common experience."[26] Thus it may reasonably be argued that the evidence must demonstrate that the criticism in fact undermined the working relationship[27] or, at the very least, was certain to do so.

Must a teacher first resort to an existing grievance procedure before bringing his criticisms of the school authorities to the attention of the public?

In *Pickering,* the U.S. Supreme Court determined that the case before it furnished "no occasion . . . for consideration of the extent to which teachers can be required by narrowly drawn grievance procedures to submit complaints about the operation of the schools to their superiors for action thereon prior to bringing the complaints before the public."[28]

Grievance procedures typically are designed to deal with personnel policies and practices affecting employees, and not with the more general policies or practices followed by the school board in fulfilling its educational mission. At least where such a typical grievance procedure is in effect, a teacher will not be required to resort to the grievance machinery before publicly criticizing school authorities on a broad issue of educational policy.

In a Texas case, for example, a federal court ruled that a teacher's public remarks concerning crime, truancy, and social problems affecting the quality of education did not constitute a proper subject matter for a grievance procedure designed to secure equitable solutions to problems affecting the welfare or working conditions of employees, and therefore the teacher (who in any event had made reasonable efforts to secure change through "proper channels") could not be terminated for failing to present his remarks initially through the grievance procedure.[29]

Even where a teacher's public comments do concern employee welfare or working conditions, the comments may touch upon issues of broader scope than those to which the grievance procedure is designed to apply.[30] In an analogous context, New York City welfare investigators complained in a letter to an HEW official of the workload in the city welfare department and also declared that the state, by not reducing the workload, failed to qualify for federal contributions. The court ruled that the letter raised issues "not personal to them" but involved "general policies and practices in carrying out the Department's function."[31] Therefore, the court held, the investigators were not required to exhaust a grievance procedure dealing with the *individual* problems of employees and not designed "to deal with such broad issues as those raised in the . . . letter."[32]

In reserving the question whether a school board by a "narrowly drawn" grievance procedure may require a teacher to submit his complaints about the operation of the schools to his superiors before bringing such complaints to the public, the court was implicitly recognizing the principle that a governmental regulation must not encroach unnecessarily upon First Amendment rights where its legitimate objectives can be achieved by a regulation more narrowly drawn—a principle that has been applied to strike down teacher dismissals based on overbroad rules.[33] Thus, where a teacher's public remarks concerned such matters of vital public interest as truancy and crime in the schools, and he had made reasonable efforts to create an awareness of these problems within the administrative structure of the school system, a federal court ruled that the termination of his employment on the basis of his remarks could not be justified by the school district's interest in channeling such matters through a grievance procedure, even assuming it was applicable.[34]

Assuming that school authorities may require a teacher, by a "narrowly drawn" grievance procedure, to submit his complaints about the operation of the schools to his superiors before bringing them to the public (a question left open by *Pickering*), and also assuming that such authorities would be justified in channeling the subject matter of the speech through the grievance procedure, this presumably would not be enough. Rather, it can be contended, the school authorities must give the teacher sufficiently clear advance notice that he is required to exhaust the grievance procedure before he makes his complaints public.[35]

Is a teacher's public out-of-class criticism of co-workers protected?

In *Pickering* the Supreme Court distinguished cases in which a teacher's statements are directed at one with whom he would normally be in contact in the course of his daily work and in which a question of maintaining "harmony among coworkers" is presented,[36] but the Court did not indicate how it would decide such cases. As with statements directed at an immediate superior, the fact that speech is aimed at co-workers seems relevant to the extent that it affects the communication's impact upon the efficient operation of the school system, and thereby becomes a factor in the *Pickering* analysis.[37] In *Connick v. Myers*, a case decided in 1983 in which a district attorney fired an aggrieved assistant after she circulated a questionnaire that called into question his and his supervisors management of the office, the Court wrote that the district attorney thought that the questionnaire "was an act of insubordination which interfered with working relationships." It then declared: "When close working relationships are essential to fulfilling public responsibilities, a wide degree of [judicial] deference to the employer's judgment is appropriate."[37a]

Certainly speech critical of co-workers will be protected where it involves "a matter of compelling public concern," such as misappropriation of public funds.[38] As one court stated, "the creation of disharmony cannot be so feared as to silence the critic who would inform the public of this misbehavior [padding of mileage claims] by public officials."[39]

Other types of public criticism of co-workers may also be protected under *Pickering*. For example, in a Virginia case a federal court held statements made by a community college professor to fellow faculty members, criticizing a faculty committee report which had stigmatized him, protected by the First Amendment.[40]

Is a teacher's public out-of-class criticism of a school system policy or practice unprotected because the criticism produces friction in his relationship with his immediate superior or co-workers?

It is unlikely that a court would hold a teacher's speech unprotected on this ground. In *Tinker v. Des Moines School District*,[41] the Supreme Court, speaking to a different but related issue involving the exercise of First Amendment rights in a school context, said that "[i]n order for . . . school officials to justify prohibition of a particular expression of opinion . . . [they] must be able to show that . . . [their] action was caused by something more than a mere desire to avoid the discomfort and unpleasantness that always accompany an unpopular viewpoint."[42] That type of unrest, the Supreme Court of California has said, "must be tolerated in the schools as well as in society generally."[43]

Thus, where a guidance counselor had advised parents of Mexican-American students to consult the local legal aid society about the placement of their children in classes for the mentally retarded on the basis of tests conducted in English rather than their native tongue, the Ninth Circuit held the counselor's communication protected even though it had "ruffl[ed] the feathers" of her co-workers.[44] And the Supreme Court of California ruled that school authorities could not constitutionally transfer a teacher on the ground that his criticism of school policies had alienated some of his fellow teachers and caused "disharmony" among the faculty.[45] In a non-school

Third Circuit case involving criticisms of administrators and co-workers, a tax department employee wrote letters to public officials accusing his supervisors of mismanagement and his co-workers of filing fraudulent returns. Finding the letters to be protected by the First Amendment, the court wrote:

> We do not underestimate the internal unease or unpleasantness that may follow when a government employee decides to break rank and complain either publicly or to supervisors about a situation which s/he believes merits review and reform. That is the price the First Amendment exacts in return for an informed citizenry.[46]

Are a teacher's public out-of-class statements on controversial political or social issues—not involving criticism of his employer or co-workers—protected?

Yes. In such a case the legitimate interests of the school authorities would not seem to be implicated. Accordingly, a teacher may well have greater freedom to speak out on issues of this kind than on school issues, even though he may have no special knowledge of the subject matter.

Thus, for example, the Second Circuit recognized that a state college faculty member had a constitutional right, and "one of great importance," to send other faculty members an invitation to participate in a peace program concerning the Vietnam War. The court further concluded that the faculty member had a constitutional right to send a letter to the president of another college suggesting that she had arbitrarily suspended a number of students.[47] And the Ninth Circuit ruled that a letter to a local newspaper by a teacher who was also chairman of the local chapter of the American Civil Liberties Union, defending the ACLU's position favoring legalization of marijuana, was protected by the First Amendment and thus did not form a valid basis for contract non-renewal.[48]

Do a teacher's out-of-class comments on an employment-related subject concern a "matter of public interest" within the meaning of Pickering?

Apparently so. The decisions of the Supreme Court indicate that to the extent a teacher's speech must be on a matter of "public interest" in order to trigger First Amendment protection, there is a public interest in matters affecting public employment. Thus, the Court has held that public employees have a First Amendment right to express their views regarding government "decisions concerning labor relations."[49] In *City of Madison Joint School District No. 8 v. Wisconsin Employment Relations Commission*,[50] the Court, addressing the right of non-union teachers to express themselves on the merits of a "fair share" proposal that would have required them to help defray the costs of collective bargaining, said:

> Surely no one would question the *absolute right* of the nonunion teachers to consult among themselves, hold meetings, reduce their views to writing, and communicate those views to the public generally in pamphlets, letters, or expressions carried by the news media.

In *Mount Healthy Board of Education v. Doyle*,[51] moreover, the Court agreed that the question of a dress code for teachers in the public schools was a matter of public interest. These decisions may be viewed as implicitly recognizing that in public agencies the public is the employer, and therefore has an interest in the efficiency of the agency, the compensation of the agency's employees, and conditions that could affect employee morale or the quality of the services performed.

Many decisions of the federal appeals courts also recognize that *Pickering*'s protection of the speech rights of public employees extends to comments on matters affecting their employment. The Fifth Circuit held that an assistant professor at a state university had a First Amendment right to distribute a questionnaire soliciting the views of the faculty on a broad range of employment-related issues, "such as the degree of mutual confidence existing between administration and faculty, the extent to which good teaching and good research were rewarded, the extent to which faculty opinions were listened to and respected, the effectiveness of the administration in dealing with grievances, the accuracy and completeness of information used to evaluate teachers, and other matters." The court concluded that "[t]hese are matters of public importance and concern. Comment upon them is protected under *Pickering v. Board of Education* . . . and similar cases."[52] And the Seventh Circuit ruled that a teacher's advocacy of a master collective bargaining contract was "clearly a matter of public concern" and therefore protected.[53] Similarly, the Third Circuit concluded that several professors' criticisms of the personnel policies and methods of the president of the state-related university at which they worked were " 'core' speech squarely encompassed within the First Amendment."[54]

The public interest in matters concerning employment in public agencies is particularly clear where a public educational institution is involved. The public, through its elected representatives, exercises control over public education, determining curriculum content, methods of instruction, and the proper allocation of school funds.[55] The public therefore has a legitimate and substantial interest in all matters bearing on the ability of public educational institutions to perform their functions. Of course, a court will be particularly inclined to find a "public interest" component in a teacher's employment-related speech where the teacher's comments reflect a concern that the employment practice in question is detrimental to students.[56]

On the other hand, a court may conclude that there is no public interest in "a mere in-house dialogue about administrative details of no concern to the public."[57] And there may, perhaps, be a matter so unique to an individual teacher's employment situation that a court might question whether it is a matter of public interest. A matter of "personal pique" or "private ambitions"[58] may fall in this category, e.g., a gripe that the speaker has not received public credit for his work[59] or that his office is too small.

This apparently was the case in *Connick v. Myers*, in which an assistant district attorney, unhappy with a proposed transfer, circulated a questionnaire that disturbed the district attorney The courst stated:

> We view the questions pertaining to the confidence and trust that Myers coworkers possess in various supervisors, the level of office morale, and the need for a grievance committee as mere extensions of Myers' dispute over her transfer . . . . [W]e do not believe these questions are of public import in evaluating the performance of the Dictrict Attorney as an elected official. Myers did not seek to inform the public that the District

Attorney's office was not discharging its governmental
responsibilities . . . .

To persume that all matters which transpire within a
government office are of public concern would mean that
virtually every remark—and certainly every criticism directed at a public offical—would plant the seeds of a
constitutional case.[59a]

The Court concluded that "Myers' questionnaire touched
upon matters of public concern in only a most limited sense;
her survey, in our view, is most accurately characterized as
an employee grievance concerning internal office policy."[59b] In
summarizing its holding, the Court stated: "We hold only
then when a public employee speaks not as a citizen upon
matters of public concern, but instead as an employee upon
matters only of personal interest, absent the most unusual
circumstances, a federal court is not the appropriate for in
which to review the widsom of a personnel decision taken by
a public agency allegedly in reaction to the employee's
behavior."[59c] This discussion and Justice Brennan's strong
dissent,[59d] which noted how the Court has often said that the
job-related concerns of public employees are generally public
concerns, make clear how difficult it is not only for public
employees, but also for the court, to draw the line between
what speech is of public concern and what speech is not.

In Arizona a federal district court held that a professor's
bitter opposition to the appointment of a new creative writing
instructor was unprotected because "the issue was limited to
a discussion of the relative qualifications of [the new instruc-
tor] in the creative writing program [and was therefore] an
internal matter not of public concern."[60] In a Texas case, a
federal district court concluded that the communications of a
teacher's aide relating to the immediate terms and conditions
of her employment were only "tangentially" on a matter of
public concern and, in part for that reason, unprotected.[61]
But the fact that speech on a public issue may be prompted
by a private concern should not diminish First Amendment
protection. For example, the possibility of race discrimination
in public employment is a matter of public concern,[62] and it
is no less so if it is brought to the public's attention by an
employee who claims that he was personally injured by the
alleged discrimination.

Are a teacher's public out-of-class comments not involving a matter of public interest wholly unprotected?

Assuming that a teacher's comments do not involve a matter of "public interest," it is far from clear that all First Amendment protection should be withheld.[63] Since *Pickering* involved speech determined by the Supreme Court to relate to a matter of public interest, the Court did not decide whether a teacher's comments lacking a "public interest" component were protected.

The First Amendment "forbids abridgement of the 'freedom of speech' "[64]—not of certain kinds of speech. As the Supreme Court said in a different context in *Winters v. New York*:[65] "Though we can see nothing of any possible value to society in these magazines, they are as much entitled to the protection of free speech as the best of literature." Thus even though a teacher's speech does not relate to "burning social issues," it would not appear to be "automatically excluded from protection."[66]

Several courts, however, have treated the extent to which the speech involves a matter of public interest as a factor in what they have viewed as the balancing required by *Pickering*. One court stated that an "extremely strong or unusual" case would have to be made by school authorities to counterbalance the interest of a teacher in speaking publicly as a citizen,[67] while another court suggested that where the only persons shown to have any interest in a professor's communications were members of his department and the dean, the communications "concerned an issue of less public interest than Pickering's," and the First Amendment interest in the protection of such communications was "correspondingly reduced."[68]

In a significant decision upholding speech not involving a matter of public interest, the 11th Circuit held to be constitutionally protected a police officer's bitter personal complaints about his police chief.[69] While acknowledging that the officer's calling the police chief a "back stabbing son of a bitch" and a "bastard" did not concern a public matter, the court wrote that the police officer,

> like every citizen, has a strong interest in having the opportunity to speak his mind, free from government censorship or sanction. . . . Although the actual words

Waters spoke cannot be said to be valuable to the public at large, the first amendment's protections do not turn on the social worth of the statements, save in a few exceptions not relevant here . . . . Similarly, that Waters chose to express his ideas in language some might find offensive is not, in and of itself, enough to override his interest in speaking freely.[70]

Even though the comments had in a sense become public when the police officer to whom the complaining officer was talking relayed the remarks to the police chief, the court emphasized the private nature of the comments, calling them "idle barroom chatter." In holding the police officer's transfer and demotion unconstitutional, the court wrote that "[a]bsent significant countervailing governmental interests, we are loathe to sanction the intrusion of the government's ear into the private lives of its employees."[71] After stating that such verbal sniping can be punished only when "the police department can show that the speech in question actually disrupts the officer's efficiency or the internal operation of the department . . ." the court concluded that there was no such disruption in this case.[72]

Does a teacher have a First Amendment right to criticize policies or practices in his school system in remarks communicated privately to his superior?

Such communications are within the scope of the First Amendment, although, like a teacher's speech in a public forum, consideration of institutional efficiency may limit protection in some circumstances.

In *Givhan v. Western Line Consolidated School District*[73] a former teacher in Mississippi alleged that her employment contract was not renewed, in violation of her free-speech rights, because she had expressed to her principal the view that the policies of her school and school district were racially discriminatory. The Fifth Circuit concluded that unless speech by a public employee is directed to a public audience it is unprotected by the First Amendment.[74] Disagreeing, the Supreme Court ruled that the First Amendment protection of freedom of speech is not "lost to the public employee who arranges to communicate privately with his employer rather than to spread his views before the public."[75] The Court did recognize, however, that private expression to an immediate superior may pose added factors for consideration in determining whether the speech is protected:

> When a teacher speaks publicly, it is generally the *content* of his statements that must be assessed to determine whether they "in any way either impeded the teacher's proper performance of his daily duties in the classroom or . . . interfered with the regular operation of the schools generally. . . ." Private expression, however, may in some situations bring additional factors into the *Pickering* calculus. When a government employee personally confronts his immediate superior, the employing agency's institutional efficiency may be threatened not only by the content of the employee's message, but also by the manner, time, and place in which it is delivered.[76]

Punishment of a teacher because of a communication addressed to his superior, in addition to implicating the free speech clause of the First Amendment, also implicates that Amendment's right to petition for redress of grievances[77]—although this right, like a teacher's free-speech right, may be subject to the type of limitations suggested in *Pickering* and *Givhan*. The right of petition "extends to all departments of the Government" including "administrative agencies."[78] A number of courts therefore have held that the right protects government employees who communicate their grievances directly to those in the administrative hierarchy having authority to deal with them.

Thus even before *Pickering* the U.S. Court of Claims ruled that the discharge of a naval shipyard worker because of his letter to the Secretary of the Navy alleging favoritism in promotions unconstitutionally infringed upon the worker's right of petition. The court concluded that "a petition by a federal employee to one above him in the executive hierarchy is covered by the First Amendment."[79] On the basis of the petition clause the same court subsequently held protected a letter by a probationary teacher in a Job Corps center to an OEO official, suggesting that the center "should get rid of its Director and other officials to make it run like it should" and asserting that too many people in high positions had come from the other side of the tracks and had no understanding of the problems the "black boys have had to face."[80]

In *City of Madison Joint School District No. 8 v. Wisconsin Employment Relations Commission*,[81] moreover, the Supreme Court ruled that a non-union teacher had a First Amendment right to speak at a public school board meeting on a "fair share" proposal which would have required all teachers (whether members of the union or not) to pay union dues. While the public nature of the session played a significant role in the Court's decision, the Court also noted the independent significance of the protected First Amendment right of teachers to communicate directly with their school board concerning the operation of the schools. Although not expressly relying on the petition clause, the Court articulated the concern that "restraining teachers' expressions *to the board* on matters involving the operation of the schools would seriously impair the board's ability to govern the district"[82] and would infringe upon the "protected right" of teachers "to communicate with the board."[83] Presumably management of the schools would also be impaired if similar communications by teachers directed to school authorities other than board members, e.g., superintendents or principals, were inhibited.

A standard limiting a public employee's speech protection to matters of public interest seems particularly dubious in applying the petition clause. Writing in the 19th century, a respected authority on constitutional law characterized the right of petition as a "generic term" which "applies to . . . appeals of every sort, and for every purpose, made to the judgment, discretion, or favor of the person or body having authority in the premises."[84]

To be constitutionally protected, must a teacher's public out-of-class speech be mild or moderate in tone?

Generally such speech, if otherwise shielded from punishment by the First Amendment, does not lose its protected character because its tone is sharp.

Thus, the Ninth Circuit has rejected the notion that "[t]he desire to maintain a sedate academic environment" is an interest "sufficiently compelling . . . to justify limitations on a teacher's freedom to express himself on political issues in vigorous, argumentative, unmeasured, and even distinctly unpleasant terms."[85] The same court, assessing whether a faculty member's speech at an academic senate meeting was constitutionally protected, acknowledged that "the proper functioning of schools and universities requires some discretion from all involved," but observed that "unrealistic sensitivity to the fragility of schools and universities is inappropriate. Robust intellectual and political discussions can and should thrive on college campuses. These discussions will not always be models of decorum." The court warned that "often those with the power to appoint will be on one side of a controversial issue and find it convenient to use their opponents' momentary stridency as a pretext to squelch them."[86]

Nor is blandness a prerequisite to constitutional protection where a teacher's speech is critical of a nominal superior. The Supreme Court in *Pickering* expressly repudiated the suggestion that a teacher's truthful criticism of his school board in a letter to a newspaper constitutionally could furnish grounds for dismissal because the statements in the letter were "critical in tone."[87] In a Pennsylvania case, the Third Circuit held to be constitutionally protected a telegram that a faculty member had sent to the Governor complaining that the president of a state-related university was "inhumane," "vicious," "vindictive," and "arrogant with power," and had engaged in "terribly irrational and destructive" conduct. The court wrote that "[s]peech with far less claim to legitimacy than a telegram by a faculty member at a state-related institution to his Governor has been held to fall within the scope of the First Amendment . . . . The possibility or even the likelihood that plaintiffs may have been misguided or obstinate . . . does not derogate from the status of their expressions as speech within the First Amendment."[88]

Similarly, in an Arizona case a federal court found constitutionally protected a state university professor's "extremely sharp" criticism of the Board of Regents—including a press release questioning the motives of the board and characterizing an action it had taken as hypocritical and a televised speech questioning the moral propriety of the board's conduct.[89] Similarly, a Mississippi federal district court held protected a teacher's "unquestionably abrasive" criticism of the policies of his school board and superintendent.[90]

Some courts have ruled that even a teacher's untruthful criticism of a nominal superior may be constitutionally protected though it is harshly articulated. In a New York case a teacher was suspended without pay for distributing to fellow teachers copies of his letter to the school board critical of its failure to renew the contract of a probationary teacher. In addition to "strident" comments, the letter contained factual inaccuracies. The court noted that there was no proof that the inaccuracies were the result of reckless or intentional falsehood, or that the teacher's indiscretions had any harmful effects on the school system. "Indiscreet bombast in an argumentative letter," the court held, "to the limited extent present here, is insufficient to sanction disciplinary action. Otherwise, those who criticize in any area where criticism is permissible would either be discouraged from exercising their right or would be required to do so in such innocuous terms as would make the criticism seem ineffective or obsequious."[91]

It should not be assumed, however, that the protection afforded to robust expression and vigorous criticism by teachers extends to profanity or vituperation. To be sure, in holding that a student could not be expelled for distributing an undergound newspaper, the Supreme Court has said that dissemination of ideas "no matter how offensive to good taste" may not be shut off in the name of "conventions of decency."[92] The courts, however, have been less tolerant of profane or vituperative speech in the employment context. The District of Columbia Circuit has said that "it is inherent in the employment relationship . . . that an employee cannot reasonably assert a right to keep his job while at the same time he inveighs against his superiors in public with intemperate and defamatory cartoons. [Dismissal in such circumstances neither] comes as an unfair surprise [nor] is so unexpected and uncertain as to chill his freedom to engage in appropriate speech."[93] Another court, in a case involving termination of a teacher's employment, observed that vituperative speech "adds very little to the world of ideas."[94] Nevertheless, in a Texas case in which a police officer called his police chief a "son of a bitch" and a "bastard" in a barroom conversation with a friend, the 11th Circuit held that even such epithets were constitutionally protected. The court wrote, "[t]hat [the police officer] chose to express his ideas in language that some might find offensive is not, in and of itself, enough to override his interest in speaking freely."[95]

Where the target of a teacher's statements is an immediate superior, a court may consider the tone of a teacher's speech relevant to the issue of whether the statements interfered with the regular operation of the school by substantially affecting the working relationship. For example, a Texas federal district court, in holding speech by a teacher's aide at a school board meeting unprotected, relied in part on its finding that she had referred sarcastically to her immediate superiors and "c[o]me very close to publicly ridiculing" her immediate supervisor as well as the assistant superintendent.[96] In another case, it was held that the non-renewal of a probationary teacher's contract because of statements he made at a public school board hearing calling his administrative supervisor a liar and challenging the integrity of the entire administrative staff did not violate his right to free speech.[97]

Must the impediment to a teacher's performance or to the operation of the school system created by his out-of-class speech be substantial before it can furnish grounds for discharge or discipline?

The case law strongly supports this view.

The Supreme Court has said that "only considerations of the greatest urgency can justify restrictions on speech."[98] Thus where a policeman challenged his dismissal based on his public statements, the District of Columbia Circuit held that since the government's action affected fundamental rights, the intrusion had to be justified by "a compelling governmental interest."[99] And the Eighth Circuit has indicated that it believes the governmental interest must be "[l]egitimate and compelling" to justify school authorities in punishing a teacher for otherwise protected speech.[100] A significant degree of interference with the teacher's performance of his own duties or substantial disruption of the school environment would appear to be the only "legitimate and compelling" interests that could render such punishment consistent with the First Amendment.

Following the *Pickering* decision, the Supreme Court in *Tinker v. Des Moines School District*[101] ruled that First Amendment rights of students to engage in symbolic classroom expression—in that case, wearing a black armband to protest government policy in Vietnam—can constitutionally be curtailed only when their exercise threatens to "materially and substantially disrupt the work and discipline of the school."[102] Federal courts of appeals addressing the question uniformly have held that the *Tinker* standard also governs the extent of disruption or interference with operations that must be shown before a public employee can be disciplined for speech under *Pickering*, i.e., the speech must be shown to have materially and substantially interfered with the legitimate function of the employing agency.[103] Several courts have intimated that in weighing the disruptiveness of the public employee's criticisms against the public's interest in hearing the criticism and the employee's right to make the criticism, they would take into account whether there were less disruptive ways for the employee to lodge the criticisms and whether the method chosen to make the criticism was calculated to disrupt.[104]

In a recent, slightly ambiguous decision, the Supreme Court, by a 5–4 vote, apparently stepped back from this position. In *Connick v. Myers*, in which the Court found the disputed speech was not of public concern, the Court wrote: "[W]e do not see the necessity for an employer to allow events to unfold to the extent that the disruption of the office and the destruction of working relationships is manifest before taking action. We caution that a stronger showing may be necessary if the employee's speech more substantially involved matters of public concern."[104a] Here, the Court was apparently adopting a sliding scale: the more that speech concerns a public matter, the stronger must be the showing of potential disruption in order to punish the speaker.

To provide a basis for discharge or discipline, must the disruption or interference be unreasonable?

A forceful argument can be made to this effect. As one court has noted, some kinds of speech are almost certain to cause substantial disruption, e.g., speech by public employee which "accurately exposes rampant corruption in her office," but society cannot afford to leave such speech unprotected.[105] Similarly, in a Fourth Circuit case in which a professor made some highly critical statements charging her school's administration with being unaware of student attitudes and insensitive toward student needs, the court wrote that this dispute "did not disrupt the college community or create any more disharmony than would be expected when a subordinate criticizes her superiors on any subject. In any event disharmony is not a *per se* defense to dismissal." The court concluded that "[w]hatever disruption might have been caused in this case is overshadowed by the public interest in these subjects and [the plaintiff's] right to express her opinions on them."[106]

Who has the burden of proof on the issue of whether the teacher's performance, or the operation of the school system, was substantially impeded by his out-of-class speech?

All federal courts of appeals addressing the allocation of the burden of proof in *Pickering* cases have placed on the public employer the burden of proving that the plaintiff's statements in fact caused disruption sufficient to override the plaintiff's First Amendment interest.[107] These decisions reflect the general rule in First Amendment cases that the exercise of First Amendment rights may not be regulated or punished unless the government demonstrates that such exercise impairs an overriding governmental interest.[108]

Is the "material and substantial disruption" test satisfied by an administrator's testimony that he was apprehensive about potential disruption?

No. An "undifferentiated fear" is "not enough to overcome the right to freedom of expression" in the school environment.[109] Thus a Mississippi federal court held that a principal's court testimony that he was "scared every day" for the remainder of the year that trouble might arise in the school as the result of a teacher's public statements criticizing his school board and superintendent was insufficient to override the teacher's free-speech rights. Accordingly, the court ruled that the non-renewal because of such statements was invalid and issued a preliminary and permanent injunction reinstating him for the 1979–80 school year.[110]

Can the school authorities satisfy their burden of proof by speculative opinion testimony concerning the likelihood of material and substantial disruption?

Probably not. Speculative opinion testimony "has limited utility in justifying a restriction of freedom of expression."[111] The Second Circuit has stated that "[a]ny limitation on the exercise of constitutional rights can be justified only by a conclusion, based upon reasonable inferences flowing from concrete facts and not abstractions, that the interests of discipline or sound education are materially and substantially jeopardized, whether the danger stems initially from the conduct of students or teachers."[112] In an Indiana case involving students who were suspended for giving out leaflets urging students to walk out of classes, a federal district court wrote that school authorities "have the burden of bringing forth evidence justifying a reasonable forecast of material interference with the school's work . . . and [that] the courts will not merely accept bare allegations on the part of the school authorities that such forecast existed."[113]

May a court accept the judgment of the school authorities with respect to the effects of a teacher's out-of-class speech on his performance or the operation of the school system without satisfying itself that the judgment was correct?

No. The District of Columbia Circuit has ruled that the trial court erred in accepting uncritically the conclusion of the commanding officer of a naval facility that a memorandum sent by a teacher employed at the facility to individuals officially responsible for matters at the school had impaired the efficiency of the service.[114] The court concluded that "[t]he balancing here of First Amendment freedoms against an asserted governmental interest requires the judgment of the District Court."[115] This ruling seems consistent with the decision in *Tinker v. Des Moines School District*,[116] in which the Supreme Court refused to defer to the administrative judgment of school officials on the effects of classroom speech by students.

Does adverse community reaction or loss of taxpayer confidence furnish a constitutionally permissible basis for discharging or disciplining a teacher for out-of-class speech?

The Fifth Circuit has ruled that a state university's interest in maintaining public confidence justified the dismissal of a teaching assistant whose speeches using profane language and criticizing the university administration had received adverse newspaper publicity.[117] To the extent this ruling suggests that sanctions may be imposed upon a teacher for otherwise protected speech because community reaction is or is likely to be adverse, the decision seems unsound and unrepresentative.

In *Cooper v. Aaron*[118] the Supreme Court ruled that the constitutional principles underlying the right of black school children in Little Rock, Arkansas, to desegregated schooling "cannot be allowed to yield simply because of disagreement with them."[119] Nor are free-speech rights contingent upon the popularity of the speaker's views.[120] Thus an Arizona federal court determined that "even loss of legislative funds and public misunderstanding, where these detriments are caused by the public's violent disagreement with the views expressed by a faculty member, are not the kind of detriments that can be balanced against a teacher's right to free expression."[121] And a Colorado federal court concluded that a state university's decision not to hire an applicant for a faculty position could not "be grounded upon a fear that a Regent's constituency would not approve the appointment of a Marxist, or that the state legislature or certain alumni would reduce the financial support received by the University."[122]

Is a teacher immunized from punishment for conduct which otherwise would justify employment termination or discipline because his conduct takes the form of speech?

No. The Sixth Circuit, for example, held unprotected a teacher's statement to an unauthorized assembly of students on school property, partly on the ground that he had impliedly contradicted statements of his superiors that the students should return to class.[123] The Fourth Circuit has warned that "[a] college has a right to expect a teacher to follow instructions and work cooperatively and harmoniously with the head of the department" and that a teacher "does not immunize himself against loss of his position simply because his noncooperation and aggressive conduct are verbalized."[124] And the same court upheld the discharge of two community college faculty members who had voiced disagreement with changes in the tenure system by failing to take part in a budget workshop and refusing to participate in commencement exercises. The court rejected their argument that the First Amendment insulated them from discharge because their violations of the terms of their employment were ingredients in a protest.[125]

Similarly, the Supreme Court of Nevada held that the refusal to renew the contract of a teacher who had persistently encouraged his daughters not to attend school and had indicated that he would continue to allow them to be truant did not violate his First Amendment rights.[126] In an Oregon case, a teacher's efforts to secure an abortion for a mentally retarded student over the opposition of the welfare department, which had custody of the student, were held unprotected in view of the strain that the teacher's activities, although embodied in speech, had produced between the school district and the welfare department.[127]

Can school authorities penalize a teacher for otherwise protected speech on the ground that the speech reveals a characteristic or attitude with which they legitimately may be concerned?

The courts generally have scrutinized such attempted justifications carefully to determine whether the attribute with which the school authorities purport to be concerned is merely a label for the speech or for the friction naturally resulting from the expression of controversial ideas. Thus the Tenth Circuit held that termination of the employment of state college faculty members because of their out-of-class speech concerning the college's administrative policies violated their First Amendment rights, notwithstanding the claim by the college authorities that the terminations were justified because, in making their statements, the faculty members had been "divisive."[128] And the District of Columbia Circuit refused to accept the contention that the discharge of a policeman for otherwise protected public statements could be justified on the ground that the statements reflected an unsatisfactory "attitude." The court ruled that the policeman's spoken words and his attitude were "inseparably intertwined," and that the free-speech clause of the First Amendment "cannot be laid aside simply on the basis that the speaker was penalized not for his speech but for a state of mind manifested thereby."[129]

There may well be cases, however, in which a court may conclude that a teacher's speech demonstrated a characteristic which the school authorities could validly take into account in determining his suitability for continued employment. The Supreme Court noted in *Pickering* that the case before it did "not present a situation in which a teacher's public statements are so without foundation as to call into question his fitness to perform his duties in the classroom. In such a case, of course, the statements would merely be evidence of the teacher's general competence, or lack thereof, and not an independent basis for dismissal."[130] As the First Circuit has held, "[t]he first amendment does not protect an employee who has revealed his incompetencies in writing, as by submitting an inept report."[131] The Fifth Circuit has held that university authorities, without violating the First Amendment, could determine that a professor's conduct in repeatedly making false public statements when their truth easily could have been ascertained "demonstrated a lack of character and intellectual responsibility needed for a tenured professor."[132] On the other hand, the Fifth Circuit has made it clear that the factual inaccuracy of a teacher's statements cannot constitutionally form the basis for a determination that he 'has an undesirable character trait unless the evidence demonstrates that he has acted with reckless disregard of their truth or falsity.[133] The doctrine is inapplicable in any event to a teacher's statement of an idea or opinion rather than a fact, since "[u]nder the First Amendment there is no such thing as a false idea."[134]

Is a teacher's out-of-class speech constitutionally protected if, without authority, he purports to speak for his school system?

No. School authorities may validly conclude that such conduct evidences lack of character or judgment. The Tenth Circuit, for example, has ruled that a state university constitutionally could terminate the employment of staff counselors for holding a press conference—otherwise protected by the First Amendment—which "was accompanied by an unjustified cloak of officialdom."[135]

Similarly, where a teacher wrote a letter to a state legislator complaining of alleged under-financing of the program in which she worked, and falsely represented that she expressed the views of the school board, the court refused to hold the letter constitutionally protected. Concluding that she "had the right to write a letter to her Representative and otherwise express her opinions as a citizen," the court held that the teacher "had no right . . . to speak for the Board or to misrepresent its position."[136]

Does a teacher have a First Amendment right to advise parents that she considers a policy or practice of her employing school system harmful to her students?

As in other cases involving a teacher's out-of-class criticism of school authorities, a court—applying the *Pickering* test—is likely to approach this question by determining whether the interests of the school system are sufficiently substantial to override the teacher's free-speech interest. To justify the imposition of a penalty for such speech, however, school officials must demonstrate more than a mere wish to be free from criticism.

In an Arizona case, a Mexican-American educator held a counseling position, uniquely suited to her talents and desires, in a school located in an area where the population consisted primarily of Mexican-Americans and Yaqui Indians. She became concerned that children were being placed in classes for the mentally retarded because they were tested in English rather than in their native tongue. After attempting unsuccessfully to deal with this problem internally within the school system and becoming frustrated by the lack of action, she advised certain parents of affected children to consult the local legal aid society. In retaliation, school authorities transferred her to a school attended primarily by well-to-do Anglo students. Holding that she had been transferred for a constitutionally impermissible reason, the Ninth Circuit concluded that "[t]he School District's interest in being free from general criticism cannot outweigh the right of a sincere, educational counselor to speak out against a policy she believes to be both harmful and unlawful."[137]

A teacher treads on shaky ground, however, when he seeks to communicate to parents views critical of school system practices by using students as couriers. In a New Jersey case, a federal court ruled that the First Amendment did not protect the attempt by a local teachers' union to circulate a letter critical of the school administration, written by the union president on union stationery, which was given by union members to their pupils with instructions to bring the message to their parents or guardians.[138] The theory of the decision—that while teachers have a First Amendment right to comment on matters of public interest in connection with the operation of the public schools in which they work, they have no First Amendment right to free, efficient delivery of such messages—also would seem to apply to an effort by an individual teacher, not under union auspices, to use his students as a "public postal service."[139]

Does the First Amendment protect a teacher's actions in helping students to publish or circulate an underground newspaper?

The First Amendment bars school officials "from regulating the material to which a child is exposed after he leaves school each afternoon."[140] Thus they cannot restrict an underground student newspaper—one conceived, executed, and distributed outside the school.[141]

The Tenth Circuit held in a Wyoming case that a teacher's acts in helping students with an underground newspaper—acts of "assistance and association"—were "protected, although no writing of her own was involved," at least where there was no showing that her actions impeded the proper performance of her classroom duties or the regular operation of the school generally.[142] The school authorities had based the non-renewal of her contract on her "insubordination" in allegedly refusing to comply with her principal's directive to stop circulation of the newspaper. The court ruled, however, that the only premise for a valid claim of insubordination was that the school properly could ban such publications in advance, and determined that such a ban constituted a prior restraint which was "plainly impermissible under the [First] Amendment."[143]

Does a teacher have a First Amendment right to circulate literature to other teachers on school grounds during his lunch hour or other off-duty time?

A teacher probably has such a right, but this right is by no means absolute in character. The effectiveness of the right will depend in large part on the surrounding circumstances.

The Supreme Court has written that "[t]he guarantees of the First Amendment have never meant 'that people who want to propagandize protests or views have a constitutional right to do so whenever and however and wherever they please.' "[144] Thus, the Second Circuit has concluded that a teacher does not have "an absolute constitutional right to use all parts of a school building for unlimited expressive purposes."[145] Rather, the state may set aside portions of its property for purposes inconsistent with the use of that property as a public forum.[146]

Whether school authorities can constitutionally prohibit teachers from circulating literature to other teachers will often hinge on such factors as whether (1) the authorities have allowed other groups to distribute literature in school, (2) there are adequate alternative means for teachers to reach their audience, and (3) the school board or other teachers have circulated material on the same topic.

If the school board allows an outside group or a rival teachers' group to distribute literature in the halls or in the teachers' lounge, that would argue in favor of allowing any teacher to circulate literature in those places.[147] The Supreme Court has stated that "under the Equal Protection Clause, not to mention the First Amendment itself, government may not grant the use of a forum to people whose views it finds acceptable, but deny use to those wishing to express less favored or more conventional views. And it may not select which issues are worth discussing or debating in public facilities."[148] The Court added that "[o]nce a forum is opened up to assembly or speaking to some groups, government may not prohibit others from assembling or speaking on the basis of what they intend to say."[149] This is one of the reasons why the Second Circuit held that a school board could not prohibit a teacher from wearing a black anti-Vietnam War armband in school while the board allowed another teacher to display a pro-Vietnam War sign in his classroom.[150]

The Supreme Court has stated, however, that where school authorities have not turned a classroom or an interschool mail system into a public forum, they may constitutionally grant access to groups whose activities are "compatible with the intended purpose of the property" and deny access to groups whose activities are inconsistent with the use of the property.[150a] In unsettling language that would allow discrimination according to a speaker's identity, but not according to a speaker's message—it is of course at times impossible to separate the two—the Court stated in dictum that a school board that opens its interschool mail system and teacher mailboxes to messages from the Cub Scouts or YMCA, which "engage in activities of interest and educational relevance to students," would not as a consequence be required to permit a teacher organization such as a union to use the mail system because in the Court's view, the union's speech "is concerned with the terms and conditions of teacher employment," a type of speech which the Court said was not of similar educational relevance to the speech of the Cub Scouts.[150b]

A second important factor to examine when school authorities seek to prevent teachers from distributing literature is "the existence of adequate alternative means to reach the intended audience."[151] Thus at least where it can be shown that the school premises are the only, or the most, effective place for teachers to communicate with one another, a prohibition forbidding a teacher to circulate literature or a petition on school premises may violate the First Amendment. The California Supreme Court has ruled invalid, as a violation of the First Amendment's free speech and petition guarantees, a school board regulation prohibiting teachers from circulating a petition on school premises during duty-free lunch periods.[152] The court observed that freedom of speech contemplates effective communication and that school premises are the most effective place for teachers to communicate with one another.[153] In the same vein, the U.S. Supreme Court has written that "[t]he place of work is a place uniquely appropriate for dissemination of views concerning the bargaining representative and the various options open to the employees."[154]

Another important factor militating in favor of letting a teacher distribute literature is whether the school board, a rival teachers' group, or an outside group has circulated literature in school on the same matter. The reason for this is that "[w]hen speakers and subjects are similarly situated, the state may not pick and choose" according to the message or viewpoint of the speech.[155]

Such discrimination occurred recently in a noteworthy Fifth Circuit case where an Alabama school board maintained regulations stating that "[a]ll material political or sectarian in nature distributed on any school campus shall have prior approval of the Assistant Superintendent of Administration." In overturning the regulation and thereby strongly affirming teachers' free-speech rights, the court wrote:

the administrators clearly interpreted [the regulations] to give authority transgressing the First Amendment rights of the teachers . . . . Letters by two Board members on the subject of teacher competency testing were distributed in the schools, while two [teacher association] papers opposing the Board's position were treated differently. One administrator said he would not have approved the [teacher association's] papers for distribution due to their tendency to incite teachers. One principal refused their distribution in his school solely on the ground they were union material. The problem lies in the fact that there was no difference between the possible disruptive effect of the Board's communications and the [teacher association's] communications on the subject in controversy. They differ only in the positions taken. School administrators and principals may not permit one side to promote its position while denying the other side the same opportunity.[156]

The court went on to say that the regulations' requirement of prior submission and prior approval was not what made the regulations offensive.[157] Rather, the court wrote, citing the district court with approval, that what condemned these regulations was that they

contain insufficient standards, purposes, or guidelines by which school authorities may be guided in determining what literature may be distributed on school campuses. [The regulations] fall far short, therefore, of the requirement that a restraint on expression must be "bounded by clear and precise standards" which are susceptible of objective measurement.[158]

The court also found that the regulations were impermissibly overbroad "because they may be applied to, and thus deter protected expression."[159] Lastly, the court stated that the regulations were employed improperly here because the principal exercised his discretion "solely on the basis of whether [he] agreed or disagreed with the statements made. This violates the First Amendment . . . ."[160] In another literature-banning case a New York federal court struck down as unconstitutionally overbroad a regulation prohibiting (with limited exceptions) distribution of all literature by teachers in all areas of the school premises at all times.[161]

Generally, before school authorities can constitutionally forbid a teacher from circulating literature in school, they should have to show either that the school, its hallways, and its mailboxes have not been opened up as public forums for distributing literature, i.e., that other groups are not allowed to give out literature,[162] or that giving out the literature would cause "a substantial and material interference with the requirements of appropriate discipline in the operation of the schools."[163]

Does a teacher have a First Amendment right to speak at a public session of his school board devoted to hearing citizen views?

Yes. In *City of Madison Joint School District No. 8 v. Wisconsin Employment Relations Commission*[164] the president of the local teachers union, during a portion of a school board meeting devoted to expression of opinion by the public, took the floor and spoke on the subject of the ongoing collective bargaining negotiations between the union, which was the exclusive bargaining representative, and the board. He concluded his remarks by presenting to the board a petition signed by over 1,300 teachers calling for expeditious resolution of the negotiations. One of the union's proposals during the negotiations called for inclusion of a so-called "fair share" clause, which would have required all teachers, whether members of the union or not, to defray the costs of collective bargaining. Following the union president's remarks, a non-union teacher was given the floor and stated that neither side had adequately addressed the "fair share" issue and that teachers were confused about the proposal, and he asked that all alternatives be presented clearly to the teachers and the public. The union then filed a complaint with the Wisconsin Employment Relations Commission, claiming that the school board had committed a prohibited labor practice by permitting the non-union teacher to speak at the meeting, illegally "negotiating" with a member of the bargaining unit other than the exclusive collective bargaining representative.

The Commission concluded that the board was guilty of the prohibited labor practice and ordered it to cease and desist from permitting employees, other than representatives of the union, to appear and speak at board meetings on matters subject to collective bargaining between the board and the union. The Supreme Court of Wisconsin affirmed, holding that such abridgment of the employees' speech was justified in order "to avoid the dangers attendant upon relative chaos in labor-management relations."[165]

The U.S. Supreme Court reversed, holding that the teacher in question had a First Amendment right to speak and that since he did not actually seek to bargain with the board the record did not show such danger to labor-management relations as would justify curtailing that speech.[166] In holding that the speech was protected, the Court stated: "Where the state

has opened a forum for direct citizen involvement, it is difficult to find justification for excluding teachers who make up
the overwhelming proportion of school employees and are
most vitally concerned with the proceedings."[167] The Court
concluded that "[t]he participation in public discussion of
public business cannot be confined to one category of interested individuals. . . . Whatever its duties as an employer,
when the board sits in public meetings to conduct public
business and hear the views of citizens, it may not be required to discriminate between speakers on the basis of their
employment, or the content of their speech."[168] The Court
was particularly concerned that the Commission's order re-
strained future speech by teachers "on matters subject to
collective bargaining,"[169] characterizing this portion of the
Commission's order as "the essence of prior restraint."[170] The
Court said: "Teachers not only constitute the overwhelming
bulk of employees of the school system, but they are the very
core of that system; restraining teachers' expressions to the
board on matters involving the operation of the schools would
seriously impair the board's ability to govern the district."[171]

Subsequently an Ohio federal district court held that a
board policy, insofar as it prohibited teachers—but not the
general public—from discussing, in the visitor recognition
period of its public meetings, matters pertaining to the terms
and conditions of their employment, relegating them instead
to the consultation and grievance procedure, was repugnant
to the First Amendment.[172] The court further concluded that
if, as the board maintained, its policy actually was to exclude
all persons from addressing the board on matters pertaining
to labor relations, the policy nevertheless would offend the
First Amendment.[173] The court determined that if the justification for such a policy was to keep labor relations matters
confined to the grievance and consultation procedure, the
board's action "clearly" was unlawful since, to justify prohibition
of a particular expression of opinion, the state must be able to
show that its action was caused by something more than a
mere desire to avoid the discomfort that always accompanies
an unpopular viewpoint.[174]

On the other hand, the court concluded, if the board was
concerned that discussion of particular topics might cause
disturbances, it could—and was constitutionally required to—
adopt narrower means of avoiding that result. For example,

the court said, the board could impose strict, content-neutral rules of conduct and eject unruly participants. Alternatively, the court indicated, in the interest of controlling its agenda and avoiding distractions it could confine public participation and comment to matters on the agenda or to specified subjects, citing a statement in *City of Madison* that "public bodies may confine their meetings to specified subject matter."[175] The court declared, however, that it did "not believe that the rationale for this statement justified opening public discussion to any and all matters *except* the disfavored topic. . . . As the Court stated in *Madison*, 'when the board sits in public meetings to conduct public business and hear the views of citizens, it may not . . . discriminate between speakers on the basis of . . . the content of their speech.' " The Ohio federal court did observe that the board could, if it wished, dispense altogether with the visitor recognition portion of its meetings.[176]

May a school board constitutionally refuse to recognize non-resident teachers during a portion of a public meeting devoted to hearing citizen views?

At least one court has ruled that a board may not. In the Ohio case the court held that a school board policy refusing to recognize non-resident teachers during the visitor recognition portion of public school board meetings violated the First Amendment in addition to the equal protection clause of the 14th Amendment.[177] The court reasoned that a teacher in the district, whether a resident or not, clearly was an "interested" individual within the meaning of the constitutional principle, enunciated in *City of Madison*, that "the participation in public discussion of public business cannot be confined to one category of interested individuals."[178]

Does a teacher who feels strongly about a political or social cause have a constitutional right to express those feelings by wearing—in the classroom—an armband, button, or other symbol identifying him with that cause?

The Second Circuit has ruled that a school board could not, without contravening the First Amendment, discharge an 11th-grade English teacher for wearing a black armband in the classroom in symbolic protest against the Vietnam War, where it was agreed that the armband did not disrupt classroom activities.[179] The court relied upon the decision of the

U.S. Supreme Court in *Tinker v. Des Moines School District*[180] in which the Court, holding that junior-high-school students could not constitutionally be suspended for wearing such an armband in the classroom, characterized the symbolic expression involved as akin to "pure speech."[181] Elaborating on the standard set forth in the *Tinker* case, the Second Circuit concluded that "[a]ny limitation on the exercise of constitutional rights can be justified only by a conclusion, based upon reasonable inferences flowing from concrete facts and not abstractions, that the interests of discipline or sound education are materially and substantially jeopardized, whether the danger stems initially from the conduct of students or teachers."[182] The mere fact that the principal believed that wearing the armband "would possibly" encourage pupils to engage in disruptive demonstrations, the court ruled, could not overcome the teacher's right to freedom of expression.[183] The court noted that the teacher had made no attempt to proselytize his students, and that it did not appear from the record that any student believed the armband to be anything more than "a benign symbolic expression of the teacher's personal views."[184] Observing that the country had recently enfranchised 18-year-olds, and that "[i]t would be foolhardy to shield our children from political debate and issues until the eve of their first venture into the voting booth," the court concluded that in the circumstances presented, the greater danger lay not in tolerating the teacher's expression but in penalizing it, with the danger that the school, by power of example, would appear to students to be sanctioning a "pall of orthodoxy" in the classroom.[185]

Does the free-speech clause of the First Amendment protect a teacher's refusal to compromise his personal beliefs by declining, for reasons of principle, to participate in the flag ceremonies?

The Supreme Court has concluded that "[i]f the First Amendment protects a public employee from discharge based on what he has said, it must also protect him from discharge based on what he believes."[186] Thus, unless the government can "demonstrate an overriding interest" of "vital importance" requiring that a person's private beliefs conform to those of the hiring authority, his beliefs cannot be the basis for depriving him of continued public employment.[187] It would appear to follow that, unless school authorities can show an "overriding interest of vital importance" requiring a teacher to utter what he does not believe, he cannot be made to forfeit his job for refusing to obey such a requirement.[188]

In *Russo v. Central School District*[189] the Second Circuit held that a probationary high-school art teacher's First Amendment rights were violated when school officials discharged her for standing silently at attention during daily classroom recitation of the pledge of allegiance in which school regulations required her to participate. The court relied upon the decision of the Supreme Court in *West Virginia State Board of Education v. Barnette,*[190] where the Court recognized that in connection with the pledge, "the flag salute is a form of utterance." In *Barnette,* the Supreme Court said: "To sustain the compulsory flag salute, we are required to say that a Bill of Rights, which guards the individual's right to speak his own mind, left it open to public authorities to compel him to utter what is not in his mind."[191]

In *Russo,* the Second Circuit recognized that schools "have a substantial interest in maintaining flag salute programs,"[192] but concluded that the state must achieve its goal by means that have a "less drastic" impact on First Amendment freedoms.[193] The court noted that Mrs. Russo neither disrupted her classes nor attempted to prevent her students from reciting the pledge, and that the record indicated that the class participated in the flag salute program each day under the supervision of the senior instructor. "In view of all the circumstances in this case," the court concluded, "it is clear that the state's interest in maintaining a flag salute program was well-served in Mrs. Russo's classroom, even without her participation in the pledge ceremonies."[194]

This type of analysis would appear to apply whether or not the teacher's beliefs are religiously based. The analysis, however, has not been uniformly accepted by the federal courts of appeals. In *Palmer v. Board of Education,*[195] the Seventh Circuit held that a public school teacher who was a member of Jehovah's Witnesses was not free to disregard the prescribed curriculum concerning patriotic matters, including participation in the pledge of allegiance, even though she claimed that such participation would violate her religious principles. The court concluded that her "right to her own religious views and practices remains unfettered, but she has no constitutional right to require others to submit to her views and to forego a portion of their education they would otherwise be entitled to enjoy." The court distinguished *Russo* on the ground that Russo's job "was not to teach patriotic matters to children, but to teach art" and stated that the court in *Russo* had "carefully indicated that through its holding it did not mean to limit the traditionally broad discretion that has always rested with local school authorities to prescribe curriculum."[196]

Palmer appears to stand for the proposition that where there is a prescribed curriculum on patriotic matters calling for pledge ceremonies, school authorities may require the teacher who is responsible for teaching that part of the curriculum to participate in such ceremonies even though such participation violates her religious principles. Presumably, the Seventh Circuit would apply this rationale to a claim based on freedom of speech as well as to a claim based on freedom of religion. *Palmer*, however, rests on the dubious proposition that school authorities may force a teacher to violate his own personal beliefs as long as such coercion is impressed with a "curricular" label.

Where a teacher claims that the termination of his employment violated his free-speech rights, will a court uphold the termination on the basis of a rationale that differs from the one advanced by the school authorities in making the termination decision?

Although the answer is not entirely clear, a strong argument can be made against upholding the termination in such circumstances.

In a well-reasoned District of Columbia decision a police officer was discharged for advocating the "blue flu"—a euphemism for concerted action of police officers falsely reporting to their superiors that they were too ill to perform their assigned duties. The District of Columbia Circuit held that the Police Department could not, consistent with the First Amendment, discharge him on the ground that his advocacy evinced an unlawful intent. After trial, however, the district court concluded that by his public advocacy of the "blue flu" the police officer put his own reputation for truthfulness in question, and that a good reputation for truthfulness is essential to the ability of a police officer to perform effectively his many testimonial duties. The District of Columbia Circuit, however, concluded that he "was discharged because he advocated strike actions, not because he lied. Because the only lawful ground on which the discharge might have been justified was constructed after the fact, this discharge cannot be sustained."[197] The court explained:

> If the *Pickering* approach to the complicated issue of freedom of speech for public employees is to have any vigor, judicial review for the discharge must be addressed solely to contemporaneous considerations. Absent the complicating factor of constitutionally protected conduct, a public employee can be discharged for a variety of reasons, and a probationary employee for even gossamer causes. That being so, any kind of reconstruction of the reasoning behind the discharge that provides the employer with a post hoc justification for his action cannot be allowed. To permit that kind of judicial "review" would eviscerate *Pickering*'s effort to prevent the state from using its control over a person's job to penalize its employees for the exercise of their First Amendment rights. Therefore, it is essential, as Judge Leventhal said in an analogous case, that the court reviewing the discharge restrict its focus to "the reasons given by the [employer] and not on reasons that may come to light if and when a court rummages throughout the record in an effort to reconstruct on what basis the [employer] might have decided the matter."[198]

Demonstrations

May a teacher be discharged or disciplined for engaging in a peaceful demonstration while off duty?

No, at least in the absence of a showing that his participation substantially impaired his teaching performance or the operation of the school system.

Thus a three-judge federal district court struck down a provision of an Alabama statute denying a pay raise to any teacher who failed to pledge that he had not participated in, "encouraged or condoned . . . any extra-curricular demonstration which was not approved by the city, county or state

Board of Education." The court held that while the state "might have some legitimate interest in the extramural speech and associational activities of its teachers, it appears to us that there is no justification for restricting the right of a teacher to engage in non-partisan advocacy of social or political reform, absent a showing that such activity reflects substantially on his or her performance in class or interferes with the regular operation of the schools."[199] The court ruled that "even though state and local school officials of Alabama might have a legitimate interest in regulating the conduct of teachers in the midst of school unrest," the challenged provision "constitutes a comprehensive interference with associational freedom which goes far beyond what might be justified in the protection of the state's legitimate interest."[200]

A teacher should be aware, however, that if the demonstration in which he participates disrupts the normal functioning of the educational institution, he may be on weak ground if he contends in a subsequent disciplinary proceeding that he was merely exercising his First Amendment rights. For example, while defending the right of professors to demonstrate peacefully against the policies of the president of a state-related school, the Third Circuit found unprotected a demonstration by several professors in the classroom of a professor who was close to the school's president.[201] In another case a professor at the University of Nebraska participated in a student occupation of a campus ROTC building to protest the military invasion of Cambodia and the killing and wounding of students at Kent State by the National Guard. Because a number of demonstrators, not including the professor, threatened violence and interference with a scheduled class, the university authorities canceled it. This was one of the factors relied upon by the Board of Regents in refusing to reappoint the professor. Upholding this ground for non-reappointment, the court said:

> It will not do for . . . [the professor] to claim that neither he nor most of the others in the group would have interfered with the class. When one chooses to join a group which is largely leaderless and unstructured, he must assume, not only the benefits of the group, but the

disabilities of the group, as well . . . When the group chooses not to communicate with a united voice, it must bear the consequences of splintered voices.[202]

The court also sustained, as grounds for the university's refusal to reappoint the professor, his intrusion into the negotiations between the students and the administration and his action in remaining and linking arms with other demonstrators notwithstanding directives from the university president—determined by the court to have been reasonable under the circumstances—to vacate the building. With respect to the latter activity, the court concluded that one fair interpretation of the professor's conduct was that he was defying the directives.[203]

Political and Ideological Activity

May a teacher constitutionally be discharged or disciplined because of his political affiliation?

Generally, no. The Supreme Court has recognized that implicit in the First Amendment is the right to join with others to pursue goals which that amendment independently protects, such as political or ideological activity.[204] In *Elrod v. Burns*[205] the Supreme Court ruled that a non-policymaking, non-confidential governmental employee cannot constitutionally be discharged on the sole ground of his political beliefs from a job he is satisfactorily performing.

Consistently with *Elrod*, where a Texas school board refused to renew the contracts of two teachers, while extending probationary one-year contracts to others, because of their relationship with a political opponent of three recently elected board members and their party leader, a federal court held that the First Amendment rights of the teachers were violated.[206] In addition, discerning "a long judicial history in our country of jealously protecting" the First Amendment rights of teachers, the court ruled that "[t]he trustees' failure to rehire these teachers because of their political associations was done in disregard of the teachers' clearly established constitutional rights and cannot reasonably be characterized as action taken in good faith." Accordingly, the court held the board members personally liable for damages.[207] A federal district court in Puerto Rico reached the same conclusion in a case involving the demotion of school administrators for their political affiliations.[208]

Since most teachers are neither policymakers nor confidential employees, they would appear to be protected under the rule that *Elrod* appeared to articulate. Subsequent to *Elrod*, moreover, the Supreme Court made it clear that "the ultimate inquiry is not whether the label 'policymaker' or 'confidential' fits a particular position; rather, the question is whether the hiring authority can demonstrate that party affiliation is an appropriate requirement for the effective performance of the office involved."[209] As an example, the Court stated: "The coach of a state university's football team formulates policy, but no one could seriously claim that Republicans make better coaches than Democrats, or vice versa, no matter which party is in control of state government."[210]

May a teacher's employment be terminated because he is a member of a radical political organization?

No. In *Keyishian v. Board of Regents*,[211] teachers at the state university of New York attacked the constitutionality of a state law making Communist Party membership "prima facie" evidence of disqualification for employment in the public school system. The Supreme Court struck down this provision insofar as it proscribed mere knowing membership in an organization found to be subversive "without any showing of specific intent to further [its] unlawful aims."[212] The Court held the provision to be an unconstitutional interference with associational rights because of its overbreadth.[213]

Recently, relying on *Keyishian* and other Supreme Court decisions,[214] a federal district court held that the public acknowledgment by an assistant professor at the University of Arkansas that he was a Communist and a member of the Progressive Labor Party was a constitutionally impermissible basis for the non-renewal of his contract. The court stated: "It is now beyond question that mere association with or membership in a communistic organization is protected activity for which a State may not impose civil disabilities such as exclusion from state employment."[215]

May state or school authorities constitutionally compel a

teacher to disclose his organizational affiliations as a condition of public employment?

Only when the subordinating interests of the state can survive close scrutiny.

The Supreme Court "has recognized the vital relationship between freedom to associate and privacy in one's associations."[216] Thus it has held that absent a "substantial relation" between the governmental interest and the information required to be disclosed, the First Amendment protects individuals from compulsory disclosure of their associational relationships.[217]

This principle protects teachers from compulsory disclosure of their membership in a teachers' organization. The Fifth Circuit has held in a suit by a teacher federation against a school board alleging harassment and intimidation that the district court abused its discretion by imposing sanctions of dismissal of the suit and payment of the school board's attorneys fees as a result of the federation's refusal to diclose the names of its members who had not authorized the release of their names. The court said: "To direct disclosure of the membership list would subject the other members to the very retaliatory measures they seek to avoid."[218] As the court noted, decisions of the Supreme Court have held that interests of the state alleged to justify compelled disclosure must survive exacting scrutiny and must be sufficient to justify the deterrent effect that the disclosure may have.[219]

It is not clear to what extent, if at all, states or school authorities may compel disclosure of a teacher's associational ties in pursuit of an inquiry into the qualifications of their teachers. In *Shelton v. Tucker*[220] the Supreme Court ruled unconstitutional an Arkansas law requiring teachers, as a condition of employment in a state-supported school or college, to file annually an affidavit listing every organization to which they had belonged or contributed. The Court ruled that the disclosure requirement, with its "unlimited and indiscriminate sweep," went "far beyond what might be justified in the exercise of the State's legitimate inquiry into the fitness and competency of its teachers," and impermissibly inhibited the teachers' rights of free association.[221]

In *Shelton* the Court cited, among other considerations, the fact that Arkansas was a non-tenure state, where a teacher's continued employment depended on the discretion of the school authorities to renew his one-year contract, and where no provision was made for notice, charges, hearing, or opportunity to explain. It is not clear to what extent the principle of the decision would protect tenured teachers, whose employment cannot be terminated except for just cause and then only after notice and hearing, from similar disclosure requirements. Nor is it clear to what extent *Shelton* would be applied to shield applicants for employment from such requirements. A strong argument can be made, however, that *Shelton* applies in these contexts as well.

May a teacher be required by a legislative committee to disclose his organizational affiliations on pain of contempt or criminal punishment?

Not if the teacher asserts a proper claim of privilege against self-incrimination.

Some teachers also have urged that they cannot be subjected to such interrogation consistently with their constitutional right of free association. Under current law, however, a legislative committee acting pursuant to a legislative authorization justified by a compelling state interest constitutionally may investigate an individual's associational relationships,[222] and the Supreme Court has held that teachers are not immune from such exposure. In *Barenblatt v. United States*[223] a teacher declined to answer questions posed by a subcommittee of the House Committee on Un-American Activities concerning his prior affiliation with Communist organizations while he was a graduate student and teaching fellow at the University of Michigan. He contended that the academic profession should have a special privilege to withhold information regarding associational activities. The Court rejected this argument, stating that Congress is not "precluded from interrogating a witness merely because he is a teacher."[224]

May a service charge, required by an agency shop clause in a collective bargaining agreement to be paid to the bargaining representative by a non-union teacher in the bargaining unit, constitutionally be used to support an ideological cause to which the teacher is opposed?

No. In *Abood v. Detroit Board of Education*[225] the Supreme Court ruled that an agency shop agreement between the Detroit school board and the Detroit Federation of Teachers was valid insofar as the service charges required of non-union members were used to finance expenditures by the union for collective bargaining, contract administration, and grievance adjustment purposes. The Court held, however, that the First Amendment prohibited the union and the board of education from requiring any teacher, as a condition of holding a teaching job, to contribute to the support of an ideological cause he might oppose. The Court indicated that while an injunction prohibiting the union from expending exacted funds for political purposes would be inappropriate, a court—in the absence of an available voluntary internal union remedy—could require a refund of a portion of the exacted funds in the proportion that union political expenditures bore to total union expenditures, or the reduction of future exactions by the same proportion.[226]

To what extent does a school board policy which restricts a teacher's political activity violate his First Amendment rights?

In *U.S. Civil Service Commission v. National Association of Letter Carriers*[227] and *Broadrick v. Oklahoma*[228] the Supreme Court rejected constitutional challenges to broad restrictions on the political activity of federal and state civil service employees, including restrictions on partisan candidacy for public office. The Court accepted the argument that these restrictions were justified by the desire to insulate public servants from political pressures[229] and by the necessity to ensure that the government and its employees not only execute the laws impartially but also appear to the public to be doing so.[230] As it had in the *Pickering* case, the Court recognized that the government's interest in regulating both the conduct and speech of its employees differs significantly from its interest in regulating those of citizens generally.[231]

In *Letter Carriers*, involving the constitutionality of the federal Hatch Act, a prior Supreme Court decision upholding the constitutionality of the Act *(United Public Workers v. Mitchell)*[232] was "unhesitatingly" reaffirmed.[233] The *Letter Carriers* approach to judging the constitutionality of restrictions on the political activity of public employees has been characterized as "some sort of 'balancing' process."[234] The First Circuit has said: "It appears that the government may place limits on campaigning by public employees if the limits substantially serve government interests that are 'important' enough to outweigh the employees' First Amendment rights."[235] Other courts have attempted to give more content to the *Letter Carriers* test. The Fifth Circuit, for example, has concluded that "restrictions on the partisan political activity of public employees and officers, where such activity contains substantial non-speech elements . . . are constitutionally permissible if justified by a reasonable necessity . . . to achieve a compelling public objective."[236] The court stated that "the requisite closeness of the means-end relation must be determined on a case-by-case basis." As the burden "comes closer to impairing core first amendment values, e.g. the right to hold particular views . . . or impairs some given first amendment value more substantially . . . the requisite closeness of fit between means and end increases accordingly."[237]

Does a state law or school board policy requiring a teacher to forfeit his teaching position if he becomes a candidate for public office violate the First Amendment?

In *Hickman v. City of Dallas*[238] a provision of the Dallas City Charter, a personnel rule, and a regulation of the Dallas city police department required a Dallas city policeman to forfeit his position with the city if he became a candidate for elective office within Dallas County. A Texas federal district court ruled that these provisions violated the First Amendment as applied to a non-supervisory Dallas city police officer who resided in the city of De Soto, which was in Dallas County, and who wished to become a candidate for the De Soto City Council. Applying the Fifth Circuit's interpretation of *Letter Carriers*, the court concluded that to restrict the right of candidacy (characterized by the court as an "important," though not "fundamental" right)[239] Dallas "must demonstrate that its objectives are 'compelling.' Second, Dallas must show that it is reasonably necessary to restrict plaintiff 's First Amendment right (to candidacy) to enable Dallas to achieve its 'compelling' objectives."[240] The court concluded that the City of Dallas had "a compelling interest in maintaining the loyalty, efficiency and nonpartisanship of its employees"—an interest "sufficiently compelling that Dallas may put reasonable restrictions on the right of its employees to become candidates for elective office. For example, conflicts might arise if an employee were to challenge his supervisor, or run for mayor or the city council, in a Dallas city election. Candidacy for elective office, whether inside or outside Dallas, by those in managerial or supervisory positions might well create the possibility and the appearance of conflicts of interest."[241] With respect to the plaintiff, however, the court did—

> not find the necessary nexus between Dallas' compelling public objectives and its consequent right to burden First Amendment activities to accomplish such objectives (on the one hand), and plaintiff's proposed candidacy for the City Council of De Soto (on the other hand). The ends to be obtained do not justify the means employed. Defendants have not shown that Hickman's candidacy would impair or affect the integrity of Dallas city government or the loyalty and efficiency of Dallas employees. Dallas prohibits Hickman's candidacy simply because it is within Dallas County. The prohibition is arbitrary, artificial and unjustified.[242]

In *Hickman* the court stated that "[t]he potential for conflict when a city employee seeks office within the city may well be sufficient to justify a restriction on candidacy."[243] The Seventh Circuit reached the same conclusion in a case in which a city employee was required to take a leave of absence when she announced that she was running for mayor. The court wrote: "The impairment of free speech brought about by the leave of absence requirement is indirect and probably very slight; the benefits in preserving order, discipline, and efficiency in public employment strike us as much greater than the cost to First Amendment interests."[244] And in *Magill v. Lynch,* also decided after *Letter Carriers,* the First Circuit ruled that a municipal government "may constitutionally restrict participation by its employees in nominally nonpartisan elections if political parties play a large role in the campaigns."[245] The court believed that heavy party involvement posed multiple dangers recognized in *Letter Carriers,* including the dangers that favoritism presented for efficient government, the possibility that a politically active public work force would give the incumbent party and the incumbent workers an unbreakable grasp on the reins of power, and the need to ensure that employees achieve advancement on their merits and be free from both coercion and the prospect of favor from political activity.[246] Even when parties are absent, the court thought, "[M]any employee campaigns might be thought to endanger at least one strong public interest, an interest that looms larger in the context of municipal elections than it does in the national elections considered in *Letter Carriers*. The city could reasonably fear the prospect of a subordinate running directly against his superior or running for a position that confers great power over his superior."[247] Under this view a statute or rule requiring a teacher to resign in order to run as a candidate against his own superintendent or a member of his own school board would not violate the teacher's First Amendment rights. Similar considerations would support the constitutionality of a rule requiring a teacher who is elected to the office of school board member or superintendent to resign his elective office or his teaching position.

Does a school board policy requiring a teacher who becomes a candidate for public office to take a mandatory leave of absence violate his First Amendment rights?

The Court of Appeals of Kentucky has held that such a policy, because it was not contingent upon a determination that a teacher's political activity as a candidate would adversely affect the performance of his teaching duties, was overbroad and thus violated the First and 14th Amendments.[248] While the decision did not discuss *Letter Carriers*, it appears consistent with the Fifth Circuit's "reasonable necessity" interpretation of that decision and with the "closeness of fit" standard.

May a teacher constitutionally be forced to relinquish his teaching position if he is elected to office as a state legislator, city councilman, or similar part-time position on a body which has responsibility for the budget of his employing institution?

Before *Letter Carriers* and *Broadrick*, a three-judge federal district court in West Virginia rejected a federal constitutional challenge to a provision of that state's constitution which, as applied, prohibited an athletic director at a state college from simultaneously holding office as a state legislator.[249] While the case was decided on the basis of a "rational basis" test, the same result may well follow under a "reasonable necessity" or similar standard. If such a provision were based on a rationale of avoiding the existence or appearance of a conflict of interest, the objective presumably would be regarded as both "important" and "compelling." The key question would be whether the end justified the means, i.e., whether the requirement was reasonably necessary to achieve the objective. Arguably, a requirement that the legislator or councilman disqualify himself from voting where a conflict actually existed would satisfy the objective of avoiding conflicts but with a less draconian effect on the First Amendment rights of teachers and voters than a requirement mandating forfeiture of the elective office or the teaching position. As the Fifth Circuit has observed, however, "The Court in *Letter Carriers* did not require that the means-end fit be perfect. Rather, it held that Congress could constitutionally restrict political activity by subordinate employees in order to prevent coercion by their superiors; the legislature did not have to rely upon a prohibition against coercion alone, a less restrictive and arguably effective alternative to the measure enacted."[250] In short, the Fifth Circuit concluded, "[T]he 'reasonable necessity' test permits a degree of prophylaxis, particularly where the state has an interest in avoiding the appearance of impropriety."[251]

Union Activity

Do teachers and other public employees have a constitutional right to form and join labor organizations?

Yes. The "freedom of association" which the Supreme Court has derived by implication from the rights of speech, press, petition, and assembly guaranteed by the First Amendment confers on public employees the right to form and join labor organizations or professional associations and to participate fully in their affairs.[252] Thus, for example, where a school board failed to renew the contracts of nine teachers—among them the leaders of the union and some of its most active members—in retribution for their union activities, the board was held to have violated their right to freedom of association.[253]

Does a policy of school authorities that denies use of school facilities by a teacher organization dedicated to organizing school employees for collective bargaining but permits

use of such facilities by other teacher organizations violate the free-speech clause of the First Amendment?

Yes. A Missouri federal district court held that a university policy which allowed use of university facilities, including campus mail and campus meeting rooms, by the AAUP but not by groups, such as the NEA affiliate on campus, deemed to be labor organizations or which had as their goal the organization of university employees for collective bargaining, violated the free-speech clause of the First Amendment, in addition to the equal protection clause of the 14th Amendment.[254] However, if school authorities do not permit other teacher organizations to use school facilities, then, because schools are not considered public forums,[255] school officials could constitutionally deny use of such facilities to a teachers' union.[256] If school authorities open up school facilities such as classrooms or auditoriums to one teachers' group to such a degree that they can be considered public forums, the school authorities then have to open them up on the same terms to any teacher's group that requests use of the facilities, because the First Amendment prohibits government officials from favoring one speaker over another.[257]

Does a policy of school authorities that allows a teacher organization serving as exclusive bargaining agent to use the interschool mail system and teacher mailboxes, but denies a rival teacher organization access to the mail system violate the free-speech clause of the First Amendment?

In *Perry Education Association v. Perry Local Educators' Association*, the U.S. Supreme Court held that the free-speech rights of the rival union were not violated when it was not allowed to use the interschool mail system.[257a] The Court, by a 5–to–4 vote, concluded that school officials had not turned the mail system into a public forum, which was to be opened to everyone who wanted to use it, but had instead left it as a system of strictly limited access.[257b] Because this was so, the Court found that school authorities could place reasonable regulations on access to the mail system so long as they were "not an effort to suppress expression merely because public officials oppose the speaker's view."[257c]

The Court stated that in giving the majority union exclusive access to the interschool mail system, the school authorities were not discriminating against the viewpoint of the rival union, but were instead facilitating the ability of the exclusive bargaining agent, regardless of its viewpoint, to communicate with all teachers.[257d] The Court also stated that it was reasonable for school authorities to exclude the rival union from the mail system as "a means of insuring labor-peace within the schools."[257e] Crucial to the Court's decision was its conclusion that there was "no indication that the school board intended to discourage one viewpoint and advance another."[257f]

Does a teacher have a right to join an employee organization that engages in unlawful strikes or other illegal activity?

An individual cannot constitutionally be punished for joining an organization which engages in unlawful activity unless he is shown to have affiliated with the organization with knowledge of the illegality and with the specific intent of furthering its unlawful aims.

In *McLaughlin v. Tilendis*[258] non-tenured teachers sued school officials under the Civil Rights Act claiming that their employment had been terminated because of their union activities. Upholding their right to bring such a claim under the Act, the court ruled that "[u]nless there is some illegal intent, an individual's right to form and join a union is protected by the First Amendment."[259] Responding to the contention that the union might engage in strikes or other activity injurious to the public interest, the court said that even if the union were "connected with unlawful activity," the bare fact of membership would not justify charging members with their organization's misdeeds. "A contrary rule would bite more deeply into associational freedom than is necessary to achieve legitimate state interests, thereby violating the First Amendment."[260]

Does the right of association protect members of a union or employee association and their representatives in advocating the objectives of the organization?

Yes. The right of association includes the right to engage in "vigorous advocacy" of the organization's goals and objectives.[261] It thus affords protection, in addition to that afforded by the free speech clause itself, for "advocacy" by members of a union or employee association concerning employee grievances or other aspects of the employment relationship. For example, in an Illinois case a federal district court found that a superintendent's policy of not giving preferred staffing and summer teaching positions to certain teachers because they were members violated their freedom of speech and of association.[262]

The right of association also includes the right of members of an organization "to consult with each other" and "to select a spokesman from their number who could be expected to give the wisest counsel."[263] One who is selected to act as spokesman, in turn, presumably has a corresponding right to perform that role.

Whether by virtue of the free-speech clause or the implied right of association, or both, the courts have given First Amendment protection to advocacy by a representative of a public employee organization concerning employment-related matters, holding the First Amendment applicable to statements made by a teacher, in his capacity as an official of a faculty association, in meetings held to discuss faculty grievances;[264] to a letter sent to a government official by two police officers, in their capacity as officials of a police union, concerning the compensation due other officers who had been required to work outside their normal hours;[265] and to the statement of a teacher, as president of the faculty association, accusing administration negotiators of attempting to "buy . . . off" the association "with little items at the expense of big ones."[266]

"The right of free association may not be abridged merely because its exercise may be annoying to some people."[267] Concluding that a teacher would have been re-employed but for her union activities, the Sixth Circuit noted that an alleged personality conflict between her and her principal had germinated from those activities. The court stated: "To allow any rancorous feelings engendered in this manner to justify a dismissal would decimate constitutional protections."[268]

The relationship between a public employee union and a public employer is inherently an adversary one and thus inevitably will produce some degree of conflict, hostility and disharmony. Some courts have recognized this reality. In a Sixth Circuit decision, the court held unconstitutional a principal's reprimand of a building representative for "unprofessional and unacceptable conduct," imposed in response to his representation of a fellow employee at a grievance meeting held pursuant to established procedures. The court noted that "[o]ne cannot separate [the building representative's] zealous advocacy from his role as a union representative."[269] In a Texas case, a fireman was suspended for certain activities as president of the union. Although the court disapproved of the "machismo" manner in which he presented grievances to city officials, and his always presenting grievances in the form of "non-negotiable demands," the court concluded that he had an "unerring instinct for exactly how far he [could] go without violating applicable rules . . . and . . . exercised this facility to press his every right to its very limit." It thus found his activities constitutionally protected.[270]

A similar recognition of the friction inherent in the adversary relationship between union and employer is reflected in opinions dealing with the termination of a teacher's employment because of speech in his capacity as a teacher association leader. In one such case the court said: "It may be that following plaintiff's statement, ill will existed between the plaintiff and the administration officials. This type of conflict could have an adverse effect on the administration of a school. However, any friction which exists may in large part be the result of an over-sensitivity to criticism on the part of the administration."[271]

A teacher's public criticism of school authorities in his capacity as a union official has been held protected even where it included "strident" and "unnecessary comments" which amounted to "excessive characterizations and inferences."[272]

In a New Hampshire case—decided before *Mount Healthy* but nevertheless relevant in this context—a teacher who was an active and outspoken member of the teachers' negotiating committee issued a series of press releases accusing the school board of "high-handed treatment" and "utter disregard" of its employees. The releases irritated the superintendent, who felt that they created public animosity toward the board and constituted unprofessional conduct. Later, after becoming chairman of the negotiating committee, the teacher severely criticized the school board at a teacher association meeting, and stated that he had no personal respect for the school board negotiating team, the school board itself, or the superintendent. The teacher's contract was not renewed. Concluding that the decision was motivated primarily by the teacher's press releases and his statements at the association meeting the court held that the non-renewal violated his constitutional rights of free speech and association, and directed that he be reinstated with back pay.[273]

The closer a teacher union leader comes to personal vilification, however, the more unwilling a court may be to place his speech under the protective shield of the First Amendment, whether the speech is uttered in his capacity as citizen or union leader. When a teacher, in her capacity as the president of the local teacher association, was invited by the school district to address a faculty orientation meeting and utilized the occasion to criticize the superintendent in "insulting and vituperative language" for "no purpose discernible other than to satisfy some personal need," her speech was held unprotected and her dismissal as a tenured teacher sustained. "Free speech and collective bargaining rights," the court said, "do not endow a teacher, as a school district employee, with a license to vilify superiors publicly. The employer-employee relationship restrains the right of the employee to the extent necessary to the efficient and successful operation of the educational system."[274]

Does the "material and substantial disruption" test apply to a teacher's union activities?

Although the issue is not firmly settled, at least one court has expressly held the test applicable. In a Florida case, the contracts of two teachers were not renewed because of their activities in steering a local teachers' organization. The trial court concluded that there had been no violation of their rights since there was "more than ample evidence that they exercised their First Amendment liberties in a manner that interfered with the normal operation of the school." The Fifth Circuit determined that the trial court's finding was not clearly erroneous but decided that the Supreme Court's ruling in *Tinker* and its own decisional law established a test "more demanding" than whether the teacher's protected conduct "interfered with the normal operation of the school," and concluded that the question was whether the teacher's union activities "materially and substantially disrupted the operation of the school.[275] Accordingly, the Fifth Circuit vacated the judgment and directed the trial court to reassess the evidence and make additional findings of fact in light of the correct legal standard.[276]

Can school authorities constitutionally terminate a teacher's employment merely because he brings unannounced representatives to a meeting with a superior and requests their presence at the meeting?

No. The Fifth Circuit has held that such termination would violate the teacher's right of free association.[277]

Can school authorities constitutionally refuse to consider or act upon grievances when filed by the union rather than by employees directly?

Yes. In *Smith v. Arkansas State Highway Employees, Local 1315*,[278] the U.S. Supreme Court upheld the constitutionality of a policy of the Arkansas State Highway Commission not to consider a grievance initiated by an employee of the Arkansas State Highway Department unless the employee by-passed the union's grievance procedure and submitted his written complaint directly to the designated employer representative. The Supreme Court noted that "[w]ere public employers . . . subject to the same labor laws applicable to private employers, this refusal might well constitute an unfair labor practice." The Court, however, rejected the contention that the policy violated the First Amendment, stating: "The public employee surely can associate and speak freely and petition openly, and he is protected by the First Amendment from retaliation for doing so. . . . But the First Amendment does not impose any affirmative obligation on the government to listen, to respond or, in this context, to recognize the association and bargain with it."[279]

Do teachers have a constitutionally protected right to strike?

The Supreme Court has indicated that encompassed within the concern of the First Amendment right of association are essential organizational activities which give an organization life and promote its fundamental purposes, [280] and arguably the strike is indispensable to the viability of a labor organization. As one federal judge has noted: "If the inherent purpose of a labor organization is to bring the worker's interests to bear on management, the right to strike is, historically and practically, an important means of effectuating that purpose. A union that never strikes, or which can make no credible threat to strike, may wither away in ineffectiveness."[281]

Nevertheless, no court has yet held that public employees have a constitutional right to strike, while many decisions hold to the contrary.[282] The Supreme Court, moreover, has summarily affirmed a lower-court decision upholding the constitutionality of an absolute ban on strikes by federal employees.[283]

Does an "agency shop" agreement requiring a teacher who is a member of the bargaining unit but not a member of the union to help finance the union's collective bargaining activities violate his freedom of association?

No. In *Abood v. Detroit Board of Education*[284] the Supreme Court acknowledged that "[t]o be required to help finance the union as a collective-bargaining agent might well be thought . . . to interfere in some way with an employee's freedom to associate for the advancement of ideas, or to refrain from doing so, as he sees fit."[285] Nevertheless, the Court concluded that such interference was constitutionally justified by the legislative assessment of the importance of the agency shop to the system of labor relations established by the state. The Court recognized that the union, as the exclusive representative, has an obligation to fairly and equitably represent all employees, union and non-union, within the relevant bargaining unit, and that an agency shop provision may be thought to distribute fairly the cost of negotiating and administering the collective agreement, settling disputes, and processing grievances.[286] The Court held, however, that First Amendment principles prohibited the union and the board of education from requiring any teacher to contribute to the support of an ideological cause—unrelated to collective bargaining—which he might oppose.[287]

Other Associational Activity

Does a school board policy prohibiting public school teachers from enrolling their own school-age children in private school violate the First Amendment guarantee of freedom of association?

While such a broad policy might raise difficult constitutional questions—possibly implicating liberty and privacy rights protected by the due process clause of the 14th Amendment in addition to the implied First Amendment right of free association—a school board rule forbidding teachers to patronize a "segregation academy" or other private school with a policy or practice of excluding certain racial groups arguably would have a greater claim to constitutional validity. Such a rule might be justified on the theory that schoolteachers who send their own children to a segregated school harm their students by manifesting a belief that segregated education is desirable and a distrust in desegregated schools. The decisions in this area thus far have been inconclusive, however. While a Mississippi federal district court upheld the constitutionality of a board policy which, as applied, prohibited teachers from sending their own children to a racially segregated private school,[288] and the Fifth Circuit affirmed its judgment by a divided vote,[289] there was no majority opinion in the court of appeals. The Supreme Court, after granting review, dismissed the writ as improvidently granted and thus did not address the merits of the questions presented.[290]

Does the First Amendment protect a teacher's freedom in his personal relationships?

Some courts have so ruled. For example, an Illinois federal court held that the relation of husband and wife is protected by the freedom of association guaranteed by the First Amendment, and accordingly that the non-renewal of a teacher's contract because of the animosity of school authorities toward her husband, who was an official of an Illinois teachers' union, would violate her First Amendment right of association.[291]

Similarly, a Mississippi federal court ruled that a teaching applicant's right of free association under the First Amendment was violated when she was denied employment because of the exercise by her husband—a controversial figure in the community who was active in the civil rights movement—of his constitutionally protected right of free speech.[292] Other federal courts have found violations of the First Amendment right of free association in the refusal to employ a teacher because of her residence on a communal farm,[293] and in the termination of a teacher's employment because out-of-town friends of her son had stayed overnight at her apartment, where there was no proof of impropriety.[294]

A substantial question exists, however, as to whether the

"freedom of association" which the Supreme Court has derived from the existence of other First Amendment rights actually protects all personal associations and communal activities, or extends only to association with others in the pursuit of goals, such as speech, assembly, or petition, having independent First Amendment significance.[295] A federal district court in Texas gave a limited definition to the freedom of association in a case in which the new school board voted not to renew the contract of the director of vocational education because he was close to a member of the board that was voted out. Rejecting the instructor's assertion that the board had violated his right of association, the court found that the teacher associated with the member of the old board out of friendship and not "for the furtherance of any particular school program, policy, or objective." Acknowledging that the Supreme Court has found it unconstitutional to discharge certain employees solely because of their political affiliation, the court wrote that it "is convinced that the Constitution will not be interpreted to protect mere personal affinity in cases where the association bears no relationship to the expression of beliefs or ideas."[296]

Loyalty Programs

Loyalty oaths for teachers have old roots. In colonial times teachers who refused to swear allegiance to the Revolutionary government or who publicly proclaimed loyalty to England suffered financial or even bodily harm. Some were driven out of the country, including President Cooper of Columbia, who fled half-dressed over the college fence, escaping to a British sloop.[297] "Patriotic" oaths commonly have been required of teachers in other times of stress—for example, during the Civil War. The practice became widespread during and after the First World War, when a number of states enacted loyalty oath legislation[298] and also during the McCarthy period, when loyalty oaths were used as devices to ensure that the teachers of our impressionable youth were "one hundred percent Americans."

Among the grounds upon which teachers have objected to loyalty oath requirements are that (1) such oaths are futile, since any person against whom society needs protection is unlikely to have scruples against subscribing to the oath and breaking it; and (2) the broad nature of the typical oath permits interested pressure groups to suppress teacher questioning of orthodox views, and such suppression is its real purpose.

May a teacher be required as a condition of employment to subscribe to a loyalty oath?

It depends on the oath. Neither the federal nor state government may condition employment on taking an oath that impinges on rights guaranteed by the First and 14th Amendments, such as rights relating to political beliefs.[299] Nor may such employment be conditioned on an oath that one has not engaged, or will not engage, in protected speech activities, such as criticizing institutions of government, discussing political doctrines that approve the overthrow of certain forms of government, or supporting candidates for political office.[300] Public employment may not be conditioned upon an oath denying past, or abjuring future, associational activities that are constitutionally protected, including membership in organizations having an illegal purpose, unless one knows of the purpose and has a specific intent to promote it.[301] Finally, an oath imposed as a condition of public employment may not be so vague that "men of common intelligence must necessarily guess at its meaning and differ as to its application, [because such an oath] violates the first essential of due process of law."[302]

An oath requiring an individual to swear, as a condition of public employment, that he will uphold the Constitution of the United States or the state, however, is constitutional, as is an oath containing a promise to oppose the overthrow of the government of the United States or the state by force, violence, or any illegal method.[303]

Free Exercise of Religion and Rights Under The "Establishment" Clause

Does the termination of a teacher's employment because of his refusal to work on a religious holiday violate the "free exercise" clause of the First Amendment?

When an important state interest is shown, the Supreme

Court's decisions require a "delicate balancing" between that interest and a "free exercise" of religion claim.[304] "The essence of all that has been said and written on the subject," however, "is that only those interests of the highest order and those not otherwise served can overbalance legitimate claims to the free exercise of religion."[305]

In the context of a teacher's dismissal for being absent without permission to observe a religious holiday, it can be argued that the dismissal violates the free exercise clause where the school district could have accommodated the teacher by employing a fully qualified substitute at no additional cost. Thus, ruling that a prohibition against religious discrimination in the California Constitution was violated by the dismissal of a teacher, a member of the Worldwide Church of God, for absence required by his religious faith, the California Supreme Court observed that "[t]here was no shortage of qualified substitute teachers who could be and were called in to replace him at no additional cost to the district."[306] Although the court took note of evidence that instruction by a regular teacher is generally preferable to instruction by a substitute, it concluded that "such evidence falls short of showing that [his] absence for five to ten holy days a year imposed a hardship sufficiently severe to warrant disqualifying him from employment as a teacher."[307] The court explained that by statute each teacher was allowed at least ten days of paid leave each year for illness or "personal necessity."[308] It concluded that a district unwilling to pay for leave for religious purposes as a personal necessity must then accommodate those purposes by allowing a reasonable amount of unpaid leave, and determined that the unpaid leave required for the religious observances in question would not be unreasonably burdensome.[309] Responding to the superintendent's objection that it takes time for the substitute to establish an effective relationship with the class and that lesson plans do not furnish the substitute with enough information, the court said:

The fact that most classes missed by [plaintiff] were on consecutive days and taught by the same substitute provided more continuous time for the substitute's orientation than if [plaintiff's] absences had been sporadic. The fact that [plaintiff] knew the dates of his absences well in advance enabled him to furnish detailed lesson plans the quality of which is not disputed. Finally, the uncontradicted evidence that teachers in nearby school districts were permitted the absences denied [plaintiff] reinforces our conclusion that as a matter of law the district, by seeking to dismiss him, failed to make reasonable accommodation for his religious practices.[310]

Dismissing a teacher for refusing to work on a religious holiday may also violate Title VII of the Civil Rights Act of 1964, which is applicable to most school districts and obligates employers, short of "undue hardship," to make "reasonable accommodations" to the religious needs of their employees.[311] While the Supreme Court has held that to require an employer to bear more than a *de minimis* cost in order to accommodate an employee's religious needs would be an undue hardship,[312] the decision leaves room for a teacher to contend that no undue hardship is borne by a school district which is made to use, at no extra cost, a substitute who is fully qualified. Thus, when a teacher's aide who belonged to the Worldwide Church of God was not rehired because she had been absent on many religious holidays, a federal district court in Virginia held that the school district had violated Title VII.[313] Although the school district, which did not hire a substitute for the teacher's aide, argued that her "failure . . . to provide the students day-to-day instruction resulted in great harm to the students' educational progress," the court concluded that the district had failed to sustain its burden of proving undue hardship.[314] The court wrote that "[w]hile sympathetic to [the school district's] fears of undue hardship suffered by the students, such a finding cannot be made on mere opinion and speculation.[315]

In several cases it has been argued that Title VII's imposition on employers of a duty of reasonable accommodation to the religious practices of employees violates the "establishment clause" of the First Amendment. This issue has not been directly decided by the U.S. Supreme Court.[316] In the California case the court rejected the school district's argument that to require it to accommodate the teacher's religious observances contravened the establishment clause.[317]

If a school board has a policy establishing Good Friday as a paid holiday for teachers, is it obligated to afford Jewish teachers a day off with pay for a Jewish holiday?

In *Mandel v. Hodges* [318] employees of the State of California had been granted three hours off with pay on Good Friday, and this was found violative of the establishment clause. The remedy in such a case, however, would be to eliminate Good Friday as a paid holiday, not to order a comparable number of days off with pay for Jewish holidays.

Is the discharge of a teacher because his answers to a student's questions on scientific and theological matters do not fit the religious orthodoxy of the local parents a violation of the First Amendment prohibition against the establishment of religion?

A North Carolina federal district court determined that the discharge of a student teacher without warning because his answers to scientific and theological questions did not fit the notions of the local parents and teachers was a violation of the establishment clause of the First Amendment. The court said: "If a teacher has to answer searching, honest questions only in terms of the lowest common denominator of the professed beliefs of parents who complain the loudest, this means that the state through the public schools is impressing the particular religious orthodoxy of those parents on the religious and scientific education of the children by force of law."[319]

Does the "free exercise" clause protect a teacher from being discharged or disciplined for refusing to participate in flag ceremonies that would violate his religious beliefs?

This issue has been discussed in the context of a free-speech claim. It was noted that the Seventh Circuit appears to have held, in *Palmer v. Board of Education*,[320] that as long as school authorities articulate a teacher's duties in relation to flag ceremonies as being part of the "curriculum," they may force him to participate in such ceremonies notwithstanding the intrusive effect that such forced participation might have on his religious principles. This proposition seems doubtful. Where the goal of the school authorities can be achieved by means which have a "less drastic" impact on First Amendment rights, moreover, such as by relying upon another teacher who would perform the function as well, *Palmer* may leave room, even in the Seventh Circuit, for a "free exercise" claim to prevail.

In any event, independently of any constitutional principle, Title VII of the Civil Rights Act of 1964 requires an employer, short of undue hardship, to make a reasonable accommodation to a teacher's religious beliefs—a requirement that may well come into play in this context, at least where the employer would suffer no financial hardship and no seniority rights of other employees are involved.

NOTES

1. Frankfurter, J., concurring in *Wieman v. Updegraff*, 344 U.S. 183, 195 (1952).
2. *Shelton v. Tucker*, 364 U.S. 479, 487 (1960); *Sweezy v. New Hampshire*, 354 U.S. 234, 250 (1957) (opinion of Warren, C.J., joined by Black, Douglas, and Brennan, J.J.).
3. *See* Frankfurter, J., *supra* note 1.
4. 391 U.S. 563 (1968).
5. *Id*. at 569–70 (emphasis added).
6. *Id*. at 570 n.3. In *Hanneman v. Breier*, 528 F.2d 750 (7th Cir. 1976), the Seventh Circuit held that in order to justify discipline of police officers for violating a police department confidentiality rule, the defendant chief of police "must show a state interest in confidentiality applicable on these facts which outweighs the public and individual interests in the particular statements made." *Id*. at 754.
7. 391 U.S. 563, 570 n.3.
8. *Id*. at 574 (emphasis added). To constitute reckless disregard, there must be proof that the speaker " 'in fact entertained serious doubts as to the truth of his publication.' " *Herbert v. Lando*, 441 U.S. 153, 156 (1979), quoting *St. Amant v. Thompson*, 390 U.S. 727, 731 (1968). There must be a "high degree of awareness of [the statements'] probable falsity." *Garrison v. Louisiana*, 379 U.S. 64, 74 (1964). Although the "recklessness" standard is a subjective one, it may be satisfied by particularly convincing circumstantial proof. Thus, "[s]uch 'subjective awareness of probable falsity,' *Gertz v. Robert Welch, Inc.*, 418 U.S. 323, 335 n.6 (1974), may be found if 'there are obvious reasons to doubt the veracity of [an] informant or the accuracy of his reports.' " *Herbert v. Lando*, 441 U.S. 153, 156–57 (1979), *quoting St. Amant v. Thompson*, 390 U.S. 727, 732 (1968). The Fifth Circuit has held that a teacher's false statements were not protected when they were made "without foundation in fact," when investigation of the facts would have been "relatively easy" and when the teacher made no such investigation. *Megill v. Board of Regents*, 541 F.2d 1073, 1083 (5th Cir. 1976).

9. 391 U.S. 563, 571–72.

10. *Id*. at 573 n.5.

11. *Id*. at 573 n.5.

12. *Id*. at 569.

13. 439 U.S. 410 (1979).

14. *Id*. at 417.

14a. *Connick v. Myers*,—U.S. ——, 103 S. Ct. 1684 (1983).

14b. *Id* at 1960.

15. *Haimowitz v. University of Nevada*, 579 F.2d 526, 530 (9th Cir. 1978) (plaintiff's accusation against his department chairman almost certainly protected; summary judgment for defendant reversed); *Ring v. Schlesinger*, 502 F.2d 479, 488 (D.C. Cir. 1974) (teacher attacked competence and ethics of principal; summary judgment for defendant reversed). *But cf. Boehm v. Foster*, 670 F.2d 111 (9th Cir. 1982) (when plaintiff wrote letter to supervisor that he said was merely a parody accusing supervisor of being a "self-styled dictator in miniature without competency," court found the letter unprotected speech because it was not of public concern and seriously undermined work relationship).

16. *E.g., Cooper v. Johnson*, 590 F.2d 559, 562 (4th Cir. 1979); *Roseman v. Indiana University of Pennsylvania*, 520 F.2d 1364 (3d Cir. 1975), *cert. denied*, 424 U.S. 921 (1976).

17. *See Porter v. Califano*, 592 F.2d 770, 773–74 (5th Cir. 1979).

18. *Swilley v. Alexander*, 629 F.2d 1018, 1021 (5th Cir. 1980).

19. *Lusk v. Estes*, 361 F.Supp. 653, 663 (N.D. Tex. 1973). *See also Gorham v. Jewett*, 392 F.Supp. 22, 26 (D. Mass. 1975), *aff'd*, 527 F.2d 642 (1st Cir. 1975) (dictum) (counselor's letter to newspaper critical of his principal's proposal for Title III funds under the Elementary and Secondary Education Act "concerned a matter of public interest" and constituted protected speech). *Cf. Roberts v. Lake Central School Corp*., 317 F.Supp. 63, 64–65 (N.D. Ind. 1970) (comment of local teacher association president and member of negotiating team at association meeting that school administration was trying to "buy off" teachers with "small items at the expense of big ones" protected, even though directed at actions of his own principal).

20. *Pickering v. Board of Education*, 391 U.S. 563, 570 (1968).

21. *See Abbott v. Thetford*, 529 F.2d 695 (dissenting opinion), *adopted as opinion of en banc court*, 534 F.2d 1101, 1103 (5th Cir. 1976), *cert. denied*, 430 U.S. 954 (1977).

22. *Id*.

23. *See Sprague v. Fitzpatrick*, 546 F.2d 560, 565–66 (3d Cir. 1976), *cert. denied*, 431 U.S. 937 (1977).

24. *See Hillis v. Stephen F. Austin State University*, 486 F.Supp. 663, 1980 *rev'd on other grounds*, 665 F.2d 547 (5th Cir.); *cert. denied*, 457 U.S. 1106 (1982).

25. *Eckerd v. Indian River School District*, 475 F.Supp. 1350, 1360 (D. Del. 1979).

26. *Hillis v. Stephen F. Austin State University, supra.*
27. *Id. Cf. Cotten v. Board of Regents,* 395 F.Supp. 388, 389, 392
    (S.D. Ga. 1974), *aff'd,* 515 F.2d 1098 (5th Cir. 1975) (where
    personality conflict existed between pharmacology professor and
    his department chairman, and mutual criticism rose to the level of
    "internecine warfare," involuntary termination of professor's em-
    ployment in order to restore harmony within department and
    university did not violate professor's First Amendment rights).
28. *Pickering v. Board of Education,* 391 U.S. 563, 572 n.4 (1968).
29. *Lusk v. Estes,* 361 F.Supp. 653, 661, 662, 663 (N.D. Tex. 1973).
30. *Cf. Hickory Fire Fighters Association v. City of Hickory,* 656 F. 2d
    917, 921 (4th Cir. 1981) (existence of grievance procedure no excuse
    for not letting fire fighters speak about working conditions at city
    council meeting).
31. *Tepedino v. Dumpson,* 24 N.Y.2d 705, 709, 249 N.E.2d 751, 753,
    301 N.Y.S.2d 967, 969 (1969).
32. 24 N.Y.2d at 709, 249 N.E.2d at 752, 301 N.Y.S.2d at 969.
33. *Russo v. Central School District No. 1,* 469 F.2d 623, 632 (2d
    Cir.1972), *cert. denied,* 411 U.S. 932 (1973); *James v. Board of
    Education,* 461 F.2d 566, 574 (2d Cir.), *cert. denied,* 409 U.S. 1042
    (1972). *See also Davis v. Williams,* 598 F.2d 916 (5th Cir. 1979).
34. *Lusk v. Estes, 361 F.Supp.* 653, 663 (N.D. Tex. 1973). *See also
    Jannetta v. Cole,* 493 F.2d 1334, 1337 (4th Cir. 1974).
35. *Cf. Jannetta v. Cole,* 493 F.2d 1334, 1337 (4th Cir. 1974) ("As to
    the charge that Jannetta by-passed the 'chain of command' proce-
    dure by presenting his petition directly to the city manager, it is
    noted that nowhere was it suggested that such a by-pass would
    result in dismissal"); *Castleberry v. Langford,* 428 F.Supp. 676,
    680 (N.D. Tex. 1977).
36. 391 U.S. at 569–70.
37. *See Jannetta v. Cole,* 493 F.2d 1334, 1337 n.4 (4th Cir. 1974).
37a. *Connick v. Myers,* ——U.S.——,——, 103 S. Ct. 1684, 1692 (1983).
38. *Atcherson v. Siebenmann,* 605 F.2d 1058, 1063 (8th Cir. 1979).
39. *Atcherson v. Siebenmann,* 458 F.Supp. 526, 539 (S.D. Iowa 1978),
    *rev'd in part on other grounds citing statement in text with approval,
    605 F.2d 1058, 1063 (8th Cir. 1979).*
40. *Phillips v. Puryear,* 403 F.Supp. 80, 88 (W.D. Va. 1975).
41. 393 U.S. 503 (1969).
42. *Id.* at 509.
43. *Los Angeles Teachers Union v. Los Angeles City Board of Education,*
    71 Cal.2d 551, 564, 455 P.2d 827, 835, 78 Cal. Rptr. 723, 731
    (1969). *See Tinker v. Des Moines School District,* 393 U.S. 503,
    508–09 (1969). *Cf. Hickman v. Valley Board of Education,* 619 F.2d
    606, 609 (6th Cir. 1980) (personality conflict between teacher and
    principal germinating from teacher's constitutionally protected union
    activities did not justify termination.

44. *Bernasconi v. Tempe Elementary School District No. 3*, 548 F.2d 857, 862 (9th Cir.), *cert. denied*, 434 U.S. 825 (1977).

45. *Adcock v. Board of Education*, 10 Cal.3d 60, 68, 513 P.2d 900, 905, 109 Cal. Rptr. 676, 681 (1973). *See also Mabey v. Reagan*, 537 F.2d 1036, 1050 (9th Cir. 1976).

46. *Monsanto v. Quinn*, 674 F.2d 990, 1001 (3rd Cir. 1982).

47. *Stolberg v. Board of Trustees*, 474 F.2d 485, 490 (2d Cir. 1973). *See also Adamian v. Jacobsen*, 523 F.2d 929, 934 (9th Cir. 1975); *Council v. Donovan*, 40 Misc. 2d 744, 750, 244 N.Y.S.2d 199, 205 (1963) (a teacher's license could not be canceled "because of . . . his scruples against nuclear warfare"); *Bekiaris v. Board of Education*, 6 Cal.3d 575, 100 Cal. Rptr. 16, 493 P.2d 280 (1972).

48. *Wagle v. Murray*, 546 F.2d 1329, 1334 (9th Cir. 1976), *vacated on other grounds*, 431 U.S. 935 (1977), *opinion on remand*, 560 F.2d 401 (9th Cir. 1977), *cert. denied*, 434 U.S. 1014 (1978). *See also Jervey v. Martin*, 336 F.Supp. 1350 (W.D. Va. 1972) (state college professor who asserted that he had been denied a discretionary salary raise because he had written letter to editor praising author of article on premarital sex stated valid claim under § 1983). *Cf. Van Ooteghem v. Gray*, 628 F.2d 488, 492–93 (5th Cir. 1980), *aff'd in relevant part by en banc court*, 654 F.2d 304 (1981), *cert. denied*, 455 U.S. 909 (1982) ("the ability of a member of a disfavored class to express his views on civil rights publicly and without hesitation—no matter how personally offensive to his employer or majority of his co-employees—lies at the core of the Free Speech Clause of the First Amendment").

49. *Abood v. Detroit Board of Education*, 431 U.S. 209, 230 (1977).

50. 429 U.S. 167, 176 n.10 (1976) (emphasis added).

51. 429 U.S. 274, 284 (1977).

52. *Lindsey v. Board of Regents*, 607 F.2d 672, 674 (5th Cir. 1979).

53. *McGill v. Board of Education*, 602 F.2d 774, 778 (7th Cir. 1979). *See also Shaw v. Board of Trustees*, 549 F.2d 929, 932 (4th Cir. 1976) (teachers "had every right to disagree with the changing of the tenure system and the trustees' failure to grant formal bargaining rights with the college administration, and to say so"); *Greminger v. Seaborne*, 584 F.2d 275, 277 (8th Cir. 1978) (allocation of funds for teachers' salaries); *Hastings v. Bonner*, 578 F.2d 136, 139 (5th Cir. 1978) (teacher salaries, benefits, and teaching conditions); *Gasparinetti v. Kerr*, 568 F.2d 311, 316 (3rd Cir. 1977), *cert. denied*, 436 U.S. 903 (1978) (police department work rules and contract negotiations); *Hanneman v. Breier*, 528 F.2d 750, 755–56 (7th Cir. 1976) (public employer-employee relations and misuse of employee discipline); *Rampey v. Allen*, 501 F.2d 1090 (10th Cir. 1974), *cert. denied*, 420 U.S. 908 (1975). *But see Clark v. Holmes*, 474 F.2d 928, 931 (7th Cir. 1972), *cert. denied*, 411 U.S. 972 (1973) (faculty member's disputes with superiors and colleagues about course content and student counseling

unprotected, in part because not "matters of public concern"); *Rowe v. Forrester*, 368 F.Supp. 1355, 1357 (M.D. Ala. 1974) (faculty member's statements about regular operations and functions of faculty and administration unprotected because not "on matters of general public concern").

54. *Trotman v. Board of Trustees of Lincoln University*, 635 F.2d 216, 225 (3d Cir. 1980), *cert. denied*, 451 U.S. 986 (1981).

55. *See, e.g., United Carolina Bank v. Board of Regents of Stephen F. Austin State University*, 665 F.2d 553 (5th Cir. 1982) (professor's charge that forestry department was misallocating research funds was a matter of public concern).

56. *See Johnson v. Butler*, 433 F.Supp. 531, 535 (W.D. Va. 1977) (complaint by teacher to her principal concerning her status as a "floating" teacher was protected by the First Amendment: "[T]he teacher sincerely believed that her status as a floating teacher contributed to classroom inefficiency and was adversely affecting her as a teacher. . . . [T]he right of a teacher to voice concerns about conditions which interfere with the education of students falls squarely within the protections afforded by the Constitution"). *But cf. Jones v. Kneller*, 482 F.Supp. 204, 209 (E.D. N.Y. 1979), *aff 'd mem.*, 633 F.2d 204 (2d Cir.), *cert. denied*, 449 U.S. 920 (1980). ("[b]ickering" among "two factions in the department" who had a constant disagreement as to the most appropriate method of teaching certain classes and certain students unprotected).

57. *Lindsey v. Board of Regents*, 607 F.2d 672, 675 (5th Cir. 1979).

58. *See Cooper v. Johnson*, 590 F.2d 559, 562 (4th Cir. 1979).

59. *Id.*

59a. *Connick v. Myers*, ——U.S.——, ——, 103 S. Ct. 1684, 1690, 91 (1983).

59b. *Id* at 1693–94.

59c. *Id* at 1690.

59d. *Id* at 1694.

60. *Harris v. Arizona Board of Regents*, 528 F.Supp. 987, 999 (D. Ariz. 1981).

61. *Barbre v. Garland Independent School District*, 474 F. Supp. 687, 698 (N.D. Tex. 1979).

62. *English v. Powell*, 592 F.2d 727, 732 n.5 (4th Cir. 1979).

63. *See Phillips v. Puryear*, 403 F.Supp. 80, 88 (W.D. Va. 1975) (community college professor stigmatized by faculty committee report had First Amendment right to criticize the report in conversations with fellow faculty members). *See also Rampey v. Allen*, 501 F.2d 1090 (10th Cir. 1974), *cert. denied*, 420 U.S. 908 (1975).

64. *Givhan v. Western Line Consolidated School District*, 439 U.S. 410, 415 (1979).

65. 333 U.S. 507, 510 (1948).

66. *Eckerd v. Indian River School District*, 475 F.Supp. 1350, 1359 (D. Del. 1979).

67. *Starsky v. Williams*, 353 F.Supp. 900, 922–23 (D. Ariz. 1972), *modified on other grounds*, 512 F.2d 109 (9th Cir. 1975).

68. *Roseman v. Indiana University of Pennsylvania*, 520 F.2d 1364, 1368 (3d Cir. 1975), *cert. denied*, 424 U.S. 921 (1976). *See also Connecticut State Federation of Teachers v. Board of Education*, 538 F.2d 471, 481 (2d Cir. 1976); *Eckerd v. Indian River School District*, 475 F.Supp. 1350, 1359 (D. Del. 1979) (content of allegedly protected speech may bear on degree of interest teacher may properly claim in his First Amendment freedom).

69. *Waters v. Chaffin*, 684 F.2d 833 (11th Cir. 1982) (citations omitted).

70. *Id.* at 837.

71. *Id.* at 839.

72. *Id.* at 839–40.

73. 439 U.S. 410 (1979).

74. 555 F.2d 1309, 1318 (5th Cir. 1977).

75. 439 U.S. 410, 415–16 (1979). *See also Columbus Education Association v. Columbus City School District*, 623 F.2d 1155 (6th Cir. 1980) (First Amendment rights of free speech and association protected zealous advocacy by building representative of fellow teacher at grievance meeting with supervising principal, held pursuant to established procedures); *Hillis v. Stephen F. Austin State University*, 665 F.2d 547, 549 (5th Cir.), *cert. denied*, 457 U.S. 1106 (1982), (university art professor's criticism, at a meeting with his department head, of the latter's directive to carry a student on his class roll and give her a "B" even though he had never seen the student or reviewed her portfolio, held protected by the First Amendment); *Eckerd v. Indian River School District*, 475 F.Supp. 1350, 1358, (D. Del. 1979) ("*Givhan* . . . establishes that the private context of [the plaintiff teacher's] speech did not automatically remove it from the protections of the First Amendment").

76. *Givhan v. Western Line Consolidated School District*, 439 U.S. 410, 445 n.4 (1979). *See Egger v. Phillips*, 669 F.2d 497, 503 (7th Cir. 1982) (FBI agent complains to his supervisor about internal corruption); *Janusaitis v. Middlebury Volunteer Fire Department*, 607 F.2d 17, 26 (2d Cir. 1979). Of course, where a teacher's private expression occurs pursuant to established procedures and at the time and place and in the manner agreed to by the parties, institutional efficiency would not seem to be threatened. *See Columbus Education Association v. Columbus City School District*, 623 F.2d 1155, 1160 (6th Cir. 1980).

77. *Hillis v. Stephen F. Austin State University*, 486 F.Supp. 663, 666–67 (E.D. Tex. 1980), *rev'd on other grounds*, 665 F.2d 547 (5th Cir.), *cert. denied*, 457 U.S. 1106 (1982).

78. *California Motor Transport Co. v. Trucking Unlimited*, 404 U.S. 508, 510 (1972).

79. *Swaaley v. United States*, 376 F.2d 857, 863 (Ct.Cl. 1967). *See also Burkett v. United States*, 402 F.2d 1002, 1008 (Ct.Cl. 1968).

80. *Jackson v. United States*, 428 F.2d 844, 846, 848 (Ct.Cl. 1970). *See also Tepedino v. Dumpson*, 24 N.Y.2d 705, 249 N.E.2d 751, 301 N.Y.S.2d 967 (1969).
81. 429 U.S. 167 (1976).
82. *Id.* at 177 (emphasis added).
83. *Id.* at 175 n.7.
84. T. Cooley, *The General Principles of Constitutional Law in the United States of America* 297 (1898).
85. *Adamian v. Jacobsen*, 523 F.2d 929, 934 (9th Cir. 1975).
86. *Mabey v. Reagan*, 537 F.2d 1036, 1050 (9th Cir. 1976).
87. 391 U.S. at 570.
88. *Trotman v. Board of Trustees of Lincoln University*, 635 F.2d 216, 225–26 (3d Cir. 1980), *cert. denied*, 451 U.S. 986 (1981).
89. *Starsky v. Williams*, 353 F.Supp. 900, 924 (D. Ariz. 1972), *modified on other grounds*, 512 F.2d 109 (9th Cir. 1975). *See also Jones v. Battles*, 315 F.Supp. 601, 607 (D. Conn. 1970) (dictum) (teacher's constitutional protection is not lost because his comments "strongly challenge or cause severe criticism of . . . his nominal superior" or are less discreet than professional ethics might have dictated).
90. *Jordan v. Cagle*, 474 F.Supp. 1198, 1210 (N.D. Miss. 1979), *aff'd mem.*, 620 F.2d 298 (5th Cir. 1980).
91. *Puentes v. Board of Education*, 24 N.Y.2d 996, 999, 250 N.E.2d 232, 233, 302 N.Y.S.2d 824, 826 (1969). *See also Jordan v. Cagle*, 474 F.Supp. 1198, 1210–11 (N.D. Miss. 1979), *aff'd mem.*, 620 F.2d 298 (5th Cir. 1980).
92. *Papish v. Board of Curators*, 410 U.S. 667, 670 (1973). *Cf. Cohen v. California*, 403 U.S. 15, 24 (1971) (state cannot constitutionally excise one particular scurrilous epithet from public discourse on theory that state is guardian of public morality).
93. *Meehan v. Macy*, 392 F.2d 822, 835 (D.C. Cir. 1968), *modified*, 425 F.2d 469, *aff'd with modifications en banc*, 425 F.2d 472 (1969), *quoted with approval in Arnett v. Kennedy*, 416 U.S. 134, 161–62 (1974) (plurality opinion). *See also Fuentes v. Roher*, 519 F.2d 379, 390 (2d Cir. 1975).
94. *Starsky v. Williams*, 353 F.Supp. 900, 917 (D. Ariz. 1972), *modified on other grounds*, 512 F.2d 109 (9th Cir. 1975). *See Megill v. Board of Regents*, 541 F.2d 1073, 1083–84 (5th Cir. 1976) (profanity at academic meeting); *Duke v. North Texas State University*, 469 F.2d 829, 840 (5th Cir. 1972), *cert. denied*, 412 U.S. 932 (1973) ("extremely disrespectful and grossly offensive remarks aimed at the administrators of the university"); *Lux v. Board of Regents of New Mexico Highlands University*, 95 N.M. 361, 622 P.2d 266 (N.M. Ct.App. 1980), *cert denied*, 454 U.S. 816 (1981) (diatribe against university president did not foster rational discourse); *Pietrunti v. Board of Education*, 128 N.J. Super. 149, 319 A.2d 262, *cert. denied*, 419 U.S. 1057 (1974) (insulting and vituperative language in speech attacking character of superintendent). *See also Adamian v. Jacobsen*, 523 F.2d 929, 933 (9th Cir. 1975).

95. *Waters v. Chaffin*, 684 F.2d 833, 837 (11th Cir. 1982).

96. *Barbre v. Garland Independent School District*, 474 F.Supp. 687, 693 (N.D. Tex. 1979).

97. *Jones v. Battles*, 315 F.Supp. 601, 608 (D. Conn. 1979). *See also Boehm v. Foster*, 670 F.2d 111, 113 (9th Cir. 1982); *Amburgey v. Cassady*, 370 F.Supp. 571, 567 (E.D. Ky.), *aff'd*, 507 F.2d 728 (6th Cir. 1974).

98. *Speiser v. Randall*, 357 U.S. 513, 521 (1958).

99. *Tygrett v. Washington*, 543 F.2d 840, 849 (D.C. Cir. 1974).

100. *Clark v. Mann*, 562 F.2d 1104, 1118 (8th Cir. 1977).

101. 393 U.S. 503 (1969).

102. *Id.* at 513.

103. *See, e.g., Trotman v. Board of Trustees of Lincoln University*, 635 F.2d 216, 230 (3d Cir. 1980), *cert. denied*, 451 U.S. 986 (1981); *Van Ooteghem v. Gray*, 628 F.2d 488 (5th Cir. 1980), *aff'd in relevant part by en banc court*, 654 F.2d 304 (1981), *cert. denied*, 455 U.S. 909 (1982); *Porter v. Califano*, 592 F.2d 770, 773–74 (5th Cir. 1979); *Hastings v. Bonner*, 578 F.2d 136, 143 (5th Cir. 1978); *Mabey v. Reagan*, 537 F.2d 1036, 1050 (9th Cir. 1976); *Smith v. Losee*, 485 F.2d 334, 339 (10th Cir. 1973) (*en banc*), *cert. denied*, 417 U.S. 908 (1974); *Fluker v. Alabama State Board of Education*, 441 F.2d 201, 206 (5th Cir. 1971); *Harris v. Arizona Board of Regents*, 528 F.Supp. 987, 999 (D. Ariz. 1981); Note, *The Non-Partisan Freedom of Expression of Public Employees*, 76 Mich.L.Rev. 365, 380–81 & nn.66–67 (1977).

104. *Foster v. Ripley*, 645 F.2d 1142, 1149 (D.C. Cir. 1981); *Shoemaker v. Allender*, 520 F.Supp. 266, 269 (E.D. Pa. 1981).

104a. *Connick v. Myers*, ——U.S.——,——, 103 S. Ct. 1684, 1692–93 (1983) The Court added: "The limited First Amendment interest involved here does not require that [the employer] tolerate action which he reasonably believed would disrupt the office, undermine his authority and destroy close working relationships." *Id.* at 1694.

105. *Porter v. Califano*, 592 F.2d 770, 773–74 (5th Cir. 1979). *See also Atcherson v. Siebenmann*, 605 F.2d 1058, 1063 (8th Cir. 1979).

106. *Daulton v. Affeldt*, 678 F.2d 487, 491 (4th Cir. 1982).

107. *E.g., Columbus Education Association v. Columbus City School District*, 623 F.2d 1155 (6th Cir. 1980) ("[p]laintiff established a *prima facie* case that the reprimand was predicated on constitutionally protected activity. The burden then shifted to defendants to prove that its [sic] interest in the efficient administration of education outweighs the plaintiffs' [sic] free speech and association rights"); *Porter v. Califano*, 592 F.2d 770, 773 (5th Cir. 1979); *Tygrett v. Washington*, 543 F.2d 840, 849–50 (D.C. Cir. 1974); *Smith v. Losee*, 485 F.2d 334, 339–40 (10th Cir. 1973) (*en banc*), *cert. denied*, 417 U.S. 908 (1974); *Hostrop v. Board of Junior College District No. 515*, 471 F.2d 488, 493 n.14 (7th Cir. 1972), *cert. denied*, 411 U.S. 967 (1973).

108. *Tygrett v. Washington*, 543 F.2d 840, 849 (D.C. Cir. 1974). See *Tinker v. Des Moines School District*, 393 U.S. 503, 509 (1969); *NAACP v. Button*, 371 U.S. 415, 439 (1963).

109. *Tinker v. Des Moines School District*, 393 U.S. 503, 508 (1969); *Hastings v. Bonner*, 578 F.2d 136, 143 (5th Cir. 1978); *Jordan v. Cagle*, 474 F.Supp. 1198, 1212 (N.D. Miss. 1979), *aff'd mem.*, 620 F.2d 298 (5th Cir. 1980).

110. *Jordan v. Cagle, supra*.

111. *Los Angeles Teachers Union v. Los Angeles City Board of Education*, 71 Cal. 2d 551, 564 n.13, 455 P.2d 827, 835 n.13, 78 Cal. Rptr. 723, 731 n.13 (1969).

112. *James v. Board of Education*, 461 F.2d 566, 571 (2d Cir.), *cert. denied*, 409 U.S. 1042 (1972).

113. *Dodd v. Rambis*, 535 F.Supp. 23, 29 (S.D. Ind. 1981), *citing Scoville v. Board of Education*, 425 F.2d 10, 13 (7th Cir.), *cert. denied*, 400 U.S. 826 (1970).

114. *Ring v. Schlesinger*, 502 F.2d 479, 490, (D.C. Cir. 1974).

115. *Id.* at 489–90. *See also Porter v. Califano*, 592 F.2d 770, 772 (5th Cir. 1979).

116. 393 U.S. 503, 514 (1969). *See also James v. Board of Education*, 461 F.2d 566, 575 n.22 (2nd Cir.), *cert. denied*, 409 U.S. 1042 (1972). *But see Lusk v. Estes*, 361 F.Supp. 653, 660 (N.D. Tex. 1973).

117. *Duke v. North Texas State University*, 469 F.2d 829, 839–40 (5th Cir. 1972), *cert. denied*, 412 U.S. 932 (1973). *But see Jordan v. Cagle*, 474 F.Supp. 1198, 1210 n.9 (N.D. Miss. 1979), *aff'd mem.*, 620 F.2d 298 (5th Cir. 1980) ("[s]ince none of plaintiff's public statements involved the use of *excessive* profanity directed toward the superintendent or board, the board's interest in avoiding loss of public respect for its faculty is not implicated under the facts of this case") (emphasis added).

118. 358 U.S. 1 (1958).

119. *Id.* at 6, *quoting Brown v. Board of Education*, 349 U.S. 294, 300–1 (1954).

120. *Cf. Bazaar v. Fortune*, 476 F.2d 570, 579, *modified*, 489 F.2d 225 (5th Cir. 1973), *cert. denied*, 416 U.S. 995 (1974). ("[s]peech cannot be stifled by the state merely because it would perhaps draw an adverse reaction from the majority of people").

121. *Starsky v. Williams*, 353 F.Supp. 900, 924 (D. Ariz. 1972), *aff'd and approved in pertinent part*, 512 F.2d 109, 111 (9th Cir. 1975). *See also Pickings v. Bruce*, 430 F.2d 595, 598 (8th Cir. 1970) (Though public statements of faculty advisers "may . . . increase the tensions . . . between the [school] and the community . . . this fact cannot serve to restrict freedom of expression").

122. *Franklin v. Atkins*, 409 F.Supp. 439, 446 (D. Colo. 1977), *aff'd*, 562 F.2d 1188 (10th Cir. 1977), *cert. denied*, 435 U.S. 994 (1978).

123. *Whitsel v. Southeast Local School District*, 484 F.2d 1222, 1229 (6th Cir. 1973). *See also Bowles v. Robbins*, 359 F.Supp. 249 (D. Vt. 1973).

124. *Chitwood v. Feaster*, 468 F.2d 359, 361 (4th Cir. 1972). *See also Peacock v. Board of Regents*, 380 F.Supp. 1081, 1085 (D. Ariz. 1974), *aff'd*, 510 F.2d 1324 (9th Cir.), *cert. denied*, 422 U.S. 1049 (1975).

125. *Shaw v. Board of Trustees*, 549 F.2d 929, 932 (4th Cir. 1976). *See also Megill v. Board of Trustees*, 541 F.2d 1073, 1084 (5th Cir. 1976) (disruptive conduct at academic meeting).

126. *Meinhold v. Clark County Board of Education*, 89 Nev. 56, 506 P.2d 420, *cert. denied*, 414 U.S. 943 (1973).

127. *Gray v. Union County Intermediate Education District*, 520 F.2d 803 (9th Cir. 1975).

128. *Rampey v. Allen*, 501 F.2d 1090, 1100 (10th Cir. 1974) (*en banc*), *cert. denied*, 420 U.S. 908 (1975).

129. *Tygrett v. Washington*, 543 F.2d 840, 845 (D.C. Cir. 1974).

130. *Pickering v. Board of Education*, 391 U.S. 563, 573 n.5 (1968).

131. *Rosado v. Garcia Santiago*, 562 F.2d 114, 118 (1st Cir. 1977).

132. *Megill v. Board of Regents*, 541 F.2d 1073, 1085 (5th Cir. 1976).

133. *Lindsey v. Board of Regents*, 607 F.2d 672, 675–76 (5th Cir. 1979). *See also Jordan v. Cagle*, 474 F.Supp. 1198, 1210–11, (N.D. Miss. 1979), *aff'd mem.*, 620 F.2d 298 (5th Cir. 1980).

134. *Gertz v. Robert Welch, Inc.*, 418 U.S. 323, 339 (1974); *Lindsey v. Board of Regents*, 607 F.2d 672, 675 (5th Cir. 1979).

135. *Butler v. Hamilton*, 542 F.2d 835, 839 (10th Cir. 1976). *See Aumiller v. University of Delaware*, 434 F.Supp. 1273, 1290 (D. Del. 1977).

136. *Long v. Board of Education*, 331 F.Supp. 193, 197 (E.D. Mo. 1971), *aff'd*, 456 F.2d 1058 (8th Cir. 1972). *See also Cook County College Teachers Union v. Byrd*, 456 F.2d 882, 888–89 n.7 (7th Cir. 1972), *cert. denied*, 414 U.S. 883 (1973); *Murphy v. Facienda*, 307 F.Supp. 353, 355 (D. Colo. 1969).

137. *Bernasconi v. Tempe Elementary School District No. 3*, 548 F.2d 857, 862, (9th Cir.), *cert. denied*, 434 U.S. 825 (1977).

138. *Reid v. Barrett*, 467 F.Supp. 124 (D. N.J. 1979), *aff'd*, 615 F.2d (1354) (1980).

139. *Id.* at 127.

140. *Thomas v. Board of Education*, 607 F.2d 1043, 1051 (2d Cir. 1979), *cert. denied*, 444 U.S. 1081 (1980).

141. *Id.*

142. *Bertot v. School District No. 1*, 522 F.2d 1171, 1183 (10th Cir. 1975). *Cf. Pickings v. Bruce*, 430 F.2d 595, 598–99 (8th Cir. 1970) (sanctions imposed on faculty advisers to student organization in reprisal for organization's invitation to controversial speaker violated First Amendment rights of advisers as well as students to free expression and association).

143. *Bertot v. School District No. 1*, *supra*.

144. *Greer v. Spock*, 424 U.S. 828, 836 (1976), *quoting from Adderley v. Florida*, 385 U.S. 39, 48 (1966).

145. *Connecticut State Federation of Teachers v. Board of Education Members*, 538 F.2d 471, 480 (2d Cir. 1976). *See also Perry Education Association v. Perry Local Educators' Association*, ———U.S. ———,———, 103 S. Ct. 948, 955–56 (1983) 4165, 4168 (U.S. Feb. 23, 1983).

146. Cases cited in note 145.

147. *Police Department v. Mosley*, 408 U.S. 92, 95–96 (1972). *See also Widmar v. Vincent*, 454 U.S. 263, 267–70 (1981).

148. *Police Department v. Mosley*, 408 U.S. 92, 96 (1980).

149. *Id. See also Widmar v. Vincent*, 454 U.S. 263, 267–70, (1981); *City of Madison v. Wisconsin Employment Relations Commission*, 429 U.S. 167, 175–76 (1976).

150. *James v. Board of Education*, 461 F.2d 566 (2d Cir.), *cert. denied*, 409 U.S. 1042 (1972).

150a *Perry Education Association v. Perry Local Educators' Association*, ———U.S.———,———, 103 Ct. 948, 957 (1983).

150b *Id.* at 956.

151. *Connecticut State Federation of Teachers, supra* note 145, at 480. *See also Perry Education Association v. Perry Local Educators' Association*, ———U.S.———,———, 103 S. Ct. 948, 959 (1983); ("the reasonableness of the limitations on . . . access to the school mail system is also supported by the substantial alternative channels that remain open for . . . communication to take place").

152. *Los Angeles Teachers Union v. Los Angeles City Board of Education*, 71 Cal. 2d 551, 455 P.2d 827, 78 Cal. Rptr. 723 (1969). *See also Downs v. Conway School District*, 328 F.Supp. 338 (E.D. Ark. 1971) (where superintendent interpreted school policy on circulation of petitions to bar teacher from sending personal notes to other teachers asking them whether they found an open incinerator on the school playground objectionable, non-renewal of teacher's contract in part for sending notes violated her First Amendment rights of free speech and petition).

153. *Los Angeles Teachers Union v. Los Angeles City Board of Education*, 71 Cal. 2d 551, 560, 455 P.2d 827, 832, 78 Cal. Rptr. 723, 728 (1969).

154. *NLRB v. Magnavox Co.*, 415 U.S. 322, 325 (1974).

155. *Perry Education Association v. Perry Local Educators' Association*, ———U.S.———,———, 103 S. Ct. 948, 955–56 (1983).

156. *Hall v. Board of School Commissioners of Mobile County*, 681 F.2d 965, 968 (5th Cir. 1982).

157. *Id.* at 969.

158. *Id.* at 971, (quoting district court). *See also Southeastern Promotions Ltd. v. Conrad*, 420 U.S. 546, 533 (1975).

159. *Hall, Supra* note 156, at 971.

160. *Id.* at 972.

161. *Friedman v. Union Free School District No. 1.*, 314 F. Supp. 223 (E.D. N.Y. 1970).

162. *Perry Education Association v. Perry Local Educators' Association*, ——U.S.——, ——, 103 S. Ct. 948, 955–56 (1983); *Police Department v. Mosley*, 408 U.S. 92, 95–96 (1972).

163. *Connecticut State Federation of Teachers v. Board of Education Members*, 538 F.2d 471, 478 (2d Cir. 1976).

164. 429 U.S. 167 (1976).

165. *Id.* at 167–73.

166. *Id.* at 173–74.

167. *Id.* at 175.

168. *Id.* at 175–76.

169. *Id.* at 176.

170. *Id.* at 177.

171. *Id.*

172. *Princeton Education Association v. Princeton Board of Education*, 480 F.Supp. 962, 969 (S.D. Ohio 1979).

173. *Id.* at 970.

174. *Id.* at 970–71.

175. *Id.* at 968, *citing* 429 U.S. at 175 n.8.

176. *Princeton Education Association v. Princeton Board of Education*, *supra* note 172, at 971.

177. *Id.* at 969.

178. *Id.*

179. *James v. Board of Education*, 461 F.2d 566 (2d Cir.), *cert. denied*, 409 U.S. 1042 (1972). *See also* opinion of trial court on remand, 385 F.Supp. 209 (W.D. N.Y. 1974).

180. 393 U.S. 503 (1969).

181. *Id.* at 505.

182. *James v. Board of Education*, 461 F.2d 566, 571 (2d Cir.), *cert. denied*, 407 U.S. 1042 (1972).

183. *Id.* at 572.

184. *Id.* at 574.

185. *Id. See also Russo v. Central School District*, 469 F.2d 623, 633 (2d Cir. 1972, *cert. denied*, 411 U.S. 932 (1973).

186. *Branti v. Finkel*, 445 U.S. 507, 516 (1980). See also *Board of Education v. Barnette*, 419 U.S. 625 (1943).

187. *Branti v. Finkel*, *supra* at 516. *Elrod v. Burns*, 427 U.S. 347, 362, 368, 373 (1976) (plurality opinion).

188. *Cf. Aurora Education Association East v. Board of Education*, 490 F.2d 431, 434 (7th Cir.), *cert denied*, 416 U.S. 985 (1974) (school board policy which, as applied, precluded a teacher from receiving full salary and perquisites if, as a mere matter of dogma, he held to the belief that teachers should be free to strike against governmental agencies, violated First Amendment: A teacher, "like any other citizen . . . is free to think as he likes"). *See also National Association*

of Letter Carriers v. Blount, 305 F.Supp. 546 (D. D.C. 1969), *appeal dismissed by stipulation,* 400 U.S. 801 (1970). Presumably, where there were multiple reasons for termination, but the teacher proves that his beliefs were a "substantial" or "motivating" factor, the *Mount Healthy* test would apply and the board would have to prove that it would have made the same decision even absent the protected conduct.

189. 469 F.2d 623 (2d Cir. 1972), *cert. denied,* 411 U.S. 932 (1973).

190. *Id.* at 632–34, *citing* 319 U.S. 624, 632 (1972).

191. *Id.* at 634.

192. *Russo v. Central School District,* 469 F.2d 623, 632 (2d Cir. 1972), *cert. denied,* 411 U.S. 932 (1973).

193. *Id.*

194. *Id.* at 633. *See also Hanover v. Northrup,* 325 F.Supp. 170, 172 (D. Conn. 1970); *State v. Lundquist,* 262 Md. 534, 278 A.2d 263 (1971).

195. 603 F.2d 1271, 1274 (7th Cir. 1979), *cert. denied,* 444 U.S. 1026 (1980)

196. *Id.* at 1273.

197. *Tygrett v. Barry,* 627 F.2d 1279, 1286–87 (D.C. Cir. 1980). *Cf. Johnson v. Branch,* 364 F.2d 177, 181 (4th Cir. 1966) (trial court's finding in § 1983 action that teacher's civil rights activities consumed so much of her time and interest that they interfered with her extracurricular activities at the school, created some dissension between her and the principal, and caused the board to refuse to renew her contract is "irrelevant because it is not the reason advanced by the board members for refusing to [renew] her contract"). *See also S.E.C. v. Chenery Corp.,* 332 U.S. 194, 196 (1947); *Williams v. Sumter School District No. 2,* 225 F.Supp. 397, 403 (D. S.C. 1966). *But see Acanfora v. Board of Education,* 491 F.2d 498, 503 (4th Cir.), *cert. denied,* 419 U.S. 836 (1974).

198. *Tygrett v. Barry, supra* at 1286.

199. *Alabama Education Association v. Wallace,* 362 F.Supp. 682–83, 685–86 (M.D. Ala. 1973).

200. *Id.* at 686.

201. *Trotman v. Board of Trustees of Lincoln University,* 635 F.2d 216, 226 (3d Cir. 1980), *cert. denied,* 451 U.S. 896 (1981).

202. *Rozman v. Elliott,* 335 F.Supp. 1086, 1097 (D. Neb. 1971), *aff'd,* 467 F.2d 1145 (8th Cir. 1972).

203. *Rozman v. Elliott, supra* at 1098.

204. *See, e.g., Cousins v. Wigoda,* 419 U.S. 477, 489 (1975). *See also Montgomery v. White,* 320 F.Supp. 303, 304 (E.D. Tex. 1969).

205. 427 U.S. 347 (1976).

206. *Guerra v. Roma Independent School District,* 444 F.Supp. 812, 819 (S.D. Tex. 1977). *See also Miller v. Board of Education,* 450 F.Supp. 106, 112–13 (S.D. W.Va. 1978) (termination of employment of school bus driver and cook due to political considerations unconstitutional).

207. *Guerra v. Roma Independent School District, supra* at 822, *citing Perry v. Sindermann,* 408 U.S. 593 (1972), and *Keyishian v. Board of Regents,* 385 U.S. 589 (1967).
208. *Soto v. Chardon,* 514 F.Supp. 339 (D. P.R. 1981).
209. *Branti v. Finkel,* 445 U.S. 507, 518 (1980).
210. *Id.*
211. 385 U.S. 589 (1967).
212. *Id.* at 610.
213. *Id.* at 605–10.
214. *Baird v. State Bar,* 401 U.S. 1 (1971); *United States v. Robel,* 389 U.S. 258 (1967); *Sweezy v. New Hampshire,* 354 U.S. 234 (1957).
215. *Cooper v. Ross,* 472 F.Supp. 802, 810 (W.D. Ark. 1979). *See also Karst v. Regents of the University of California,* 4 College Law Bull. 47 (Cal. Ct. App. Jan. 26, 1972).
216. *Gibson v. Florida Legislative Committee,* 372 U.S. 539, 544 (1963); *NAACP v. Alabama,* 357 U.S. 449, 462 (1958).
217. *Buckley v. Valeo,* 424 U.S. 1, 64 (1975); *Gibson v. Florida Legislative Committee, supra; NAACP v. Button,* 371 U.S. 415 (1963); *Shelton v. Tucker,* 364 U.S. 479 (1960); *Bates v. Little Rock,* 361 U.S. 516 (1960); *NAACP v. Alabama, supra.*
218. *Hastings v. North East Independent School District,* 615 F.2d 628, 632 (5th Cir. 1980).
219. *Id.*
220. 364 U.S. 479 (1960).
221. *Id.* at 490.
222. *Barenblatt v. United States,* 360 U.S. 109, 127 (1959).
223. 360 U.S. 109 (1959).
224. *Id.* at 112.
225. 431 U.S. 209 (1977).
226. *Id.* at 240.
227. 413 U.S. 548 (1973).
228. 413 U.S. 601 (1973).
229. 413 U.S. at 564–67.
230. 413 U.S. at 565.
231. *Id.*
232. 330 U.S. 75 (1947).
233. 413 U.S. at 556.
234. *Alderman v. Philadelphia Housing Authority,* 496 F.2d 164, 171 n.45 (4th Cir.), *cert denied,* 419 U.S. 844 (1974); *accord, Magill v. Lynch,* 560 F.2d 22, 27 (1st Cir. 1977), *cert. denied,* 434 U.S. 1063 (1978).
235. *Magill v. Lynch, supra.*
236. *Morial v. Judiciary Commission,* 565 F.2d 295, 300 (5th Cir. 1977) *(en banc), cert. denied,* 435 U.S. 1013 (1978).
237. *Id. See also Barry v. District of Columbia Board of Elections,* 448 F.Supp. 1249, 1252 (D. D.C.), *appeal dismissed,* 580 F.2d 695 (D.C. Cir. 1978).

238. 475 F.Supp. 137 (N.D. Tex. 1979).

239. *Id.* at 140.

240. *Id.*

241. *Id.* at 140–41. *Accord Otten v. Schicker*, 655 F.2d 142, 144 (8th Cir. 1981).

242. 475 F.Supp. at 141. *See also Stone v. City of Wichita Falls*, 477 F.Supp. 581, 584–85 (N.D. Tex. 1979) *aff'd*, 646 F.2d 1085 (5th Cir.), *cert. denied*, 454 U.S. 1082 (1981) (city charter provision barring city employees from becoming a candidate for public office violated First Amendment as applied to city fireman who sought election to county commission in adjoining county).

243. *Hickman v. City of Dallas*, 475 F.Supp. 137, 141 (N.D. Tex. 1979).

244. *Bart v. Telford*, 677 F.2d 622, 625 (7th Cir. 1982).

245. 560 F.2d 22, 29.

246. *Id.* at 27–29.

247. *Id.* at 29.

248. *Allen v. Board of Education*, 584 S.W.2d 408 (C.A. Ky. 1979); *but cf. Bart v. Telford*, 677 F.2d 622 (7th Cir. 1982) (upholding requirement that city employee take leave of absence when running for mayor).

249. *Wilson v. Moore*, 346 F.Supp. 635 (W.D. W.Va. 1972). *Cf. Lay v. City of Kingsport*, 454 F.2d 345 (6th Cir.), *cert. denied*, 409 U.S. 846 (1972) (assistant superintendent constitutionally could be forbidden on conflict-of-interest rationale from simultaneously holding office as alderman).

250. *Morial v. Judiciary Commission, of State of Louisiana*, 565 F.2d 295, 300 (5th Cir. 1977) (*en banc*), *cert. denied*, 435 U.S. 1013 (1978).

251. *Id.* at 303.

252. *Smith v. Arkansas State Highway Employees*, 441 U.S. 463, 464 (1979); *Hanover Township Federation of Teachers v. Hanover Community School Corp.*, 457 F.2d 456 (7th Cir. 1972); *Orr v. Thorpe*, 427 F.2d 1129 (5th Cir. 1970); *McLaughlin v. Tilendis*, 398 F.2d 287 (7th Cir. 1968). *See also American Federation of State, County and Municipal Employees v. Woodward*, 406 F.2d 137 (8th Cir. 1969); *Gerrin v. Hickey*, 464 F.Supp. 276, 282–83 (E.D. Ark. 1979).

253. *Hanover Township Federation of Teachers v. Hanover Community School Corp.*, 318 F.Supp. 757 (N.D. Ind. 1970), *aff'd*, 457 F.2d 456 (7th Cir. 1972). *See also Gerrin v. Hickey*, *supra*; *Tischler v. Board of Education*, 37 App. Div.2d 261, 323 N.Y.S.2d 508 (1971).

254. *University of Missouri v. Dalton*, 456 F.Supp. 985 (W.D. Mo. 1978).

255. *Connecticut State Federation of Teachers v. Board of Education Members*, 538 F.2d 471, 478 (2d Cir. 1976).

256. *Perry Education Association v. Perry Local Educators' Association*, ————U.S.————, ————, 103 S. Ct. 948, 955–57 (1983) (U.S. Feb.

23, 1983); *Police Department v. Mosley*, 408 U.S. 92, 95–96 (1972). *See also National Socialist White People's Party v. Ringers*, 473 F.2d 1010 (4th Cir. 1973) (*en banc*).

257. *Perry Education Association v. Perry Local Educators' Association*, ——U.S.——,——, 103 S. Ct. 948, 954–57 (1983); (U.S. Feb. 23, 1983); *Police Department v. Mosley*, 408 U.S. 92, 95–96 (1972); *see also City of Madison v. Wisconsin Employment Relations Commission*, 429 U.S. 167, 175–76 (1976).

257a. ——U.S.——,——, 103 S. Ct. 948 (1983), *rev'd*, 652 F.2d 1286 (7th Cir. 1981).

257b. *Id.* at 955–56, *citing Greer v. Spock*, 424 U.S. 828, 836 (1976); *Adderley v. Florida*, 385 U.S. 39, 48 (1966).

257c. *Id.* at 955.

257d. *Id.* at 958–59.

257e. *Id.* at 959.

257f. *Id.* at 957.

258. 398 F.2d 287 (7th Cir. 1968).

259. *Id.* at 289.

260. *Id.*

261. *See NAACP v. Button*, 371 U.S. 415, 429 (1963); *Lee v. Smith*, GERR No. 383, B–15, B–16 (E.D. Va. 1971).

262. *Lake Park Education Association v. Board of Education of Lake Park*, 526 F.Supp. 710 (N.D. Ill. 1981).

263. *Brotherhood of Railroad Trainmen v. Virginia*, 377 U.S. 1, 6 (1964). *See also United Transportation Union v. State Bar*, 401 U.S. 576 (1971); *United Mine Workers v. Illinois State Bar Association*, 389 U.S. 217 (1967); *NAACP v. Button*, 371 U.S. 415 (1963).

264. *Smith v. Losee*, 485 F.2d 334, 338–39 (10th Cir. 1973) (*en banc*), *cert. denied*, 417 U.S. 908 (1974). *See also Castleberry v. Langford*, 428 F.Supp. 676 (N.D. Tex. 1977) (statements made by fireman, as union president, in presenting grievances of other fire fighters, are constitutionally protected).

265. *Bence v. Brier* 501 F.2d 1185 (7th Cir. 1974), *cert. denied*, 419 U.S. 1121 (1975).

266. *Roberts v. Lake Central School Corp.*, 317 F.Supp. 63, 64-65, (N.D. Ind. 1970). *See also Gieringer v. Center School District No. 58*, 477 F.2d 1164 (8th Cir.), *cert. denied*, 414 U.S. 832 (1973); *Los Angeles Teachers Union v. Los Angeles City Board of Education*, 71 Cal. 2d 551, 455 P.2d 827, 78 Cal. Rptr. 723 (1969).

267. *Hastings v. Bonner*, 578 F.2d 136, 141–42 (5th Cir. 1978), *citing Coates v. City of Cincinnati*, 402 U.S. 611, 615 (1971).

268. *Hickman v. Valley Board of Education*, 619 F.2d 606, 609 (6th Cir. 1980). *See also Columbus Education Association v. Columbus City School District*, 623 F.2d 1155, 1160 (6th Cir. 1980).

269. *Columbus Education Association v. Columbus City School District*, 623 F.2d 1155, 1159 (6th Cir. 1980).

270. *Castleberry v. Langford*, 428 F.Supp. 676, 685 (N.D. Tex. 1977).

271. *Roberts v. Lake Central School Corp.*, 317 F.Supp. 63, 65 (N.D. Ind. 1970). *See also Hastings v. Bonner*, 578 F.2d 136, 141 (5th Cir. 1978). *Cf. Mabey v. Reagan*, 537 F.2d 1036, 1050 (9th Cir. 1976) (warning, in another context, against "unrealistic sensitivity to the fragility of schools and universities").

272. *Puentes v. Board of Education*, 24 N.Y.2d 996, 998, 250 N.E.2d 232, 233, 302 N.Y.S.2d 824, 826 (1969) (invalidating suspension of teachers' union president for writing letter criticizing school administration's failure to renew contract of probationary teacher).

273. *Chase v. Fall Mountain Regional School District*, 330 F.Supp. 388, 390–91, 400 (D. N.H. 1971).

274. *Pietrunti v. Board of Education*, 128 N.J. Super. 149, 166, 319 A.2d 262, 271, *cert. denied*, 419 U.S. 1057 (1974). *But see Papish v. Board of Curators*, 410 U.S. 667 (1973).

275. *Hastings v. Bonner*, 578 F.2d 136, 143 (5th Cir. 1978). *Compare Pietrunti v. Board of Education*, 128 N.J. Super. 149, 166, 319 A.2d 262, 271, *cert. denied*, 419 U.S. 1057 (1974).

276. *Hastings v. Bonner*, *supra*.

277. *Id*. at 140–42 (5th Cir. 1978).

278. 441 U.S. 463 (1979).

279. *Id. at 465. See also Local Union No. 370 v. Detrick*, 592 F.2d 1045 (9th Cir. 1979).

280. *Williams v. Rhodes*, 393 U.S. 23 (1968); *United Mine Workers v. Illinois State Bar Association*, 389 U.S. 217 (1967).

281. *United Federation of Postal Clerks v. Blount*, 325 F.Supp. 879, 885 (D. D.C.) (Wright, J., concurring), *aff'd*, 404 U.S. 802 (1971).

282. *See, e.g., United Federation of Postal Clerks v. Blount*, 325 F.Supp. 879 (D. D.C. 1971) and cases cited at 882; *Anderson Federation of Teachers v. School City*, 252 Ind. 558, 251 N.E.2d 15 (1969), *cert. denied*, 399 U.S. 928 (1970) and cases cited at 17. *See also, e.g., School District of the Town of Westerly v. Westerly Teachers Association*, 111 R.I. 96, 299 A.2d 441 (1973). *Cf. Shaw v. Board of Trustees*, 549 F.2d 929, 932 (4th Cir. 1976).

283. *United Federation of Postal Clerks v. Blount*, 404 U.S. 802 (1971).

284. 431 U.S. 209, 222 (1977).

285. *Id*. at 221–22.

286. *Id*. at 235–36.

287. *Id*.

288. *Cook v. Hudson*, 365 F.Supp. 855 (N.D. Miss. 1973).

289. 511 F.2d 744 (5th Cir. 1975).

290. 429 U.S. 165 (1976). *Compare Berry v. Macon County Board of Education*, 380 F.Supp. 1244 (M.D. Ala. 1971) (refusal to rehire public school employees because they sent their children to private segregated schools violated employees' constitutional rights).

291. *Newborn v. Morrison*, 440 F.Supp. 623, 627 (S.D. Ill. 1977).

292. *Randle v. Indianola Municipal Separate School District*, 373 F.Supp. 766 (N.D. Miss. 1974).

293. *Doherty v. Wilson*, 356 F.Supp. 35, 41 (M.D. Ga. 1973).

294. *Fisher v. Snyder*, 346 F.Supp. 396, 398–99 (D. Neb. 1972), *aff'd on other grounds*, 476 F.2d 375 (8th Cir. 1973).

295. See L. Tribe, *American Constitutional Law* 700–01 (1978).

296. *Burris v. Willis Independent School District*, 537 F.Supp. 801, 806 (S.D. Tex. 1982).

297. H. Beale, *A History of Freedom of Teaching in American Schools* 60 (1941).

298. H. Beale, *Are American Teachers Free?* 65 (1936).

299. *Cole v. Richardson*, 405 U.S. 676, 680 (1972); *Law Students Civil Rights Research Council, Inc. v. Wadmond*, 401 U.S. 154 (1971).

300. *Cole v. Richardson, supra; Keyishian v. Board of Regents*, 385 U.S. 589 (1967); *Baggett v. Bullitt*, 377 U.S. 360 (1964); *Cramp v. Board of Public Instruction*, 368 U.S. 278 (1961).

301. *Cole v. Richardson, supra; Whitehill v. Elkins*, 389 U.S. 54 (1967); *Law Students Civil Rights Research Council, Inc. v. Wadmond, supra; Keyishian v. Board of Regents, supra; Elfbrandt v. Russell*, 384 U.S. 11 (1966); *Wieman v. Updegraff*, 344 U.S. 183 (1952).

302. *Cole v. Richardson, supra; Cramp v. Board of Public Instruction*, 368 U.S. 278, 287 (1961).

303. *Cole v. Richardson, supra; Ohlson v. Phillips*, 397 U.S. 317 (1970).

304. *McDaniel v Paty*, 435 U.S. 618, 628, n.8 (1978); *Wisconsin v. Yoder*, 406 U.S. 205, 215 (1972); *Sherbert v. Verner*, 374 U.S. 398 (1963).

305. *Wisconsin v. Yoder*, 406 U.S. 205, 215 (1972). See *McDaniel v. Paty*, 435 U.S. 618, 628 n.8 (1978).

306. *Rankins v. Commission on Professional Competence*, 24 Cal. 3d 167, 593 P.2d 852, 857, 154 Cal. Rptr. 907 (1979).

307. *Id*.

308. *Id*.

309. *Id*.

310. *Id*.

311. 42 U.S.C. § 2000e(j).

312. *See Trans World Airlines v. Hardison*, 432 U.S. 63, 84 (1977) (seniority system in collective bargaining agreement not required to give way so that airline employee could accommodate clerk whose religious beliefs prohibited him from working on Saturdays).

313. *Edwards v. School Board of City of Norton*, 483 F.Supp. 620, 627 (W.D. Va), *vacated and remanded on damages question*, 658 F.2d 951 (4th Cir. 1981).

314. *Id*. at 626–27.

315. *Id*. at 627.

316. *See Trans World Airlines v. Hardison*, 432 U.S. 63, 89–91 (1977) (Marshall, J., dissenting); *Cummins v. Parker Seal Co*., 516 F.2d

544 (6th Cir. 1975) (2–1 decision upholding constitutionality), *aff 'd by equally divided court*, 429 U.S. 65 (1976). *See Wheeler, Establishment Clause Neutrality and the Reasonable Accommodation Requirement*, 4 Hastings Const. L.Q. 901, 915 (1977).

317. *Rankins v. Commission on Professional Competence*, 24 Cal. 3d 167, 593 P.2d 852, 858–59, 154 Cal. Rptr. 907 (1979).

318. 54 Cal. App. 3d 596, 610–15, 127 Cal. Rptr. 244 (1976).

319. *Moore v. Gaston County Board of Education*, 357 F.Supp. 1037, 1043 (W.D. N.C. 1973).

320. 603 F.2d 1271 (7th Cir. 1979), *cert. denied*, 444 U.S. 1026 (1980).

III

Freedom of Expression in the Classroom

Academic freedom, the Supreme Court has observed, is "a special concern of the First Amendment, which does not tolerate laws that cast a pall of orthodoxy over the classroom."[1] Recalling the words of Judge Learned Hand, the Court said:

The classroom is peculiarly the "marketplace of ideas." The Nation's future depends upon leaders trained through wide exposure to that robust exchange of ideas which discovers truth "out of a multitude of tongues [rather] than through any kind of authoritative selection."[2]

While the Court was speaking in the context of higher education, its words are also relevant in grade- and secondary-school settings. In *Tinker v. Des Moines Independent Community School District* the Court, speaking about high schools, declared that "students may not be regarded as closed-circuit recipients of only that which the state chooses to communicate," and cautioned that schools may not be used to "foster a homogeneous people."[3] More recently, in the famous book-banning case *Board of Education, Island Trees Union Free School District v. Pico*, the Court plurality, emphasizing the paramount importance of free access to ideas, stated:

[J]ust as access to ideas makes it possible for citizens generally to exercise their rights of free speech and press in a meaningful manner, such access prepares students for active participation in the pluralistic, often contentious society in which they will soon be adult members.[4]

As one court has noted, "much of what was formerly taught in many colleges in the first year or so of undergraduate studies is now covered in the upper grades of high school."[5] Another court has commented on the inequity of denying academic freedom to high-school students who do not go on to college:

> For many people, the formal educational experience ends with high school. To restrict the opportunity for involvement in an open forum for the free exchange of ideas to higher education would not only foster an unacceptable elitism, it would also fail to complete the development of those not going on to college, contrary to our constitutional commitment to equal opportunity. Effective citizenship in a participatory democracy must not be dependent upon advancement toward college degrees. Consequently, it would be inappropriate to conclude that academic freedom is required only in the colleges and universities.[6]

Finally, it has been judicially observed that "even those who go on to higher education will have acquired most of their working and thinking habits in grade and high school" and thus need an early opportunity to "operate in an atmosphere of open inquiry, feeling always free to challenge and improve established ideas."[7]

Although the Supreme Court has yet to confront directly the issue of a teacher's freedom of speech in the classroom, the lower federal courts, consistently with these judicial statements, have accorded a measure of constitutional protection to classroom expression by teachers in the grade and secondary schools.

To what extent, if any, does the First Amendment give teachers the right, free of control by the school authorities, to determine the content or manner of their teaching?

Because the Supreme Court has not yet spoken directly to this question, the answer is not clear. A plurality of the Court has said, however, that "local school boards have broad discretion in the management of school affairs"[8] and "must be permitted 'to establish and apply their curriculum in such a way as to transmit community values.'"[9] Nevertheless, in a case involving a school board's removal of several controversial books from a school library, a plurality of the Court stated that if such a removal had as its purpose the "contract[ing of] the spectrum of available knowledge,"[10] the removal would be unconstitutional because "[o]ur Constitution does not permit the official suppression of *ideas*."[11] The Court expressly stated that its decision was "not intrud[ing] into the classroom"[12] and because that was the case, it left open the question of how much latitude teachers have in determining the content and manner of their teaching once the school board and administration have established the curriculum.

Lower federal courts have given somewhat more, but still superficial attention to the issue of a teacher's freedom of expression in the classroom. Decisions affording protection to a teacher's teaching methods or classroom discussion often pay homage to "academic freedom" without explaining how that concept is enshrined in the Constitution. In particular, these courts have not begun to grapple with the basic question of how a teacher who is hired by school authorities to teach a subject in school, and who presumably is their agent, gains a constitutional right to teach it the way he wishes even at the elementary or secondary levels, where, because of compulsory school attendance laws, students constitute a captive audience. And although there is some authority tending to support the notion that a student may have a First Amendment right to receive a teacher's classroom communication even when the utterance itself is not protected by the Amendment,[13] the Seventh Circuit has stated that "[i]t is difficult to conceive how a student may assert a right to have the teacher control the classroom when the teacher herself does not have such a right."[14]

It may be argued in some cases, however, that the classroom in question was conceived and established, at least in part, as a forum for the expression of opinion on the subject matter of the course, and that to this extent the classroom is in substance a free-speech forum in which both teacher and student have the free speech rights possessed by a participant in the forum. One federal appeals judge has written that "[t]eaching implies that the strengths and weaknesses of ideas will be closely examined. Some will be favored, others criticized. That is the academic freedom that has its own strong claim to First Amendment protection."[15] With this idea of the classroom as a "marketplace of ideas" in mind, it may be urged that a teacher's classroom discussion is entitled to constitutional protection provided it remains within curricular guidelines.[16]

In any event, it seems apparent that the Constitution does not give a teacher a blanket of immunity preventing superiors from evaluating his classroom performance and acting on the basis of that evaluation. The Sixth Circuit has ruled that a public university, without violating the First Amendment, can refuse to renew a non-tenured teacher's contract because of displeasure with her "pedagogical attitudes."[17] The court concluded that the Constitution does not insulate the teaching style of a non-tenured teacher "from review by her superiors when they determined whether she has merited tenure status just because her methods and philosophy are deemed acceptable somewhere within the teaching profession."[18] Similarly, the Eighth Circuit has stated that "included within the [school] board's discretion [to run the schools] is the authority to determine the curriculum that is most suitable for students and the teaching methods that are to be employed, including the educational tools to be used. . . . These decisions may properly reflect local community views and values as to educational content and methodology."[19]

Other decisions, and logic as well, also indicate that a teacher has no absolute right to use a particular teaching method contrary to the wishes of her superiors. A teacher who opts for team teaching plainly has no right to compel her principal to provide her with a teaching partner.[20] And if a teacher decides that she can best impart knowledge to her students through hypnosis, it seems likely that her principal can direct her to desist without disturbing the sleep of the Founding Fathers. Thus, the Tenth Circuit stated that, at least at the secondary level, teachers do not have "a constitutional right absolute in character to employ their methods in preference to more standard or orthodox ones."[21] And the Supreme Court of Washington held that "if Global Studies detracts from the scope of a conventional history course—because it emphasizes small groups, independent reading and writing, and inquiry discovery techniques—petitioners may be compelled to abandon their own preferred techniques and to teach history in a more conventional manner. While teachers should have some measure of freedom in teaching techniques employed, they may not ignore or omit essential course material or disregard the course calendar."[22]

The implication of the Washington decision is that a teacher *does* have "some measure of freedom" in the choice of teaching techniques, provided he teaches the essential course material and observes the course calendar. The Fifth Circuit, in the context of the dismissal of a social studies teacher for using a simulation technique to teach the history of the post-Civil War Reconstruction period, held that classroom discussion is protected activity, and that school authorities could not constitutionally penalize her for using the technique.[23] And the Tenth Circuit also has expressed the view, without explanation, that "[u]ndoubtedly [teachers] have some freedom in the techniques to be employed."[24]

The courts have not been uniform in their approach to this issue. Thus, in rejecting a teacher's constitutional attack on a dress code requiring him to wear a tie, the Second Circuit addressed his claim that tielessness enabled him to achieve closer rapport with his students and enhanced his ability to teach. This claim, the court said, "does not implicate the First Amendment. It is merely an assertion that one teaching technique is to be preferred over another. It has no more to do with a constitutional interest than would a claim that closer rapport could be achieved by arranging students' desks in circles rather than rows."[25]

In any event, as the Washington decision reflects, even a court which is ready to accord "some" freedom to a teacher in his choice of teaching technique is likely to recognize that the legitimate interests of the school authorities may justify limits on that freedom. Avoiding the formulation of rigid standards in this area, and framing the question as whether a teacher had a constitutional right to employ a particular "teaching method"—the discussion of "taboo words" in the classroom— the First Circuit could "see no substitute for a case-by-case inquiry into whether the legitimate interests of the school authorities are demonstrably sufficient to circumscribe a teacher's speech."[26]

Where choice of teaching method is involved, the legitimate interests of the school authorities might include not only coverage of the curriculum and compliance with the course calendar, but also considerations of financial and physical feasibility and the effect upon a child of being taught in alternate years by new and old methods. Thus school authorities might conclude that while the new math, or phonetic spelling, is a technique superior to the traditional method, it would not serve the interests of sound education to shuttle the child back and forth between methods, since this might result in confusion and lack of continuity. A school principal might also conclude that sound education would best be furthered by teaching methods determined to be effective by experienced educators such as "master teachers," rather than by allowing even the most inexperienced teachers freedom to select their own methods.

Where the classroom speech does not involve use of a teaching "method," but merely the expression of opinion, a similar test, based on whether school authorities have a legitimate interest justifying limitations on the speech, may apply. While the First Circuit has said that "free speech does not grant teachers a license to say or write in class whatever they may feel like . . ."[27] the Seventh Circuit has stated that school boards "are not free to fire teachers for every random comment in the classroom."[28] And the Tenth Circuit has expressed the view that "teachers do have some rights to freedom of expression in the classroom, teaching high school juniors and seniors."[29] In that court's view such teachers "cannot be made to simply read from a script prepared or approved by the [school] board. . . . Censorship or suppression of opinion, even in the classroom, should be tolerated only where there is a legitimate interest of the state which can be said to require priority."[30]

What interests of school authorities have been considered legitimate and sufficient to justify circumscribing a teacher's classroom speech?

Generally, the courts have agreed that school authorities have a legitimate interest in ensuring that a teacher's classroom speech is relevant to the subject matter of the course and appropriate to the age level of the students.[31]

Some courts have concluded that these are the only interests which would justify prohibiting or penalizing a teacher's classroom expression. For example, a Texas federal district court held that a teacher has a constitutional right "to use the tools of his profession as he sees fit," at least within the constraints of relevance and appropriateness to the age level of

the students. On this basis the court upheld a teacher's right
to assign materials on the Vietnam War and race relations in a
civics class.[32] On similar reasoning an Oregon federal district
court upheld a teacher's First Amendment right to invite a
Communist, among other political speakers, to a political
science class, because such speakers were the teacher's
"medium" for exposing students to a diversity of ideas.[33] A
rule that a teacher has a constitutional right to use the tools of
his profession as he sees fit, subject only to the limitations of
relevance and appropriateness to the age level of the students,
however, is open to the objection that it ignores other legitimate interests of school authorities, including their interest in
assuring the quality of classroom instruction.

**How strictly does the First Amendment permit school
authorities to enforce their interest in the relevance of a
teacher's classroom speech to the subject matter?**
The courts have provided only limited guidance on this
question.

The District of Columbia Circuit refused to hold that an
Air Force teacher of a basic English class for foreign officers
had a First Amendment right to make classroom observations
on Vietnam and anti-Semitism where the lesson plan he was
supposed to follow at the time in question called for language
instruction on the subjects "At the Dentist" and "How to Test
a Used Car." Noting that the observations "would appear to
have, at best, minimal relevance to the immediate classroom
objectives," the court implied that the result might have
been different had he been teaching current events, political
science, sociology, or international relations.[34] Another court
expressed doubt that a teacher "had a constitutional right to
teach politics in a course in economics."[35] And a third court
rejected a high-school biology teacher's claim that his classroom remarks were entitled to First Amendment protection,
relying in part upon the ground that he "left legitimate areas
of discussion" when he began relating his personal experi-
ences with prostitutes in Japan.[36]

It can be argued, however, that in the interest of academic
freedom and sound education, any requirement of relevance
should be interpreted liberally. Disparaging the argument
that a junior-college English teacher cannot teach notions of
campus freedom in a literature course, the Fifth Circuit has

stated: "[I]t would obliterate cherished ideas about the relationship of teacher-pupil and the teacher's role in character building were instruction so closely confined to the technicalities of a particular subject or academic discipline. With its inexorable logic and predictability there may even be a great moral lesson in 2 × 2 equal 4."[37] One judge on the Seventh Circuit, moreover, has expressed the view that "[t]he appropriateness of a particular classroom discussion topic cannot be gauged solely by its logical nexus to the subject matter of instruction. A teacher may be more successful with his students if he is able to relate to them in philosophy of life, and, conversely, students may profit by learning something of a teacher's views on general subjects. [Footnote omitted.] Academic freedom entails the exchange of ideas which promote education in its broadest sense."[38]

Would a purpose to indoctrinate students be constitutionally sufficient to justify school authorities in prohibiting or penalizing a teacher's classroom speech?

Presumably, school authorities would have a "legitimate" interest in instilling respect for democratic institutions, obedience to law, and other values basic to the health and prosperity of our society. It can be argued, however, that the values school authorities legitimately may seek to inculcate in the young are not unlimited. Arguably, it is an abuse of power for such authorities to regulate the content of education for the purpose of instilling doctrinaire views on matters of current political or social controversy. As the Supreme Court stated in *West Virginia State Board of Education v. Barnette:*[39] "If there is any fixed star in our constitutional constellation, it is that no official, high or petty, can prescribe what shall be orthodox in politics, nationalism, religion, or other matters of opinion." It seems evident, therefore, that a school board cannot properly use the public schools, for example, to promote allegiance to a particular political party, to instill in students a particular view on a current social or political issue such as the propriety of affirmative action programs or the desirability of legalized abortion, or to imbue students with a particular opinion on the merits of labor unions. As the Supreme Court's plurality opinion stated in the *Island Trees* book-banning case:

If a Democratic school board, motivated by party affiliation, ordered the removal of all books written by or in favor of Republicans, few would doubt that the order violated the constitutional rights of the students denied access to those books. The same conclusion would surely apply if an all-white school board, motivated by racial animus, decided to remove all books authored by blacks or advocating racial equality and integration. Our Constitution does not permit the official suppression of *ideas*.[40]

Along the same lines, the Eighth Circuit stated, in a case overturning a school board's removal of a film from the curriculum because several parents had ideological and religious objections to it, "At the very least, the First Amendment precludes local authorities from imposing 'a pall of orthodoxy' on classroom instruction which implicates the state in the propagation of a particular religious or ideological viewpoint."[41] Accordingly, it should not be hard to argue that if the motives of school authorities in prohibiting or penalizing a teacher's classroom speech are impermissibly indoctrinative, they are illegitimate and render the prohibition or penalty unconstitutional.

Is the desire to avoid offending any student or parent a legitimate interest sufficient to justify circumscribing a teacher's classroom speech?

No. In *Keefe v. Geanakos*[42] the First Circuit ruled that a teacher cannot, consistently with the First Amendment, be punished for the content of his discussions in the classroom or his selection of materials for assignment, at least where the discussion or assignment is pursuant to a demonstrated educational purpose, relevant to the prescribed curriculum, not obscene, and appropriate to the age level of the students. The court enjoined a school board from firing a high-school English teacher because of his assignment of an essay in the *Atlantic Monthly* by Dr. Robert J. Lifton of Yale Medical School on dissent, protest, radicalism, and revolt and the teacher's discussion in class of the word "motherfucker," which was used repeatedly in the article. In another leading case— *Parducci v. Rutland*[43]—Judge Frank Johnson overturned, on a similar rationale, the dismissal of another high-school English instructor because he had assigned a short story by Kurt

Vonnegut, Jr., a comic satire which the school authorities construed as condoning, if not encouraging, "the killing off of elderly people and free sex."[44] In both cases the fact that some students or parents were offended was held not to be controlling.[45]

Do school authorities have a legitimate interest in avoiding material and substantial disruption, sufficient to circumscribe a teacher's classroom speech?

Some decisions suggest that school authorities have a "legitimate interest" in avoiding "material and substantial disruption" to the operation of the school and that accordingly a teacher may be disciplined for classroom discussion that has such a disruptive effect.[46] The Fifth Circuit, however, has held that the test is not whether substantial disruption occurs "but whether such disruption overbalances the teacher's usefulness as an instructor."[47] Applying this standard, the court upheld the district court's finding that a Texas teacher whose contract had not been renewed because she had employed a technique known as "Sunshine simulation" to teach American history of the post-Civil War Reconstruction period—a technique which involved role playing by students in order to recreate the period of history and which evoked strong feelings by students on racial issues and resulted in parental complaints—had "sustained her prima facie burden of showing a violation of her constitutional rights."[48] In any event it can be argued, as a Texas federal district court has ruled, that "material" disruption does not occur merely because members of the community are upset by presentation of a controversial issue in the schools.[49]

Does a teacher have a constitutional right to state his personal political or philosophical opinions in the classroom?

The courts have shed only faint light on this question. The Supreme Court has cautioned that "[a] teacher works in a sensitive area in a schoolroom. There he shapes the attitude of young minds toward the society in which they live. In this, the state has a vital concern."[50] Thus the courts have been "keenly aware of the state's vital interest in protecting the impressionable minds of its young people from any form of extreme propagandism in the classroom."[51] For example, where "there was substantial evidence that a teacher had abused his position by using his classroom 'as his personal forum to promote union activities, to sanction polygamy, to attack marriage, to criticize other teachers and to sway and influence the minds of young people without a full and proper explanation of both sides of the issue,' " a federal court held that the school board did not violate his First Amendment rights by denying him tenure for such conduct.[52]

More recently, an Arkansas federal court held that an assistant professor at the University of Arkansas had a First Amendment right to acknowledge his Communist beliefs inside the classroom. The court concluded that "at least in the context of a university classroom [he] had a constitutionally protected right simply to inform his students of his personal political and philosophical views."[53] The court "intimate[d] no view as to whether the same expression by a teacher in a public grade school or high school classroom would also be constitutionally protected."[54] It emphasized that its holding was "strictly limited to a teacher's right simply to inform his students of his views and does not imply that a teacher has the right to proselytize students or to devote so much class time to such matters that his coverage of the prescribed subject matter is impaired."[55]

Even at the secondary level it can be argued that where a teacher makes a reasonable effort to give a balanced classroom presentation he has a constitutional right to express to his students his personal view on a controversial question. Thus, a Texas federal district court held that a high-school civics teacher had a constitutional right to express in class his personal opinions on the Vietnam War and race relations where he fairly presented other views and no material and substantial disruption resulted.[56]

Many questions in this area remain unanswered. For example, even if a teacher does balance the expression of his personal opinion by presenting other viewpoints, isn't there a danger that his own opinion will carry greater weight because of his status as an authority figure? At what age level, if any, are students sufficiently mature and independent so that the risk of subtle indoctrination, whether or not intended, is obviated? Does it make any difference that the teacher's personal opinion is delivered in response to a student's direct request? Because the answers to these and other questions in this area are not yet clear, and because the Supreme Court has not provided authoritative guidance, a teacher, at least at the grade- or secondary-school level, cannot be certain that he may safely disregard the directives of those in higher authority to refrain from expressing in the classroom his personal view on a controversial issue. Indeed, such uncertainty is inherent in any jurisdiction where the courts apply the rule that a teacher's classroom speech is unprotected if it results in "material and substantial disruption"—presumably requiring a teacher to successfully predict whether his speech will be disruptive or to forfeit his job.

Does a teacher have a constitutional right to criticize school authorities in the classroom?

The courts generally have rejected the contention that a teacher has a constitutional right to use the classroom as a forum for disparaging his superiors or attacking school system policies.

A Florida federal district court, for example, while recognizing "that from time to time it may be necessary for a school teacher to delve into thought-provoking discussions with students that may well concern areas of interest other than English, Biology, American History, or the like,"[57] refused to hold constitutionally protected the actions of a high-school biology teacher who utilized as much as a full class period in criticism of the superintendent, the school board, and the school system, including lengthy discussions on the inadequacy of teacher salaries and such comments as "You'd better tell your parents to get off their ass and elect a new school board" and "You can't call yourself a Christian if you vote for" the superintendent.[58]

Even at higher levels of education, a teacher should not assume that because he is employed by a public institution he has a constitutional right to criticize the administration or faculty in the classroom. Indeed, the Seventh Circuit has ruled to the contrary.[59]

A court may reach a different result where a teacher's classroom criticism of school authorities is closely related to the subject matter being taught—particularly where the criticism originates with his students. An Arkansas court, for example, ruled that an elementary-school teacher had a constitutional right, during an authorized class on nutrition, to add her signature to a student-initiated letter protesting the serving of cooked rather than raw carrots in the school cafeteria.[60]

Does the Constitution require that a teacher be given clear guidelines showing what types of classroom discussion or assignments are prohibited?

Yes, unless the activity is one which the teacher plainly ought to have recognized as forbidden.

In 1967 the U.S. Supreme Court invalidated laws of New York which required removal of a teacher from the public school system for "treasonable or seditious" utterances or acts and barred employment in the system of any person who "by word of mouth or writing willfully or deliberately advocates, advises, or teaches the doctrine" of forceful overthrow of government.[61] The statutes required an annual review of every teacher to determine whether any utterance of his, inside the classroom or not, came within the reach of the laws.[62] Holding these provisions unconstitutionally vague, the Court said: "When one must guess what conduct or utterance may lose him his position, one necessarily will 'steer far wider of the unlawful zone.' . . . The danger of that chilling effect upon the exercise of vital First Amendment rights must be guarded against by sensitive tools which clearly inform teachers what is being proscribed."[63]

Several decisions have held that the due process clause of the 14th Amendment bars punishment of a teacher for allegedly offensive classroom discussion or assignments without prior notice that such conduct was forbidden.[64] As one court said, this protection is afforded because in his teaching capacity the teacher is engaged in the exercise of what may plausibly be considered "vital First Amendment rights" and should not be forced to guess what speech may cost him his job.[65]

The courts have left open the possibility, however, that a teacher "may be on notice of impropriety from the circumstances of a case without the necessity of a regulation." One court has suggested that such notice might be inferred from an informal rule, an understanding among teachers at the school generally, a body of disciplinary precedents, or precise canons of ethics, and that warning would not be required if the teacher engaged in "unforeseeable outrageous conduct which all men of good will would, once their attention is called to it, immediately perceive to be forbidden."[66]

Whatever the source of the notice, it cannot constitutionally be too vague. In Lawrence, Massachusetts, an 11th-grade English teacher, in the context of a discussion of the use of vulgar words whose traditional counterparts were socially acceptable, chalked the word "fuck" on the blackboard and asked if anyone could define it. One boy volunteered that the word meant "sexual intercourse." The teacher observed that the term "sexual intercourse" was socially acceptable and the "word on the board" was not. "It is a taboo word." After discussing other aspects of taboos, the teacher went on to other matters. Dismissed for "conduct unbecoming a teacher," the teacher challenged his dismissal on constitutional grounds. In response to his contention that he was not warned that his conduct was improper, the school authorities relied on a statement in the Code of Ethics of the Education Profession that the teacher "recognizes the supreme importance of the pursuit of the truth, devotion to excellence and the nature of democratic citizenship." Rejecting the argument that this constituted sufficient warning, the First Circuit said: "As notice to the plaintiff that he should not have engaged in the act in question, this standard, though laudable, is impermissibly vague."[67]

In another case, however, a teacher intercepted a note circulating among her students, read the note to her class, and explained that three vulgar colloquialisms contained in the note were not obscene when used in different contexts. In a questionable ruling, the Fourth Circuit held that regulations penalizing "neglect of duty" gave a teacher reasonable prior notice that her classroom conduct was unacceptable, in light of a statute defining a teacher's duties to include "maintaining discipline and encouraging morality."[68]

The lack of notice that particular classroom expression by a teacher is forbidden, or overly vague notice, may also be subject to challenge on the ground that it leaves school authorities free to pick and choose, on the basis of personal whim, which speech to punish and which to tolerate.[69] This vice is not cured by a supervisor's warning, when he is displeased by a teacher's classroom expression, that a repeat performance will result in discipline, but only by a clear policy or regulation of general applicability containing ascertainable standards.

Most of the cases applying the doctrine that a teacher is constitutionally entitled to prior notice that particular teaching conduct is forbidden involve classroom expression. The doctrine may also be applicable to teaching method. The Wyoming Supreme Court relied on this doctrine as one reason for invalidating the termination of a teacher's employment for giving more D and F grades than would appear on a normal probability curve, where the teacher was never told to grade on the curve and the school district had no formal grading policy.[70]

May a faculty adviser to a student publication which is sponsored by the school board be dismissed or disciplined because of the publication's contents?

Academic freedom concepts underlying decisions holding that a teacher has a measure of constitutional protection in employing the tools of his profession would seem applicable to faculty advisers to student publications sponsored or sanctioned by the board. A New Jersey court has ruled that the faculty adviser to a community college student newspaper was deprived of her First Amendment rights when she was discharged for writing an editorial accusing the chairman of the board of trustees of a conflict of interest in making a "deal" whereby his nephew's company received a contract from the college for furnishing audiovisual equipment.[71]

Where the editorial or article which provokes the wrath of the school authorities is authored not by the adviser but by students, a sanction imposed upon the adviser nevertheless may be vulnerable to constitutional challenge. By advising student editors and authors, the adviser arguably becomes a party to the publication of information and ideas with which the First Amendment is concerned.[72] This may be so, for example, where the newspaper is conceived and established as a forum for the expression of opinion and accordingly is "in substance a free speech forum."[73] In such a case the adviser may share in the First Amendment protections accorded the students. In particular, at least where the adviser's teaching position is so structured as to include the dissemination of ideas, it can be argued that he cannot be disciplined for counseling or contributing to the publication of articles espousing controversial views. [74]

On a similar theory, an adviser's own First Amendment rights may also be implicated when his employment is terminated for refusing to censor a student newspaper. In addition, the adviser may have a constitutional right, grounded in the supremacy of the First Amendment over state law, to refuse to execute state directives that would violate the constitutional rights of students [75]—rights implicated by such censorship. [76] In a Ninth Circuit case, however, where the newspaper adviser refused to follow a school policy requiring him to show controversial articles to the principal for pre-publication review for accuracy, the court held that the teacher's First Amendment rights were not infringed when he was penalized for insubordination. [77] The court found that the principal's desire to check articles for accuracy, as distinguished from censoring them, did not infringe upon the adviser's constitutional rights or those of his students because the principal was helping educate students about the "need for a *responsible* press." [78] To buttress its decision, the court added that the teacher's refusal to submit the articles to review contributed to a deterioration of the working relationship between the teacher and principal and that the articles not submitted for review contained inaccuracies that stirred up conflict within the school. [79] The adviser in this case was allowed "third-party" standing to challenge, on behalf of students, the constitutionality of school policies that restricted the students' rights. [80]

To what extent, if any, can a teacher's First Amendment rights be infringed by an action of a legislature or school board prescribing curriculum?

It seems clear that in a public educational system, curricular decisions must be made by a public body accountable to the people. Thus, the state has the power to establish the curriculum of its public schools or to delegate all or some of its authority to local agencies such as school boards. [81] Exclusion of a particular subject from the curriculum would not appear to violate the constitutional rights of either students or teachers. It would be difficult to quarrel with Mr. Justice Stewart's view that "[a] state is entirely free . . . to decide that the only foreign language to be taught in its public school system shall be Spanish." [82]

Until a plurality of the Supreme Court stated in 1982 in *Board of Education, Island Trees School District v. Pico* that school authorities could not remove a book from the library if their intent was to suppress ideas,[83] it seemed clear that even if the basis for a school board's decision to remove a subject from the curriculum were the subject's controversial nature, that decision would not violate First Amendment rights. In a pre-*Island Trees* decision summarily affirmed by the Supreme Court, a three-judge federal district court rejected a teacher's contention that his First Amendment rights were being infringed by a Michigan statute prohibiting discussion of birth control in the public schools. The Court concluded that "[t]here is nothing in the First Amendment that gives a person employed to teach the constitutional right to teach beyond the scope of the established curriculum."[84] As the court observed, "The whole range of knowledge and ideas cannot be taught in the limited time available in public school. . . . The authorities must choose which portions of the world's knowledge will be included in the curriculum's programs and courses, and which portions will be left for grasping from other sources, such as family, peers or other institutions."[85] Previously Mr. Justice Black, in a concurring opinion, stated that he could not "imagine why a State is without power to withdraw from its curriculum any subject deemed too emotional and controversial for its public schools."[86]

The state also would appear to have the power to designate the basic texts to be used in public school courses, or to delegate that power to school boards. This is generally so even if the text is chosen to promote a particular point of view.[87] Nevertheless, the Supreme Court's book-banning decision calls into question how one-sided a school board can be in selecting books promoting a particular point of view.[88] The thrust of the book-banning decision is that a school board may remove a book from its library if the basis of its decision is educational suitability, but not if the basis is to suppress ideas.[89] Because the Court plurality explicitly stated that its decision did not reach the shaping of curriculum or the selection of textbooks,[90] the Court left open the question whether a school board's selecting a textbook or removing a subject from the curriculum with the intention of suppressing certain ideas would violate the Constitution.

Among the little that seems clear at this point is that if a

basic text is chosen primarily to further religious beliefs, that
would violate the First Amendment's establishment clause.[91]
Similarly, a school board's conscious selection of textbooks
portraying a particular minority group as inherently inferior
would probably violate the right of minority schoolchildren to
the equal protection of the law. The High Court's book
removal decision leaves few clues, however, whether it would
be unconstitutional for a school board to select intentionally,
for example, history textbooks that deliberately ignore or
even disparage the role of labor unions or women in American history. Keeping in mind that courts are reluctant to
interfere in basic educational policymaking, there would have
to be a balancing of the school board's interest in promoting
community values and the Constitution's protections against
the suppression of ideas.

Another, similar difficult question is presented where the
state legislature or a school board attempts to bar from
the schools a particular type of thinking falling within the
general parameters of a prescribed subject. In a 1968 case in
which one of the plaintiffs was a public school biology teacher,
the Court refused to decide whether an Arkansas "monkey"
law, prohibiting consideration of evolutionary theory in a
state-supported school, violated the teacher's "freedom to
teach." Avoiding what it termed this "difficult terrain,"[92] the
Court instead struck down the law on the ground that it was
enacted for religious reasons and conflicted with the First
Amendment ban on establishment of a religion. In a concurring opinion, however, Mr. Justice Stewart stated:

> It is one thing for a state to determine that "the subject
> of higher mathematics, or astronomy, or biology" shall or
> shall not be included in its public school curriculum. It is
> quite another thing for a state to make it a criminal
> offense for a public school teacher so much as to mention
> the very existence of an entire system of respected hu-
> man thought. That kind of criminal law, I think, would
> clearly impinge upon the guarantee of free communica-
> tion contained in the First Amendment.[93]

Serious constitutional questions might therefore arise if a
legislature or school board sought to prevent a teacher from
suggesting to his history class that respected historians had

advanced views of the Revolutionary War, the Civil War, or the Mexican-American War in conflict with those in the prescribed text, or otherwise made a systematic effort to bar mention in the classroom of a particular type of thinking. Such an effort at censorship or suppression of opinion might not be tolerated by the courts if there were "no legitimate interest of the state" which could "be said to require priority."[94]

Where, however, high-school English teachers in a Colorado school district challenged the constitutionality of the action of the school board barring teachers in elective contemporary literature courses from assigning or giving students credit for reading ten specified books, while approving 1275 books for such use, the court took note of the stipulation of the parties that "no systemic effort was made to exclude any particular type of thinking or book." Thus, "even though the decision was a political one influenced by the personal views of the members" the court did "not see a basis in the constitution" to grant the teachers' wish to be "freed from the 'personal predilections' of the board."[95] Similarly, the Seventh Circuit has concluded that "it is in general permissible and appropriate for local boards to make educational decisions based upon their personal, social, political and moral views."[96] The court noted, however, that "[a]t the very least, academic freedom at the secondary school level precludes a local board from imposing a pall of orthodoxy on the offerings of the classroom . . . which might either implicate the state in the propagation of an identifiable religious creed or otherwise impair permanently the students' ability to investigate matters that arise in the natural course of intellectual inquiry." The court said that "[n]othing in the Constitution permits the courts to interfere with local educational discretion until local authorities begin to substitute rigid and exclusive indoctrination for the mere exercise of their prerogative to make pedagogic choices regarding matters of legitimate dispute." The court noted that the amended complaint, which complained, among other things, of the removal of a book from one course, the deletion of certain materials from another, the excision of "objectionable" parts of the textbook, and the discontinuance of certain courses, "nowhere suggests that in taking these actions defendants have been guided by an interest in imposing some religious or scientific orthodoxy or a desire to eliminate a particular kind of inquiry generally."[97]

The court granted the plaintiffs leave to amend their complaint again so as to include, if they could, the allegations necessary to make out a claim under the court's ruling.[98]

In another case involving the removal of books from a school, a Second Circuit judge wrote:

The plenary power of school officials transgresses First Amendment limits . . . when their actions tend to suppress ideas. It is one thing to teach, to urge the correctness of a point of view. But it is quite another to take any action that condemns an idea, that places it beyond the pale of free discussion and scrutiny.[99]

NOTES

1. *Keyishian v. Board of Regents*, 385 U.S. 589, 603 (1967).
2. *Id. See also United States v. Associated Press*, 52 F.Supp. 362, 373 (S.D. N.Y. 1943).
3. 393 U.S. 503, 511 (1969).
4. ———U.S.———, 102 S.Ct. 2808 (1982) (plurality opinion). *See also Right to Read Defense Committee of Chelsea v. School Committee*, 454 F.Supp. 703, 715 (D. Mass. 1978) ("The most effective antidote to the poison of mindless orthodoxy is ready access to a broad sweep of ideas").
5. *Albaum v. Carey*, 283 F.Supp. 3, 10 (E.D. N.Y. 1968).
6. *Cary v. Board of Education*, 427 F.Supp. 945, 953 (D. Colo. 1977), *aff'd on other grounds*, 598 F.2d 535 (10th Cir. 1979).
7. *Albaum v. Carey, supra* at 10–11.
8. *Board of Education, Island Trees School District v. Pico,*———U.S. ———, ———, 102 S.Ct. 2799, 2806 (1982) (plurality opinion).
9. *Id.*
10. *Id.* at 2808, *citing Griswold v. Connecticut*, 381 U.S. 479, 482 (1965).
11. *Id.* at 2810 (emphasis in original). *See also id.* at 2814–15 (Blackmun, J., concurring in part and concurring in the judgment).
12. *Id.* at 2805.
13. *Id.* at 2808–09; *Pratt v. Independent School District No. 831, Forest Lake*, 670 F.2d 771, 776–77 (8th Cir. 1982); *Right to Read Defense Committee of Chelsea v. School Committee*, 454 F.Supp. 703, 714 (D. Mass. 1978). *See also Procunier v. Martinez*, 416 U.S. 396, 408–09 (1974).
14. *Zykan v. Warsaw Community School Corp.*, 631 F.2d 1300, 1307 (7th Cir. 1980).

15. *Pico v. Board of Education, Island Trees School District*, 638 F.2d 404, 433 (2d Cir. 1980) (Newman, J., concurring in the result), *aff'd,*———U.S.———, 102 S.Ct. 2799 (1982).

16. *Cf. Gambino v. Fairfax City School Board*, 429 F.Supp. 731, 734 (E.D. Va.), *aff'd*, 564 F.2d 157 (4th Cir. 1977).

17. *Hetrick v. Martin*, 480 F.2d 705, 708 (6th Cir.), *cert. denied*, 414 U.S. 1075 (1973).

18. *Id.* at 709.

19. *Pratt v. Independent School District No. 831, Forest Lake*, 670 F.2d 771, 775 (8th Cir. 1982).

20. *Cf. McElearney v. University of Illinois*, 612 F.2d 285, 288 (7th Cir. 1979) ("Academic freedom does not empower a professor to dictate to the University what research will be done using the school's facilities or how many faculty positions will be devoted to a particular area").

21. *Adams v. Campbell City School District*, 511 F.2d 1242, 1247 (10th Cir. 1975).

22. *Millikan v. Board of Directors*, 93 Wash. 2d 522, 611 P.2d 414 (1980).

23. *Kingsville Independent School District v. Cooper*, 611 F.2d 1109, 1113 (5th Cir. 1980).

24. *Adams v. Campbell City School District*, 511 F.2d 1242, 1247 (10th Cir. 1975).

25. *East Hartford Education Association v. East Hartford Board of Education*, 562 F.2d 838, 857 n.5 (2nd Cir. 1977).

26. *Mailloux v. Kiley*, 448 F.2d 1242, 1243 (1st Cir. 1971).

27. *Id.*

28. *Zykan v. Warsaw Community School Corp.*, 631 F.2d 1300, 1305 (7th Cir. 1980).

29. *Cary v. Board of Education*, 598 F.2d 535, 543 (10th Cir. 1979). *See also Minarcini v. Strongsville City School District*, 541 F.2d 577, 582 (6th Cir. 1976) (removal of books from school library based solely on the social or political tastes of school board members constituted unconstitutional "burden on freedom of classroom discussion" by making it difficult for a student to find and read a book discussed in class: "If one of the English teachers considered Joseph Heller's *Catch 22* [sic] to be one of the more important modern American novels . . . we assume that no one would dispute that the First Amendment's protection of academic freedom would protect . . . his right to say so in class").

30. *Cary v. Board of Education, supra.*

31. *Keefe v. Geanakos*, 418 F.2d 359 (1st Cir. 1969); *Sterzing v. Fort Bend Independent School District*, 376 F.Supp. 657 (S.D. Tex. 1972), *vacated on other grounds*, 496 F.2d 92 (5th Cir. 1974); *Parducci v. Rutland*, 316 F.Supp. 352 (M.D. Ala. 1970).

32. *Sterzing v. Fort Bend Independent School District, supra* at 662.

33. *Wilson v. Chancellor*, 418 F.Supp. 1358, 1364 (D. Or. 1976). *See also Downs v. Conway School District*, 328 F.Supp. 338 (E.D. Ark. 1971).

34. *Goldwasser v. Brown*, 417 F.2d 1169, 1177 (D.C. Cir. 1969), *cert. denied*, 397 U.S. 922 (1970).

35. *Ahern v. Board of Education*, 327 F.Supp. 1391, 1397 (D. Neb. 1971), *aff'd*, 456 F.2d 399 (8th Cir. 1972). *See also Birdwell v. Hazelwood School District*, 491 F.2d 490 (8th Cir. 1974).

36. *Moore v. School Board*, 364 F.Supp. 355, 361 (N.D. Fla. 1973).

37. *Pred v. Board of Public Instruction*, 415 F.2d 851, 857 n.17 (5th Cir. 1969).

38. *Brubaker v. Board of Education*, 502 F.2d 973, 991–92 (7th Cir.), *aff'd by an equally divided en banc court*, 502 F.2d 1000 (Fairchild, J., dissenting), *cert. denied*, 421 U.S. 965 (1975). *See also Moore v. School Board*, *supra* note 36, at 360–61.

39. 319 U.S. 624, 642 (1943).

40. *Board of Education, Island Trees School District v. Pico*,———U.S. ———,———, 102 S.Ct 2799, 2810 (1982) (opinion of Brennan, J.).

41. *Pratt v. Independent School District No. 831, Forest Lake*, 670 F.2d 771, 776 (8th Cir. 1982).

42. 418 F.2d 359 (1st Cir. 1969).

43. 316 F.Supp. 352 (M.D. Ala. 1970).

44. *Id.* at 353–54.

45. *Keefe v. Geanakos*, 418 F.2d 359, 361–62 (1st Cir. 1969); *Parducci v. Rutland*, 316 F.Supp. 352, 354 (M.D. Ala. 1970).

46. *Sterzing v. Fort Bend Independent School District*, 376 F.Supp. 657, 662 (S.D. Tex. 1972), *vacated on other grounds*, 496 F.2d 92 (5th Cir. 1974); *Parducci v. Rutland*, 316 F.Supp. 352, 355 (M.D. Ala. 1970).

47. *Kingsville Independent School District v. Cooper*, 611 F.2d 1109, 1113 (5th Cir. 1980).

48. *Id.*

49. *Dean v. Timpson Independent School District*, 486 F.Supp. 302 (E.D. Tex. 1979).

50. *Shelton v. Tucker*, 364 U.S. 470, 485 (1960), *quoting Adler v. Board of Education*, 342 U.S. 485, 493 (1952).

51. *Parducci v. Rutland*, 316 F.Supp. 352, 355 (M.D. Ala. 1970). *See also Sterzing v. Fort Bend Independent School District*, *supra* note 46, at 601.

52. *Knarr v. Board of School Trustees*, 317 F.Supp. 832, 836 (N.D. Ind. 1970), *aff'd*. 452 F.2d 649 (7th Cir. 1971).

53. *Cooper v. Ross*, 472 F.Supp. 802, 811 (E.D. Ark. 1979).

54. *Id.* at 811 n.5.

55. *Id.*

56. *Sterzing v. Fort Bend Independent School District*, 376 F.Supp. 657, 658, 661 (S.D. Tex. 1972), *Vacated or other grounds*, 496 F.2d 92 (5th Cir. 1974).

57. *Moore v. School Board*, 364 F.Supp. 355, 360–61 (N.D. Fla. 1973).

58. *Id.* at 361.

59. *Clark v. Holmes,* 474 F.2d 928, 931 (7th Cir. 1972), *cert. denied,* 411 U.S. 972 (1973).

60. *Downs v. Conway School District,* 328 F.Supp. 338 (E.D. Ark. 1971).

61. *Keyishian v. Board of Regents,* 385 U.S. 589, 599 (1967).

62. *Id.* at 601–02.

63. *Id.* at 604.

64. *See Mailloux v. Kiley,* 448 F.2d 1242 (1st Cir. 1971), *aff'g* 323 F.Supp. 1387 (D. Mass. 1971); *Keefe v. Geanakos,* 418 F.2d 359, 362 (1st Cir. 1969); *Sterzing v. Fort Bend Independent School District,* 376 F.Supp, 657, 662 (S.D. Tex. 1972); *See also Webb v. Lake Mills Community School District,* 344 F.Supp. 791 (N.D. Iowa 1972); *Parducci v. Rutland,* 416 F.Supp. 352, 356–58 (M.D. Ala. 1970).

65. *Keefe v. Geanakos,* 418 F.2d 359, 362 (1st Cir. 1969). *See also Mailloux v. Kiley,* 436 F.2d 565, 566 (1st Cir. 1971); *Parducci v. Rutland,* 316 F.Supp. 352, 357 (M.D. Ala. 1970).

66. *Mailloux v. Kiley,* 323 F.Supp. 1387, 1392–93 (D. Mass.), *aff'd,* 448 F.2d 1242 (1st Cir. 1971). *Compare Fern v. Thorp Public School,* 532 F.2d 1120, 1130 (7th Cir. 1976).

67. *Mailloux v. Kiley,* 448 F.2d 1242, 1243 (1st Cir. 1971).

68. *Frison v. Franklin County Board of Education,* 596 F.2d 1192 (4th Cir. 1979).

69. *See Davis v. Williams,* 598 F.2d 916, 921–22 (5th Cir. 1979), *modified,* 617 F.2d 1100 (*en banc*), *cert. denied,* 449 U.S. 937 (1980).

70. *Board of Trustees v. Holso,* 584 P.2d 1009, 1018 (Wyo. 1978).

71. *Endress v. Brookdale Community College,* 144 N.J. Super. 109, 364 A.2d 1080 (1976).

72. *Cf. Pickings v. Bruce,* 430 F.2d 595, 598–99 (8th Cir. 1970).

73. *See Gambino v. Fairfax City School Board,* 429 F.Supp. 731, 734 (E.D. Va), *aff'd,* 564 F.2d 157 (4th Cir. 1977) (student newspaper conceived and established for the expression of opinion was in substance a free-speech forum).

74. *See Antonelli v. Hammond,* 308 F.Supp. 1329, 1337, (D. Mass. 1970).

75. *See* United States Constitution, Art. 6, ¶2; *Nash v. Florida Industrial Commission,* 389 U.S. 235 (1967); *In re Grand Jury Subpoena,* 382 F.Supp. 1205 (W.D. N.Y. 1974). *Cf. In re Neagle,* 135 U.S. 1 (1890). *Accord Clifton v. Cox,* 549 F.2d 722 (9th Cir. 1977); *Harley v. Schuylkill County,* 476 F.Supp. 191 (E.D. Pa. 1979).

76. *See Gambino v. Fairfax County School Board,* 564 F.2d 157 (4th Cir. 1977); *Joyner v. Whiting,* 477 F.2d 456 (4th Cir. 1973); *Shanley v. Northeast Independent School District,* 462 F.2d 960 (5th Cir. 1972); *Fujishima v. Board of Education,* 460 F.2d 1355 (7th Cir. 1972); *Eisner v. Stamford Board of Education,* 440 F.2d 803 (2d Cir. 1971); *Leibner v. Sharbaugh,* 429 F.Supp. 744 (E.D. Va. 1977); *Pliscou v. Holtville Unified School District,* 411 F.Supp. 842 (S.D.

Cal. 1976); *Antonelli v. Hammond*, 308 F.Supp. 1329, 1335 (D. Mass. 1970).

77. *Nicholson v. Board of Education Torrance Unified School District*, 682 F.2d 858, 866 (9th Cir. 1982).

78. *Id.* at 863 (emphasis in original).

79. *Id.* at 865–66.

80. *Id.* at 863 & n.3. *See also Craig v. Boren*, 429 U.S. 190, 194–97 (1976); *Carey v. Population Services International*, 431 U.S. 678, 682–84 (1977); *Eisenstadt v. Baird*, 405 U.S. 438, 443 (1972); *Singleton v. Wulff*, 428 U.S. 106, 112 (1976); *United States v. Lyman*, 592 F.2d 496, 502 (9th Cir. 1978), *cert. denied*, 442 U.S. 931 (1979); *Mancuso v. Taft*, 476 F.2d 187, 190 (1st Cir. 1973); *Wilson v. Chancellor*, 418 F.Supp. 1358, 1367 (D. Or. 1976).

81. *Mercer v. Michigan State Board of Education*, 379 F.Supp. 580, 585 (E.D. Mich.), *aff'd mem.*, 419 U.S. 1081 (1974).

82. *Epperson v. Arkansas*, 393 U.S. 97, 115–16 (1968) (Stewart, J., concurring).

83. *Board of Education, Island Trees School District v. Pico*,———U.S. ———,———, 102 S.Ct. 2799, 2810 (1982).

84. *Mercer v. Michigan State Board of Education*, 379 F.Supp. 580, 585 (E.D. Mich.), *aff'd mem.*, 419 U.S. 1081 (1974). *But see Epperson v. Arkansas*, 393 U.S. 97, 115–16 (1968) (Stewart, J., concurring) (While a state could decide that only one foreign language is to be taught in the public schools, the state could not constitutionally "punish a teacher for letting his students know that other languages are also spoken in the world").

85. *Mercer v. Michigan State Board of Education*, *supra* at 586.

86. *Epperson v. Arkansas*, *supra* note 84, at 113.

87. *See West Virginia Board of Education v. Barnette*, 319 U.S. 624, 631 (1943); *Cary v. Board of Education*, 598 F.2d 535 (10th Cir. 1979).

88. *Board of Education, Island Trees School District v. Pico*,———U.S. ———,———, 102 S.Ct. 2799, 2810 (1982) ("discretion to determine the content of . . . school libraries . . . may not be exercised in a narrowly partisan or political manner").

89. *Id.*

90. *Id.* at 2805 ("Our adjudication . . . does not intrude into the classroom, or into the compulsory courses taught there. Furthermore, even as to library books, the action before us does not involve the *acquisition* of books").

91. *See Epperson v. Arkansas*, 393 U.S. 97 (1968).

92. *Id.* at 105.

93. *Id.* at 116 (Stewart, J., concurring).

94. *Cary v. Board of Education*, 598 F.2d 535 (10th Cir. 1979). *Cf. Board of Education, Island Trees School District v. Pico*,———U.S. ———,———, 102 S.Ct. 2799, 2810 (1982); *id.* at 2814 (Blackmun, J., concurring in part and concurring in the judgment) ("school

officials may not remove books for the *purpose* of restricting access to the political ideas or social perspectives discussed in them, when that action is motivated simply by the officials' disapproval of the ideas involved"); *Minarcini v. Strongsville City School District*, 541 F.2d 577, 582 (6th Cir. 1967); *Right to Read Defense Committee v. School Committee of Chelsea*, 454 F.Supp. 703 (D. Mass. 1978) (school board's removal of books from school library based solely on "social or political tastes" of board members unconstitutional). *See also Salvail v. Nashua Board of Education*, 469 F.Supp. 1269 (D. N.H. 1979).

95. *Cary v. Board of Education*, 598 F.2d 535 (10th Cir. 1979).

96. *Zykan v. Warsaw Community School Corp.*, 631 F.2d 1300, 1306 (7th Cir. 1980).

97. *Id.*

98. *Id.* at 1308–09.

99. *Pico v. Board of Education, Island Trees School District*, 638 F.2d 404, 432–33 (2d Cir. 1980) (Newman, J., concurring in the result), *aff'd*,———U.S.———, 102 S.Ct. 2799 (1982).

IV

The Right of Privacy

Teachers historically have been held to a standard of personal conduct that might have suffocated Caesar's wife. For example, until World War I, "[d]ancing, card-playing, smoking, drinking, theatre-going, and Sabbath-breaking were still regarded by multitudes as sinful. . . . The teacher was expected in all these matters to be exemplary."[1]

In 1883 Josiah Royce wrote that a teacher "may find of a sudden that his non-attendance at church or the fact that he drinks beer with his lunch, or rides a bicycle, is considered of more moment than his power to instruct."[2] Even before he got into difficulties over teaching evolutionary theory, John Scopes was criticized in Dayton for cigarette smoking and dancing.[3]

In one contract, signed in 1915, female teachers promised "not to keep company with men; to be home between the hours of 8:00 p.m., and 6:00 a.m. unless in attendance at a school function;" "not to loiter downtown in ice cream stores;" and not to get in a carriage or automobile with any man except her father or brother.[4]

Similar restraints were imposed even after the First World War. For example, a Virginia contract signed in 1935 specified that teachers could not keep company with "sorry young men." A Tennessee contract stipulated that the teacher was "to refrain from any and all questionable pastimes." An Alabama contract required the teacher to promise that, if employed, she "will not have company or go automobile riding on Monday, Tuesday, Wednesday and Thursday

140

nights . . . ."[5] One young teacher echoed Royce's remark: "How I conduct my classes seems to be of no great interest to the school authorities . . . but what I do when school is not in session concerns them tremendously."[6]

Such attitudes survive in some school districts today, particularly in small towns and rural communities. In the 1970s a Wyoming federal jury found that one of the reasons for the non-renewal of a teacher's contract was her lack of church attendance and the conduct of her personal life. She testified that the principal had informed her, among other things, that "there was dissatisfaction in the community with the fact that she played cards . . . ."[7]

Although there is no provision in the Constitution expressly establishing a right of privacy, the Supreme Court has concluded that the Constitution nevertheless creates zones of protected privacy. As Mr. Justice Brandeis observed:

> The makers of our Constitution undertook to secure conditions favorable to the pursuit of happiness. They recognized the significance of man's spiritual nature, of his feelings and of his intellect. They knew that only a part of the pain, pleasure, and satisfaction of life are to be found in material things. They . . . sought to protect Americans in their beliefs, their thoughts, their emotions and their sensations. They conferred, as against the government, the right to be let alone—the most comprehensive of rights and the right most valued by civilized men.[8]

The constitutional right of privacy is far from fully defined. Some components of the right, however, have emerged from decisions of the Supreme Court. One, derived directly from the Fourth Amendment, is the freedom of an individual, in his private affairs, from governmental surveillance and intrusion. A second is the right of an individual not to have personal matters disclosed by the government. A third is an individual's right to think as he chooses, free from governmental compulsion.

An action taken by school authorities may simultaneously violate a teacher's constitutional right of privacy and his First Amendment right of expression or association. And in some cases the "privacy" right may be implied, at least in part, from a First Amendment right.

Is a teacher's constitutional right of privacy infringed by a school board requirement that he participate in the flag ceremonies?

Arguably, his constitutional right to privacy, as well as his right of free speech (see Chapter II), is infringed by such a requirement.

The Supreme Court has derived from the First Amendment a purpose "to reserve from all official control" the "sphere of intellect and spirit."[9] Thus in *West Virginia State Board of Education v. Barnette*[10] the Court enjoined enforcement of a state statute requiring the expulsion of school children for failure to salute the flag and give the pledge of allegiance. The vice of the statute, the Court concluded, was that it "left it open to public authorities to compel [an individual] to utter what [was] not in his mind."[11] Speaking for the Court with characteristic eloquence, Mr. Justice Jackson said:

> If there is a fixed star in our constitutional constellation, it is that no official, high or petty, can prescribe what shall be orthodox in politics, nationalism, religion, or other matters of opinion or force citizens to confess by word or act their faith therein. If there are any circumstances which permit an exception, they do not now occur to us.[12]

In a number of cases the *Barnette* decision has been applied to protect teachers against compulsion by school authorities to participate in flag ceremonies.[13]

The *Barnette* decision can be read as holding that the right to freedom of speech guaranteed by the First Amendment implies (1) the right to decide whether to speak or remain silent, or (2) freedom of belief. *Barnette* also conceivably may be interpreted as gleaning from the "penumbra"[14] of the First Amendment a right of privacy in the realm of beliefs. In *Russo v. Central School District No. 1,*[15] for example, the Second Circuit held that a teacher could not constitutionally be dismissed for a silent refusal to participate in her school's daily flag salute ceremonies. Relying upon the language from *Barnette* quoted above, the court said: "Beliefs . . . are most at home in a realm of privacy, and are happiest in that safe and secluded harbour of the mind that protects our innermost thoughts."[16]

In the Seventh Circuit, however, which has rejected a teacher's claim that his freedom of religion is unconstitutionally violated because he has been compelled to lead a curricular flag salute contrary to his religious beliefs,[17] a claim that such compulsion violates his constitutional right of free speech or privacy seems unlikely to prevail.

Do school authorities invade a teacher's constitutional right of privacy where they discipline him for the books he reads, or the films he views, within his own home?

Yes. In *Stanley v. Georgia*[18] the Supreme Court struck down an obscenity statute insofar as it punished an individual for possessing "obscene" films in his home. The Court relied in part upon the First Amendment right—subsumed in the freedom of speech and press—to receive information and ideas.[19] But the Court also ruled that the right had an "added dimension."[20] The defendant, said the Court, is asserting the "right to satisfy his intellectual and emotional needs in the privacy of his own home," the "right to be free from state inquiry into the contents of his library."[21] The Court stated:

> [We] think that mere categorization of these films as "obscene" is insufficient justification for such a drastic invasion of personal liberties guaranteed by the First and Fourteenth Amendments. Whatever may be the justifications for other statutes regulating obscenity, we do not think they reach into the privacy of one's own home. If the First Amendment means anything, it means that a State has no business telling a man, sitting alone in his own house, what books he may read or what films he may watch. Our whole constitutional heritage rebels at the thought of giving government the power to control men's minds.[22]

On the basis of the *Stanley* decision, it seems doubtful that a teacher could be penalized by school authorities because of his personal reading or viewing habits, at least where they are indulged at home. A Louisiana federal district court has remarked that "it could hardly be thought," in light of *Stanley v. Georgia*, "that any [government] employee could be discharged for possessing in his personal residence materials deemed obscene."[23]

Does the constitutional right of privacy extend to conduct, other than reading books and viewing films, that occurs in the privacy of one's home?

While the parameters of the constitutional right of privacy are still fuzzy, neither reading nor viewing would appear to exhaust the realm of private conduct within the home coming within the purview of the right. For example, a Nebraska federal district court held that a teacher's dismissal because male friends of her son visiting from out-of-town stayed overnight at her apartment violated her constitutional right of privacy,[24] among other rights. The court of appeals upheld the decision on other grounds without reaching or discussing the privacy issue.[25]

Do school authorities invade a teacher's constitutional right of privacy where they penalize him for using a drug, such as marijuana, in the privacy of his home?

With some exceptions, the courts generally have rejected claims that governmental efforts to control use of marijuana in the home violate the right of privacy, either under a state or the federal constitution.[26] Since significant federal constitutional questions are raised by such efforts, however, it can be argued that any statute authorizing discipline of a teacher for possession or use of marijuana in his home must be construed to require a showing that such possession or use renders him unfit to teach.[27]

Does a "no-spouse" rule adopted by school authorities prohibiting a husband and wife from teaching at the same school violate the constitutional right of privacy?

An Arizona federal district court has so held in an unreported opinion.[28] The court reasoned that the Supreme Court has established a fundamental right to marry, and that under that Court's decision in *Zablocki v. Redhail*,[29] a rule which interferes "significantly" with the decision to enter into the marriage relationship must be subjected to rigorous constitutional scrutiny.[30] Thus, the court determined, the no-spouse rule could be sustained only if the district showed a compelling interest in support of the rule. The court concluded that no compelling interest was shown by the school district, distinguishing cases arising in a supervisor-employee context, where "there is a strong interest in avoiding favoritism and conflicts of interest."[31]

The Arizona decision appears substantially to extend the *Zablocki* principle, which actually was based on an equal protection rationale. In *Zablocki* the Supreme Court dealt with a Wisconsin statute requiring a parent who did not have child custody, but who was obligated by court order to provide support, to obtain court approval before remarrying. The Court struck down the statute as a violation of the equal protection clause. The Court ruled that the "right to marry" is "part of the fundamental 'right of privacy' implicit in the Fourteenth Amendment's Due Process Clause"[32] and that "when a statutory classification significantly interferes with the exercise of a fundamental right, it cannot be upheld unless it is supported by sufficiently important state interests and is closely tailored to effectuate only those interests."[33] The state interests in court approval for remarriage were to ensure that the parent had met his outstanding support obligations and that the children covered by the support order were "not then and [were] not likely thereafter to become public charges."[34] Yet, the Court noted, an unemployed parent or one who had a low income could not keep his child off welfare even if he met his support obligations. Since under the state's law such a parent never could obtain approval to remarry,[35] the statute in *Zablocki* absolutely deprived certain poor people of a fundamental right in violation of the equal protection clause.

A "no-spouse" rule does not implicate the equal protection clause in this manner. It is at least questionable, moreover, whether a rule requiring transfer of one spouse to another school could properly be characterized as significantly interfering with a decision to marry so as to require the state to show that the rule is justified by compelling, or even important, interests in the absence of a showing that the transfer would produce real hardship, i.e., where the school to which the transfer is made is a substantially greater distance from the teacher's home, or where the new teaching assignment is substantially more burdensome in other respects. In such a case, a teacher might argue that the governmental interests in support of the no-spouse rule are not sufficiently important to justify it or that the rule is not closely tailored to effectuate only those interests. In either case, it might be urged, the

rule interferes significantly with the right to marry by imposing a substantial penalty upon·the marriage decision.[36] The
school authorities, of course, would be entitled to show, if
they can, that the governmental interests *are* important and
that the rule is "closely tailored" to the interests involved.

**Is a pregnant teacher's constitutional right of privacy in-
fringed by a school board policy requiring her to take maternity leave at a fixed point in her pregnancy several months
in advance of the expected date of delivery?**

Yes. In *Cleveland Board of Education v. LaFleur*,[37] the
Supreme Court invalidated maternity leave regulations requiring pregnant teachers to take leave at least four months
before the expected birth, and to remain on leave for several
months after giving birth. The Court concluded that "there is
a right to be 'free from unwarranted governmental intrusion
into matters so fundamentally affecting a person as the decision whether to bear or beget a child.' "[38] The Court ruled
that the mandatory leave provisions, by penalizing the pregnant teacher for deciding to bear a child, constituted a burden on the exercise of this right.

In *LaFleur* the Court rejected both justifications for the
regulations advanced by the school boards involved. It concluded that the regulations were not justified by the goal of
continuity of classroom instruction since such continuity could
be attained just as well by simply requiring ample advance
notice of the date upon which the teacher wished to com-
mence her leave.[39] The Court also rejected the contention
that by keeping the pregnant teacher out of the classroom
during the final months of pregnancy, the mandatory leave
rules protected the health of the teacher and her unborn
child while at the same time assuring that students had a
physically capable instructor in the classroom at all times.
The Court concluded that the regulations "cannot pass mus-
ter under the Due Process clause of the Fourteenth Amendment, because they employ irrebuttable presumptions [of
physical incapacity] that unduly penalize a female teacher for
deciding to bear a child."[40] The Court also held that a rule
adopted by the Cleveland school board requiring the teacher
to wait until her child reached the age of three months before
she was eligible to return to work "serve[d] no legitimate
state interest, and unnecessarily penalize[d] the female teacher

for asserting her right to bear children."[41] The Court, however, upheld a rule of the Chesterfield County, Virginia, school board making a teacher eligible for re-employment upon submission of a medical certificate from her physician and guaranteeing return to work no later than the beginning of the next school year following the eligibility determination.[42]

Subsequent to the *LaFleur* decision, Congress passed the Pregnancy Discrimination Act as an amendment to Title VII of the Civil Rights Act of 1964. Under the amendment, discrimination by an employer—including a school board—on the basis of pregnancy, childbirth, or a related medical condition constitutes unlawful discrimination under Title VII.[43] Guidelines issued by the Equal Employment Opportunity Commission provide that employment policies and practices involving matters including "the commencement and duration of leave" shall "be applied to disability due to pregnancy, childbirth, or related medical conditions on the same terms and conditions as they are applied to other disabilities."[44] In questions and answers accompanying the guidelines, the EEOC states that "[a]n employer may not single out pregnancy-related conditions for special procedures for determining an employee's ability to work." Thus "if an employer allows its employees to obtain doctor's statements from their personal physicians for absences due to other disabilities or return dates from other disabilities it must accept doctor's statements from personal physicians for absences and return dates connected with pregnancy-related disabilities."[45] The questions and answers further state that an employer may not have a rule which prohibits an employee from returning to work for a predetermined length of time after childbirth.[46]

Because of the importance of the Pregnancy Discrimination Act and the widespread effect of the Act on teachers, I have reproduced the new EEOC Guidelines about the Act and accompanying questions and answers in the Appendix.

Do school authorities violate a teacher's constitutional right of privacy where they terminate her employment or otherwise discipline her for becoming pregnant while unwed or for bearing a child out of wedlock?

The Supreme Court has stated: "If the right of privacy means anything, it is the right of the individual, *married or single*, to be free of unwarranted governmental intrusion into matters so fundamentally affecting a person as the decision whether to bear or beget a child."[47] The Court also has ruled that "where a decision as fundamental as that whether to bear or beget a child is involved, regulations imposing a burden on it may be justified only by compelling state interests, and must be narrowly drawn to express only those interests."[48]

Applying these principles, a Delaware federal district court held that the plaintiff, who had been denied re-employment as director of residence halls at a state college because she had borne a child out of wedlock, was entitled to a preliminary injunction reinstating her. Ruling that she had made a strong showing of probable success on the merits of her case, the court considered it "virtually a foregone conclusion that the defendants will not be able to establish a compelling state interest sufficient to justify the intrusion upon the plaintiff's right to decide to bear an illegitimate child." The court noted that there was "no evidence to suggest that plaintiff would advise students to engage in premarital sex, bear an illegitimate child or do anything else the defendants might find objectionable." The court further observed that "the majority of students at Delaware State College are adults between the ages of 18 and 24" and consequently "much less likely than younger children to accept uncritically the advice and lifestyle of those in positions of authority."[49]

Using a somewhat different analysis, the Fifth Circuit reached the same conclusion and overturned a school board's discharge of an unmarried remedial reading teacher who had become pregnant. The board said it was dismissing her for "immorality" and for having neglected to follow a board policy requiring pregnant teachers to inform their principals no later than the fourth month of pregnancy. The court rejected out of hand the board's assertion that unwed parenthood is per se proof of immorality and that the parent of an out-of-wedlock child is necessarily an unfit role model.[50] Employing a *Mount Healthy* analysis, the court found that the other reason proffered for her dismissal—failure to notify the principal in time—was pretextual and not possibly sufficient reason for discharging her.[51] The court concluded that the board's policy of automatically firing unmarried pregnant teachers was an irrational classification that violated the plaintiff's equal protection rights.[52]

In contrast, a Nebraska federal district court concluded

that the termination of a junior-high-school teacher's contract because she had become pregnant while unwed did not violate her constitutional right of privacy. The court concluded that "the interests of the plaintiff in determining her own familial relationships and associating with whom she chooses do not outweigh the interests of the school in providing the kind of teachers it chooses for imparting social values and educational subject matter to junior high school students."[53]

Similarly, a Texas federal district court rejected a teacher's claim that her transfer to a non-classroom position because she had become pregnant while unmarried violated her constitutional right to privacy, to procreate, and to decide whether to marry or not to marry. Conceding that her right "to become pregnant," to "have her child," and "to decline to marry" were protected by the due process clause, the court concluded that the interests of the school authorities in avoiding disruption of the educational process resulting from anticipated public reaction to her unconventional lifestyle, and in providing students "a learning environment free of the disruption, disturbance and tension likely to be engendered by any public controversy that might arise" justified the transfer decision.[54]

Nevertheless, the arguments advanced by school authorities in this context may be vulnerable. In the Delaware case, the state college had refused to renew the residence hall director's contract in part due to "the possibility of an adverse public reaction." The court concluded that "interference with constitutional rights cannot be justified on the grounds that the community is hostile to their exercise and vigorously displays its feelings."[55]

Another argument that may be advanced by school officials is that a policy of terminating the employment of a teacher because she becomes pregnant out of wedlock is a justifiable means of weeding out "immoral" faculty members. A policy encroaching upon a teacher's constitutional right of privacy, however, arguably may not be premised upon the view of school authorities, or on the prevalent view in the community, that particular behavior is "immoral" at least without a showing that fitness to teach is implicated.[56] Even assuming such a policy were otherwise constitutionally permissible, moreover, it might be overbroad.[57] The Fifth Circuit has noted, for example, that a policy which is so broad that it penalizes all teachers who bear out-of-wedlock children, even a teacher who has been raped and chooses to bear rather than abort the child, irrationally punishes her innocent conduct along with conduct by other unwed mothers which some might view as morally culpable.[58]

School authorities also may argue that a policy providing for the termination of the employment of a teacher who is an unwed parent or becomes pregnant out of wedlock is justified because a teacher serves as a "role model" for students, who may emulate the teacher's behavior. To the extent that the school authorities are seeking to discourage such behavior because of their personal moral code or to enforce conventional morality in the community, this rationale may be vulnerable. Even if the rationale of school authorities is that they wish to discourage out-of-wedlock pregnancies among students because such pregnancies are having a harmful effect on the educational process, the school authorities may be unable to prove that the particular teacher is in fact a role model for the behavior they are seeking to discourage. For example, the teacher may not be recognizably pregnant, or the students in question may be ignorant of the teacher's marital status, or they may not have reached an age at which they would be conscious of the teacher's behavior. While such consciousness may increase in proportion to the age of students, school authorities may still be unable to prove their case if the students have reached that point in their development where they do "not indiscriminately imitate all responses by all potential models."[59]

The family lifestyle of the teacher, moreover, may determine the outcome of the "role model" issue. Thus, where each of two unwed teacher aides in a Mississippi school system was living, with an illegitimate offspring, under the same roof as her parents, brothers, and sisters, the Fifth Circuit observed that "[i]t would be a wise child indeed who could infer knowledge of either plaintiff's unwed parent status based on the manner of plaintiff's existence."[60] Affirming a decision holding unconstitutional a rule of the school authorities under which an unwed parent was ineligible to be hired as a teacher's aide, the Fifth Circuit quoted approvingly the following language from the trial court's opinion:

In the absence of overt, positive stimuli to which children can relate, we are convinced that the likelihood of inferred learning that unwed parenthood is necessarily good or praiseworthy is highly improbable, if not speculative. We are not at all persuaded by defendants' suggestions, quite implausible in our view, that students are apt to seek out knowledge of the personal and private family life-styles of teachers or other adults within a school system, (*i.e.* whether they are divorced, separated, happily married or single, etc.), and, when known, will approve them and seek to emulate them.[61]

On this point, by analogy to First Amendment cases, it can be argued that school authorities may not encroach on constitutionally protected privacy interests, any more than on free-speech interests, based on speculative justifications.[62]

Finally, in some cases it may be urged that at a minimum the "least drastic means" principle requires school authorities to pursue their objective by an alternative less draconian than termination. Available alternatives might include (1) asking the teacher to take a leave of absence for maternity reasons and granting such leave,[63] or (2) temporary transfer to a non-teaching position.[64]

A termination for unwed pregnancy or for bearing a child out of wedlock also is potentially vulnerable to challenge on grounds other than privacy. A policy or practice of terminating unwed employees for pregnancy or parenthood arguably violates the prohibition against sex discrimination in employment contained in Title VII of the Civil Rights Act of 1964. Such a policy or practice, it can be contended, has a disproportionate adverse impact on women and therefore is presumptively invalid under the Supreme Court's decision in *Griggs v. Duke Power Co.*[65] As the Sixth Circuit has noted: "Pregnancy is a condition unique to women, so that termination of employment because of pregnancy has a disparate and invidious impact upon the female gender."[66] And a practice of terminating employees for unwed parenthood arguably is presumptively invalid because a male's parental status is not physically demonstrable. As Chief Justice Burger remarked in his dissenting opinion in *Stanley v. Illinois*:

In almost all cases, the unwed mother is readily identifiable, generally from hospital records, and alternatively by physicians or others attending the child's birth. Unwed fathers, as a class, are not traditionally quite so easy to identify and locate. Many of them either deny all responsibility or exhibit no interest in the child or its welfare; and, of course, many unwed fathers are simply not aware of their parenthood.[67]

In any event, proof that the board never has terminated the employment of any male single teacher because of putative fatherhood should suffice to establish a disparate impact without the need to rely on a presumption. Whether the board's policy is based on alleged "immorality" or on an asserted interest in preserving (or reawakening) marital values in the students, the brunt of the policy falls on the female gender.[68]

Under the *Griggs* analysis, once a disparate impact is shown, the policy or practice violates Title VII unless it is job-related and justified by business necessity. If the teacher were to demonstrate that there was a less restrictive alternative,[69] such as temporarily transferring her to a non-teaching position or offering her a maternity leave of absence, the termination of her employment would violate Title VII as well as her constitutional right of privacy.[70]

Can school authorities, consistently with a teacher's constitutional right of privacy, terminate his employment, or otherwise discipline him, because of his sexual preferences or his private consensual sexual practices?

This issue has not been clearly resolved, although one's sexuality certainly lies at the core of his "feelings," "emotions," and "sensations."

The Supreme Court has invalidated, as violations of the constitutional right of privacy, restrictions on the sale and use of contraceptives by married and unmarried persons.[71] The Court has based these decisions on what it has held to be the protections afforded by the Constitution to "individual decisions in matters of childbearing from unjustified intrusion by the state."[72] Courts applying these decisions have taken conflicting positions on whether private consensual sexual conduct—heterosexual or homosexual—can be made criminal or otherwise penalized by the government.[73]

In *Doe v. Commonwealth's Attorney*,[74] a divided three-judge federal district court in Virginia refused to bar enforcement, against male homosexuals, of the state's criminal sodomy statute. The Supreme Court, three Justices dissenting, summarily affirmed.[75] The meaning of the summary affirmance is unclear, since there appears to have been no evidence that any of the parties was threatened with prosecution, and the Supreme Court's decision therefore may have rested on a conclusion that the district court correctly denied relief, not on the ground—articulated by the district court—that the statute was constitutional, but because the case was not "ripe" for adjudication.[76]

Before the *Doe* decision many courts—influenced at least in part by the prospect that the constitutional right of privacy might otherwise be infringed—had held that the government may not constitutionally concern itself with the private sex habits of its employees, or take adverse action against an employee for what it perceives to be sexual impropriety, without a clear showing that the employee's conduct affected his ability to perform his job.[77] As the District of Columbia Circuit put it, "the notion that it could be an appropriate function of the federal bureaucracy to enforce the majority's conventional codes of conduct in the private lives of its employees is at war with elementary concepts of liberty, privacy, and diversity."[78]

The leading teacher case applying these principles is *Morrison v. State Board of Education*,[79] where the state board of education had revoked a teacher's credentials because he had privately engaged in a brief homosexual relationship with a fellow teacher. Although the applicable statute authorized revocation for "immoral conduct," "unprofessional conduct," and "acts involving moral turpitude," the court held that the statute could only be constitutional if those terms were construed to "denote immoral or unprofessional conduct or moral turpitude which indicates unfitness to teach."[80] The court ruled that if the statute were construed to authorize revocation of a teacher's certificate for private conduct not shown to impede his fitness to teach, "serious constitutional problems" would be raised concerning the right of privacy.[81] "Conscientious school officials concerned with en-

forcing such a broad prohibition might be inclined to probe
into the private life of each and every teacher, no matter how
exemplary his classroom conduct."[82] To avoid these constitutional problems, the court construed the statute to authorize
revocation only for such conduct as rendered the teacher
unfit to perform his job, and held that "an individual can be
removed from the teaching profession only upon a showing
that his retention in the profession poses a significant danger
of harm to either students, school employees, or others who
might be affected by his actions as a teacher."[83]

A similar result was reached by the Iowa Supreme Court in
Erb v. Iowa State Board of Public Instruction,[84] which involved the revocation of a teacher's certificate because he had
engaged in an adulterous affair with a fellow teacher. The
court adopted as its standard the following observation from
an opinion in an Ohio case:

> The private conduct of a man, who is also a teacher, is a
> proper concern to those who employ him only to the
> extent it mars him as a teacher, who is also a man.
> Where his professional achievement is unaffected, where
> the school community is placed in no jeopardy, his pri-
> vate acts are his own business and may not be the basis
> of discipline.[85]

Applying this standard, the court held that the teacher's
certificate was illegally revoked for adultery because there
was no evidence of any reasonable likelihood that his retention in the profession would adversely affect the school
community. The court cited evidence to the contrary, including evidence showing him "to be a teacher of exceptional
merit,"[86] "[o]verwhelming and uncontroverted evidence of
local regard and support"[87] reflected in his employing school
board's rejection of his offer to resign, evidence that the
conduct involved was unlikely to recur,[88] and the fact that the
conduct "was not an open or public affront to community
mores," but had become public "only because it was discov-
ered and made public by others."[89]

Although such evidence is helpful, of course, the teacher
may argue that the burden is not on him to prove the absence
of the requisite nexus, but on the school authorities to prove
the existence of such a nexus, and that speculation does not

suffice. Thus, for example, speculation that a male faculty member's extramarital relationship with a female faculty member would impair public confidence in his ability to teach was held by a Wisconsin federal district court in an unreported opinion to be insufficient to justify non-renewal of his contract where there was "no evidence that the educational environment surrounding plaintiff's school-related activities suffered because of [his] private life."[90]

A question also may arise on whether it is sufficient merely that *some* connection be shown between the teacher's private conduct and fitness to teach or whether the school authorities must meet a higher standard. There is some authority supporting the view that a higher standard similar to that applied by the Supreme Court in *Tinker v. Des Moines School District*[91] should be applied. In a Nebraska case a teacher's contract was terminated because she had allowed out-of-town male friends of her son to stay overnight at her apartment, where she lived as a divorcee. Concluding that there was no permissible inference of immorality, the court held the termination unconstitutional. Citing the *Tinker* standard, the court declared:

> [T]o justify a dampening of the rights of assembly or association and privacy the state . . . must show that the termination of the teacher's contract was caused by conduct which *"materially and substantially"* interfered with the school's work or rights of students . . . .[92]

On appeal, the Eighth Circuit did not reach the privacy issue, affirming the judgment on other grounds.[93]

At least one other decision is in accord with the ruling in the Nebraska case on the applicability of the *Tinker* standard. A Georgia federal district court concluded that "for a state governmental body to justify controlling [the] private off-duty conduct [of a policeman, it] must show that the employee's usefulness as a police officer would be *substantially and materially* impaired by the conduct in question."[94]

Notwithstanding these decisions, the absence of clear guidance from the Supreme Court has left this area unsettled. In a Pennsylvania case a federal court, in a decision affirmed by the Third Circuit, held that the discharge of two public library employees for living together in a state of "open

adultery" did not violate their constitutional right of privacy.[95]
In a South Dakota case a young single female elementary-
school teacher in a small town was discharged as "incompetent"
to continue teaching because she insisted upon sharing her
mobile home, furnished by the school board and located near
the school, with a single man over protests from parents and
others. She challenged her dismissal as an infringement upon
her constitutional right of privacy, seeking damages against
the school board members as individuals. On appeal from the
federal trial court's dismissal of her suit, the Eighth Circuit
noted that it was not clear whether her conduct was embraced within the parameters of the constitutional right of
privacy, but suggested that if it were, her right would be
subject to a *Pickering*-type "balancing" test which would take
into account the interests of the school authorities, including
the local mores of the community and the concern that
"teachers teach by example as well as by lecture."[96] Without
expressing any view on whether the trial court should have
applied a balancing test, or how the balance should be struck,
the court ruled that since the right to cohabit out of wedlock
had not been held to fall within the contours of the constitutional right of privacy at the time of her dismissal, it could not
be said that the board members either knew or reasonably
should have known that their action would violate the teacher's
constitutional right, if any, and therefore they could not be
held personally liable.[97]

In a Delaware case a federal district court upheld a jury's
finding that the school board had violated the privacy rights
of a principal by refusing to renew his contract because he
was dating an assistant principal in his school who had recently separated from her husband. Several board members
had expressed chagrin over the affair, especially after the
principal's arm was broken in an altercation with the assistant
principal's husband. The judge awarded the principal $51,000
in compensatory damages and $7750 in punitive damages for
not only the violation of his privacy rights, but also due
process violations.[98]

Whatever the ultimate resolution of these privacy issues
may be, a teacher, at least at the elementary or secondary
level, will have an uphill battle where he is shown to have
engaged in sexual activity with a student.[99] Even the discharge of a teacher, or the revocation of his teaching certificate,

for behavior indicating a *potential* for misconduct with a student, e.g., perversity in an out-of-school relationship with a minor, probably would be upheld against attack on privacy grounds.[100] In such a case a court is likely to conclude that the teacher's conduct posed a sufficient threat of damage to the teacher-student relationship, and thus to the school district, to justify the sanction imposed.[101]

Even at the college level it would appear that a teacher constitutionally may be discharged for a "meretricious" relationship with a student.[102] At least one court has observed that the integrity of the educational system, under which teachers wield considerable power in the grading of students and the granting or withholding of certificates and diplomas, is jeopardized by such a relationship.[103]

Where a teacher is discharged or disciplined for having a sexual relationship with a *former* student, he may have a stronger claim that the school board's action violates his constitutional right of privacy or freedom of association. His claim may be rejected, however, if, without the contribution of school officials, his conduct has become the subject of public notoriety. Where a school board charged in substance that a high-school teacher had slept with a former student during the summer following her graduation at her home while her parents were away, a New York state court indicated that proof of either prior relationship or public notoriety might warrant discipline of the teacher.[104] Such a teacher might urge, however, that it is only where the public notoriety "materially and substantially" impairs his ability to discharge the responsibilities of his position that he can be disciplined without violating his constitutional rights of privacy and freedom of association.

Can school authorities, consistently with a teacher's constitutional right of privacy, terminate his employment or otherwise discipline him because of his public sexual conduct?

Whether or not a teacher's consensual sexual acts performed in discreet privacy are constitutionally protected, it is reasonably clear that such protection, if any, is unlikely to be extended to sexual conduct performed in public. A teacher dismissed on the ground that she has posed in the nude for the centerfold of *Playboy* magazine should anticipate judicial resistance if she argues that the dismissal violated her right of "privacy." Similarly, a teacher dismissed for skinny-dipping in a river near the center of town in public view is unlikely to find a source of redress in the U.S. Constitution.[105] Where substantial evidence supported the charge that a teacher had undressed and caressed a dress mannequin on his property in public view, the First Circuit rejected his claim that his dismissal for "conduct unbecoming a teacher" violated his constitutional right of privacy.[106] The right, said the court, "may be surrendered by public display"[107] and does not extend "to conduct displayed under the street lamp on the front lawn."[108]

In a California case the teaching credentials of an elementary-school teacher were revoked on the ground that she had engaged in certain acts of sexual misconduct evidencing her unfitness to teach. The hearing examiner found, among other things, that she had joined a "swingers" club and engaged in acts of oral copulation with men other than her husband. Upholding revocation of her certificate, the California Supreme Court distinguished the *Morrison* case in part on the ground that "in *Morrison* the conduct at issue occurred entirely in *private* and involved only two persons, whereas plaintiff's indiscretions involved three different 'partners,' were witnessed by several strangers, and took place in the semi-public atmosphere of a club party."[109] In dissent Judge Tobriner, noting that the teacher's acts "occurred in the bedroom of a private home," and that the only persons witnessing the conduct were members of The Swingers, a private club limited to persons who desired to view or engage in such activity, concluded that "the acts occurred in a private place, not a public one or one open to public view."[110]

Whether or not the public nature of a teacher's conduct automatically defeats his claim that punishment by school authorities for such conduct violates his constitutional right of privacy, it is reasonably clear that the sanction imposed does not violate the teacher's privacy right where the public conduct has gained sufficient notoriety so as to impair his relationship with the school community[111]—at least where the impairment is material and substantial.

Do school authorities violate a teacher's constitutional right of privacy when they prohibit her from breast-feeding her baby in private in school?

Arguably. In a Florida case, the Fifth Circuit ruled that a teacher has a constitutionally protected privacy right to breast-feed her baby free of governmental interference, but stated that a school board's interests in not having teachers bring their children to school might overcome the teacher's privacy interests.[112] In the Florida case the teacher's husband or baby-sitter would bring her baby to school during her lunch hour, and she would breast-feed the baby in a locked room with no one else present. The principal threatened her with disciplinary action because her actions violated the district policy prohibiting teachers from bringing their children to school. She asked permission to breast-feed her baby in a camper van in the school parking lot, but the principal forbade such a practice because of the policy prohibiting teachers from leaving the premises during school hours. She also sought to have her baby-sitter bottle-feed the baby, but the baby refused the formula. Finally she went to court, asserting that her constitutional right of privacy was being violated.

The court stated that "[t]he Constitution protects from undue state interference citizens' freedom of personal choice in some areas of marriage and family life" and added that "[t]he Supreme Court has long recognized that parents' interest in nurturing and rearing their children deserves special protection against state interference."[113] "Breastfeeding," the court continued, "is the most elemental form of parental care. It is a communion between mother and child that, like marriage, is 'intimate to the degree of being sacred . . . . Nourishment is necessary to maintain the child's life, and the parent may choose to believe that breastfeeding will enhance the child's psychological as well as physical health. In light of the spectrum of interests that the Supreme Court has held specially protected we conclude that the Constitution protects from excessive state interference a woman's decision respecting breastfeeding her child."[114]

The court then decided to send the case back to the district court for trial.[115] There it was to be decided whether the school district's reasons against allowing teachers to bring their children to school—avoiding disruption in the educational process, ensuring that teachers perform their duties without distraction, and avoiding potential liability for accidents involving the teachers' children—justified prohibiting the plain-

tiff from breast-feeding her child in school. The court also
ordered the trial court to examine whether the school district
regulations were more restrictive than was necessary.[116]

**May a teacher constitutionally be dismissed based on infor-
mation secured through a doctor's breach of a confidential
relationship with a teacher who is his patient?**

Generally, no. In an Alabama case a school superintendent,
learning of rumors that an unmarried teacher in the school
system was a hospital patient and was pregnant, called her
doctor, who told the superintendent that the teacher had
asked for an abortion because she would lose her job if she
had a baby. Based on this information, the school board
cancelled her contract based on the statutory ground of
"immorality." A three-judge federal district court held that
this application of the statute violated the teacher's constitutional right of privacy, stating:

> The Board made no finding that [her] claimed immoral-
> ity had affected her competency or fitness as a teacher,
> and no such nexus was developed in the evidence. No
> "compelling interest" . . . was established by the evi-
> dence which would justify the invasion of [her] constitu-
> tional right of privacy. Under the testimony that [she]
> was in the early months of pregnancy, she in consultation
> with her physician would be free to determine, without
> regulation by the State, whether pregnancy should be
> terminated [citing a Supreme Court decision on the con-
> tours of the constitutional right to an abortion]. For the
> State, in the absence of any compelling interest, to base
> cancellation of [her] employment contract on evidence
> growing out of her consultations with her physician was,
> in our opinion, an unconstitutional invasion of her right
> of privacy.[117]

**Under what circumstances, if any, would an investigation
by school authorities into a teacher's private life violate his
constitutional right of privacy?**

Such a violation would occur if there were no connection
between the investigation and a legitimate concern of the
school authorities.

While the matters into which a public employer legitimately may inquire conceivably may be broader than those which would justify an employee's dismissal, the courts have indicated that the employer should be required to make some showing of job-relatedness before investigating areas that are wholly private.[118] A federal court has held that in the absence of a showing that a policeman's private, off-duty personal activities have an impact upon his on-the-job performance, inquiry into those activities by police officials violates his constitutional right of privacy.[119]

It is not clear to what extent, if any, school authorities constitutionally may conduct an inquiry into a teacher's off-duty personal activities where they have evidence that such activities are sufficiently "open and notorious" to impair his performance on the job. Where, however, the activities bear only a tenuous relationship to his on-the-job performance, they would appear clearly beyond the scope of any reasonable, or constitutional, investigation by school officials.

A wider inquiry into private areas of the lives of employees or an inquiry into the private lives of dependents may require stronger justification. Striking down a Department of Energy directive requiring employees to answer a questionnaire prying into the religious, social, political, educational, and fraternal associations of the employee, his spouse, and his minor children and dependents as an unreasonable invasion of privacy, one court stated: "People, even people working for the government, have within reason the right to be left alone." The court concluded: "Before data can be gathered in these privacy areas, the government must convincingly show a substantial relation between the information sought and a subject of overriding and compelling state interest."[120]

In what circumstances, if any, would a law imposing a financial disclosure requirement violate a teacher's constitutional right of privacy?

Such financial disclosure requirements generally have been upheld.[121] Recent decisions, however, indicate that a violation of a public employee's constitutional right of privacy would occur if the law were not justified by compelling—or at least substantial—state interests; not narrowly drawn to deal only with those interests, or not sufficiently clear to provide adequate guidance to individuals interested in complying.[122] One court stated that public employees who were challenging a financial disclosure requirement "seem correct in arguing that the legislature should be required to make a stronger showing of need in regulating spouses than it may be required to make in regulating employees."[123]

If the statute contains a mechanism for protecting privacy, it nevertheless may be vulnerable to constitutional challenge if, to assert a privacy claim under the statute, an employee must make a detailed written explanation and the statute affords insufficient safeguards against circulation of the explanation to individuals likely to abuse it.[124]

Moreover, if the disclosure requirement exempts only material that is "highly personal" or contains language to that effect, and the reports are made public, the public will be placed on notice that some aspect of the employee's financial life is highly personal. As one federal court has noted in such a context: "That the aspect of their lives that is withheld will have been found to have no relationship to their duties, or to raise no actual or potential conflict of interest, seems unlikely to [guarantee] that no effort will be made by members of the public to discover the underlying facts. Indeed, some investigators may be more interested in uncovering non-job related "highly personal" facts than in examining less intensely personal information, however job related."[125]

Does a teacher have any constitutional protection against unreasonable searches of his desk or office by school authorities?

Yes. The Fourth Amendment to the U.S. Constitution, which bars unreasonable searches and seizures, was designed to "safeguard the privacy and security of individuals against arbitrary invasion by government officials."[126] Fourth Amendment protection is not limited to situations in which the search is aimed at uncovering evidence of criminal conduct. The Supreme Court has recognized that "[i]f the government intrudes on a person's property, the privacy interest suffers whether the government's motivation is to investigate violations of criminal laws or breaches of other statutory or regulatory standards."[127]

A government employee, however, may claim the protection of the Fourth Amendment only if the area searched was one in which he had a "reasonable expectation of freedom from governmental intrusion."[128] Such an expectation can exist notwithstanding the government's ownership of the searched premises.[129] Thus, the Third Circuit has held that a guidance counselor charged with maintaining sensitive student records enjoys, in the absence of an accepted practice or regulation to the contrary, a reasonable expectation of privacy in his school desk.[130] An anonymous cartoon had appeared in a local newspaper ridiculing the financial and personnel policies of the Fair Lawn, New Jersey, Board of Education by depicting the board members as poker players, apparently gambling away employees' salaries and jobs. Suspecting the guidance counselor as the offending cartoonist, a board member entered the guidance counselor's school at night, found a janitor with a pass key, directed him to unlock the door to the guidance counselor's suite, and observing a slightly opened drawer in the guidance counselor's desk, pulled it completely open, revealing copies of the cartoon. The court ruled that this action violated the guidance counselor's Fourth Amendment rights.[131]

An employer, however, may conduct a search in accordance with a regulation or practice that would dispel in advance any expectation of privacy.[132] In the New Jersey case, moreover, there was no evidence that the board member was acting to recover government property, or was undertaking as an employer to monitor the guidance counselor's performance of his official duties. The cases indicate that even where an area is reserved for the exclusive use of a government employee, a public employer may conduct a search of the area where it is justified by business necessity.[133] Such an employer may be unable to demonstrate business necessity, however, where a less intrusive means of accomplishing the business purpose exists.

Can a school board, consistently with a teacher's constitutionally protected privacy rights, order a teacher to undergo a physical examination?

In many cases, yes. In a California case, the court upheld the school board's refusal to employ a teaching applicant after she refused to have a chest X-ray.[134] The court wrote that the board's requirement for such an X-ray before a teacher starts classes is "constitutional as a health measure for the protection of society" and is not an unconstitutional invasion of privacy.[135] In a New York case, a federal district judge upheld a school board's suspension and subsequent dismissal of a teacher who in the fourth month of a sick leave refused to send her medical records to or submit to an examination with the school district's physician, who was a male.[136] Rejecting the notion that there is a constitutionally protected privacy right for a tenured female teacher to refuse to submit to an examination with a district-employed male physician, the court concluded: "Her argument is based on personal preference, not upon a well-recognized principle of liberty and justice. There simply is no constitutionally recognized right to refuse a medical examination because the physician is a male.[137]

Does a statutory or contractual provision authorizing a school board to subject a teacher to a compulsory mental examination infringe upon his constitutional right of privacy?

It seems clear that "[p]rotection of school children from teachers who have shown evidence of harmful, significant deviation from normal mental health" is not only a valid legislative concern but a compelling state interest.[138] Nevertheless, any statutory or contractual provision authorizing a school board to subject a teacher to a compulsory mental examination impinges upon his constitutionally protected privacy interest.[139] Such a provision, therefore, must be narrowly drawn so as not to encroach upon this interest more than is necessary to protect the legitimate concerns of the school system.[140]

Thus a New Jersey statute authorized a school board to require any employee to submit to a mental examination "whenever, in the judgment of the board, an employee shows evidence of deviation from normal physical or mental health." In order to save the constitutionality of the statute, a New Jersey court construed the term "deviation from normal . . . mental health" to mean "harmful, significant deviation from mental health affecting the teacher's ability to teach, discipline or associate with children of the age of the children subject to the teacher's control in the school district."[141]

Before being compelled to undergo a mental examination, a teacher may be constitutionally entitled to a hearing. The Ninth Circuit has recognized that a directive requiring a teacher to submit to a mental examination is stigmatizing because it "implie[s] that there exist[s] both reasonable grounds for the order and mental unfitness for the job."[142] In *Paul v.*

Davis the U.S. Supreme Court held that official defamation does not deprive a person of liberty so as to trigger the due process protections of the 14th Amendment unless, in conjunction with the defamatory remarks, "a right or status previously recognized by state law [is] distinctly altered or extinguished."[143] (See Chapter V.) It can be argued, however, that whether or not a liberty or property interest sufficient to invoke due process requirements is implicated, a statutory or contractual provision authorizing such a compulsory mental examination would violate the employee's constitutional right of privacy unless adequate procedural safeguards were observed before such compulsion were exercised; otherwise, mental examinations would be required even where they were unnecessary to achieve the admittedly valid governmental purpose.[144] Of course, where a teacher is found to be mentally ill, and as a result of that finding "a right or status" conferred upon him by state law is "distinctly altered or extinguished"[145]—e.g., where he is discharged or placed on an involuntary leave of absence—he is at that point deprived of liberty, a deprivation which cannot be imposed without first affording him procedural due process.[146]

NOTES

1. H. Beale, *A History of Freedom of Teaching in American Schools* 170–71 (1941).

2. J. Royce, *The Freedom of Teaching*, Overland Monthly, 235, 239 (1883).

3. L. Allen, *Bryan and Darrow at Dayton* 109 (1925).

4. *New York State Education*, May 1971 at 32.

5. D. Cooke, "Blue Law Blues," *The Nation's Schools*, Oct. 1935 at 33.

6. *Id.* at 32.

7. *Stoddard v. School District No. 1*, 590 F.2d 829, 831, 833 (10th Cir. 1979).

8. *Olmstead v. United States*, 277 U.S. 438, 478 (1928) (dissenting opinion).

9. *West Virginia State Board of Education v. Barnette*, 319 U.S. 624, 642 (1943).

10. *Id.*

11. *Id.* at 634.

12. *Id.* at 642.

13. *Russo v. Central School District No. 1*, 469 F.2d 623 (2d Cir. 1972), *cert. denied*, 411 U.S. 932 (1973); *Hanover v. Northrup*, 525 F.Supp.

170 (D. Conn. 1970); *State v. Lundquist*, 262 Md. 534, 278 A.2d 263 (1971).

14. *Griswold v. Connecticut*, 381 U.S. 479, 484 (1965).

15. 469 F.2d 623 (2d Cir. 1972), *cert. denied*, 411 U.S. 932 (1973).

16. *Id.* at 634.

17. *Palmer v. Board of Education*, 603 F.2d 1271 (7th Cir. 1979), *cert. denied*, 444 U.S. 1026 (1980).

18. 394 U.S. 557 (1969).

19. *Id.* at 564.

20. *Id.*

21. *Id.* at 565.

22. *Id.*

23. *Major v. Hampton*, 413 F.Supp. 66, 70 n.2 (E.D. La. 1976).

24. *Fisher v. Snyder*, 346 F.Supp. 396, 400 (D. Neb. 1972).

25. 476 F.2d 375 (8th Cir. 1973).

26. *See Louisiana Affiliate of National Organization for Reform of Marijuana Laws v. Guste*, 380 F.Supp. 404, 406–07 (E.D. La. 1974), *aff'd*, 511 F.2d 1400 (5th Cir.), *cert. denied*, 423 U.S. 867 (1974); *National Organization for Reform of Marijuana Laws v. Gain*, 100 Cal. App. 3d 586, 161 Cal. Rptr. 181, 184 (1979) and cases cited.

27. *Cf. Morrison v. State Board of Education*, 1 Cal. 3d 214, 461 P.2d 375, 82 Cal. Rptr. 175 (1969) (statute authorizing revocation of a teacher's life diploma for "immoral" or "unprofessional" conduct construed to permit revocation only for such conduct as renders him unfit to perform his job).

28. *Bromley v. Wilks*, No. Civ. 79–657, slip Op. at 2 (D. Ariz., filed Aug. 28, 1979).

29. 434 U.S. 374 (1978).

30. *See Voichahoske v. City of Grand Island*, 194 Neb. 175, 231 N.W.2d 124, 128 (1975) (city policy denying employment to spouses of employees seriously impeded constitutional right to marry and free personal choice in matters relating to family life, requiring showing that policy was warranted by a substantial state interest and that there was no less restrictive alternative). Such policies may also be vulnerable under Title VII of the Civil Rights Act of 1964 when a disparate impact on one sex can be shown. *See Yuhas v. Libbey-Owens Ford Co.*, 562 F.2d 496, 498 (7th Cir. 1977), *cert. denied*, 435 U.S. 934 (1978) (policies violate Title VII unless employer shows rule is job-related). *Cf. Sanbonmatsu v. Boyer*, 8 EPD ¶9704 (N.Y. App. Div. July 5, 1974) (state university violated sex discrimination provisions of New York Human Rights Law by denying employment to professors whose spouses were currently teaching at the university).

31. *Bromley v. Wilks*, *supra* note 28, at 3.

32. 434 U.S. at 680.

33. *Id.* at 682.

34. *Id.* at 675.
35. *Id.* at 681.
36. *Thompson v. Board of Trustees*, 627 P.2d 1229 (Mont. 1981) (interpreting Montana statute prohibiting discrimination due to marital status so that it overturns school district policy barring administrator from working in same district as spouse).
37. 414 U.S. 632 (1974).
38. *Id.* at 640.
39. *Id.* at 642.
40. *Id.* at 648. *See also, e.g., Rodgers v. Berger*, 438 F.Supp. 713, 726 (D. Mass. 1977) (provision in collective bargaining agreement between school committee and teachers association requiring plaintiff to take mandatory maternity leave violated due process clause of 14th Amendment); *Bradley v. Cothern*, 384 F.Supp. 1216 (E.D. Tex. 1974).
41. *Cleveland Board of Education v. LaFleur, supra* note 37, at 650.
42. *Id.*
43. Pub.L. 95–555, 92 Stat. 2076.
44. 29 C.F.R. §1604.10(b) (1982).
45. 29 C.F.R. app. §1604.10 (1982). See appendix to this book for more information on discrimination based on pregnancy.
46. *Id.*
47. *Eisenstadt v. Baird*, 405 U.S. 438, 453 (1972) (emphasis added).
48. *Carey v. Population Services International*, 431 U.S. 678, 686 (1977).
49. *Lewis v. Delaware State College*, 455 F.Supp. 239, 249–50 (D. Del. 1978).
50. *Avery v. Homewood City Board of Education*, 674 F.2d 337, 341–42 (5th Cir. 1982).
51. *Id.* at 340–41.
52. *Id.* at 342 & n.6
53. *Brown v. Bathke*, 416 F.Supp. 1194, 1200 (D. Neb. 1976), *rev'd on other grounds*, 566 F.2d 588 (8th Cir. 1977).
54. *Wardlaw v. Austin School District*, 10 FEP Cases 892, 895 (W.D. Tex. 1975).
55. *Lewis v. Delaware State College*, 455 F.Supp. 239, 248 (D. Del. 1978), *quoting from Langford v. City of Texarkana*, 478 F.2d 262, 267 (8th Cir. 1973). *See also Cooper v. Aaron*, 358 U.S. 1, 16 (1958).
56. *See Avery v. Homewood City Board of Education*, 674 F.2d 337, 340–41 (5th Cir. 1982); *Norton v. Macy*, 417 F.2d 1161, 1165 (D.C. Cir. 1969); *Mindel v. United States Civil Service Commission*, 312 F.Supp. 485 (N.D. Cal. 1970). *Cf. Morrison v. State Board of Education*, 1 Cal. 3d 214, 461 P.2d 375, 82 Cal. Rptr. 175 (1969) (statute authorizing revocation of teacher's certificate for "immoral conduct" could only be constitutional if term were construed to denote immoral conduct which indicates unfitness to teach).

57. *Cf. Cleveland Board of Education v. LaFleur*, 4:.S. 632, 650 (1974) (mandatory leave requirement unnecessarily penalized female teacher for asserting her right to bear children).

58. *Andrews v. Drew Municipal Separate School District*, 507 F.2d 611, 615 (5th Cir.), *cert. granted*, 423 U.S. 820 (1975), *cert. dismissed*, 425 U.S. 559 (1976).

59. Sarason et al., *Modeling and Role-Playing in the Schools; A Manual with Special Reference to the Disadvantaged Student*, Human Interaction Research Institute, Los Angeles, Calif. (April 1973) at 6.

60. *Andrews v. Drew Municipal Separate School District*, 507 F.2d 611, 616 (5th Cir.), *cert. granted*, 423 U.S. 820 (1975), *cert. dismissed*, 425 U.S. 559 (1976).

61. *Id.* at 616–17.

62. *James v. Board of Education*, 461 F.2d 566, 571 (2d Cir.), *cert. denied*, 409 U.S. 1042 (1972) ("Any limitation on the exercise of constitutional rights can be justified only by a conclusion, based on reasonable inferences flowing from concrete facts and not abstractions, that the interests of discipline or sound education are materially and substantially jeopardized, whether the danger stems initially from the conduct of students or teachers"). *See Olbert v. Sparta Area Schools*, Opinion and Order 76–C–373 (W.D. Wis. Mar. 31, 1977).

63. *Cf. Brown v. Bathke*, 566 F.2d 588, 592 (8th Cir. 1977) (leave of absence for remainder of term was alternative which "could have alleviated the Board's concern for the moral welfare of the students while affording some protection of Ms. Brown's rights"—an alternative no longer available because of delay in affording post-termination hearing); *id.* at 594 (Miller, J., concurring) (alternatives available to board included requesting teacher to take maternity leave).

64. *See Wardlaw v. Austin School District*, 10 FEP Cases 892, 895 (W.D. Tex. 1975). *Cf. Brown v. Bathke, supra.*

65. 401 U.S. 424 (1971).

66. *Jacobs v. Martin Sweets Co., Inc.*, 550 F.2d 364, 370 (6th Cir.), *cert. denied*, 431 U.S. 917 (1977). *But see Grayson v. Wickes Corp.*, 450 F.Supp. 1112, 1119 (E.D. Ill. 1978), *aff'd*, 607 F.2d 1194 (7th Cir. 1979) (no Title VII violation: employee "failed to show she was treated any differently than similarly situated male employees had been or would have been treated. She failed to prove that unmarried male employees who engaged in sexual relations and produced illegitimate offspring would have been treated differently by Wickes").

67. 405 U.S. 645, 665 (1972).

68. *Brown v. Bathke*, 566 F.2d 588, 593 (8th Cir. 1977) (concurring opinion of Miller, J.).

69. In a Title VII case the burden of proof appears to be on the plaintiff to demonstrate the presence of a less restrictive alternative—not on the employer to demonstrate the absence of such an alternative.

See *Dothard v. Rawlinson*, 433 U.S. 321, 329 (1977); *Albermarle Paper Co. v. Moody*, 422 U.S. 405, 425 (1975); *Scott v. University of Delaware*, 455 F.Supp. 1102, 1123 (D. Del. 1978), *aff'd in part and rev'd in part*, 601 F.2d 76 (3d Cir.), *cert. denied*, 444 U.S. 931 (1979).

70. See *Brown v. Bathke*, 566 F.2d 588, 594 (8th Cir. 1977) (Miller, J., concurring).

71. *Griswold v. Connecticut*, 381 U.S. 479 (1965); *Eisenstadt v. Baird*, 405 U.S. 438 (1972); *Carey v. Population Services International*, 431 U.S. 678 (1977).

72. *Carey v. Population Services International*, 431 U.S. 678, 687 (1977).

73. Compare, *e.g.*, *Baker v. Wade*, 553 F.Supp. 1121 (N.D. Tex. 1982) (overturning state's anti-sodomy statute); *New York v. Onofre*, 51 N.Y. 2d, 415 N.E. 2d 936, 434 N.Y.S. 2d 947 (1980), *cert. denied*, 451 U.S. 987 (1981); *Acanfora v. Board of Education*, 359 F.Supp. 843 (D. Md. 1973), *aff'd on other grounds*, 491 F.2d 498 (4th Cir.), *cert. denied*, 419 U.S. 836 (1974) (teacher's private consensual homosexual activity is a fundamental right); and *State v. Saunders*, 75 N.J. 200, 381 A.2d 333 (1977) (statutory ban on fornication violates right of privacy) with *Velez-Lozano v. Immigration and Naturalization Service*, 463 F.2d 1305 (D.C. Cir. 1972) (upholding Virginia sodomy law as applied to consensual homosexuality), and *Hugh v. State*, 14 Md. App. 497, 287 A.2d 299 (Ct. Spec.App.), *cert. denied*, 409 U.S. 1025 (1972).

74. 403 F.Supp. 1199 (E.D. Va. 1975).

75. 425 U.S. 901 (1976).

76. See L. Tribe, *American Constitutional Law* 943 (1978).

77. See, *e.g.*, *Norton v. Macy*, 417 F.2d 1161 (D.C. Cir. 1969); *Gayer v. Laird*, 332 F.Supp. 169 (D. D.C. 1971); *Mindel v. United States Civil Service Commission*, 312 F.Supp. 485 (N.D. Cal. 1970). For a relevant post-*Doe* decision, see *benShalom v. Secretary of Army*, 489 F.Supp. 964, 976 (E.D. Wis. 1980).

78. *Norton v. Macy*, 417 F.2d 1161, 1165 (D.C. Cir. 1969). *See also Mindel v. United States Civil Service Commission*, 312 F.Supp. 485 (N.D. Cal. 1970).

79. 1 Cal. 3d 214, 461 P.2d 375, 82 Cal. Rptr. 175 (1969).

80. 1 Cal. 3d at 225, 461 P.2d at 382, 82 Cal. Rptr. at 182.

81. 1 Cal. 3d at 233, 461 P.2d at 390, 82 Cal. Rptr. at 190. *See also Acanfora v. Board of Education*, 359 F.Supp. 843, 853 (D. Md. 1973), *aff'd on other grounds*, 491 F.2d 498 (4th Cir.), *cert. denied*, 419 U.S. 836 (1974) (school board policy of not knowingly employing any homosexuals is constitutionally objectionable). *But see Gaylord v. Tacoma School District No. 10*, 88 Wash. 2d 286, 559 P.2d 1340 (*en banc*), *cert. denied*, 434 U.S. 879 (1977).

82. 1 Cal. 3d at 233–34, 461 P.2d at 390, 82 Cal. Rptr. at 190.

83. 1 Cal. 3d at 235, 461 P.2d at 391, 82 Cal. Rptr. at 191.

84. 216 N.W.2d 339 (Iowa 1974).

85. 216 N.W.2d at 343, *quoting from Jarvella v. Willoughby-Eastlake City School District*, 12 Ohio Misc. 288, 291, 233 N.E.2d 143, 146 (1967). *Cf. Stoddard v. School District No. 1*, 429 F.Supp. 890, 892 (D. Wyo. 1977), *aff'd*, 590 F.2d 829 (10th Cir. 1979) (teacher's constitutional right of privacy embraces the right to determine with whom he or she will associate); *Board of Trustees v. Holso*, 584 P.2d 1009, 1018 (Wyo. 1978), (quoting *Stoddard* language).

86. 216 N.W.2d at 344.

87. *Id*.

88. *Id*.

89. *Id*.

90. *Olbert v. Sparta Area Schools*, Opinion and Order 76–C–373 (W.D. Mar. 31, 1977) at 4. *Cf. James v. Board of Education*, 461 F.2d 566, 571 (2d Cir.), *cert. denied*, 409 U.S. 1041 (1972). *See also benShalom v. Secretary of Army*, 489 F.Supp. 964, 976 (E.D. Wis. 1980) ("This court . . . will not defer to the Army's attempt to control a soldier's sexual preferences absent a showing of actual deviant conduct and absent proof of nexus between the sexual preference and the soldier's military capabilities. The Army, in this case, has not even tried to show that such a nexus exists").

91. 393 U.S. 503, 509 (1969).

92. *Fisher v. Snyder*, 346 F.Supp. 396, 401 (D. Neb. 1972) (emphasis added).

93. 476 F.2d 375 (8th Cir. 1973).

94. *Smith v. Price*, 446 F.Supp. 828, 834 (M.D. Ga. 1977), *rev'd on other grounds*, 616 F.2d 1371 (5th Cir. 1980) (emphasis added).

95. *Hollenbaugh v. Carnegie Free Public Library*, 436 F.Supp. 1328, 1333–34 (W.D. Pa. 1977), *aff'd*, 578 F.2d 1374 (3d Cir.), *cert. denied*, 439 U.S. 1052 (1978). *Cf. Childers v. Dallas Police Department*, 513 F.Supp. 134 (N.D. Tex. 1981) (employing "material and substantial" standard in assessing decision not to hire a gay activist).

96. *Sullivan v. Meade Independent School District*, 530 F.2d 799, 804 (8th Cir. 1976). *See Ambach v. Norwick*, 441 U.S. 68, 78–79 (1979).

97. *Sullivan v. Meade Independent School District*, *supra* at 808.

98. *Schreffler v. Board of Education of Delmar School District*, 506 F.Supp. 1300 (D. Del. 1981).

99. *Goldin v. Board of Education*, 78 Misc. 2d 972, 359 N.Y.S.2d 384 (Sup.Ct. 1973), *aff'd in part, modified in part*, 35 N.Y.2d 534, 324 N.E.2d 106, 364 N.Y.S.2d 440 (1974). *Cf. Board of Trustees v. Stubblefield*, 16 Cal. App. 3d 820, 94 Cal. Rptr. 318 (1971) (college teacher can be discharged for "meretricious" relationship with current student).

100. *See Tomerlin v. Dade County School Board*, 318 So.2d 159 (Fla. App. 1975); *Moser v. State Board of Education*, 22 Cal. App.3d 988, Cal. Rptr. 86 (1972); *Denton v. South Kitsap School District*, 10 Wash. App. 69, 516 P.2d 1080 (1973).

101. *Denton v. South Kitsap School District, supra.*

102. *Board of Trustees v. Stubblefield,* 16 Cal. App. 3d 820, 94 Cal. Rptr. 318 (1971).

103. *Id.*

104. *Jerry v. Board of Education,* 35 N.Y.2d 534, 364 N.Y.S.2d 440, 324 N.E.2d 106 (1974). *See Moser v. State Board of Education,* 22 Cal. App.3d 988, 101 Cal. Rptr. 86 (1972).

105. As in other cases, there may be a state law ground on which to attack the dismissal. One state court, for example, ruled that public skinny-dipping by a teacher neither constituted unfitness to teach nor rendered his services "unprofitable" to the school, as charged in the dismissal proceedings. *Rubino v. Orland School Committee,* Docket No. CV–76–148 (Super Ct. Me. Nov. 10, 1978) (decision on motion for summary judgment).

106. *Wishart v. McDonald,* 500 F.2d 1110, 1116 (1st Cir. 1974).

107. *Id.* at 1114.

108. *Id.*

109. *Pettit v. State Board of Education,* 10 Cal. 3d 29, 513 P.2d 889, 109 Cal. Rptr. 665 (1973).

110. *Id.* at 41, 513 P.2d at 897, 109 Cal. Rptr. at 673.

111. *Moser v. State Board of Education,* 22 Cal. App. 3d 988, 101 Cal. Rptr. 86 (1972). *Cf. Jerry v. Board of Education,* 35 N.Y.2d 534, 324 N.E. 2d 106, 364 N.Y.S. 2d 440 (1974) (applying "notoriety" rule to private conduct known to the public).

112. *Dike v. School Board of Orange County, Florida,* 650 F.2d 783 (5th Cir. 1981).

113. *Id.* at 785–86.

114. *Id.* at 787.

115. *Id.*

116. *Id.*

117. *Drake v. Covington County Board of Education,* 371 F.Supp. 974, 979 (M.D. Ala. 1974). Under the Pregnancy Discrimination Act a school board may not discharge or refuse to hire a woman because she has had or is contemplating having an abortion. *See* Appendix, section A; section B, fourth-to-last question.

118. *Shuman v. City of Philadelphia,* 470 F.Supp. 449, 460 n.9 (E.D. Pa. 1979). *See American Federation of Government Employees v. Schlesinger,* 443 F.Supp. 431 (D. D.C. 1978).

119. *Shuman v. City of Philadelphia,* 470 F.Supp. 449, 459 (E.D. Pa. 1979).

120. *American Federation of Government Employees v. Schlesinger,* 443 F.Supp. 431, 434 (D. D.C. 1978).

121. *See* Note, *The Constitutionality of Financial Disclosure Laws,* 59 Cornell L. Rev. 345 (1974).

122. *Slevin v. City of New York,* 477 F.Supp. 1051, 1055–56 (S.D. N.Y. 1979).

123. *Id.* at 1057.
124. *Id.* at 1058.
125. *Id.*
126. *Camera v. Municipal Court,* 387 U.S. 523, 528 (1967); *Gillard v. Schmidt,* 579 F.2d 825, 827–28 (3d Cir. 1978).
127. *Marshall v. Barlow's, Inc.,* 436 U.S. 307, 312 (1978).
128. *Gillard v. Schmidt,* 579 F.2d 825, 828 (3d Cir. 1978); *United States v. Speights,* 557 F.2d 362, 363 (3d Cir. 1977), *quoting United States v. White,* 401 U.S. 745, 751–52 (1971).
129. *Mancusi v. DeForte* 392 U.S. 364, 368 (1967); *Gillard v. Schmidt.* 579 F.2d 825, 829 (3d Cir. 1978).
130. *Gillard v. Schmidt,* 579 F.2d 825, 828 (3d Cir. 1978).
131. *Id.*
132. *Id.* at 829; *United States v. Bunkers,* 521 F.2d 1217 (9th Cir.), *cert. denied,* 423 U.S. 989 (1975); *United States v. Donato,* 269 F.Supp. 921, 924 (E.D. Pa.), *aff'd,* 379 F.2d 288 (3d Cir. 1967).
133. *See United States v. Nasser,* 476 F.2d 1111, 1123 (7th Cir. 1973); *United States v. Hagarty,* 388 F.2d 713 (7th Cir. 1968); *United States v. Collins,* 349 F.2d 863, 867–68 (2d Cir. 1965), *cert. denied,* 383 U.S. 960 (1966); *United States v. Blok,* 188 F.2d 1019, 1021 (D.C. Cir. 1951); *United States v. Kahan,* 350 F.Supp. 784, 791, 798 (S.D. N.Y. 1972), *rev'd on other grounds,* 479 F.2d 290 (2d Cir. 1973), *rev'd,* 415 U.S. 239 (1974).
134. *Garrett v. Los Angeles City Unified School District,* 116 Cal App. 3d 472, 172 Cal. Rptr. 170 (1981).
135. *Id.* at 480, 172 Cal. Rptr. at 174–175.
136. *Gargiul v. Tompkins,* 525 F.Supp. 795 (N.D. N.Y. 1981).
137. *Id.* at. 798.
138. *Kochman v. Keansburg,* 124 N.J. Super. 203, 305 A.2d 807 (1973).
139. *Id.*
140. *Id.* at 211, 305 A.2d at 811.
141. *Id* at 211–12, 305 A.2d at 812; *see also Dusanek v. Hannon,* 677 F.2d 538, 542 (7th Cir. 1982) (only disabilities which impair the efficiency of a teacher may be the basis for requiring a health examination).
142. *Stewart v. Pearce,* 484 F.2d 1031, 1034 (9th Cir. 1973).
143. 424 U.S. 693, 711 (1976).
144. *But see Hoffman v. Jannarone,* 401 F.Supp. 1095, 1099 (D. N.J. 1975), *modified mem.,* 532 F.2d 746 (3d Cir. 1976).
145. 424 U.S. 693, 711 (1976).
146. *See Lombard v. Board of Education of City of New York,* 502 F.2d 631 (2d Cir. 1974), *cert. denied,* 420 U.S. 976 (1975). *See also Dusanek v. Hannon,* 677 F.2d 538, 542–43 (7th Cir. 1982) ("when the result of [a] medical examination is adverse to a teacher, the Illinois procedure permits the teacher either to request a medical leave of absence, or to fight his or her removal by refusing to take

such a leave, thereby triggering rights to a hearing. The teacher is given the option of a hearing before any property interest is taken away. . . . We conclude that it is not a deprivation of due process of law to be put to the option of defending oneself in a proper dismissal hearing or voluntarily accepting a change in one's job status, when the state's action in first initiating the medical investigation is reasonable").

V

The Right to Due Process of Law

This chapter discusses the rights of teachers under the due process clause of the 14th Amendment. The length of the chapter reflects the mushrooming litigation in this area following the decisions of the Supreme Court in *Board of Regents v. Roth* and *Perry v. Sindermann*. These decisions had the effect of inviting lawsuits by adopting rules which made the question whether a teacher is entitled to reasons and a hearing in connection with the termination of his employment depend on the particular circumstances of the employment relationship and of the termination.

The chapter discusses what constitutes a property or liberty interest triggering due process protection under the *Roth* and *Sindermann* decisions; what rights are embraced within the concept of due process; the remedies to which a teacher deprived of due process is entitled; and the substantive protections afforded teachers by the due process clause.

A. Procedural Due Process

Under what circumstances does the Constitution require that a teacher be afforded procedural due process in connection with the proposed termination of his employment?

The 14th Amendment provides that no state shall "deprive any person of life, liberty or property without due process of law."[1] In *Board of Regents v. Roth*[2] and *Perry v. Sindermann*[3] the Supreme Court, construing this language literally, con-

cluded that a teacher is entitled to due process in connection
with the termination of his employment only if the termination would deprive him of "liberty" or "property."

When does the termination of his employment deprive a teacher of a constitutionally protected "property" interest?

In *Roth*, the Supreme Court stated that "[t]he Fourteenth
Amendment's procedural protection of property is a safeguard of the security of interests that a person has already
acquired in specific benefits."[4] "To have a property interest
in a benefit," the Court declared, "a person clearly must have
more than an abstract need or desire for it. He must have
more than a unilateral expectation of it. He must, instead,
have a legitimate claim of entitlement to it."[5] In *Sindermann*,
the Court ruled that a teacher had a property interest in
continued employment if he had a legitimate claim of entitlement to continued employment "absent sufficient cause."[6]

How does a court determine the "legitimacy" of a teacher's claim of entitlement to continued employment?

Generally by reference to state law.

In *Roth* the Court stated that "[p]roperty interests, of
course, are not created by the Constitution. Rather, they are
created and their dimensions are defined by existing rules or
understandings that stem from an independent source such as
state law—rules or understandings that secure benefits and
that support claims of entitlement to those benefits."[7] In
Perry v. Sindermann[8] the Court, while concluding that a
Texas state junior-college professor might be able to show
from the circumstances of his service and other relevant facts
that he had a legitimate claim of entitlement to job tenure,
stated: "If it is the law of Texas that a teacher in the
respondent's position has no contractual or other claim to job
tenure, the respondent's claim would be defeated."[9]

Subsequently, in *Bishop v. Wood*,[10] a North Carolina
police officer was dismissed without a hearing for failing
properly to discharge his duties, even though he was classified as a "permanent employee" by a city ordinance which
specified that he could be dismissed if certain grounds existed.
In *Still v. Lance*,[11] the North Carolina Supreme Court had
held that an enforceable expectation of continued public employment could exist only if the employer by statute or con-

tract had actually granted some form of guarantee. Construing the ordinance before it, the federal district court in *Bishop* concluded that the policeman held his position at the pleasure of the city—an interpretation upheld by the Fourth Circuit. The U.S. Supreme Court concluded that "the sufficiency of the claim of entitlement [to continued employment] must be decided by reference to state law."[12] Without independently examining the state law issue, except to find the interpretation of the two lower federal courts plausible in light of *Still v. Lance*, the Supreme Court concluded that the policeman had no property interest.[13] Similarly, in *Paul v. Davis*, the Supreme Court stated that an interest gains constitutional status as a property interest by virtue of the fact that it has been "initially recognized and protected by state law."[14]

The Seventh Circuit, construing *Bishop* and *Paul*, has interpreted these decisions to mean that "the existence of a property interest cognizable under the due process clause depends on whether state law has affirmatively created an expectation that a particular employment relationship will continue unless certain defined events occur."[15] The court, however, indicated that such an affirmative obligation may stem from "a statutory, regulatory, or judicial source."[16] Although a Wisconsin federal district court has stated that "an examination of the enforceability of an alleged property interest must be directed at the existence of "affirmative recognition in state law" either through formal state enactments, or through judicial interpretation of relevant enactments,"[17] this conclusion is questionable, since a "judicial source" for a property interest arguably includes the common law.

Since *Bishop v. Wood*, moreover, the Supreme Court has instructed that "federal constitutional law determines whether [an] interest rises to the level of a legitimate claim of entitlement protected by the Due Process Clause."[18] Thus, "although the primary source of property rights is state law, the state may not magically declare an interest to be '*non* property' after the fact for Fourteenth Amendment purposes . . . ."[19] In short, the state may not defeat what would otherwise be a property interest through "definitional gamesmanship."[20]

Does a tenured teacher have a property interest in continued employment?

Yes. In *Slochower v. Board of Higher Education*[21] a tenured

professor at a city university was dismissed under a provision
of the municipal charter terminating the employment of any
city employee who invoked his Fifth Amendment privilege
against self-incrimination to avoid answering a question relating to his official conduct. The Supreme Court ruled:

> The state has broad powers in the selection and dis-
> charge of its employees, and it may be that proper in-
> quiry would show Slochower's continued employment to
> be inconsistent with a real interest of the State. But
> there has been no such inquiry here. We hold that the
> summary dismissal of appellant violates due process of
> law.[22]

In *Board of Regents v. Roth* the Supreme Court characterized the *Slochower* decision as holding "that a public college
professor dismissed from an office held under tenure provisions . . . [has an interest] in continued employment that . . .
[is] safeguarded by due process."[23]

This constitutional requirement of procedural fairness in
connection with the termination of a tenured teacher's employment is independent of, and may be more comprehensive than, the procedural protections afforded by state tenure
statutes or tenure policies of the teacher's employing institution.
The requirement is equally applicable to tenured public school
teachers at the elementary and secondary levels.[24]

Must tenure be formal in order to confer a property interest?

No. In *Sindermann* the Supreme Court ruled that proof by
a junior-college professor that his employer had a *"de facto"*
tenure program, based on an unwritten "common law" in the
institution under which he was entitled to continued employment absent "sufficient cause," would obligate the college to
afford him a hearing on the non-renewal of his contract.[25]

In a Tennessee case a university "objectively acted toward"
a professor "in such a manner as to reasonably lead him to
believe that he was a person with a relative degree of permanency in the academic community" of the university. The
university's acts included permitting him to participate in a
university retirement program restricted to "permanent type
personnel," allowing him to vote on tenure for other teachers,

and representing that he would be treated like any other tenured professor. On these facts the Sixth Circuit ruled that he had acquired a property interest in continued employment entitling him to a due process hearing when the university proposed not to renew his contract.[26]

The Fifth Circuit has held that where a college's faculty handbook contained a section entitled "Tenure" stating that "[t]enure is expected to be stable," and where under established procedure, a teacher was placed on probation if her contract was not annually renewed, a discharged faculty member who had taught in the college for six years, had been department chairman for five, and was the senior member of the Psychology Department had a "property interest entitling her to invoke due process protection."[27]

If a tenured teacher is also a coach, does his property interest as a tenured teacher give him due process rights in connection with an attempt to strip him of his coaching position?

No. In an illustrative Ohio case the plaintiff, who had been a teacher and football coach in the school system for 20 years, had tenure as a teacher, but his status as a coach under state law was probationary. The Sixth Circuit ruled that he was not entitled to procedural due process in connection with the non-renewal of his coaching contract even though he had tenure as a teacher.[28]

Does a non-tenured teacher who has a written contract for a specified term have a property interest in continued employment during that term?

Generally, yes. The Supreme Court has recognized that an untenured teacher dismissed during the unexpired term of an express contract has a property interest in continued employment safeguarded by due process.[29]

Where the contract gives the employer unfettered discretion to terminate the teacher's employment, however, the contract probably confers no property interest on the employee. In *Bishop v. Wood* the Supreme Court stated that a holding that a public employee holds his position at the will of his employer establishes that he has no property interest.[30] Previously the Ninth Circuit found "a great deal of merit" in a university's contention that the contractual appointment of a department head "should be read as merely delimiting the term during which . . . [he] was to serve at sufferance . . . and that, as the position was terminable at will, he had no protected interest in it."[31]

Can a teacher have de facto tenure in a school district or educational institution covered by a formal tenure system?

The decisions conflict on this issue. In *Perry v. Sindermann* the Supreme Court stated that the possibility of an unwritten "common law" that certain employees shall have the equivalent of tenure was "particularly likely in a college or university . . . that has no explicit tenure system even for senior members of its faculty."[33] It did not say, as it might have said, that such a "common law" could never exist in an institution with a formal tenure system. The Sixth Circuit ruled, therefore, that a professor at the University of Tennessee had acquired a reasonable expectation that his employment would continue on a permanent basis with the Department of Mathematics— and therefore a property interest in continued employment— even though the university had a well-established tenure system and the professor had not been granted formal tenure status.[34] The Seventh Circuit has thus far declined the opportunity to "say that there could never be a case in which a university had a *de facto* tenure policy on which faculty could justifiably rely which was inconsistent with a codified tenure plan."[35]

The law in the Fourth Circuit also "appears to be that the existence of explicit contractual provisions governing tenure does not necessarily negate the existence of a legitimate extracontractual expectation of continued employment."[36] Thus a Maryland federal district court refused to dismiss the complaint of two former University of Maryland professors who alleged that they had a legitimate claim of entitlement to job tenure stemming from practices and understandings at the university even though their contracts purported to set forth the exclusive means of achieving tenure, and accordingly that they were denied procedural due process when their employment was terminated without a hearing.[37] In an opinion also refusing to grant summary judgment for the defendants the court noted, among other things, that the plaintiffs had made or altered personal and professional commitments or priorities in reliance on the understanding that they had tenured status.[38]

The First Circuit, on the other hand, has concluded that "the existence of a highly structured system of de jure [formal] tenure argue[s] against a parallel system of de facto tenure."[39] The Fifth Circuit has held that because the University of Florida had an "explicit written tenure program," a professor who had not been granted tenure had "failed to prove that he had a reasonable expectancy of continued employment."[40] In the Ninth Circuit, "the existence of a formal code governing the granting of tenure precludes a reasonable expectation of continued employment absent extraordinary circumstances,"[41] and that the court has refused to recognize a *"de facto"* tenure claim where the educational institution had a written tenure system of which the plaintiff was aware.[42] A federal judge in Arizona found such "extraordinary circumstances" in a case involving a well-known author who was given a two-year contract which provided him with certain tuition benefits for his children, coupled with a promise of "automatic tenure" upon the expiration of that contract.[43] But a Delaware federal district court ruled that where there were detailed statutory tenure regulations under which renewal of a teacher's contract for the 1973–74 school year would have conferred tenure, the teacher "could not have had an objective expectation of employment beyond the 1972–73 school year absent some unambiguous assurance of school authorities to that effect."[44]

Does a statute, contract, rule, or policy which furnishes assurance against arbitrary employment actions create a property interest?

Arguably. In one case a Virginia federal district court held that procedural guarantees for law enforcement officers set out in the Virginia Code, calling for extensive procedural safeguards including an adversary, trial-type hearing, were "designed . . . to minimize arbitrary governmental decision-making" and accordingly gave Virginia policemen a legitimate claim of entitlement to continued employment, "at least to the extent that it furnished insurance against arbitrary employment actions."[45]

Can a property interest be conferred by a provision in a faculty handbook?

Yes. The Fourth Circuit, for example, ruled that a faculty handbook provision stating that after temporary or probationary status for three years a teacher would be "employed on a continuing contract basis" and that "cases of dismissal are rare and result from *incompetence* or from *immoral* or disreputable conduct" conferred a legitimate claim of entitlement to continued employment, and therefore a property interest, upon a teacher employed under the policy for five years.[46]

Even where a faculty handbook provision is ambiguous, the provision, coupled with the manner in which school authorities have interpreted it in actual practice, may support a teacher's argument that he has a legitimate claim of entitlement to continued employment. In a Delaware case, for example, a college handbook provided that professional unclassified employees, of whom plaintiff was one, could be terminated only "for cause" if they had served more than 90 days. The defendants argued that the word "termination" referred to dismissals during a contract term and not to non-renewals. A federal court concluded that this argument conflicted with the college president's testimony that such employees could "expect to have their contracts renewed from year to year 'unless there is cause.' The Court concludes that plaintiff has made more than a *prima facie* showing that in light of the policies and practices of the College, she had a legitimate claim of entitlement to continued employment . . . and therefore was deprived of a constitutionally protected property interest."[47]

Can a property interest be conferred by a collective bargaining agreement?

Yes. As the Supreme Court recognized in *Roth*, "understandings that secure certain benefits and that support claims of entitlement to those benefits" can furnish the source of a property interest.[48] An unexpired collective bargaining agreement can constitute such an "understanding."[49] Thus, for example, where a collective bargaining agreement to which a state university was a party provided that suspension of a non-tenured faculty member could only be for "cause," a Michigan federal district court ruled that the agreement created "a contractually based claim of entitlement under Michigan law" and therefore a property interest sufficient to invoke the procedural protections of the due process clause.[50]

Where a collective bargaining agreement had expired, however, and subsisted only by virtue of a day-to-day informal understanding which had terminated in response to a strike, "itself a substantial breach of the understanding," the Sixth Circuit ruled that teachers discharged for striking did not have a property interest entitling them to procedural due process in connection with their discharges.[51]

Does a "continuing contract" statute which provides for automatic renewal of a teacher's contract in the absence of affirmative action by the board to terminate his employment confer a property interest in continued employment?

No. For example, in a series of decisions the Eighth Circuit has held that no such property interest is created by statutes of this type, which do not limit the causes for which a teacher may be terminated.[52]

Does a statute, rule, policy, individual contract, or collective agreement requiring that a teacher receive a hearing or other procedural rights in connection with the termination of his employment confer a property interest in a continued employment?

Arguably it does not. That state law mandates certain procedures, the contention would run, does not in itself give those procedures a federal constitutional dimension. In short, a school system may argue that the mere existence of such a requirement does not confer the requisite "legitimate claim of entitlement" to continued employment. Holding that a collective bargaining contract requiring that probationary teachers be accorded a pre-termination hearing did not confer a property interest in continued employment, a New York federal district court stated: "A probationary teacher does not gain a 'legitimate claim of entitlement' . . . to a tenured position merely because the termination procedure becomes more complex and formal than it was previously. A probationary teacher who is by contract entitled to a hearing before termination is still a probationary teacher subject to termination, not a tenured teacher entitled to continuing employment."[53]

A school system may also contend that the same principle applies where school authorities voluntarily adopt a more formal or more complex termination procedure. Thus the Seventh Circuit approved a federal district court opinion concluding that "[t]he fact that defendants voluntarily afforded plaintiff a grievance hearing and internal appellate review is insufficient to allow plaintiff to invoke federal constitutional protections for defects in the hearing process."[54]

Nevertheless, there may be countervailing arguments available to a teacher in these situations. He may contend that procedural safeguards designed to minimize arbitrary termination decisions confer a property interest at least to the extent that they furnish protection against the arbitrary actions which those safeguards are designed to prevent,[55] and therefore entitle a teacher for whose benefit the safeguards exist to the procedural protections of the due process clause. Where the procedural safeguards are not followed, the teacher may argue that he has a broader property interest which not only protects him against arbitrary termination, but gives him a legitimate claim of entitlement to continued employment. Thus, there are decisions holding that policies which, if followed, would have served to protect a public employee's employment status confer a property interest in continued employment.[56]

One way of making such an argument in terms consistent with *Bishop v. Wood* is that in such circumstances state law gives him the right to continued employment.[57] In a pre-*Bishop* Hawaii case a counselor at a community college in the University of Hawaii system was denied tenure without compliance with evaluation procedures in effect at the college. A federal court concluded that he "had a legitimate expectation of future employment unless and until the administration of the University deprived him of that expectation in a manner consistent with the established procedures in effect . . . [at the] college. This expectation was sufficient to create a property interest protected by the Fourteenth Amendment."[58] Because he had not received the notice or hearing required by the due process clause, the court held that he had been denied his 14th Amendment rights.[59] Although the court's conclusion that the counselor had a legitimate expectation of continued employment was not expressly predicated on the existence of an enforceable right to continued employment under state law, the decision may be rationalized on that ground.

Where the same statute, rule, policy, or contract confers a legitimate claim of entitlement to continued employment

absent sufficient cause and specifies the procedures to govern termination in terms less comprehensive than due process requires, is the teacher's property interest limited so that his procedural rights are confined to those specified?

No. In *Arnett v. Kennedy*[60] the Supreme Court considered this question in a case involving the Lloyd-La Follette Act. A section of the Act (1) conferred upon non-probationary federal employees the right not to be discharged except "for such cause as will promote the efficiency of the service" and (2) prescribed the procedural means by which that right was to be protected. The plaintiff argued that this section created an expectancy of job retention requiring procedural protection under the due process clause of the Fifth Amendment beyond that afforded by the Act and related agency regulations. Justice Rehnquist, in an opinion for himself and two other Justices, believed that because the grant of the substantive right was "inextricably intertwined" with the limitations on the procedures to be employed in determining that right, the plaintiff "must take the bitter with the sweet"[61] and that therefore the federal employee was entitled only to the statutory procedures. Six Justices, however, disagreed with that position, concluding that while the legislature may elect not to create a property interest, once the legislature has conferred such an interest, the Constitution—not the statute—determines the scope of the employee's due process rights.[62]

Can custom be the source of a property interest?

Yes. In *Perry v. Sindermann*[63] the Supreme Court recognized that "[a] teacher . . . who has held his position for a number of years . . . might be able to show from the circumstances of his service—and from other relevant facts—that he has a legitimate claim of entitlement to job tenure. Just as this Court has found there to be a 'common law of a particular industry or of a particular plant' that may supplement a collective bargaining agreement . . . so there may be an unwritten 'common law' in a particular university that certain employees shall have the equivalent of tenure. . . . This is particularly likely in a college or university . . . that has no explicit tenure system even for senior members of its faculty, but that nonetheless may have created such a system in practice."[64]

Thus, the Fifth Circuit concluded that the "common law"

of a Texas school district gave a superintendent the equivalent of tenure in his administrative post for a two-year term. Although the court relied in part upon a written rule providing that after the first year the superintendent was to be elected for a term of "from two to five years," the court also cited, among other things, evidence that his predecessor and his successor were hired pursuant to this understanding.[65]

In a relevant case involving several police officers who had scored well on a promotional exam and had sued because they were passed up for promotions, a federal judge in Illinois wrote that "[w]ell-established patterns of practice and existing understandings are recognized as alternative sources of protected property interests. . . . Plaintiffs' allegations that the unwavering custom and state policy of the [Village] Board is to promote the highest ranking qualified person adequately assert the type of 'mutually explicit understanding' stemming from state law which has received protection and recognition under the due process clause."[66]

Can a school system's unwritten practices in dealing with a particular teacher confer a property interest?

Yes. The Sixth Circuit ruled that a professor at the University of Tennessee had a property interest in continued employment where the university "objectively acted toward" him "in such a manner as to reasonably lead him to believe that he was a person with a relative degree of permanency" in the university's academic community.[67] Among the factors upon which the court relied were assurances by the acting head of his department that he would be treated like any other tenured professor; the professor's inclusion in a retirement program ordinarily available only to permanent personnel; and his participation in voting on tenure for other teachers. On the basis of such factors, the court of appeals agreed with the trial court's conclusion that he "had a viable understanding that his employment would continue on a permanent basis," notwithstanding a letter he received from his department chairman stating that the professor's "position was one without tenure."[68]

In a number of cases, however, the faculty member involved had not been granted the perquisites of tenure or led to believe that he had been awarded a permanent position, and had been fully aware of his probationary status. In such circumstances de facto tenure claims were rejected.[69]

Can a teacher have a property interest where, solely because of an assurance contained in a policy, practice, or representation of school authorities, he reasonably believes that he may expect continued employment if his work is satisfactory, or that his employment will be terminated only for good cause?

Yes. The District of Columbia Circuit held that a non-investigative FBI employee had a property interest in continued employment by virtue of an FBI handbook explaining: "You may assume that your position is secure, if you continue to do satisfactory work." The court concluded that "[t]he Bureau could hardly have conveyed more precisely the understanding that . . . [he] did not hold his position at the whim of his superiors and that he would lose his position only for behavior which impairs his efficiency or that of the Bureau." Thus, said the court, he "could properly be dismissed only for failing to perform his duties satisfactorily and without prejudice to the FBI's achievement of its law-enforcement mission."[70]

Many courts, however, have rejected claims that a teacher acquires a property interest by a school official's assurance of continued employment[71] or tenure[72] if his work is satisfactory, or statement to the effect that a teacher can expect tenure if he satisfies certain standards of competence,[73] although the premise of such rulings is not always clear. Such an outcome is likely if the assurance or policy is ambiguous.[74] Or the court may feel that in light of the customs and practices in the academic community, there could not have been an intent by the employer to create a binding obligation, or an understanding by the teacher that one was being created. For example, the Seventh Circuit, accepting as true the plaintiff's allegation that he was informed he could eventually expect tenure if he met certain standards of professional competence, stated that "[t]his is of course true of most neophyte members of university faculties, including this very institution,"[75] and ruled that no property interest was created. Similarly, the First Circuit rejected a professor's assertion that he had obtained a property interest after his department chairman had stated that "it is my intention to promote . . . [the professor] to a tenured position . . . when his book is published."[76]

The 11th Circuit found that a school employee had not been deprived of a protected property interest when a university board refused to give her a salary increase after the salary review committee had recommended her for one.[77] In a Delaware case a federal judge held that a teacher was not given a property entitlement by guidelines stating that in considering promotions "[p]rimary consideration shall be given to performance in current position."[78] The court wrote, "[W]hat plaintiff seeks . . . if carried to its logical conclusion, is the judicial supervision of the most delicate part of every state school's academic operation, a role federal courts have neither the competency nor resources to undertake."[79]

A court may also conclude that the school system or educational institution lacks power under state law to give the assurance or adopt the policy.[80] The Fifth Circuit ruled that no property interest was created by the policy of a Texas school district that teachers could expect to be rehired if they satisfactorily performed their jobs. Following the direction of the Supreme Court in *Bishop v. Wood,* the court looked to Texas law and concluded that such a policy did not confer a property interest under the law of that state, which the Texas courts had construed as forbidding an agreement, express or implied, "which would have resulted in a term that was not limited by three years [as required by state law] but by the failure of the teacher to render satisfactory service."[81] Similarly, where the teacher relies on an oral assurance, a court may conclude that no binding obligation was created, when state law requires that contracts of the type in question must be in writing.[82]

Finally, the school official making the assurance or adopting the policy may be acting outside the scope of his authority,[83] although there may be circumstances in which apparent authority may be sufficient.[84] Where the power to hire lay exclusively within the province of the board, an Alabama federal court held that a promise of continued employment by the principal "carries about the same weight as a promise by the weatherman that there is no chance of rain on Saturday."[85] The Ninth Circuit concluded that where written procedures provided that the university president made final decisions to grant tenure, no authority to make tenure decisions was vested in a department chairman, whose conversation with an associate professor did not, and could not reasonably have been expected to, establish a binding contract guaranteeing tenure.[86]

Is a property interest conferred merely because a statute authorizes termination of a teacher's employment if he engages in particular conduct?

No. The Sixth Circuit ruled that a provision in Michigan's Public Employment Relations Act authorizing discharge of public employees who strike did not create a property interest because the statute did not contain a promise that public employees would retain their jobs absent specified cause for discharge. Accordingly, the court ruled, the plaintiff teachers— discharged for allegedly participating in an illegal strike—had no "legitimate claim of entitlement to continued employment" and thus no property interest entitling them to due process protection.[87]

Can the suspension of a teacher deprive him of a property interest?

Yes. Where, for example, a statute, rule, policy, or agreement provides that a public employee may be suspended without pay only for cause, the employee has a protectable property interest and such a suspension—at least to the extent that it "finally" deprives him of pay during the suspension period[88]—cannot be effectuated without due process procedures.[89]

In *Goss v. Lopez*, a student suspension case, the Supreme Court stated: "The Court's view has been that as long as a property deprivation is not *de minimis*, its gravity is irrelevant to the question whether account must be taken of the Due Process Clause."[90] Relying upon *Goss*, the Seventh Circuit held that due process procedures were required in connection with a 29-day suspension of a fireman with a property interest in continued employment who allegedly had violated a hair regulation by wearing a goatee.[91] The court observed: "Not only are alleged transgressions justifying suspension [of public employees] more serious than school discipline problems, but the corresponding penalties are potentially more damaging, for reputations, careers, and substantial amounts of lost pay are at stake."[92] The court further observed: "Here, appellant lost some $1,400 in pay during the 29-day suspension. Such a financial blow can be disastrous to many civil servants."[93] Quoting from a concurring opinion by a Court of Claims judge in *Ricucci v. United States*,[94] the court said: "Few [government employees] earn more than enough to pay their living expenses from month to month, and when their salaries are cut off they may be in the same destitute circumstances as a welfare recipient whose aid has been discontinued."[95]

Does the suspension of a teacher deprive him of a property interest if he continues to be paid?

A substantial argument can be made to this effect. The contours of the property interest a teacher may have in continued employment, it may be contended, embrace more than the pecuniary benefits associated with his teaching position and include continued performance of the teaching function.[96]

A teacher who has a legitimate claim of entitlement to continued employment has more than a reasonable expectation of continued pay. Employment as a teacher provides something of value wholly apart from the salary. This may be so in the sense that teaching may involve significant nonmonetary rewards. But it also is so in the sense that it is no small thing for a teacher to be separated from his profession and as a result lose the opportunity both to demonstrate and sharpen career skills.

Thus, independently of the loss of pay, where a faculty member is deprived of the "opportunity to teach" and "separated from the mainstream of his occupation as a teacher," he is deprived of a property interest and entitled to the procedural protections of the due process clause.[97]

Can the transfer of a teacher to a different position deprive him of a property interest?

Only if, under state law, he has an enforceable right to continued employment in the position from which he is transferred.

Thus, where the Tennessee legislature, in enacting the Tennessee Teacher Tenure Act, "did not intend that a teacher or principal have an entitlement to the specific job to which he [was] assigned," the Sixth Circuit ruled that a tenured teacher was not deprived of a property interest when she was transferred from one high school to another with no reduction in compensation.[98] The same court had already ruled that because a principal in Tennessee had no right under state law to continued employment as a principal, but had tenure only as a teacher, his transfer to a teaching position, even though it resulted in lower pay, did not deprive him of a property interest.[99] Similarly, the Fourth Circuit held that a principal who was reassigned to teaching with a 25 percent cut in salary was not deprived of a property interest because Virginia law states that someone's contractual status as principal does not prohibit a school board from reassigning him to a teaching position.[100] In an Oklahoma case the Tenth Circuit found that a teacher was not deprived of a property interest when he was reassigned from teaching vocational agriculture to teaching regular subjects.[101]

In a Maryland case, however, a federal court held that a non-tenured teacher was deprived of a property interest by his mid-year transfer from the classroom to the department of curriculum. The court ruled that the teacher, who had been hired under a "formal contract," had a "clearly implied promise of continued employment" as a classroom teacher.[102] And in a Texas case a federal judge, construing state law, found that an administrator who had a one-year contract to serve as an assistant principal was denied his legitimate claim of entitlement to that position when he was reassigned to be a teacher and truancy officer.[103]

Can a teacher have a property interest in continued employment entitling him to procedural due process in connection with a proposed termination or layoff because of asserted financial exigency?

Yes. Several courts have held, for example, that the due process clause of the 14th Amendment entitles a tenured teacher to procedural due process in connection with a proposed termination of his employment based on alleged financial exigency.[104] Some courts have expressed the view that a layoff is less drastic than a discharge and may not require all the procedural safeguards necessary in connection with a discharge.[105] Nevertheless, a teacher may have a property interest in his continued active employment requiring procedural due process protection in the event of a layoff as well as a termination for alleged financial exigency.[106]

Thus a tenured teacher might be denied due process in connection with such a termination or layoff if he does not receive adequate notice[107] and an appropriate hearing. The scope of the hearing, as in all other cases, depends on the nature of his property interest.

Several courts have held that the hearing must afford the teacher the opportunity to show that the purported reasons for the termination or layoff are not the actual ones.[108] In addition, there is authority for the proposition that the hearing must encompass the issue of the existence of the claimed financial exigency. For example, the AAUP's 1940 Statement on Academic Freedom and Tenure, adopted by many institutions of higher education, states that a tenured professor's employment shall be terminated only for "adequate cause," except "under extraordinary circumstances because of financial exigencies . . . . Termination of a continuous appointment because of financial exigency should be demonstrably bona fide."[109] In an Idaho case a teacher who had *"de facto* tenure" was terminated because of alleged financial exigency. On the assumption that "tenure" at the college was understood to embody the "financial exigency" standard contained in the 1940 AAUP statement, the Ninth Circuit indicated that the teacher was entitled to a due process hearing embracing the issue of whether a financial exigency actually existed, and placed the burden of proof on the college at such a hearing.[110]

Where the teacher's property interest includes retention rights over another faculty member, or the right to be judged for retention in a reasonable or non-arbitrary manner, and it is contended that the right in question is being violated, the scope of the hearing must embrace this issue as well. For example, where a community college had adopted criteria for determining which faculty members would not be rehired in the event of a reduction in force, the Fifth Circuit held that a tenured faculty member, in connection with a contemplated non-renewal for this reason, was entitled to a hearing embracing the question whether the trustees "made their decision pursuant to their previously announced criteria."[111] And where a statute required that the contracts of non-tenured teachers should be canceled before those of tenured teachers, "there were factual determinations to be reviewed at a hearing including whether [the plaintiff, a tenured teacher] was qualified to fill positions held by nontenured teachers and whether teachers could have been assigned different courses so as to allow [his] retention. Regarding such issues, due process requires that [the plaintiff] not be forced to submit to *ex parte* determinations affecting his continued enjoyment of a constitutionally protected property right."[112]

Even where no explicit criteria have been adopted governing the selection of faculty members to be terminated or laid off in the event of a reduction in force, the nature of the property interest may imply a right to a reasonable selection method. For example, where a college's policy required that the termination of a tenured faculty member's employment because of financial exigency be attributable to "extraordinary circumstances" and be "demonstrably bona fide," the Ninth Circuit ruled that a tenured teacher terminated for financial exigency was entitled to a hearing at which the college had to prove, among other things, that "a uniform set of procedures for all the faculty" governing the selection of faculty for termination had been "adopted and used."[113] On the other hand, the property interest involved may be more limited in nature, so as not to place the burden on the school authorities but nevertheless be sufficient to entitle the faculty member to show at a hearing that the selection method was arbitrary or unreasonable.[114]

Although the issue of whether a financial exigency sufficient to warrant the termination of a tenured teacher's employment actually exists may fall within the scope of the required hearing, a court nevertheless may be unwilling to permit inquiry into the wisdom of decisions by the school authorities on the programs or areas in which cuts must be made. Thus a Wisconsin federal district court, in a decision affirmed by the Seventh Circuit, concluded that tenured faculty members who under state law could be terminated or laid off only "for cause," and whose pay and teaching functions were involuntarily stopped in order to achieve faculty reductions on the ground of reduced enrollments and fiscal exigency, did not have a due process right to be heard on "whether any reduction in appropriations for the university system was in order; if so, at what campuses and in what amounts; if so, within a particular campus, whether in the credit-producing, academic areas or in the non-credit-producing, non-academic areas."[115] The court stated:

It is reasonable to suppose that, apart from their individual economic stakes, tenured faculty members of the university system might have a livelier interest in these matters, and that they might be better informed than those persons wholly outside the university system. But I am not persuaded that the Fourteenth Amendment should be construed to compel that opportunity be provided tenured faculty members for the expression of their opinions at these levels and times in the decision-making process but not to compel that the same opportunity be provided for the expression of the opinions of students or prospective students, for example, or the opinions of those who would accord a higher claim on limited public funds to an improved correctional program or to a program for the conservation of natural resources, or the opinions of taxpayers generally.[116]

Can a teacher have a property interest in a promotion?

As a general matter, a government employee has no property interest in promotion and therefore is not constitutionally entitled to a hearing in connection with a non-promotion decision.[117] Where, for example, in denying a promotion to a tenured associate professor a university violated "no tacit agreements or quasi contracts or mutual understandings," a federal court ruled that he was not deprived of a property interest.[118] The courts have recognized, however, that there may be situations in which such a property interest would exist, as where "a promotion would be virtually a matter of right—for example, where it was solely a function of seniority or tied to other objective criteria . . ."[119] or where there is a "common law" of promotion sufficient to create a de facto "right" to promotion.[120]

The Seventh Circuit has ruled that an Illinois statute which provided that promotions to principalships shall be made "for merit only" did not confer a property interest in promotion upon a teacher who possessed a principal's certificate and was otherwise eligible for promotion to a position as principal, since the statute did not create an entitlement to a principalship under state law. The court stated that there was "no indication that the Board of Education was merely a "formalistic 'rubber stamp' in the promotion process." The statute, said the court, "states that promotions shall be made by the Board and by no other. That they are only to be made for merit and not for patronage reasons surely does not prevent the Board from exercising its judgment against a given applicant."[121]

The District of Columbia Circuit, however, has indicated that a protected property interest in promotion might exist where a statute required promotions in the foreign service to be made on the basis of an evaluation of performance and relative merit conducted by boards whose findings were to form the basis for the Secretary of State's recommendations, and where continued non-promotion resulted in termination of employment.[122]

Can a teacher have a property interest in an annual salary increment?

Yes. The First Circuit, for example, held that teachers in a Massachusetts school system had a property interest in the annual salary increment because, by contract, it could not be denied unless the teacher's performance was determined to be "unsatisfactory."[123] Accordingly, the court ruled, the increment could not be taken away without due process of law.[124]

Can a teacher have a property interest in the acquisition of tenured status?

Arguably. In one case a federal court held that the plaintiff, a former college teacher who had been denied tenure, "should be given an opportunity to prove that under state law . . . he had a property interest in the expectation of tenure."[125]

The West Virginia Supreme Court has held that by meeting the objective eligibility criteria for tenure, an assistant professor at a state college obtained a sufficient entitlement so that she had a due process right under the state constitution to notice of the reasons why tenure was not extended and the right to show at a hearing before an unbiased tribunal that the reasons were "wholly inadequate or without a factual basis."[126] The decision was influenced by the court's perception of what the due process clause of the 14th Amendment requires. It is not clear, however, whether the West Virginia decision is compatible with the property interest analysis in *Roth* or with *Bishop v. Wood*. In any event, the issue has not been directly confronted by the U.S. Supreme Court.

It may be argued, however, that where standards have been adopted which purportedly govern a discretionary tenure decision, e.g., the typical higher-education standard that an applicant for tenure will be judged on the basis of his teaching, research work, and community service, the tenure candidate has a sufficient property interest to invoke procedural due process requirements with respect to the question whether the adopted criteria were the criteria actually applied. At least one federal court has so ruled.[127] Of course, a university or other educational institution may be obligated to adhere to its tenure criteria as a matter of state law or pursuant to the terms of a collective bargaining agreement.

Can a tenured teacher have a property interest in continued tenured status?

Yes. A property interest in continued tenured status would exist where, for example, a college policy permitted the college to strip a teacher of tenure, but only on specified grounds.

When does the termination of a teacher's employment deprive him of "liberty"?

In *Roth* the Supreme Court concluded that the non-renewal of a teacher's contract would deprive him of "liberty" if (1) it was based on a charge "that might seriously damage his standing and associations in his community" or (2) the state, in declining to re-employ him, imposed on him "a stigma or other disability that foreclosed his freedom to take advantage of other employment opportunities."[128]

What types of charges "might seriously damage" a teacher's "standing and associations in his community" within the meaning of Roth?

Any charge implicating his good name, reputation, honor or integrity.[129] Perhaps the clearest examples, specifically cited as illustrations in *Roth*, are charges of dishonesty or immorality.[130] Charges smacking of deliberate fraud[131] or lack of veracity[132] would qualify. One court found a deprivation of a liberty interest where a community college guidance counselor, who also had been acting as registrar, was denied tenure under charges circulated on all campuses of the university system, asserting that he had been seriously delinquent and had deliberately suspended university rules, with a resultant heavy financial loss to his employer, and containing the implication that the charges might be serious enough to warrant legal action.[133] Public statements implying untrustworthiness, e.g., statements accompanying the termination or suspension of a faculty member declaring university facilities off limits to him, may also satisfy the *Roth* test.[134]

Similarly, the test would be met by charges of sexual harassment[135] or public accusations or innuendoes of sexual misconduct with students[136] or others.[137] And a ground which may be perceived in the community as one involving moral turpitude, e.g., homosexual conduct or status, arguably qualifies even where the school authorities do not rationalize their decision in moral terms—for example, in the case of a homosexuality charge, justifying their action on the ground that students would be confused about their gender identity or their appropriate sex roles.[138]

Because "in the view of the community" the stain of exclusion from public employment on disloyalty grounds is deep, and indeed "has become a badge of infamy,"[139] termination of a teacher's employment on such a ground would satisfy the requirement. Discharge because of "poor attitude" or inability to get along is not usually found to satisfy the requirement.[140] But termination based on a public charge of intoxication—a degrading label—would impose the requisite mark of opprobrium.[141] The Fifth Circuit ruled that public statements by two school board members that a teacher's contract was not renewed because he had a "drinking problem" might seriously damage his standing and associations in his community whether or not the stigma "foreclosed his freedom to take advantage of other employment opportunities." The court concluded that this was "self-evident," but also cited evidence that the charge "was likely to blacken his name in the conservative and closely-knit community" in which he had taught.[142] A public charge of drug addiction also might sufficiently besmirch a teacher's reputation in his community to qualify under the test.

A teacher publicly charged with abusing his position also may be deprived of liberty under this standard.[143] Willful neglect of duty is one example of such a charge.[144] Use of the classroom as a soapbox for propaganda may be another. A teacher's personal reputation may also be seriously blemished, with a resulting deprivation of "liberty," where incident to his termination he is publicly branded as detrimental to the welfare of his educational institution[145] or as being a racist.[146]

On the other hand, some charges may be too innocuous to constitute a "badge of infamy." In the Fifth Circuit's view, for example, public knowledge that a teacher refused to shave his beard "clearly bore no such taint" and moreover would have no effect on his ability to earn a livelihood, and consequently his dismissal for that reason did not deprive him of a liberty interest.[147]

Can a termination be based on charges which "might seriously damage" the teacher's "standing and associations in his community" within the meaning of Roth where the charges are not made public?

No. In *Bishop v. Wood*[148] a former police officer contended that his discharge violated his due process rights. He contended that the reasons given for the discharge—failure to follow certain orders, poor attendance at police training classes, causing low morale, and conduct unsuited to an officer—were "so serious as to constitute a stigma that [might] severely damage his reputation in the community."[149] The reasons were communicated orally to the plaintiff in private and also were stated in writing in answer to interrogatories filed after he brought suit. The Supreme Court concluded:

> Since the former communication was not made public, it cannot properly form the basis for a claim that [plaintiff's] interest in his good name, reputation, honor, or integrity was thereby impaired. And since the latter communication was made in the course of a judicial proceeding which did not commence until after [plaintiff] had suffered the injury for which he seeks redress, it surely cannot provide retroactive support for his claim.

A contrary decision, the Court felt, "would penalize forthright and truthful communication between employer and employee in the former instance, and between litigants in the latter."[150] Another court has stated that "[a] contrary rule would destroy the ability of a governmental entity to investigate in any manner any derogatory reports concerning the employees."[151]

In order to constitute a deprivation of liberty under the

theory that the plaintiff's termination was based on charges which might damage his standing and associations in his community, the plaintiff must show that the charges became public or inevitably would have become so as a result of actions taken by the defendants; it is not enough if the charges became public due solely to the plaintiff's actions.[152] Nor are the charges deemed to have become public if they are discussed by board members at a closed meeting[153] or have been told to investigators.[154]

Must the charge which "might seriously damage the teacher's standing and associations in his community" be formal?

No. As the Second Circuit has noted:

A subtle campaign designed by city officials to make plaintiff the scapegoat for an episode of municipal misfeasance may impose no less an indelible stigma than a public proclamation announced at high noon from the steps of City Hall. Indeed, a carefully conceived scheme of suggestion and innuendo may be all the more devastating to individual liberty because it is more difficult to refute, especially when its architects sit in the highest offices of local government.[155]

What is required is "simply . . . dissemination of a false and defamatory impression, not a detailed bill of particulars."[156]

Must the charge which "might seriously damage" a teacher's "standing and associations in his community" cause the termination?

No. The Supreme Court has made it clear that it is enough that the defamatory charge occurred in the course of the termination of employment.[157]

What kind of proof is required to demonstrate that school authorities, in declining to rehire a teacher, "imposed on him a stigma or other disability that foreclosed his freedom to take advantage of other employment opportunities"?

In *Roth* the Supreme Court indicated that had the state, for example, invoked any regulations to bar the respondent from all other public employment in state universities, a deprivation of liberty would have occurred, presumably by imposing a "disability" that foreclosed his freedom to pursue his chosen profession. The Court indicated that where the state forecloses a "range" of opportunities for a particular type of professional employment, it deprives the victim of liberty.[158]

The Court in *Roth* stated that "[m]ere proof . . . that [the professor's] record of nonretention in one job, taken alone, might make him somewhat less attractive to some other employers would hardly establish the kind of foreclosure of opportunities amounting to deprivation of 'liberty.'" The Court left open the question whether proof that non-retention is likely to have a "substantial adverse effect" upon the career interests of a teacher "amounts to a limitation on future employment opportunities sufficient to invoke procedural due process guaranties," but made it clear that the likelihood of such an effect, even if it were sufficient to establish a deprivation of liberty, could not be assumed, but would have to be proved.[159]

Is a teacher who would be stigmatized by charges made by school authorities in connection with the proposed termination of his employment, but who does not dispute the charges, entitled to a due process hearing where he may attempt to explain his behavior or demonstrate that it does not warrant so drastic a sanction?

No. In *Codd v. Velger*[160] a former probationary city police officer contended that he was entitled to a hearing before his dismissal because of the stigmatizing effect of certain material placed by the police department in his personnel file—material which indicated that while still a trainee he had put a revolver to his head in an apparent suicide attempt. The Second Circuit held that the police officer was deprived of liberty because the city made personnel files available to prospective employers with the employee's consent, and the former employees had no practical alternative but to consent to the release of such information if they wished to be considered for further employment. The Supreme Court noted that the police officer had not affirmatively asserted in his pleadings or elsewhere that the report of the apparent suicide attempt was substantially false. Observing that the hearing that is required where a non-tenured public employee has been stigmatized in the course of a decision to terminate his employment is solely "to provide the person an opportunity to clear his name," the Court said: "If he does not challenge the substantial truth of the material in question, no hearing would afford a promise of achieving that result for him." Accordingly, the Court determined that the policeman had "made out no claim under the Fourteenth Amendment that he was harmed by the denial of a hearing," even assuming that he was otherwise stigmatized within the meaning of *Roth*.[161]

In an Eighth Circuit case an instructor at a police training academy was discharged for using offensive language and for unzipping his trousers in front of his students. The court found that no liberty interest was implicated because the fired instructor "freely admit[ted] that on at least one occasion he either unzipped or simulated unzipping his trousers in front of several students . . . and that he might have used obscene language." Thus, the court ruled that because he did "not challenge the substantial nature of the conduct that was the basis of his dismissal," there was no problem of false stigma and therefore no need for a hearing.[162] This case means that to contend that a stigma is unfair, teachers should challenge the substance of, rather than minor details about, the charges against them.

A Wisconsin federal district court has held, however, that a teacher makes a sufficient allegation of falsity by charging that the school authorities "acted without any reason, justification or basis in fact" in refusing to renew his contract.[163] Further, the Seventh Circuit has ruled that a teacher's "continuing attempt to secure a delayed *Roth* hearing can be viewed as an implied assertion that the charges are substantially false," and that in such case, assuming the defendants are not otherwise entitled to summary judgment, he "should be allowed to amend his complaint by including the indispensable 'falsity' allegation."[164] There may also be circumstances in which a teacher remains mute at a procedurally deficient disciplinary hearing and does not dispute the truth of the charges in his complaint because of possible self-incrimination problems stemming from the pendency of a criminal action based on the same events. It is at least arguable that in such a situation the teacher's right to a due process hearing should not be negated by his failure to plead falsity in his complaint.[165]

Do public statements accompanying termination which "might seriously damage a teacher's standing and associations in his community" also impose a "stigma or other disability foreclosing his freedom to take advantage of other employment opportunities" within the meaning of Roth?

Generally yes, although job foreclosure is not a prerequisite to a liberty interest deprivation if the teacher's termination is based on charges carrying the potential for serious damage to his reputation in the community. Since the statements are public ones, prospective employers are likely to learn about and be substantially influenced by them.

Thus where a former employee of a state commission was discharged without a hearing, and commissioners who granted interviews to reporters publicly attributed her discharge to the result of an investigation of financial scandal, the Fourth Circuit held that her ability to obtain other employment was impaired, and that she was therefore deprived of liberty without due process.[166] The Tenth Circuit ruled that a school superintendent publicly charged with willful neglect of duty and incompetence was deprived of liberty on both of the *Roth* "liberty" rationales.[167] And where school authorities publicly charged that an acting school principal failed to demonstrate leadership necessary to effectively deal with the educational program; was responsible for the rapid deterioration of the school; had not provided for the basic safety of children and staff; and had created a climate of confusion and discontent, the Second Circuit decided that his chances of obtaining a supervisory position in the public school system had been "drastically impaired," and that accordingly he had been deprived of liberty.[168]

Can a teacher be deprived of liberty where no school official makes a stigmatizing charge against him in connection with the termination of his employment but the circumstances indicate that the board acted on the basis of stigmatizing charges made by parents or students?

Yes. In an Oklahoma case a school board, in rescinding the renewal of a non-tenured teacher's contract and then declining to re-employ her, stated no charges or findings against her. Public board minutes, however, focused attention on student allegations that she had distributed allegedly pornographic books in the classroom and improperly changed grades, and affidavits held by the board charged her with misconduct with male students and drunkenness. The Tenth Circuit ruled that her "discharge against this immediate background raised a substantial question whether the board declining to reemploy had imposed a stigma or other disability which foreclosed . . . [her] freedom to take advantage of other employment opportunities."[169] The court noted the superintendent's testimony that the circumstances surrounding the discharge would make it more difficult for her to get a job.[170] The court also determined that a factual question was presented as to "whether the board's actions in effect created and disseminated an allegedly false impression about the plaintiff."[171] Accordingly, the court held that it was error for the trial court to direct a verdict against the teacher for the absence of proof that she had been deprived of a liberty interest.[172]

Are there reasons which would not necessarily bear the requisite potential to seriously damage a teacher's standing and associations in his community, but which nevertheless would stigmatize him so as to foreclose his freedom to take advantage of other employment opportunities?

Yes. For example, one court stated: "Although the matter is not entirely free from doubt, it may be that the general public has developed a sufficient understanding of mental illness so that a finding of mental disability does not necessarily injure a person's 'standing and associations in his community.' " Nevertheless, the court concluded that—

> A finding of mental illness severely diminishes a person's "freedom to take advantage of other employment opportunities." This is true not because employers are bigoted or narrow minded, but because they may have doubts as to whether a person found to be mentally ill will function adequately on the job. These doubts will probably be particularly great where the employment . . . involves extensive contacts with the public.[173]

Can school authorities, in terminating a teacher's employment, impose a "stigma . . . foreclosing his freedom to take advantage of other employment opportunities" within the meaning of Roth even though they have made no statement of charges to the general public?

Yes. For example, a Wisconsin federal district court ruled that where the charges upon which the board of education decided not to renew the plaintiff's teaching contract, and related documents, had been placed in his personnel file and disclosed to other school districts prior to litigation, the plaintiff was deprived of liberty under the stigma-foreclosure test even though the charges had not been made public before such dissemination.[174]

In order to satisfy the stigma-foreclosure test, must the stigmatizing reason actually be disclosed to a prospective employer?

As long as the potential for disclosure is sufficiently strong, actual disclosure probably is not a prerequisite. The Supreme Court has indicated that a student's liberty interest would be implicated where his suspension "*could* seriously . . . interfere with later opportunities for higher education and employment."[175] Thus the courts have held that the termination of a teacher's employment based on a stigmatizing reason may foreclose a teacher's freedom to take advantage of other employment opportunities within the meaning of *Roth*, and therefore deprive him of liberty, if the reason is incorporated into a file that is available to prospective employers.[176] For example, "foreclosure" within the meaning of this branch of the *Roth* liberty interest test occurred where a teacher was refused re-employment on the ground that he was a racist and the charges were placed in a file to which prospective employers were likely to have access.[177] On the other hand, if by statute or school system rule the file is confidential, incorporation of the stigmatizing reason in the file will not foreclose other employment opportunities within the meaning of the rule.[178] The Fifth Circuit has ruled, however, that the district court erred in finding that a teacher was not deprived of liberty when a letter of reprimand containing false information was placed in the teacher's file where there was "not one shred of evidence in the record showing that the letter of reprimand will be *'merely present'* and kept 'confidential.'"[179] Another court has held that the act of an employer in making available a discharged employee's personnel file with the employee's consent sufficed to place responsibility for the stigma on the employer, since the former employee would have no practical alternative but to consent to the release of such information if he wished to be seriously considered for other employment.[180]

Is the stigma-foreclosure test satisfied where a school district refuses to renew a teacher's contract for a reason which, though not stated in the non-renewal notice or incorporated into a file, would be stigmatizing if known and the proof shows that under prevailing practice the district would be contacted before he was hired by another district and would divulge the reasons for his non-renewal?

A Delaware federal district court appears to have said yes to this question, stating:

> It is, of course, true that the Board members did not directly accuse [the teacher] of persistent insubordination by so stating in her notice of termination or in a filed report. Under the practice which prevailed in the school district and other Delaware school districts, however, a district which had not renewed a teacher would be contacted before the teacher was hired by another district and the reason for the termination would be discussed. Members of the . . . Board testified at trial that they would expect that districts making inquiries of this kind would be told the reasons for termination. In this case, we know that this expectation was justified: [The superintendent], in fact, told a prospective employer of [the teacher's] insubordination. Accordingly, when the . . . School Board acted, it must have appreciated the potential for injury to [her] career. That potential was made no less real or substantial by the fact that the reasons for termination would be disseminated orally in the natural course of events rather than in writing.[181]

Under the stigma-foreclosure test, what kind of proof is necessary to demonstrate the requisite potential for serious impairment of a teacher's ability to pursue his profession?

Testimony from persons knowledgeable about employment practices in the state and surrounding jurisdictions may demonstrate this potential, and school officials in the district where the termination occurs may even feel compelled to concede the point.[182] For example, a Delaware federal district court concluded that the non-renewal of the plaintiff's teaching contract for "persistent failure to obey administrative directives held the potential for severely impairing her ability to pursue her profession." The court explained:

> This was apparent from the testimony of the Board members, [her principal] and a professional in the teacher placement field having experience with employment practices in Delaware and the surrounding states. This testimony satisfied the Court that the vast majority of school hiring officers, upon learning of a non-renewal for a reason of this kind, would not initiate an investigation of the matter and would give no further consideration to the application. In light of this fact, [the teacher's] discharge cannot be dismissed as merely a factor which 'might make . . . [her] somewhat less attractive to some other employers.' See *Board of Regents v. Roth, supra* . . . .[183]

Testimony from the plaintiff or the superintendent of the terminating district may show that the superintendent sought to persuade the plaintiff that it would be in her interest to resign, and that in seeking other employment resignation would be more advantageous than the contemplated dismissal or non-renewal. At least one superintendent testified that he had told the plaintiff teacher "that in the case of resignation other superintendents would probably not ask more questions about the circumstances, while they would ask why a nonrenewal occurred; and that it would be more difficult for her to get a job in view of circumstances and reasons in the background."[184] The Tenth Circuit found this testimony "significant" in connection with the plaintiff's liberty interest claim.[185]

What types of reasons for terminating a teacher's employment have been recognized by the courts as having the potential to stigmatize him in the eyes of a prospective employer?

Insubordination is one such reason. In addition to the Delaware decision discussed in the answer to the previous question, an earlier unreported ruling by the same court, referred to in the later decision, found a due process violation where the evidence showed that a school administrator's non-renewal for "insubordination and failing to fulfill administrative directives" would "substantially impair her ability to obtain subsequent employment in teaching and educational administration."[186] A court in the Virgin Islands has also held that liberty was implicated by the discharge of a public employee for insubordination and continued failure to comply with regulations—charges placed in his permanent record.[187]

The Third Circuit has held that, depending on the facts, a charge that a public employee was intoxicated on the job could be stigmatizing in the sense of foreclosing subsequent employment opportunities.[188] A Michigan federal district court ruled that the plaintiff faculty member was stigmatized, and his liberty implicated because the stigma foreclosed subsequent employment opportunities by his supension without pay because of alleged sexual improprieties with students.[189] And a Hawaii federal district court ruled that where charges of serious delinquency and deliberate suspension of university rules were circulated throughout the state's academic community by the university's highest executive officer in connection with the denial of tenure, with the implication that they might be serious enough to warrant legal action, the assertion by the defense that his termination "would not preclude . . . [him] from seeking employment elsewhere in the University system . . . [was] unrealistic."[190]

Does a termination for inadequate performance deprive a teacher of liberty under the stigma-foreclosure test?

Many courts have concluded that it does not.[191] To the extent that these decisions encompass terminations for performance deficiencies which imply an *inability* to perform competently, however, they conflict with the views expressed by other courts. For example, in rejecting the claim that a university's denial of tenure based on lack of scholarly publication deprived her of liberty, the First Circuit would say only that "[d]ue process does not protect an individual from essentially neutral evaluations *that do not cast aspersions on her ability to perform her duties competently.*"[192] The Second Circuit has said: "[W]e believe the [Supreme] Court was thinking of something considerably graver than a charge of failure to perform a particular job, *lying within the employee's power to correct* . . . ."[193] And the Eighth Circuit ruled that a medical school's action in dismissing a student for "[l]ack of intellectual ability," as "distinguished from his performance, . . . imposed on him a stigma or other disability that [foreclosed] his freedom to take advantage of other . . . opportunities."[194]

It can be argued, of course, that a label of inadequate performance imposes a "stigma or disability" upon a teacher whether or not the inadequacy is a function of lack of ability, and that a prospective employer apprised of the alleged inadequacy is not likely to be enthusiastic about offering him the opportunity to replicate his performance. The question is primarily an issue of fact, upon which the nature of the evidence should control. A strong argument can be made that termination deprives a teacher of liberty under the stigma-foreclosure test where, for example, the facts show that (1) the teacher's personnel file contains unexplained charges of unsatisfactory performance which would have a substantial impact upon his employment opportunities; (2) he is highly specialized and it would be unrealistic to believe that a school system would give serious consideration to employing him without a full disclosure of his past record; and (3) his refusal to consent to the release of information "would only raise the spectre of much more serious misconduct than that contained in the personnel file," giving him no real choice but to consent to the release of his file.[195]

Does the termination of a teacher's employment for engaging in an illegal strike deprive him of liberty under either of the Roth "liberty" tests?

In *Lake Michigan College Federation of Teachers v. Lake Michigan Community College,*[196] a federal district court held that protected interests in liberty were infringed under both of the *Roth* "liberty" tests when plaintiffs were discharged for violating a state statute prohibiting strikes. The court explained:

> The teachers are accused of breaking state law, and Lake Michigan College has already imposed the maximum penalty allowed by law, forfeiture of their jobs. In a society which values law and order, a finding by a state agency that a person has broken the law is *per se* an infringement of the person's interests in his good name, reputation, honor or integrity, and is in itself a stigma

which strongly tends to foreclose his freedom to take advantage of other employment opportunities, at least where the finding is widely publicized and is coupled with the imposition of a severe statutorily authorized penalty.[197]

On appeal, however, the Sixth Circuit held that the district court had "erred in announcing a sweeping rule to the effect that whenever a person is accused of breaking a law, his fourteenth amendment liberty interests are implicated automatically." The court said: "[W]e fail to see how [the allegation that the teachers had violated the no-strike law] discredited their honesty, morality, and integrity or damaged their standing in the community." The court declared:

The . . . [Public Employment Relations Act] provides no criminal penalties for illegal strikes. Furthermore, through their pickets and placards the teachers openly announced the fact that they were on strike. Apparently they did not believe that their conduct was dishonest or immoral or that it would seriously damage their reputation in the community. At trial three of the teachers testified that there was no hostile community reaction to their participation in the strike. Similarly, we see nothing in this record to indicate that by discharging the striking faculty, the College foreclosed other employment opportunities that were available to them. The College favorably recommended several of the discharged teachers to prospective employers and generally assisted the teachers in their search for employment elsewhere. Many of the faculty members did succeed in obtaining other jobs, some of which were teaching positions.[198]

On the other hand, the Wisconsin Supreme Court has stated that a charge that a teacher had breached his contract and engaged in a strike "could detrimentally affect" his "reputation in the labor market and thereby significantly undermine his opportunities for re-employment."[199] Thus where a teacher is charged with striking illegally and disputes the charge, a liberty interest may well be implicated, especially where the teacher can prove that his opportunities for future employment might be seriously impaired. And where there is a hostile community reaction to the strike, he may be able to show that his "standing and associations in his community" might also be seriously damaged by the charge.

Must a teacher remain permanently unemployed in order to satisfy the stigma-foreclosure test?

At least one court has held to the contrary. Acknowledging that the plaintiff, a former college teacher, was "admittedly employed by another university," the court stated: "While his reemployment might be evidence that the defendants' actions have not 'imposed a stigma . . . that [has] foreclosed his freedom to take advantage of other employment opportunities,' as required by *Roth*, we do not believe that a discharged employee must remain permanently unemployed in order to prove a deprivation of a liberty interest."[200]

Are the courts more likely to find the requisite stigma where the teacher is dismissed during the school year rather than not renewed at the end of the school year?

Yes. It has been recognized that "dismissing a teacher abruptly during the year rather than simply failing to renew her contract leaves a stigma that clouds her professional status and limits her future opportunities."[201]

An Arkansas federal district court, concluding that a teacher's mid-year dismissal violated due process, determined that in addition to depriving her of a property interest the dismissal deprived her of a liberty interest, noting that "[a]n employment history of plaintiff, showing that her contract and teaching duties were terminated prior to the end of the school year, even without communication of the derogatory reasons therefor, might clearly be expected to have an adverse effect upon her future employment opportunities, and would carry a professional stigma."[202]

Is a teacher deprived of "liberty" where school authorities make a charge against him which might seriously damage his reputation in his community, or place stigmatizing material in his file, but his employment is not terminated and his employment status is not otherwise changed?

No. In *Paul v. Davis*,[203] the Supreme Court held that reputation alone does not implicate a liberty interest sufficient to invoke the procedural protection of the due process clause. Thus the Court determined that actions of police chiefs in distributing to merchants a flier captioned "Active Shoplifters" and containing the plaintiff's name and photograph did not deprive him of liberty so as to entitle him to a due process hearing.[204] The Court seemed to acknowledge that due process protections come into play where, as a result of the state action complained of, "a right or status previously recognized by state law" is "distinctly altered or extinguished."[205] And the Court also reaffirmed the conclusion in *Roth* that a liberty interest is impaired where the government stigmatizes an employee "in the course of the termination of employment" —even though continued employment is not guaranteed by state law.[206] The Court, however, stated that there was "no suggestion in *Roth* to indicate that a hearing would be required each time the State in its capacity as employer might be considered responsible for a statement defaming an employee who continues to be an employee."[207]

Every court to face the issue appears to have held that suspension without pay on the basis of stigmatizing charges satisfies the "plus" requirement of *Paul's* "stigma-plus" test.[208] But the courts have been less sympathetic to the claim that a liberty interest is implicated by a suspension *with* pay for stigmatizing reasons.[209]

The Fifth Circuit has concluded that "[t]he internal transfer of an employee, unless it constitutes such a change in status as to be regarded essentially as a loss of employment, does not provide the additional loss of a tangible interest necessary to give rise to a liberty interest meriting protection under the due process clause of the fourteenth amendment."[210] Thus a principal's transfer to a teaching position (in circumstances in which he had no property interest in the principalship) was held not to deprive him of liberty even though he was transferred for stigmatizing reasons.[211] The Fifth Circuit has suggested, however, that the result might be different if the position to which the employee is transferred is one which does not entail "significant and important" activities, e.g., where a policeman is transferred from a post as corporal to a position as janitor.[212]

Is a teacher deprived of his "liberty" where after he has been terminated school authorities make public a charge

against him which might seriously damage his reputation in his community?

Most courts have answered no, but the answer apparently depends on how proximate the defamatory statement is to the actual termination. While *Paul v. Davis* requires the stigmatizing statement be tied to loss of employment or other injury, *Paul* fails to explain where the connection between the two stops. Thus the Fifth Circuit found that a school board had deprived a teacher of her liberty when at a meeting a month after she was terminated, the board made public that she had been terminated because of an alleged drinking problem.[213] However, the Second Circuit found that a teacher who was discharged for falsifying evaluation reports was not deprived of her liberty when school officials reported to state authorities about her malfeasance after her termination. Citing *Paul v. Davis*, the court concluded that the stigmatizing statement was made "in the absence of an employment relationship" and thus there was no stigma-plus.[214] A district court in Maryland reached the same conclusion in a case in which a police chief was forced to resign because of his alleged ties to organized crime and in which a town official made a stigmatizing statement to a radio station four months after his termination.[215] The court wrote that "the allegations directed against [the police chief] may very well damage his reputation and affect his ability to obtain future employment. . . . There comes a point in time when post termination publication of defamation becomes sufficiently remote from the termination itself so as to make it no longer within 'the course of termination of employment.' "[216] Thus it appears that the best a discharged person can do is argue that the stigmatizing statement was very close in time to his termination or other injury.

What rights does a teacher who is entitled to procedural due process in connection with the termination of his employment possess?

"Once it is determined that due process applies, the question remains what process is due."[217] The Supreme Court has cautioned that "[t]he very nature of due process negates any concept of inflexible procedures universally applicable to every imaginable situation."[218] Thus, the content of due process "varies according to specific factual contexts."[219] In *Mathews v. Eldridge*[220] the Supreme Court announced guidelines for deciding "what process is due" once it is determined that due process applies:

> [O]ur prior decisions indicate that identification of the specific dictates of due process generally requires consideration of three distinct factors: First, the private interest that will be affected by the official action; second, the risk of an erroneous deprivation of such interest through the procedures used, and the probable value, if any, of additional or substitute procedural safeguards; and finally, the Government's interest, including the function involved and the fiscal and administrative burdens that the additional or substitute procedural requirement would entail.[221]

Among the procedural protections which the *Mathews* test may require in a particular teacher termination case are notice; adequate time to prepare a defense; the right to present evidence and confront and cross-examine accusers; disclosure of documents relied on; counsel; having the decision based on the record; statement of grounds for decision and evidence relied on; transcript; pre-deprivation hearing; impartial decision maker; and voir dire of tribunal members.

Notice

"The fundamental requisite of due process of law is the opportunity to be heard."[222] A corollary of this right is the right to "notice reasonably calculated, under all the circumstances, to apprise interested parties of the pendency of the action and afford them an opportunity to present their objections."[223] Reasonable notice of the substance of the charges to be considered is required.[224] Thus on the assumption that a teacher had been deprived of a liberty interest, the Tenth Circuit ruled that where hearings were held on a "wide array of complaints" from persons in the community, and the school board did not make charges or identify any causes for removal which it considered, the board hearings did not satisfy due process requirements even though the teacher had "some notions of the rumors and protests against" her before the hearings.[225] The Supreme Court has stated in another context, moreover, that the appellant's " 'knowledge' of the charge . . . does not excuse the lack of adequate notice."[226]

"Reasonable" notice of the substance of the charges means clear notice.[227] The Tenth Circuit held that a school board did not comply with due process notice requirements when it dismissed a superintendent, who possessed both property and liberty interests, on charges of "incompetency" and "willful neglect of duty." The court stated: "[W]e cannot agree that this, without more, shows meaningful notice of what one must be prepared to meet."[228] A Kentucky court concluded, apparently on state grounds, that a charge of "incompetency," without "specific details by way of names, dates and places upon which such an allegation is based," "did not permit [the teacher] to prepare an adequate defense and, therefore, denied him due process of law."[229]

The Ninth Circuit has ruled that letters informing a college instructor with de facto tenure only that "she had been non-retained because the Board had said two people must go and she was one of them" were inadequate to comply with due process requirements, since the letters "nowhere refer[red] to the Board's later position that the school had exigent financial difficulties" and the court could "perceive no sound reason for the College's failure to disclose its financial situation in writing as the basis for the proposed termination prior to the . . . hearing."[230] The Ninth Circuit ruling indicates that in the context of the termination of a teacher's employment, where due process requirements are applicable, written notice generally is required.[231] A written notice containing illegible charges, moreover, does not meet due process requirements.[232] While there are cases in the teacher termination context in which oral notice of the reason for termination has been held adequate, in each case the court relied upon the fact that the teacher had not requested a written specification of the charges against her.[233]

In a pre-*Roth* decision, the Fifth Circuit held that where due process applies, a teacher is entitled to be advised not only of "the cause or causes for his termination in sufficient detail to fairly enable him to show any error that may exist," but also of "the names and the nature of the testimony of witnesses against him."[234] The Eighth Circuit, in a post-*Roth* ruling, has required notice of both the names of those who have made allegations against the teacher and the specific nature of and factual basis for the charges.[235] Where, however, the evidence indicated that the public employee was aware of the individuals who would testify or reasonably could have expected that they would be called, the Fifth Circuit refused to find a due process violation.[236]

In requiring school officials to state the source of their charges against a teacher, a Wisconsin federal district court expressed concern lest he be left "fighting shadows."[237] In a later case decided by the same court, a teacher was accused of screaming at her pupils, inflicting degrading punishments, failing to prepare lesson plans, and failing to abide by various minor rules of the school. The charges were vague and unspecific in time and place, and the teacher did "not even know the events from which they arose." The court concluded that "[w]hen reports amount to blanket conclusions which leave the teacher no meaningful chance to reply and when, as here, the reports purport to be the sole source of disputed factual charges, the hearing on those charges is not adequate unless the source of the reports is disclosed."[238]

Where due process requirements apply, the charged party must "be given reasonable notice prior to the hearing, not only of the particulars of the alleged misconduct but also of the possible adverse consequences of the hearing."[239] This requirement serves to prevent waiver of procedural rights under a misconception concerning the maximum penalty.

Since a teacher who is entitled to invoke procedural due process protection must "be accorded a meaningful opportunity to be heard in his own defense," it would appear that another aspect of his due process right to notice is the right to be informed of the rules and regulations governing the termination proceedings. Thus where a tenured professor "had no way of knowing the rules to be applied in the dismissal proceedings," an Alabama federal district court ruled that he was deprived "of an adequate opportunity to defend himself" and hence of due process.[240] "If a set of rules was to be followed," the court held, the university was under a duty to notify plaintiff of these rules and to use them."[241] If the school authorities have a rule requiring a teacher to request a hearing in order to obtain one, they have a due process obligation, where due process is applicable, to advise him of this requirement.[242]

Adequate Time to Prepare a Defense

Since "[d]ue process requires that there be an opportunity to present every available defense" and "a *meaningful* opportunity to be heard,"[243] it requires that the teacher be furnished an adequate period of time in which to prepare a defense.[244] There must be a reasonable time interval to marshal facts and evidence.[245] In a Delaware case, for example, a federal court, ruling that a school board employee was denied due process owing to a number of deficiencies in the procedure leading to his termination, concluded that a Sunday telephone call by school authorities to an employee regarding a 10:00 a.m. Monday meeting "did not afford plaintiff an opportunity to secure documents . . . relevant to his case."[246] In another Delaware case a federal court found it wholly inadequate that the discharged principal only received notice on the very morning of the board meeting considering whether to renew his contract.[247]

Right to Present Evidence and to Confront and Cross-Examine Accusers

Where a teacher has the right to a due process hearing, he is entitled to present evidence in his behalf[248] and—at least where there are disputed issues of fact—to confront and cross-examine his accusers.[249] Where the charges are not contested, the teacher has no right to confrontation or cross-examination.[250] It is not yet clear whether, or to what extent, such a right exists where "wholly subjective professional judgments about a teacher's intellectual and psychological qualifications" are involved.[251] The fact that the issue involves the adequacy of a teacher's performance, however, will not automatically negate the right to confrontation and cross-examination, since reliance by school authorities upon alleged shortcomings may cause the termination decision to turn on the truth or falsity of disputed facts.[252] In an Eighth Circuit case involving the dismissal of a public employee, the court held that the employee's right to cross-examine available witnesses and confront adverse evidence was violated when the person adjudicating his case was having extensive ex parte communications with witnesses against him.[253]

Right to Disclosure of Documents upon
Which School Authorities Rely

Where a teacher has an interest sufficient to invoke the procedural protections of the due process clause in connection with adverse action by school authorities, his due process right may include the right to disclosure of reports and other documents upon which they rely.

Generally, assuming a public employee has an interest sufficient to invoke due process protection, "discovery must be granted [by his employer in a proceeding seeking to remove him] if in the particular situation a refusal to do so would so prejudice [the employee] as to deny him due process."[254] Thus the District of Columbia Circuit held that a Park Service employee had a due process right to a copy of a report on the personnel management practices of his supervisor for use in administrative proceedings resulting in his discharge.[255] Similarly, the Second Circuit ruled that where a tenured teacher was placed on involuntary leave of absence without pay on the ground of mental unfitness, the school board, "having assumed the burden of proving [the teacher] to be medically unfit, should as a matter of fundamental fairness and rudimentary due process have made available to [her] doctors copies of the medical reports received from its own doctors" so that she could test the credibility, weight, and accuracy of the reports, offer a point-by-point rebuttal, and furnish a meaningful response based on the "far more extensive" examinations and interviews of her conducted by her own psychiatrists.[256]

In a case involving the termination of a doctor's hospital privileges where governmental involvement in the hospital made its actions subject to constitutional requirements, the Fourth Circuit held that the refusal of the hospital's medical board to allow the doctor's lawyer access to the report of a tissue committee indicating that the doctor had conducted unjustified surgery deprived the doctor of due process. The court ruled that the hospital should be required to permit the doctor or his attorney, at their own expense, to inspect and copy all documents in the hospital's possession bearing on each charge.[257] Additionally, the U.S. District Court for the District of Columbia has held that a foreign service officer with a property interest in continued employment, before being "selected out," had a due process right "to have full access" to "all materials concerning him that were considered by" the selection board.[258]

Right to Counsel

The Supreme Court has said that "[t]he right to be heard would be, in many cases, of little avail if it did not comprehend the right to be heard by counsel."[259] In non-criminal proceedings, however, no fixed rule has been developed regarding the right to counsel.[260]

In *Goldberg v. Kelly*[261] the Supreme Court held that while the government is not constitutionally compelled to provide welfare recipients with publicly financed counsel at termination hearings, it cannot deny recipients the right to retain and be represented by counsel at their own expense. It is not clear whether this rule extends to a public employee who is entitled to invoke due process in a termination or disciplinary proceeding, but several courts have concluded that it does[262] A Florida federal district court, after holding that the termination of a university faculty member's employment had deprived him of a liberty interest, ruled that a policy which permitted him to retain counsel in an advisory capacity but barred counsel from making statements concerning his client or cross-examining witnesses violated the due process clause.[263] The Fifth Circuit reversed the decision on the ground that the faculty member had not been deprived of a liberty interest, without reaching the question of the validity of the university's policy in a case in which due process applied.[264]

The Sixth Circuit, however, has held that the due process clause did not require a university to permit a tenured associate professor's retained counsel to conduct direct and cross-examination of witnesses at a pre-termination hearing.[265] The court rejected the professor's proffered "analogy between the problems which beset an unrepresented welfare recipient confronted with an administrative court and the position of a professional academic who, under the direction of his attorney, presents his case to a panel of fellow faculty members."[266] The Ninth Circuit has suggested that "college professors dealing with their peers" are less likely to be in need of the services of counsel than welfare recipients dealing with state officials.[267] And the First Circuit has ruled that a university regulation preventing a discharged employee—in that case a mentally retarded groundskeeper—in a grievance hearing before the personnel director, from having a representative who was not a university employee did not violate due process.[268] The court also rejected the argument that the employee had a due process right to be represented at the hearing by an outside representative who was not a lawyer, concluding that "[m]any laymen, such as a professional union negotiator, could have the same formalizing impact on the proceedings as a lawyer would, without whatever contribution to orderly proceedings can be expected from the lawyer's discipline."[269] The court also thought the employee's interest in choosing an outside lay representative, rather than a layman from the university, was "comparatively weak."[270] Among the considerations motivating its decision were the fact that it was dealing with "a relatively routine personnel action" and with factual charges that were "not highly complex";[271] and the fact that a large reservoir of fellow employees (several thousand) was available to represent an aggrieved employee.[272] The court also noted that the employee and his employee representative could have "the continuing services of counsel in discussing his problem, planning his defense, and preparing his presentation," the "only limitation" being that a non-employee could not appear at the grievance meeting.[273]

The logic of these decisions is debatable. It is difficult to perceive a legitimate governmental interest in avoiding an adversarial proceeding in a context in which a public employee is exposed to the loss of his livelihood.[274] To the extent that the presence of counsel would cast a "litigation chill" on the decision to terminate,[275] as the First Circuit suggested, such a chill may be warranted. A second rationale offered by that court, that the presence of counsel may tend to convert an "otherwise ordinary" personnel action into a "cause celebre,"[276] also does not seem persuasive, since such a result may also be justified by the wrongful conduct of the school authorities.

Furthermore, it is an oversimplification to suggest, as the Sixth and Ninth Circuits have suggested, that a teacher or a professor is so well educated that he can take care of the cross-examination himself. Where presentation of a teacher's case requires the exercise of rights of confrontation and cross-examination, it is questionable whether it is consistent with fundamental fairness to deny a teacher or professor, however well educated in non-legal disciplines, the right to have his retained counsel question witnesses in a proceeding which may lead to termination of his employment. As one court has put it, "Of what value would be the right to confrontation and cross-examination without the right of counsel skilled in those arts?"[277]

Even assuming, however, that there may be circumstances in which a teacher has a due process right to retain counsel in an adjudicatory disciplinary proceeding, and that this right includes the right to have counsel confront and cross-examine witnesses, it is by no means clear that such a right would extend to the preliminary stage where an investigation has begun to focus on him and he is called by a superior for a meeting or interview. At least one court has rejected a claim by a public employee—in this case a policeman—that he had a constitutional right to be represented by retained counsel at this stage.[278] A teacher may have a stronger case for the right to have such representation where he is the target of a criminal charge as well as the subject of potential administrative discipline.[279]

Right to a Decision Based on the Record

Due process generally has been understood to include the right to a decision based on the evidence presented at the hearing.[280] A teacher cannot have a fair or meaningful hearing where the decision maker relies on evidence of which the teacher may have been unaware and which he has had no chance to answer.[281] The right to a decision based "on the record" serves to safeguard the right of confrontation and to avoid the potential for, and appearance of, injustice in the reliance upon ex parte evidence.

Thus a three-judge federal district court held that a New York statute setting forth procedures for the removal of a tenured teacher violated due process in the absence of administrative regulations requiring the decision to be based upon evidence elicited before a hearing panel established by the statute to conduct the hearing and make findings and recommendations.[282] In another case a New York federal judge, in holding that school authorities had deprived a teacher of due process in the course of placing him on "health leave" without pay, directed the defendants to afford him the opportunity to rebut the finding of mental unfitness at a hearing before an independent decision maker, and the right "to a decision based only on the evidence presented at the hearing."[283]

The right to a decision based on the record does not necessarily mean that the decision maker must read personally all or even any of the evidence. Although the Supreme Court, in construing a statutory requirement that a full hearing be provided, stated in a decision known as the "First *Morgan* case" that "the officer who makes the determinations must consider and appraise the evidence which justifies them,"[284] and a similar requirement arguably is imposed by the due process clause, a leading commentator has interpreted the *Morgan* decision not to require the decision maker to personally read the record:

> The requirement is not that deciding officers must personally read the record but . . . that they must personally "consider and appraise" the evidence. The court declared: "Evidence may be taken by an examiner. Evidence thus taken may be sifted and analyzed by competent subordinates." Since the only purpose of sifting and analyzing of evidence by subordinates is to save the time of the deciding officers, this necessarily means that deciding officers may "consider and appraise" the evidence by reading a summary or analysis prepared by subordinates. . . . The requirement [in *Morgan*] has to do with personal understanding of the evidence, not with the mechanics by which the understanding is developed.[285]

Thus the Sixth Circuit ruled that reports of a faculty senate grievance committee and the university president provided a sufficient basis for a board of regents to acquire a "personal understanding" of the evidence supporting the charges against a tenured faculty member in a discharge hearing. Accordingly, the court held, the board did not violate the faculty member's due process rights either by failing to take testimony directly or by failing to review the evidence in the form in which it was submitted to the grievance committee.[286]

A due process violation occurred, however, where the information presented to the hearing official by a school employee was not communicated to the Board of Education "in any fashion, summary or otherwise."[287] A due process violation arguably occurs, moreover, where the report of the hearing body or official does not contain a statement of the reasons for the recommendation or of the evidence relied upon. Where due process requirements are applicable, most courts have held that the decision maker must provide a statement of the reasons for its decision and the evidence relied upon in order to ensure compliance with the requirement that the decision maker's conclusion rest "solely on the . . . evidence adduced at the hearing."[288] Arguably the failure of the hearing tribunal to furnish a similar statement to the decision maker with respect to the tribunal's recommendation would make it impossible for the decision maker to determine whether the recommendation is based solely on the record evidence, and thus impossible for the decision maker to "consider and appraise" the *evidence*, as distinguished from the hearing tribunal's report.

Right to Statement of Grounds for Decision and Evidence Relied Upon

As previously indicated, in most teacher termination cases addressing the issue the courts have held that procedural due process, where it applies, requires the decision maker to state the reasons for the decision and the evidence relied upon.[289] "The purpose," as the Tenth Circuit has stated, "is to assure that *ex parte* proofs are not relied on and a reasoned decision is made."[290] The requirement also serves to ensure that there will be an adequate basis for judicial review. Where a New York statute authorizing discharge of a tenured teacher failed to require a school board to set forth its reasoning and the factual basis for its discharge decision, a three-judge federal district court held the statute unconstitutional, concluding that the availability of an appeal to a state court did not cure the defect. "Since the school board is not required to set forth reasons in support of its decision," the court concluded, "a review of the factual determination [of the hearing panel] relied upon by the board becomes illusory.

Simply stated, there will not be an adequate record for a state court to review."[291]

In a Kansas case a federal district court ruled that "[d]ue process requires the decisionmaker to set forth findings at the time of its decision, which state *clearly* the reasons for its determination and the evidentiary basis relied upon. Conclusory terms such as 'conduct unbecoming an instructor' are not sufficient."[292]

Right to a Transcript of the Proceeding

In the Fifth Circuit's decision in the *Sindermann* case, the court ruled that in a teacher termination hearing governed by due process requirements, the hearing must afford "a meaningful opportunity to develop a record which can, if necessary, later form a substantial part of any court proceeding—a transcript which should demonstrate that the academic tribunal based its decision upon matters adduced before it."[293] The rationale for this requirement is similar to the rationale of the rule requiring a statement of the grounds of the decision and the evidence relied upon.

A corollary of the Fifth Circuit rule was adopted in a post-*Roth* New York federal court decision that where due process applies, the teacher has the right "to have a transcript of the proceeding if he so desires."[294] An unsettled question is whether due process requirements, where applicable, obligate school authorities to bear the expense of making the record or furnishing the transcript. Although the law on this issue is not definitive, a pre-*Roth* Arkansas decision suggests an affirmative answer. In that case a school board failed to comply with the request of a teacher's representative for a copy of the record of her non-renewal hearing. Under an Arkansas statute the board was required to make and preserve a record of the hearing at its own expense and furnish a copy to the teacher without cost. The federal court ruled that in addition to violating the statute, the board had "not shown that [her] constitutional right of due process was respected and protected."[295]

The Right to a Pre-Deprivation Hearing

In the *Roth* case the Supreme Court said that "[w]hen protected interests [in liberty or property] are implicated, the right to some kind of prior hearing is paramount."[296] The Court indicated that a "weighing process" plays a part in determining the "form" of the hearing required,[297] but stated that "[t]he requirement of opportunity for *some* form of hearing before deprivation of a protected interest . . . does not depend upon such a narrow balancing process."[298]

Subsequently, in *Arnett v. Kennedy*,[299] the Supreme Court upheld the constitutionality of procedures by which a federal employee could be dismissed for cause even though they did not provide for a trial-type evidentiary hearing until after the actual termination of employment. In *Arnett* the procedures, while not affording a trial-type hearing prior to termination, did provide for pre-termination notice of the charges and an opportunity to respond and mandated a post-termination evidentiary hearing before an impartial tribunal (the Civil Service Commission) empowered to award reinstatement and back pay.

After the *Arnett* decision an Arkansas federal district court held that a pre-termination evidentiary hearing is constitutionally required before dismissal of a teacher in mid-contract.[300] A Delaware federal district court ruled that due process required a pre-termination evidentiary hearing in the case of the discharge of a tenured college associate professor, indicating that the circumstances would have to be "extraordinary" to permit dispensing with this requirement.[301] And a Mississippi federal district court ruled that a non-tenured teacher deemed by the court to have a property interest in continued employment had the right to "*prior* notice and hearing" before being denied re-employment.[302] In post-*Arnett* decisions, however, the Supreme Court has referred to the "ordinary principle" that "something less than an evidentiary hearing is sufficient prior to adverse administrative action,"[303] although it has made it clear that its three-part balancing test to identify the specific dictates of due process applies to this question, i.e., an assessment of (1) "the private interest that will be affected by the official action;" (2) "the risk of an erroneous deprivation of such interest through the procedures used and the probable value, if any, of additional or substitute procedural safeguards," and (3) "the Government's interest, including the function involved and the fiscal and administrative burdens that the additional or substitute procedural requirements would entail."[304]

Arguably, under this balancing test the due process scales should tip in favor of the right to a pre-deprivation evidentiary hearing in many if not most cases involving the termination of a teacher's employment. First, where a teacher's job is at stake, "the private interest that will be affected by the official action" is a vital one. The loss of one's livelihood, even for a brief period of time, can have serious consequences. As one court has observed, "Few [government employees] earn more than enough to pay their living expenses from month to month, and when their salaries are cut off they may be in the same destitute circumstances as a welfare recipient whose aid has been discontinued. In any event, if there is any difference, it is only a matter of degree."[305] And in the case of a teacher who is dismissed in mid-contract, or a tenured faculty member who is dismissed, the private interest is particularly significant since termination is likely to be stigmatizing.[306]

Second, in teacher termination cases not only is a pre-deprivation evidentiary hearing likely to minimize "the risk of an erroneous deprivation" of the teacher's interest, but the "probable value" of such a hearing as compared to a post-deprivation evidentiary hearing[307] will be high in many if not most such cases. Where a teacher's employment has already been terminated, the school board may have acquired a vested interest in ratifying the termination decision. A decision favorable to the teacher following a post-deprivation hearing also may expose the school district treasury to back-pay liability and potentially open the board members to personal liability. A post-termination decision in the teacher's favor, moreover, would constitute an admission that the board had erred in its original decision—an admission that school board members, like most human beings, naturally would be reluctant to make. The Supreme Court implicitly has recognized the vice in such a procedure by holding that "when review of an initial decision is mandated, the decisionmaker must be other than the one who made the decision under review."[308] Additionally, as the Third Circuit has pointed out:

[T]here is a substantial difference in the position of the parties once termination has actually occurred. First, the employee, cutoff [sic] from the payroll, is greatly disadvantaged in his ability to pursue the hearing remedy. He may be forced by the necessity for survival to seek other employment which will foreclose the pursuit of reinstatement. Second, the institution will have made substitute teaching arrangements, thus introducing into the hearing consideration of the interests of other faculty members. This inevitability will increase whatever tendency may already exist for the hearing officials to defer to the administration's decision.[309]

Finally, the governmental interest in dispensing with a prior evidentiary hearing may be insubstantial. For example, where the decision to terminate is made long before the termination will take effect—such as where a school board decides not to renew a teacher's contract but the non-renewal will not take effect for several months—it may be difficult for the school board to show that it would incur "fiscal . . . [or] administrative burdens"[310] if required to hold the hearing prior to rather than after non-renewal. As the Ninth Circuit has said in the context of the dismissal of a physician from a veterans' hospital residency program: "In a case where the decision to terminate is made long before the termination date, as was true here, we see no interest of the state which is furthered by delaying the resident physician's right to examine the evidence and tell an opposing version of the story until after termination."[311] A teacher may argue, moreover, that the "Government's interest" includes its interest in attracting competent teachers to assume teaching positions in the public schools by the assurance that their employment will not be terminated unfairly or through error.[312]

In a case involving a teacher with 16 years' experience who was discharged for sexually harassing students, the Ninth Circuit held that the school board had violated the teacher's due process rights by not holding the pre-deprivation hearing.[313] Doing a *Matthews v. Eldridge* balancing, the court first noted that "[t]he weight of the private interests affected is apparent" and that "the stigma arising from a midyear dismissal on the grounds" asserted would "seriously impair" the teacher's job opportunities. Next, the court stated that "[t]he interest of the school district in dismissing, rather than merely suspending, [the teacher] without affording him a hearing is less clear. The lower court found no emergency situation requiring immediate dismissal . . . ." After noting that "[t]he risk of an erroneous deprivation was substantial, since [the teacher] was dismissed without the opportunity to confront the evidence and . . . respond to charges" and that "[t]he administrative burdens of permitting" him to "rebut the charges made against him . . . were minimal," the court concluded a pre-deprivation hearing was required.[314]

Even where a pre-deprivation evidentiary hearing is not constitutionally required, school authorities may be obligated by the due process clause to adopt pre-deprivation procedures which at least minimize the risk of error. In *Arnett v. Kennedy*, where the Supreme Court upheld procedures calling for an evidentiary hearing only after termination, the procedures required pre-deprivation notice of the proposed action and the reasons for the contemplated action, as well as the opportunity to respond. A substantial array of decisions have held that a public employee with a property interest in continued employment has a due process right to such pre-deprivation procedures.[315] The Fifth Circuit, however, has held that a defect in the pre-deprivation procedures may be cured in a subsequent hearing before the same tribunal[316]—a questionable conclusion since the court expressly or in effect upheld the action of a government body in sitting in review of its own prior decision on the merits, an action which would appear to violate due process under the Supreme Court's decisions.[317]

Where the deprivation involved is not as severe as termination of employment, the procedures required by due process may not be as stringent. For example, the First Circuit ruled that where a teacher had a property interest in a salary increment, the school authorities satisfied procedural due process requirements in denying her a salary increase where she had full written notice of the charges against her and a chance to meet those charges in writing, full access to information in her file permitting her to mold her response, the right to an evaluation by another principal, and the protections afforded by a four-level grievance procedure following the school committee's adverse determination, culminating in arbitration if the teacher's grievance committee pressed the appeal.[318]

Even assuming that a pre-deprivation evidentiary hearing is not required in the circumstances of a particular termination case, a teacher may be denied due process where the board does not "wipe the slate clean" in the post-deprivation evidentiary hearing but places upon the teacher the burden of proving that the deprivation was unjustified.[319] Or the board may unduly delay the provision of a post-deprivation hearing.[320] The Supreme Court has stated that the fundamental requirement of due process is the opportunity to be heard "at a meaningful time and in a meaningful manner."[321] Where delay in affording the teacher a hearing is substantial, the teacher may suffer prejudice beyond the harm resulting from a lack of an opportunity for a hearing prior to the deprivation. In a Nebraska case the Eighth Circuit concluded that a teacher terminated for an unwed pregnancy was denied procedural due process where she was not given a hearing until two years after termination. The court stated:

> [I]n the present case the lack of a pre-termination hearing did more than merely deprive [her] of her salary. The two-year delay substantially handicapped her ability to protect her interests. At the 1975 hearing, she suffered the difficult burden of seeking a reversal of an administrative decision and two years' worth of consequences flowing from that decision. Moreover, the delay itself served virtually to destroy any possibility of reaching a compromise solution less harsh than dismissal. Alternatives other than dismissal existed at the time of original dismissal. A leave of absence for the remainder of the term or a transfer to a nonteaching position could have alleviated the Board's concern for the moral welfare of the students, [footnote omitted] while affording some protection for [her] rights. These options were no longer available at the time of the hearing in 1975. Because the delay in obtaining a hearing hampered [her] in vindicating her rights, the post-termination hearing did not satisfy the requirements of due process.[322]

Delay in affording a teacher an evidentiary hearing also may be prejudicial where facts are in dispute and witnesses have disappeared or memories are no longer fresh.

One recurring question is whether, on the basis of evidence presented in a lawsuit asserting a procedural due process challenge to the failure of school authorities to afford a pre-deprivation hearing, a court properly may substitute its judgment on the merits of the deprivation and deny relief if it resolves the merits against the teacher. The courts are divided on this question.[323] A substantial argument can be made, however, that it is improper for the court to address the merits.

The practice of retrospectively substituting the district court's judgment for that of the administrative tribunal seems fundamentally at odds with the Supreme Court's approach in *Carey v. Piphus*, where the Court made clear that the school board, in order to avoid compensating the plaintiff for losses flowing from a due process violation, must prove that it would have made the same decision even if it had afforded due process. The court did not authorize the district court to make its own substantive determination on the merits[324] As the Third Circuit has said, moreover:

> Such a retrospective substitution of the district court's judgment for that of the administrative hearing officers seriously undermines the hearing requirement. A district court cannot exercise the discretion which is vested in an administrative hearing board, nor can it bring to the dispute the same expert knowledge of the academic environment which should enlighten the deliberation of an academic hearing agency. . . . A board of his academic peers might say [the plaintiff professor] is guilty of misconduct, but [that] he should not be fired for that kind of misconduct. The district judge could not exercise such discretion. Furthermore, if we countenance the practice of making findings which the institution should have made, a substantial incentive toward affording procedural due process prior to contract termination will be removed.[325]

The Right to a Pre-Suspension Hearing

A question related to the pre-termination hearing issue is whether a teacher with a protected interest has the right to a hearing prior to *suspension*, as distinguished from *termination*, of employment, and if so, what kind of hearing. In *Goss v. Lopez*[326] the Supreme Court ruled that students deprived of property and liberty interests by suspensions from school for ten days or less are constitutionally entitled to notice and an informal hearing *before* removal from the school, except where the student's presence "poses a continuing danger to persons or property or an ongoing threat of disrupting the academic process," in which case "the necessary notice and a rudimentary hearing should follow as soon as practicable."[327] Relying upon *Goss*, the Seventh Circuit ruled in *Muscare v. Quinn* that a fireman suspended for 29 days for allegedly violating departmental hair regulations had a right to a pre-suspension hearing at which he could be fully informed of the reasons for the proposed suspension and challenge their sufficiency.[328] The court noted that alleged transgressions of public employees justifying suspension are "often more serious than school discipline problems" and "the corresponding penalties are potentially more damaging, for reputations, careers, and substantial amounts of lost pay are at stake."[329] Moreover, as an Alabama federal court noted in holding that the summary suspension of teachers without pay deprived them of property without due process, "the summary suspension of an employee from the payroll without notice or opportunity to be heard may . . . hamper that individual's ability to pursue even a post-termination hearing, due to the economic repercussions of suspension without pay."[330]

In a recent case, however, the Supreme Court held that the due process clause did not entitle a horse trainer with a property interest in his license to an evidentiary hearing before his suspension.[331] Under state law his license could have been suspended only upon a satisfactory showing that his horse had been drugged and that he was at least negligent in failing to prevent the drugging.[332] The Court concluded that while the magnitude of a trainer's interest in avoiding suspension was "[u]nquestionably" substantial, the State also had an important interest in assuring the integrity of the racing carried on under its auspices.[333] In these circumstances, it seemed to the Court, "the State is entitled to impose an interim suspension, pending a prompt judicial or administrative hearing that would definitely determine the issues, whenever it has satisfactorily established probable cause to believe that a horse has been drugged and that a trainer has been at least negligent in connection with the drugging."[334] The Court concluded that under this standard the trainer received all the process that was due him prior to the suspension of his license, since the state's testing official, who had purported to examine the trainer's horse pursuant to prescribed testing procedures, had asserted that the horse had been drugged.[335] "To establish probable cause," the Court said, "the State need not postpone a suspension pending an adversary hearing to resolve questions of credibility and conflicts in the evidence. At the interim suspension stage, an expert's affirmance, although untested and not beyond error, would appear sufficiently reliable to satisfy constitutional requirements."[336] The Court accepted as defensible the rebuttable presumption of the trainer's culpability, based on the fact of drugging, established by the court-approved state trainer's responsibility rules.[337] The Court noted that although he "was not given a formal hearing prior to the suspension of his license, he was given more than one opportunity to present his side of the story to the State's investigators."[338]

The Court, however, held that the trainer had not been assured a sufficiently timely post-suspension hearing.[339] The statutory provision for an administrative hearing, the Court ruled, neither on its face nor as applied assured a prompt proceeding and prompt disposition of the outstanding issues between the trainer and the state.[340] In fact, the Court pointed out, insofar as the statutory requirements were concerned, it was as likely as not that the trainer and others subject to relatively brief suspensions would have no opportunity to put the state to its proof until they had suffered the full penalty imposed.[341] "Once suspension has been imposed," the Court said, "the trainer's interest in a speedy resolution of the controversy becomes paramount." The Court discerned "little or no State interest . . . in an appreciable delay in going forward with a full hearing" at that point.[342]

The following aspects of this decision should be noted:

1. In holding that the trainer was not entitled to a pre-suspension hearing, the Court relied upon "the State's inter-

est in preserving the integrity of the sport and in protecting the public from harm."[343] There may be circumstances in a teacher termination case in which a school district has analogous interests—for example, where it has probable cause to believe that a teacher has sexually assaulted or has otherwise engaged in sexual improprieties with a student. In a Michigan case a university faculty member was suspended for alleged sexual liaisons with some of his female students. Both property and liberty interests of the faculty member were implicated, but the suspension was imposed without a prior hearing, although the suspension was preceded by an investigation and followed by a prompt post-suspension trial-type hearing at which the plaintiff cleared his name and secured reinstatement and back pay. A federal district court ruled that a pre-suspension hearing was not required, relying in part upon the "strong" governmental interest in avoiding "even the appearance of what might be characterized as sexual blackmail of students, at worst, and unprofessional conduct, at best."[344]

The strength of the government's interest in protecting students and others in the school environment from harm is reflected in a Second Circuit ruling that a tenured teacher was not entitled as a matter of due process to an adversary hearing before being placed on leave of absence for mental unfitness. The court concluded that "the risk of harm that might occur if a teacher believed to be mentally unfit were permitted to continue teaching is too great to insist on retention while the issue of mental fitness is being resolved."[345]

2. Under the Court's standard, the state must "satisfactorily" establish probable cause.[346] While an expert's assertion, made after he had purported to follow prescribed investigative procedures, was deemed sufficiently reliable by the Court, other information may not be reliable enough to establish probable cause. Examples might be gossip, rumor or a hearsay report.

3. The trainer was afforded a pre-suspension opportunity to tell his side of the story to the state's investigators.[347] Arguably, one entitled to invoke due process protection is, at the least, constitutionally entitled to notice of the charges against him and an opportunity to respond in some fashion prior to suspension so that the risk of error is minimized.[348]

Where an adequate hearing is not provided until after a public employee's income is suspended, moreover, the Ninth Circuit held that such a suspension constitutes a "final" deprivation and subject to the due process procedures applicable to such deprivations—unless it is possible to award back pay when the hearing is ultimately held.[349] And it is always important to determine whether an action labeled a "suspension" is in reality a termination of employment. The Fifth Circuit ruled that a procedure under which city employees were suspended without pay and lost all benefits of employment—a suspension which automatically became a termination unless the employees were reinstated with back pay on review by the Civil Service Board—was "no more than a facade," agreeing with the trial court that the "suspension" was "the functional equivalent of permanent discharge subject to the condition subsequent that an employee may be reinstated with back pay upon successful appeal." Since suspension without pay was "in reality termination," the court ruled, the city was required to afford the employees a prior hearing. Although the court did not mandate a prior evidentiary hearing, it did require, prior to "suspension," written notice of the reasons therefor and an effective opportunity to rebut those reasons, including the right to respond in writing to the charges and to respond orally before the official charged with making the decision.[350]

Since a teacher's property interest in continued employment arguably is not limited to the income from his position but also embraces the opportunity to continue practicing his profession, it can be contended that "some form of hearing" —and, depending on the circumstances, an evidentiary hearing—is constitutionally required before suspension even where the teacher continues to be paid. It may be urged that such a suspension constitutes a "final" deprivation, i.e., an irretrievable loss, for the period of the suspension, of the opportunity to teach—an opportunity which may contribute to the maintenance and development of the teacher's career skills.[351] In upholding the suspension with pay of a professor of surgery from his position as department head without a pre-suspension hearing, the Ninth Circuit noted that different considerations might have obtained had he been suspended from his position as professor, since, "while the record indicates that the administrative position was important to him, its deprivation did not remove him from the 'mainstream of his occupation' " as a teacher and surgeon.[352] Because monetary relief cannot adequately compensate a teacher for removal from the "mainstream of his occupation" it can reasonably be argued that a presuspension evidentiary hearing is constitutionally required, except where the teacher's presence "poses a continuing danger to persons or property or an ongoing threat of disrupting the academic process,"[353] in which case due process mandates pre-suspension procedure to minimize the risk of error and a prompt post-suspension hearing on the merits, thus limiting the duration of the suspension.[354]

The question frequently arises whether a plaintiff who is entitled to certain procedural due process rights before termination or suspension is entitled to a preliminary injunction against such termination or suspension where the required procedures have not been followed. Arguably, where an alleged deprivation of a constitutional right is involved no further showing of irreparable injury is necessary to justify the award of a preliminary injunction.[355] Thus while the temporary loss of income, ultimately to be recovered, does not usually constitute irreparable injury,[356] a procedural due process violation, i.e., a violation of the Constitution, may not fall within the "usual" category and itself may constitute irreparable injury.[357] Other factors may also lead a court to find irreparable injury in a particular case. Among these are a showing that employability is highly dependent upon professional reputation and past employment performance;[358] the possibility, for example in higher education cases, that back pay may be barred by the 11th Amendment;[359] the prospect that the plaintiff will be unable to secure employment in his field for another year because the hiring season will have passed;[360] and the impact of the plaintiff's absence from the mainstream of the teaching profession, including loss of contact with professional colleagues, inability to develop or maintain career skills, and loss of opportunity to build or enhance professional reputation.[361]

The Right to a Pre-Termination or Pre-Suspension Hearing in the Context of a Liberty Deprivation

Where only a deprivation of liberty is involved, the issue of the right to a pre-termination or pre-suspension hearing is complicated by additional considerations. The *Roth* decision indicates that the state cannot "foreclose a range" of employment opportunities without a "full prior hearing."[362] It is not entirely clear from this language whether the "full prior hearing" must occur before the termination of the teacher's employment, or whether it is sufficient that the hearing merely precede the actual foreclosure. For example, if school authorities terminate a teacher's employment for stigmatizing reasons incorporated into his file, but schedule a prompt post-termination hearing which occurs before he seeks another job, the termination may not "foreclose" his employment opportunities, and, if the termination is sustained after the post-termination hearing, he arguably would have had a pre-"foreclosure"—even though not a pre-termination—hearing. The Second Circuit, however, has ruled that the due process clause entitled a principal to a fair hearing before the school board's public announcement of charges—made in the course of terminating his employment and incorporated into his employment record—which went to the heart of his professional competence.[363]

Where the deprivation of liberty consists of a termination or suspension based on charges which may damage the teacher's standing and associations in his community, the Supreme Court has indicated that the purpose of the hearing is to give the employee "an opportunity to clear his name."[364] The Court, however, has not indicated whether the hearing must precede the injury to reputation.[365] Arguably it must, since the damage, once done, may be difficult to undo. Those who may have seen or heard the charges against the teacher are not likely to be present at any subsequent hearing, and the Court thus far has imposed no constitutional obligation to retract the charge following the "name-clearing" hearing, nor to publish the retraction, even assuming that this would effectively restore the teacher's reputation.

Even if a pre-termination or pre-suspension hearing is required in a "liberty" interest case, where a possible danger to persons or property or a threat to the integrity of the teacher-student relationship is involved a court may be reluctant to hold that a prior *evidentiary* hearing is required—whether the case involves the deprivation of a property interest, a liberty interest, or both. Thus where a proposed suspension is based on a charge involving an alleged sexual impropriety with a student,[366] a court might conclude that due process is satisfied by pre-suspension notice of the charge and an opportunity to respond, coupled with a prompt post-suspension opportunity for a more formal evidentiary hearing.

The Right to an Impartial Decision Maker

The Supreme Court has said that a "fair trial in a fair tribunal is a basic requirement of due process. . . . This applies to administrative agencies which adjudicate as well as to courts. . . . Not only is a biased decisionmaker constitutionally unacceptable but 'our system of law has always endeavored to prevent even the probability of unfairness.' "[367]

Conflict of Interest

A decision maker may be disqualified from adjudicating a case in which he has a conflict of interest. The Supreme Court has held that the due process clause of the 14th Amendment bars a decision maker from deciding a case where he has a "substantial pecuniary interest" in the outcome.[368] The leading case is *Tumey v. Ohio*,[369] where a unanimous Court ruled that the due process clause barred a town from awarding its mayor, as compensation for services as a judge in cases involving an alleged violation of the State's Prohibition Act, the court costs assessed against those defendants who were convicted.

The *Tumey* principle has been applied in an administrative context, and to a situation in which the financial stake of the decision maker was not as "direct or positive as it appeared to be in *Tumey*."[370] Thus the Court held repugnant to due process a proceeding in which a board of optometry composed solely of independent practitioners decided whether optometrists employed by an optical company were engaged in "unprofessional conduct." The Court upheld the reasoning of the trial court that the optical company did a large business in the state and if forced to suspend operations the individual members of the board, along with other private practitioners of optometry, would fall heir to that business.[371]

In at least some contexts, procedural due process may also

require disqualification of a decision maker from deciding a case where, although he has no personal financial interest in the outcome, he represents an institution which has a substantial financial stake in the decision. In *Ward v. Village of Monroeville*[372] the Court held repugnant to the due process clause of the 14th Amendment a state statute authorizing mayors to sit as judges on cases involving traffic offenses. The majority opinion observed that "[a] major part of village income is derived from the fines, forfeitures, costs, and fees imposed . . . in [the] mayor's court,"[373] and concluded that " 'possible temptation' may . . . exist when the mayor's executive responsibilities for village finances may make him partisan to maintain the high level of contribution from the mayor's court."[374]

In *Hortonville Joint School District No. 1 v. Hortonville Education Association*, the Supreme Court, in dictum, raised but did not decide the question whether *Tumey* and *Ward* "state the governing standards when the decisionmaker is a public employer dealing with employees."[375] To the extent that the principles of these cases do apply, however, it is possible to conceive of teacher termination cases in which the decision maker would be constitutionally disqualified.

For example, a school board member might have a substantial personal financial interest in the outcome of a teacher discharge proceeding where the teacher who may be discharged is also the head coach of the basketball team and the board member's spouse is the assistant coach and the likely heir to the head coaching position. One can also conceive of situations in which the institution represented by the school board—the school system—might have a substantial financial stake in the outcome comparable to that of the judge in *Ward v. Monroeville*. For example, where, as in New York, state law mandates loss of pay for teachers determined to have participated in an illegal strike, and as a result the coffers of the school system may be swelled by a determination that such participation has occurred, it is questionable whether the school board, or its chief executive officer, can be an impartial decision maker.[376] And where a school board in a teacher discharge case hires a replacement before the hearing, it arguably cannot sit impartially, since a decision in the teacher's favor might require the school board to pay two teachers instead of one.[377]

On the other hand, the Supreme Court held in the *Hortonville* case that "in light of the important interest in leaving with the Board the power given by the state legislature," a school board's pecuniary interest as employer in the expense of paying a tenured teacher is not enough to disqualify the board from making a policy decision as to the appropriate response to teachers who admittedly had been on strike.[378] And a Pennsylvania federal district court applied the *Hortonville* decision to reject a contention that a school board's pecuniary interest as employer in the expense of paying a tenured teacher impermissibly biased its fact-finding, as distinguished from its policymaking.[379]

A conflict of interest may exist where the teacher is involved in collateral litigation with the officials constituting the tribunal. The Second Circuit has acknowledged the "possibility of prejudgment by a decisionmaker himself engaged in litigation with the defending party."[380] A South Carolina state court concluded that a school board could not impartially decide a teacher non-renewal case, relying in part upon the fact that the members of the board had "set in motion actions against the plaintiff which have caused him to institute suit against them as defendants personally and officially."[381] A California federal court, concluding that there was an unacceptable risk of bias in a student expulsion proceeding, relied in part upon the fact that the decision of the board members might subject them to personal liability in a pending lawsuit.[382] It seems safe to say, however, that a court will not lightly permit a teacher to disqualify a school board on the ground that he is embroiled in a lawsuit against the board where the lawsuit has been filed for the purpose of laying a basis for a bias claim.

Personal Animosity

The decisions of the Supreme Court also indicate that a decision maker may not "give vent to personal spleen or respond to a personal grievance" in reaching a decision.[383] Where personal animosity has been shown to exist in a criminal case or a criminal contempt proceeding, the Court has sometimes found the probability of bias. This may occur where the adjudicator "has been the target of personal abuse or criticism by the party before him."[384]

For example, in *Mayberry v. Pennsylvania*, the Court held that if a defendant who has previously "vilified" and "cruelly slandered" the trial judge is cited for contempt after rather than during the trial, he should be tried for the contempt "before a judge other than the one reviled by the contemnor," since "[n]o one so cruelly slandered is likely to maintain that calm detachment necessary for fair adjudication."[385] And in *Taylor v. Hayes* the Court held that contemptuous conduct, though short of personal attack, may still provoke a trial judge and so embroil him in controversy that the contempt issue should be finally adjudicated by another judge.[386]

In *Hortonville*, the Supreme Court implied without deciding the question that cases such as *Mayberry* and *Hayes*, like *Tumey* and *Ward*, might not "state the governing standards when the decisionmaker is a public employer dealing with employees."[387] The decisions, far from definitive, provide limited guidance.

In *Arnett v. Kennedy*,[388] decided before *Hortonville*, Justice White, in an opinion concurring in part and dissenting in part, would have concluded that a preliminary proceeding before a supervisor prior to dismissal of a civil service employee failed to provide the impartial hearing required by statute because the grounds for the proposed discharge included the employee's alleged public attacks on the personal reputation of the supervisor.[389] A majority of the Court, however, determined that this potential bias did not contravene the impartial hearing requirement of the statute because of the availability of a hearing subsequent to the termination before an impartial decision maker (the Civil Service Commission), empowered to award reinstatement and back pay.[390]

In another pre-*Hortonville* decision the Second Circuit suggested that to place the final decision on dismissal charges against a school superintendent in the hands of a school board whose members had been the target of "personal abuse and criticism" from him—including the charge that one member had been a "liar"—would violate the due process clause.[391] The court, however, upheld a procedure under which the school board initiated the charge against the superintendent, the case was heard by an independent and impartial examiner, and the school board's decision was reviewable by the city board and the commissioner of education. The protections afforded by the independent examiner and review by the city board and commissioner were held to save the constitutionality of the procedure.[392] The court was influenced by the intimate nature of the relationship between the superintendent and the school board, concluding that disputes between them "must of necessity engender some degree of personal involvement by the superior." The court also was motivated by its reluctance to require "going outside the agency or employment relationship before dismissal could be effected."[393] The court indicated that a "more detached relation" was "necessary" "between school board and teacher," as it was "between judge and defendant."[394]

The Fifth Circuit, however, has "decline[d] to establish a rule that would *per se* disqualify a [university president's] Cabinet composed of the President and two Vice-Presidents . . . from conducting a hearing pertaining to the dismissal of one of its employees, a part-time teacher, merely because [she] ha[d] made a broadside attack on the administration of the University" in vulgar and profane terms.[395] The court was influenced by the failure of the record to disclose "actual bias or prejudice,"[396] and expressed concern that a rule forbidding a university administrator, cabinet, or board to try a teacher in a dismissal proceeding if the offending statements by the teacher include an attack on the university administration and its board "would make it too easy for a teacher to disqualify University authorities from controlling personnel in the University."[397] The court noted, however, that the offending remarks "were directed against the university administration in general, not against particular members thereof."[398]

As the Fifth Circuit decision reflects, courts have held that to be disqualifying, bias in the sense of personal animosity must be actual bias; the possibility of bias is not enough. In a Ninth Circuit case in which a teacher was charged with making improper glances at and sexual comments to students, the discharged teacher claimed that he was denied due process because a board member whose son dated one of the girls who filed charges against him had refused to recuse himself from the teacher's hearing. Rejecting this claim, the court wrote that "[m]embers of a school board in smaller communities may well have some knowledge of the facts and individuals involved in incidents which they must evaluate," and concluded that the board member had acted fairly.[399] In a Second Circuit case, the court ruled that school board members who had engaged in heated negotiations with a non-tenured teacher serving as collective bargaining representative were not thereby disqualified from acting on the superintendent's recommendation that the teacher's contract not be renewed "absent a showing of actual, rather than potential, bias."[400]

Prejudgment

A tribunal may also be unconstitutionally biased where it has prejudged the merits of the case. As the Second Circuit has said in a teacher termination case, "Any other collateral procedural guarantees are largely without meaning if the deciding tribunal has in some way adversely prejudged the merits of the case."[401]

In *Withrow v. Larkin*,[402] the Supreme Court stated that "if the initial view of the facts based on the evidence derived from non-adversarial processes as a practical or legal matter foreclosed fair and effective consideration at a subsequent adversary hearing leading to ultimate decision, a substantial due process question would be raised."[403]

The Supreme Court in *Withrow* also acknowledged in a footnote its prior holdings that "when review of an initial decision is mandated, the decisionmaker must be other than the one who made the decision under review.[404] Thus a Rhode Island federal district court concluded that "[b]y sitting in review of its own final decision that . . . teacher suspensions were justified, the [school] Committee lost . . . the impartiality that procedural due process requires."[405]

Where disciplinary action is taken against a teacher on the basis of an ex parte hearing, moreover, "fair and effective consideration at a subsequent adversary hearing" would be foreclosed if the burden of proof were shifted. The tribunal must "wipe the slate clean" rather than merely offer the teacher the opportunity to prove that the earlier ex parte decision was unjustified."[406] Thus in a Fourth Circuit case in which a teacher's certificate had been invalidated ex parte by the state superintendent, a notice to the teacher telling her that she could appear with counsel to show why the board should reinstate the certificate was constitutionally defective in that it was premised on the ex parte invalidation, and placed the burden on the teacher to prove that the invalidation was unwarranted.[407]

In a pre-*Withrow* case arising in Delaware, a federal court in effect applied both of these principles in holding that a teacher did not receive an impartial hearing because—

> the Board of Education not only examined virtually all of the relevant evidence concerning plaintiff's teaching performance, but it also weighed that evidence and reached the conclusion that there was "just cause" for dismissal. Additionally, the Board members testified that unless new evidence were presented at a subsequent termination hearing, they would vote the same way. Thus the Board had concluded its investigative and deliberative task before the termination hearing required by Delaware law and the due process clause, and plaintiff was confronted with a fait accompli.[408]

Constitutionally impermissible prejudgment may also occur where, before the hearing, members of the tribunal make statements on the merits implying conclusions on critical controverted facts in the case. The Tenth Circuit, for example, held that a school superintendent was denied procedural due process where publicly elected school board members, prior to the hearing, made firm public campaign statements calling for the superintendent's removal. The court noted that the case involved "statements on the merits by those who must make factual determinations on contested fact issues of alleged incompetence and willful neglect of duty, where the fact finding is critical.[409]

The courts have drawn a distinction between prejudgment of factual issues and prejudgment on matters of policy. For example, in *Hortonville Joint School District No. 1 v. Hortonville Education Association*[410] teachers had been discharged for admittedly engaging in a strike prohibited by state law. The teachers claimed bias because the school board which discharged them had been "involved in the negotiations that preceded and precipitated" the discharges. The Court held that a decision maker is not disqualified "simply because he has taken a position, even in public, on a policy issue related to the dispute, in the absence of a showing that he is not 'capable of judging a particular controversy fairly on the basis of its own circumstances.' "[411]

Furthermore, prejudgment of the merits of the case must be distinguished from prior familiarity with the facts. In *Hortonville* the Supreme Court held that a Wisconsin school board's familiarity with the facts stemming from its involvement in negotiations on contract issues constituting the subject matter of an illegal strike did not disqualify the board under the due process clause from acting as the decision maker in discharge proceedings against the teachers. Among the Court's conclusions was: "Mere familiarity with the facts of a case gained by an agency in the performance of its statutory role does not . . . disqualify a decisionmaker.[412]

The Court also has held that "[t]he mere exposure to evidence presented in non-adversary investigative procedures is insufficient in itself to impugn the fairness of the [members of the tribunal] at a later adversary hearing."[413] Even where the decision maker, on the basis of such an investigation, has made a preliminary determination that there are sufficient facts to warrant institution of a termination proceeding, it would not appear to be unconstitutionally biased on that ground alone. In *Withrow v. Larkin*[414] the Supreme Court held that administrative officials were not automatically disqualified as decision makers because they had conducted an initial investigation and issued a "probable cause" determination which triggered the hearing over which they would preside. The Court articulated the following test by which to determine whether a combination of investigative and adjudicative functions presents a constitutionally unacceptable risk of bias: "under a realistic appraisal of psychological tendencies and human weakness," whether the combination poses "such a risk of actual bias or prejudgment that the practice must be forbidden if the guarantee of due process is to be adequately implemented."[415] The Court found no such risk posed by the combination of functions involved in *Withrow*, concluding that—

just as there is no logical inconsistency between a finding of probable cause and an acquittal in a criminal proceeding, there is no incompatibility between the agency filing a complaint based on probable cause and a subsequent decision, when all the evidence is in, that there has been no violation of the statute. Here, if the Board now proceeded after an adversary hearing to determine that appellee's license to practice should not be temporarily suspended, it would not implicitly be admitting error in its prior finding of probable cause. Its position most probably would merely reflect the benefit of a more complete view of the evidence afforded by an adversary hearing.[416]

Similar reasoning arguably would allow a school board to act as the decision maker in a teacher discharge proceeding even though the board has suspended the teacher—based on evidence secured through non-adversarial procedures—pending the final hearing outcome.[417]

In an Eighth Circuit case involving the issues raised in *Hortonville* and *Withrow*, a school board dismissed its superintendent because of the poor shape of the system's finances and because he held a second job. The superintendent went to court to challenge his dismissal on the ground that two of the four board members had said openly that no evidence could change their minds to discharge him. Overturning the district court's decision and upholding the dismissal, the court wrote:

At least in the absence of a claim of personal animosity, illegal prejudice, or a personal or financial stake in the outcome, school board members are entitled to [a] presumption of honesty and integrity. . . . Merely by its involvement in the events preceding [the superintendent's] discharge, the Board did not become so tainted as to lose this presumption.[418]

The court added that the testimony of two board members that nothing would change their minds was "insufficient as a matter of law to demonstrate irrevocable prejudgment." It concluded that "[a]t the most, the record as a whole demonstrates that the board members tentatively, but not irrevocably, had formed an opinion concerning [the superintendent's] termination based on their previous official involvement with [him]."[419]

Dissenting, one judge wrote:

In *Hortonville*, the Board of Education had no factual issues to decide. Here, there were a number of such issues to be determined and two members of the Board closed their minds on the factual disputes before [the superintendent] had a chance to give his version of the facts.[420]

To the dissenting judge, that the board members had closed their minds on factual determinations had vitiated their decision and critically affected the due process issue.

In *Withrow* the Court did note that "we should be alert to the possibilities of bias that may lurk in the way particular procedures actually work in practice." It concluded, however, that "[t]he processes utilized by the Board . . . do not in themselves contain an unacceptable risk of bias," noting that "[t]he investigative proceeding had been closed to the public, but appellee and his counsel were permitted to be present throughout; counsel actually attended the hearings and knew the facts presented to the Board."[421]

It is not entirely clear whether a school board would satisfy due process requirements where it conducted an ex parte proceeding to determine whether there was probable cause to discharge a teacher without permitting the teacher's counsel to attend the proceeding, and then adjudicated the case on the merits. Such a procedure arguably entails an unacceptable risk that the board will rely in adjudicating the merits of the case upon evidence not subject to effective confrontation and cross-examination.[422]

In *Withrow* the Court discussed its earlier decision in *In re Murchison*,[423] in which a state judge, empowered under state law to sit as a one-man grand jury and to compel witnesses to testify before him in secret about suspected crimes, charged two such witnesses with criminal contempt, one for perjury and the other for refusing to answer certain questions, and then himself tried and convicted them. As the Court in *Withrow* characterized the *Murchison* holding: "This Court found the procedure to be a denial of due process of law not only because the judge in effect became part of the prosecution and assumed an adversary position, but also because as a judge, passing on guilt or innocence, he very likely relied on 'his own personal knowledge and impression of what had occurred in the grand jury room,' an impression that 'could not be tested by adequate cross-examination.' "[424] Counsel's presence during a school board's preliminary investigation would diminish the likelihood of the board's reliance upon evidence presented there and not subject to cross-examination.

An unacceptable risk of bias also arguably exists where it can be demonstrated that a board member personally witnessed the alleged event that forms the basis for the proposed termination, e.g., an altercation with a student. In such a case it would be difficult if not impossible for the board member to reach a decision free of his own personal observations. As in *Murchison*, he would very likely rely on "his own personal knowledge and impression of what had occurred" —"the accuracy of which could not be tested by adequate cross-examination."[425]

The Court in *Withrow* was also careful to qualify its holding by stating: "That the combination of investigative and adjudicative functions does not, without more, constitute a due process violation does not, of course, preclude a court from determining from the special facts and circumstances present in the case before it that the risk of bias is intolerably high."[426] Taking note of this qualification, a Virginia federal district court expressed "grave doubt" that the president of a community college—a "tightly-knit community"—was able to judge a dismissal case impartially where, although not "consciously partial in making his decision," he had nevertheless "prejudged the credibility of some of the witnesses" and "his decision was to an extent influenced by his prior determinations and the negative feelings toward plaintiff among certain persons at the college."[427]

"Special facts and circumstances" may also exist where a member of the tribunal receives unnecessary pre-hearing exposure to one side of the controversy. Without reaching the federal due process issue, and disposing of the case on the basis of a state constitutional provision, a Massachusetts state court, in an unreported decision, held that a superintendent's ex parte approach to three new board members in a teacher termination case "created substantial and wholly unnecessary risk of pre-hearing prejudice" and "unnecessarily impaired" their "ability to decide in an impartial manner."[428]

"Special facts and circumstances" similarly may exist where an administrator identified with the prosecution participates in the school board's deliberations. Where a superintendent testified in a teacher dismissal hearing as an adverse witness against the teacher, and then participated in the board's deliberations, a Pennsylvania state court held that the board had violated the teacher's statutory right to an impartial and unbiased decision maker.[429] The Supreme Court of Hawaii concluded in another case that although the superintendent was the secretary of the board, "where the action of the Superintendent is the subject matter of the hearing, he should not participate in or even attend executive sessions where decisions are reached by the Board," since such actions "cast suspicion on the integrity of the hearing conducted by the Board."[430] This decision, while apparently based on state law, is instructive, as is the Pennsylvania decision, on the federal due process issue.

Indeed, the very presence during the board's deliberations of an administrator identified with the prosecution, whether or not he actually participates in those deliberations, may violate due process. In a California case the superintendent sat with the board during student expulsion hearings and on at least one occasion acted as secretary to the board. The federal court held that the superintendent's involvement with the board contravened the due process clause of the 14th Amendment. The court noted that while by statute the superintendent was the board's chief adviser, he was also the chief of the "prosecution" team. Although the defendants' counsel maintained that the superintendent did not participate in the deliberations, and "did no more, perhaps, than serve cookies and coffee to the Board members," the court concluded that "whether he did or did not participate, his presence to some extent might operate as an inhibiting restraint upon the freedom of action and expression of the Board."[431]

Dual Role of Board Counsel

A due process question of impartiality is also posed when counsel who represents the board in other matters presents the prosecution's case against the teacher. A state court, in an unreported decision, has "ponder[ed] on the fairness and impartiality" of a proceeding in which "[t]he attorney presenting the prosecution to the board has been the attorney of record for the school board in various civil actions over the past years and was, in fact, representing them in an action pending in this court at the time of the hearing." Calling such a situation "untenable," the court said that "the board no doubt had supreme confidence and trust in this attorney who was representing them in other matters at that time. This very fact should have disqualified the whole board from sitting in judgment on" the teacher.[432]

An Ohio federal court, however, ruled that where it was clear from the outset of the hearing that the university's legal counsel represented the president who had already determined that the plaintiff should be dismissed, and the committee was aware that the plaintiff and the university's legal counsel were adversaries, no violation of due process resulted from such counsel's participation in the hearing.[433] Similarly, although it recognized the potential for prejudice in such a practice and recommended that the school board hire separate attorneys for each role, a Michigan appeals court refused to adopt a per se rule prohibiting board attorneys from acting as legal adviser and prosecutor.[434]

A stronger case for a due process violation exists where, in its decision-making function, the board consults the lawyer who has prosecuted the case against the teacher. The Supreme Court of Hawaii, apparently as a state law matter, has expressly disapproved of this practice.[435] It would seem particularly offensive to due process if the lawyer's advice is privately conveyed. In such circumstances the procedure—characterized by the Wyoming Supreme Court as "clumsy and irregular,"[436] involves the vice of ex parte communications, a practice abhorrent to traditional notions of fair play. As the Court of Claims has declared: "It is difficult to imagine a more serious incursion on fairness than to permit the representative of one of the parties to privately communicate his recommendations to the decision makers."[437] Such a procedure, the court ruled, would "render the hearing virtually meaningless," and "due process forbids it."[438]

In *Morgan v. United States*[439] the Secretary of Agriculture, after an ostensibly "full hearing," delegated to the attorneys for the prosecution the task of preparing the findings and discussed the proposed findings with the prosecution. The Supreme Court held this procedure fatally defective as lacking "those fundamental requirements of fairness which are the essence of due process in a proceeding of a judicial nature."[440] The Court stated:

> If in an equity cause, a special master or the trial judge permitted the plaintiff's attorney to formulate the findings upon the evidence, conferred ex parte with the plaintiff's attorney regarding them, and then adopted his proposals without affording an opportunity to his opponent to know their contents and present objections, there would be no hesitation in setting aside the report or decree as having been made without a fair hearing. The requirements of fairness are not exhausted in the taking or consideration of evidence but extend to the concluding parts of the procedure as well as the beginning and intermediate steps.[441]

More recently, a Massachusetts federal district court, in interpreting a statute requiring "a full and fair hearing," concluded:

> While lay proceedings cannot be held to the due process standards required in a court of law, it offends notions of fundamental fairness to have the prosecutor present and taking an active part in the deliberations of any fact-finding tribunal. Regardless of how limited his role or how noble his purpose, such a practice permits the possibility of a prosecutor characterizing the evidence presented, or substituting his recollection for that of the hearing officers. It goes without saying that a prosecutor with less than noble motives might subvert such a practice into an occasion for presenting additional evidence, without . . . any opportunity for rebuttal by those involved. Finally, but not at all unimportant . . . anyone subject to such a practice could hardly be blamed for doubting that he had been treated fairly and impartially.[442]

The court concluded that what the prosecutor "actually said during those deliberations is not crucial. What is crucial is that he was in fact present and participated in those deliberations. By permitting such a practice, the defendant deprived the plaintiffs of their right to a full and fair hearing."[443]

Where the tribunal, such as the typical school board, consists of non-lawyers, a procedure under which a lawyer serves as both prosecutor and adviser to the tribunal may be particularly objectionable. Since the tribunal "enjoys no legal expertise and must rely heavily upon its counsel," the prosecutor arguably is placed "in a position of intolerable prominence and influence."[444]

Some federal courts have suggested in teacher termination cases that it does not offend due process for the school board's attorney to act in a dual capacity, as prosecutor and adviser to the board.[445] By contrast, in an Illinois ruling, the school board attorney, who was prosecuting the case against a teacher, conferred privately with his clients. Over the teacher's objection, he held conferences with the board chairman concerning the admissibility of evidence and, pursuant to the board attorney's advice, the scope of cross-examination was limited. The discharge of the teacher following these proceedings was set aside by the circuit court. Affirming this decision, the state court of appeals was troubled by the dual role in which the board's attorney functioned, as well as by the fact that the board was acting "as prosecutor, judge and jury." The court concluded that the teacher "was prevented from having a fair trial by the multiple capacities in which the school board *and its attorney* were functioning."[446] Similarly, other courts have held repugnant to the due process clause of the state constitution a process under which the same lawyer serves both as prosecutor of the case against the teacher and as adviser to the board.[447]

Although in *Withrow v. Larkin*[448] the Supreme Court held that the combination of investigative and adjudicative functions in one agency did not necessarily create an unconstitutional risk of bias, the Court's decision did not discuss, and would not appear to foreclose, the argument that an unacceptable risk of bias is created where a single lawyer both prosecutes the case and advises the tribunal with respect to matters arising at the hearing or with respect to the disposition of the case, and that the due process clause of the 14th Amendment is therefore contravened by such a practice.

Bias of a Single Member of the Tribunal

A question arising with some frequency is whether the bias of one voting member of a tribunal is sufficient to invalidate the decision where the vote was unnecessary to the result. Several federal courts of appeals have held that such a decision is invalid.[449] As the Third Circuit has said: "Litigants are entitled to an impartial tribunal whether it consists of one man or twenty and there is no way which we know of whereby the influence of one upon the others can be quantitatively measured."[450]

Right to "Voir Dire" Members of Tribunal

A related question is whether a teacher with a protected interest has a due process right in a termination hearing to "voir dire" a member of the tribunal, i.e., to question the member in order to determine whether he is biased and should be disqualified. Some state courts have held that state law accords this right.[451] The Wyoming Supreme Court, by a divided vote, has rejected a tenured teacher's claim that the due process clause of the 14th Amendment afforded him such a right.[452] A state district court in Idaho, however, has ruled that it is "certainly unconstitutional to permit participation in the decision-making process by a board member who holds an actual bias against the particular [tenured] teacher," and accordingly that the plaintiff "was entitled to voir dire examination, to be conducted by the hearing officer under precisely set guidelines, in order to determine whether actual bias did in fact exist."[453]

What remedies are available to a teacher whose employment has been terminated, or who has been disciplined, without due process of law?

An understanding of this question involves the application of a principle enunciated by the Supreme Court in *Mount Healthy City School District Board of Education v. Doyle*.[454] In that case the Court, having concluded that a school board had impermissibly relied upon a teacher's exercise of First Amendment rights in deciding not to renew his contract, indicated that the "constitutional principle at stake" required that the teacher be "placed in no worse a position" than he would have been in had the constitutional violation not occurred.[455] The Court further indicated that implementation of this principle required reinstatement of the teacher with full back pay unless the board could show "by a preponderance of the evidence that it would have reached the same decision as to [the teacher's] reemployment even in the absence of the protected conduct."[456]

In *Carey v. Piphus*[457] the Supreme Court applied a similar analysis to a question involving the remedy for a procedural due process violation. In *Carey* the plaintiffs, public school students, had been deprived of a property interest—their entitlement to attend school—in a manner which violated their procedural due process rights. The Court of Appeals for the Seventh Circuit noted that plaintiffs had "submitted data . . . tending to show the pecuniary value of the time lost" and concluded that plaintiffs were entitled to this compensation unless the defendants could show that the plaintiffs "would have been suspended even if a proper hearing had been held."[458] The Supreme Court agreed, leaving the question whether the plaintiffs were entitled to compensation for the loss of their property to be decided by the district court on remand, with the outcome hinging on whether the defendants could show that they would have deprived the plaintiffs of their property even if constitutionally required procedures had been followed.[459]

The decisions in *Mount Healthy* and *Carey* strongly suggest—and several courts have construed *Carey* to establish—that a teacher or other public employee with a property interest in continued employment who is discharged without procedural due process is entitled to be made whole for the loss of that employment—including reinstatement and back pay—unless the employer can show that the employee would have been discharged even if proper procedures had been followed.[460] Absent such a showing, the employee presumably also would be entitled to any consequential damages stemming from the loss of employment.[461] For as the Court broadly stated in *Carey*, "the purpose of §1983 would be defeated if injuries caused by the deprivation of constitutional rights were uncompensated."[462]

Some courts, however, have taken an approach to the remedial question which does not seem consistent with *Mount*

Healthy and *Carey*. The Fifth Circuit, for example, which has held that a post-termination hearing "cured" the school board's failure to provide adequate pre-termination procedures, has ruled that the employee was nevertheless entitled to damages accruing during the period between his dismissal and the date of his post-termination hearing. The court so ruled without inquiring, as the *Mount Healthy* and *Carey* decisions would seem to require, whether the school board had shown that it would have terminated the teacher's employment even if it had afforded due process prior to termination.[463]

The remediation principles articulated in *Mount Healthy* and *Carey* also seem applicable to deprivations of liberty without due process. Where a school board terminates a teacher's employment based on "charges that might seriously damage his standing and associations in the community," or "imposes on him a stigma . . . that forecloses his freedom to take advantage of other employment opportunities"[464] without affording him notice and a proper hearing, he arguably should have his liberty interest restored through reinstatement as well as compensation for its deprivation unless the board can prove that it would have taken the same action even if it had afforded him procedural due process. Substantial damages may flow from actions which injure a teacher's reputation in the community or which stigmatize him and adversely affect his professional career and ability to obtain employment.[465] Although several court of appeals decisions have held that a *post hoc* hearing is the only remedy available to restore a liberty interest taken away without procedural due process,[466] these decisions are questionable. Restoration of the teacher's liberty interest arguably requires reinstatement because the stigma cannot be removed, and the liberty interest returned to him, unless he is given his job back. Until he is re-employed, it can be contended, the board will continue to convey the message that it credits the accusations against him.

Seeds of confusion in this area have been sown by the Supreme Court opinions in *Board of Regents v. Roth*[467] and *Codd v. Velger*.[468] Taken together, *Roth* and *Codd* teach that when a proposed termination is based on a charge which might damage the employee's standing in the community or would tend to foreclose other employment, and when the charge is denied by the employee, "an opportunity to refute the charge" is "mandated by the Due Process Clause."[469] These cases establish that "[t]he purpose of such notice and hearing is to provide the person an opportunity to clear his name."[470] *Roth* states, moreover, that "[o]nce a person has cleared his name at a hearing, his employer, of course, may remain free to deny him future employment for other reasons."[471] Some courts have concluded from this language that the only remedy to which an employee deprived of liberty without procedural due process is entitled is a court-ordered hearing. But it does not follow from the fact that the due process clause requires a public employer to grant an employee a hearing to clear his name, or from the fact that after the hearing the employee could be terminated for other reasons, that if the employee is denied a hearing, and is terminated not for other reasons but for the very reason which impairs his liberty, that his exclusive remedy is a court-ordered *post hoc* hearing.

The *Codd* opinion further confuses the issue by stating that "the remedy mandated by the Due Process Clause of the Fourteenth Amendment is an 'opportunity to refute the charge.' "[472] The word "remedy," however, has a dual meaning, and in context, it can be argued, the Court used the word in the sense of "[t]he means by which a right is enforced or the violation of a right is *prevented*" rather than in the sense of "[t]he means by which . . . the violation of a right is *redressed*."[473] It reasonably can be contended that what the Court was saying is that the "remedy" a public employer must afford to an employee whose employment it proposes to terminate on the basis of a stigmatizing charge is "an opportunity to refute the charge." The Court had no occasion to consider the relief to which an employee would be entitled if his rights were violated, since the Court ruled that the plaintiff's failure in *Codd* to allege that the charges against him were false was "fatal to [his] claim under the Due Process Clause that he should have been given a hearing."[474]

Even if not necessary to return a liberty interest to a teacher from whom it has been wrongfully taken, reinstatement may still be required to make him whole for loss of a job which occurred as a *consequence* of a due process violation. If a trier of fact were to find that the plaintiff would not have been terminated had he received the due process to which he was entitled, it would necessarily follow that the loss of employment was the consequence of the violation—that but for the violation, he would have continued teaching in the school system. In that event, to place the plaintiff in the position he would have occupied necessarily would require reinstatement.[475] On this issue, the burden of proof presumably would be on the plaintiff.

In addition to reinstatement, back pay may be available on this theory, as may consequential damages. In any event, such damages may be proper where, because of the continued refusal to provide a hearing, lapse of time, or other reason not due to the plaintiff's volition, a hearing now would be impossible or ineffectual, and the failure to afford the plaintiff a hearing caused damage to his reputation.[476]

Where the procedural due process violation consists of school board bias, the board may argue that *Carey* permits the board to show that it would have terminated the teacher's employment even if bias had not infected its decision. A strong argument can be made, however, that while in light of *Carey* a school board should be permitted to prove, based on contemporaneous circumstances, that it would have terminated a teacher's employment even absent the due process violation, *Carey* does not permit a speculative reconstruction of what the school board's decision would have been had it been impartial.

Assuming a school board proves that it would have terminated a teacher's employment even if it had afforded him due process, under *Carey* the teacher would still be entitled to damages for injury actually caused by the procedural violation, apart from its effect on the termination decision.[477] If, for example, a teacher could persuade a court that he suffered physical or emotional distress as a result of a "star chamber" dismissal proceeding, damages might be available under this theory.[478] And if a school board dismissed a teacher after a hearing without stating the reasons for its decision or the evidence upon which it relied, and the teacher demonstrated that this failure thwarted the judicial review to which he was entitled under state law, arguably the teacher would be entitled to damages even if the school board could prove that it would have terminated the teacher's employment even absent the procedural due process violation. Even if no actual damages can be proved, moreover, under *Carey* nominal damages can be awarded,[479] a consideration which may be significant in connection with a potential award of attorneys' fees.

Does the due process clause afford substantive protections in addition to conferring procedural rights?

Yes. The Supreme Court has recognized that the due process clause has a substantive component barring at least some types of arbitrary governmental action.[480]

Where the action of the school authorities in terminating a teacher's employment is involved, other potential claims—some of which may prove to be more viable than a substantive due process claim in the circumstances of the case—should be considered. Such claims might include, in addition to a substantive due process claim, one sounding in tort for "abusive" or "retaliatory" discharge.[481] Common-law doctrines holding at-will employees unprotected against discharge are changing, and tort as well as contract theories are being employed by courts to remedy wrongful discharges of at-will employees in the private sector.[482] Some of these doctrines may protect public employees as well. For example, a teacher with a one-year contract whose employment is terminable at will may argue that the school board has an implied duty not to dismiss him for a bad-faith reason or a reason which is against public policy. Or a teacher may argue that the school authorities commit a tort when they refuse, for such a reason, to renew his contract, although in either case the argument may become less persuasive where the teacher's status is probationary.[483]

Who is entitled to invoke the substantive protections of the due process clause?

Most federal appeals courts considering the issue—following the lead of then Judge (now Justice) Stevens in an opinion written while he was on the Seventh Circuit[484]—have ruled that substantive due process rights, like procedural due process rights, can be invoked only by one with a "liberty" or "property" interest at stake.[485] The Supreme Court has not squarely decided this question. Its decisions, however, do make clear that "the due process clause of the Fourteenth Amendment protects substantive aspects of liberty against impermissible governmental restrictions."[486] Arguably, the "substantive aspects of liberty" protected by the due process clause include freedom from substantively arbitrary government action. If so, the due process clause would invalidate an arbitrary termination or other arbitrary disciplinary decision whether or not it deprived the teacher of a property interest or an independent liberty interest.

One court has suggested that "it would be anomalous indeed to conclude that the same element—'freedom from arbitrariness'—should at once entitle a person to due process and also be a part of the process which is due.[487] This anomaly, however, has not deterred the Supreme Court from "incorporating" particular provisions of the Bill of Rights into the due process clause of the 14th Amendment. Here the same element, e.g., freedom of speech, constitutes both the liberty interest entitling one to substantive due process and a part of the substantive process which is due.

Even if a teacher without a liberty or property interest in continued employment is not entitled to invoke the substantive protections of the due process clause, the teacher may have protections against arbitrary action by his employer on some other theory, not based on the due process clause of the 14th Amendment. For example, such a teacher may have state constitutional or statutory protections; and in many states, common-law doctrines giving at-will employees no protection against arbitrary discharge are changing. Tort or implied contract doctrines are being applied in many states so as to protect employees against "abusive" or "retaliatory" discharge for conduct protected by public policy, e.g., refusing to respond to a supervisor's sexual advances.[488]

Where a teacher has a sufficient interest at stake to invoke the substantive protections of the due process clause, what standard will a court use in determining whether his "substantive due process" rights have been violated?

The Supreme Court has indicated that where the challenged government action burdens the exercise of a liberty which the Court regards as "basic" or "vital," it will scrutinize the action to determine not only whether it is arbitrary or capricious, but also whether it is unnecessary. Thus in *Cleveland Board of Education v. LaFleur*[489] the Supreme Court held unconstitutional a school board rule requiring a pregnant teacher to begin maternity leave five months before the expected birth of her child and precluding re-employment sooner than three months following birth. Noting that "freedom of personal choice in matters of marriage and family life is one of the liberties protected by the Due Process Clause of the Fourteenth Amendment" and that the right to procreate is one of the "basic civil rights of man," the Court observed that "by acting to penalize the pregnant teacher for deciding to bear a child, overly restrictive maternity leave regulations can constitute a heavy burden on the exercise of these protected freedoms." Accordingly, the Court ruled, the due process clause requires that such rules "must not *needlessly*, arbitrarily, or capriciously impinge upon this vital area of a teacher's constitutional liberty."[490] The Court concluded that the mandatory leave regulation contravened the due process clause because it employed an irrebuttable presumption that every pregnant teacher who reached the fifth month of pregnancy was physically incapable of teaching—a presumption which applied even when the medical evidence on an individual woman's status might be wholly to the contrary.[491] On similar reasoning the Court struck down the provision barring re-employment sooner than three months following birth.[492] Similarly, the Third Circuit held that a school board had acted arbitrarily and violated a teaching applicant's substantive due process rights when it adopted an irrebuttable presumption that blind people are unable to teach and consequently prohibited them from taking competitive examinations to become teachers.[493]

The Supreme Court appears to have applied a less stringent standard of review in determining whether government action not affecting a liberty perceived by the Court as "basic" or "vital" violates substantive due process. In *Kelley v. Johnson*[494] the Court assumed that a citizen had "some sort of 'liberty' interest within the meaning of the Fourteenth Amendment in matters of personal appearance,"[495] but concluded that a police department rule limiting the length of a policeman's hair did not violate the due process clause. The Court held that the question was "not, as the court of appeals conceived it to be, whether the state can 'establish' a 'genuine public need' for the specific regulation. It is whether [plaintiff] can demonstrate that there is no rational connection between the regulation, based as it is on the county's method of organizing its police force, and the promotion of safety of persons and property."[496] The Court held that the rule was rational since it could be justified either by a desire to make police officers readily recognizable to the members of the public or by a desire for esprit de corps which similarity in appearance might be felt to inculcate within the police force.[497]

Does a school board policy restricting a teacher's hairstyle or mode of dress violate substantive due process?

The justifications for a policy regulating hairstyle accepted by the Supreme Court in *Kelley v. Johnson* may be rational in a paramilitary organization such as a police force, but do not seem rational in a school context. A Fifth Circuit judge, in a concurring opinion, has stated that "[i]t hardly seems possible that such considerations apply to a high school teacher . . . ."[498]

Nevertheless, the courts have identified other interests which they have determined to be sufficiently rational to justify regulations governing a teacher's hairstyle or mode of dress in the face of a substantive due process challenge. Following the decision in *Kelley*, the Second Circuit upheld the constitutionality of a dress code for teachers, relying on "the school board's interest in promoting respect for authority and traditional values, as well as discipline in the classroom, by requiring teachers to dress in a professional manner."[499] Prior to the *Kelley* decision, the Seventh Circuit had upheld the dismissal of a complaint by a junior-high-school teacher which alleged that he had been discharged for reasons of dress and grooming. The court concluded that "the public's reaction to an official, and a student's reaction to his teacher, is undoubtedly affected by the image [the latter] projects."[500]

Both the Second and the Seventh Circuits indicated that they would not go behind the school board's conclusion that the teacher's style of dress or plumage had an adverse effect on the educational process,[501] although *Kelley v. Johnson*—subsequently decided—indicates that the courts should themselves assess the rationality of the board's conclusion. Indeed to the extent that the Seventh Circuit's decision categorically exempts the government employee's liberty interest in choice of personal appearance from constitutional protection, that holding was rejected in a post-*Kelley* decision of the Seventh Circuit holding that where there appeared to be no rational basis for a school district policy of not permitting a person with a mustache, no matter how neatly trimmed, to drive a school bus, school authorities would be required to justify the policy by showing a "rational relationship between the rule and a public purpose."[502] A court also might well conclude that no rational basis exists for a policy restricting a teacher's hairstyle at the higher-education level, even if it determined that such a policy would be rational at the elementary and secondary level.[503]

Challenges to regulations governing a teacher's appearance may, where appropriate, be framed in First Amendment terms in addition to claimed infringements on "liberty." In a particular case, a teacher may seek to articulate a message through his mode of dress or plumage. For example, a black teacher may wish to assert pride in his black heritage by wearing a goatee or a dashiki.[504]

Where a teacher alleges that his style of dress or grooming constitutes "symbolic speech," however, a court is not likely to require substantial justification for encroaching on such "speech" unless the communicative intent is clear. For example, the Second Circuit, considering a teacher's claim that by refusing to wear a necktie he wished to present himself to his students as a person not tied to "establishment conformity,"[505] viewed his claims of symbolic speech as "vague and unfocused," and said that "[a]s conduct becomes less and less like 'pure speech,' the showing of governmental interest required for its regulation is progressively lessened."[506] In such a case, the court is likely to require no more than the "rational basis" required to support an incursion on a teacher's liberty interest in his personal appearance. Similarly, although a California state court held that a teacher who wore a beard was engaging in "symbolic speech"—an expression of personality—protected by the First Amendment,[507] most courts have rejected "the notion that . . . hair length is of a sufficiently communicative character to warrant the full protection of" the Amendment.[508]

Conceivably it might nevertheless be argued that a dress code or hair regulation is tantamount to a forced utterance and a compelled falsification of the self, akin to a compelled flag salute and for that reason proscribed by the First Amendment and the constitutional right of privacy.[509] As Judge Wisdom of the Fifth Circuit has stated in a dissenting opinion:

Hair . . . for centuries has been one aspect of the manner in which we hold ourselves out to the rest of the
world. . . . A person shorn of the freedom to vary the
length and style of his hair is forced against his will to
hold himself out symbolically as a person holding ideas
contrary, perhaps, to the ideas he holds most dear. Forced
dress, including forced hair style, humiliates the unwilling complier, forces him to submerge his individuality
in the "undistracting" mass, and, in general, smacks of
the exaltation of organization over member, unit over
component, and state over individual.[510]

**What type of governmental action in terminating a teacher's
employment, or otherwise disciplining him, would be so
"irrational" as to violate the due process clause?**

This is an evolving area of the law, but the decisions provide
some guidance.

A Decision Made for Reasons Without Any Basis in Fact

The due process clause bars a state from depriving a person
of liberty or property where there is no basis in fact for the
reasons which are claimed to warrant the deprivation. The
Supreme Court has articulated and applied this principle in
many different contexts. In 1927 the Court stated in an
immigration case that "[d]eportation . . . on charges unsupported by any evidence is a denial of due process.[511] In
Schware v. Board of Bar Examiners[512] and *Konigsberg v.
State Bar*[513] the Court ruled that a state cannot, consistently
with the due process clause, turn down an application for
admission to the bar where there is no evidence rationally
supporting the conclusion that the applicant failed to satisfy
the state's admission standards. Similarly, in a series of cases
beginning with *Thompson v. Louisville*,[514] the Court has
held that it is "a violation of due process to convict and
punish a man without evidence of his guilt."[515]

This principle has been applied frequently in teacher termination and public employee dismissal cases. While some of
these cases were decided before the Supreme Court's rulings
in *Roth* and *Sindermann*, and others do not discuss the

question of whether one must be deprived of a liberty or property interest to invoke substantive due process rights, they nevertheless provide guidance on the extent to which actions of school authorities are vulnerable to a substantive due process challenge by one entitled to invoke the substantive protections of the due process clause.

In a Nebraska case, a middle-aged teacher who was a divorcee lived alone in a one-bedroom apartment in a small town. Her 26-year-old son lived and taught in a neighboring town. On several occasions friends of her son, young ladies, married couples, and young men, visited her town. Because hotel and motel accommodations were generally sparse and unavailable, she followed the advice of the school board's secretary and allowed these guests to stay overnight at her apartment. Based on this conduct, the board dismissed her for "conduct unbecoming a teacher."

Holding that the board's decision was arbitrary and capricious, and a violation of substantive due process, the Eighth Circuit stated that there was "no proof of improper conduct. The only whit of evidence offered as support for the board's conclusion that [she] was guilty of unbecoming conduct was the fact that she had overnight guests." The court stated that "the presence of these guests in her home provides no inkling beyond subtle implication and innuendo which would impugn [her] morality. Idle speculation certainly does not provide a basis in fact for the board's conclusory inference that 'there was a strong potential of sexual misconduct' and that, therefore, [her] activity was social misbehavior that is not conducive to the maintenance of the integrity of the public school system." The Eighth Circuit agreed with the district court that "[a]t most, the evidence may be said to raise a question of [her] good judgment in her personal affairs, when measured against an undefined standard which someone could suppose exists in a small town in Nebraska."[516]

In a New Hampshire case, a federal court invalidated the failure to rehire a high-school teacher after the superintendent and school board, on the basis of uninvestigated complaints and unverified rumors that he had made sexual advances toward female students, concluded—without any evidence—that he had "lost his effectiveness." Holding that the nonrenewal violated the teacher's right to due process, the court said:

To dismiss a teacher on the basis of uninvestigated complaints and unverified rumors and to admit that the decision does not depend on the truth or falseness of the complaints and rumors is patently unjust, arbitrary, and capricious. If the possibility, let alone the probability of the truth of the facts involved is not known, a decision cannot be reasoned or based on substantial evidence. The implications of such a decision are frightening. It means that any student with a personal dislike for a teacher could bring his career to an end by a complaint wholly unjustified and unsubstantiated in fact. In the same sense, a malicious group in the community could start unsubstantiated rumors resulting in dismissal. Further, an administrator or another teacher bent on a personal vendetta could, by insidiously starting false rumors, bring about the dismissal of a totally innocent teacher.[517]

In a Kansas case, a teacher was dismissed in mid-year on public charges of "conduct unbecoming an instructor" based on a jury verdict of guilty on a charge of possessing marijuana. The judge presiding over the teacher's trial, however, subsequently set aside the verdict and acquitted him as a matter of law, stating there was no evidence presented at trial to raise even an inference of guilt. The school board refused to reinstate the teacher. A federal court ruled that the real reason for this refusal involved speech and beliefs protected by the First Amendment, i.e., his responses to questions by the board giving his views on marijuana and revealing his mental conflict, at the time of his son's arrest on a related marijuana charge, between protecting his son and obeying the law. With respect to the board's charges of perjury and prior problems within the school system, the court concluded that there was "no factual justification" for the allegations, and that these and other charges leveled against him were "completely spurious in substance and were made in an attempt to validate an obviously invalid administrative action."[518] The court stated:

Substantive due process requires the decision-maker to be presented with and to consider a minimal amount of credible evidence sufficient to support a legal basis for its ultimate action. . . . [W]hat constitutes sufficient evidence may vary from situation to situation, although it need be only enough to prevent the decision from being wholly arbitrary and capricious . . . .[519]

A Decision Made for Reasons Unrelated to Teaching Fitness or the Effective Operation of the Schools

A school board's decision may be irrational, and therefore violate the substantive due process rights of a teacher entitled to invoke such protection, if it is made for reasons which bear no substantial relationship to teaching fitness or the effective operation of the schools.

Before the Supreme Court's decisions in *Board of Regents v. Roth* and *Perry v. Sindermann,* the First Circuit stated in *Drown v. Portsmouth School District*[520] that a school board would violate the due process clause if its reason for not renewing a teacher's contract were "unrelated to the educational process or to working relationships within the educational institution.[521] A teacher, said the court, "may not be dismissed for the type of automobile she drives or for the kinds of foods she eats."[522]

The court in *Drown* did not consider whether a teacher must be deprived of a property interest or an independent liberty interest in order to qualify for substantive due process protection. Nevertheless, the court's view is instructive in defining the boundaries of irrationality in those circumstances in which, under the prevailing law of the circuit in which the case arises, irrational termination of a teacher's employment is forbidden by the due process clause.

Decisions subsequent to *Roth* and *Sindermann* support the conclusion that where a public employee has an interest sufficient to invoke due process protection he may successfully attack the termination of his employment on substantive due process grounds where there is no rational connection between the employee's alleged misconduct and his suitability for continued employment. For example, where a public employee is stigmatized, and thus deprived of a liberty interest, by a discharge for homosexual activity, due process requires that some nexus be shown between the homosexual conduct and suitability for service.[523] This principle would appear to invalidate the termination of a teacher's employment—regardless of tenure status—on a charge of having committed private homosexual acts or being a homosexual, at least absent a showing that such conduct or status had become publicly known prior to the termination. The same principle may also serve as one basis for attacking the termination of a teacher's employment for allegedly "immoral" conduct, such as living together out of wedlock,[524] at least in circumstances where such conduct is not open and notorious. Where conduct of this sort becomes publicly known the teacher's case may be weaker because a court may view the teacher as a poor "role model" for students, or perceive the teacher as losing respect in the community and among the students.[525] Such defenses by school officials, however, may be vulnerable. It can be argued that as a factual matter a teacher is not a role model for behavior outside the classroom. And it can be contended that the teacher's conduct must have a nexus to a *legitimate* interest of the school authorities, and that they do not have a legitimate interest in enforcing conventional morality, even as a device for ensuring that the community, or the teacher's students, maintain their "respect" for the teacher.

Arguably a school board's decision may be unrelated to teaching fitness or to the effective operation of the schools if it is based on personal animus rather than the legitimate interests of the school authorities. A Massachusetts federal district court ruled that "[w]hile it may be perfectly legitimate for a private superior not to promote an employee whom he personally dislikes, a government employer may not stand in the way of the developing career of a subordinate for personal reasons not related to job function.[526] The court concluded that while a police chief might have legitimately decided that the working relationship between himself and a sergeant under his command had deteriorated to a point that they could not effectively work together, "the current state of the record presents a serious question of fact as to whether such a legitimate concern motivated [the police chief] or whether he illegitimately acted purely out of personal pique" stemming from a personal remark made by the sergeant to the man who later became his superior when they were both patrolmen on the police force.[527]

A school board's policy or decision may purport to relate to teaching fitness or to the effective operation of the schools, but may lack any rational basis. In a Georgia case a teacher who had been convicted of the felony of refusing induction into the armed forces was denied a teaching certificate by the State Board of Education. Despite a hearing examiner's recommendation that he be reconsidered for the certificate without regard to the conviction, the State Board refused to reconsider, and denied him a certificate solely because of his refusal to be inducted. The information before the hearing examiner and the Board was all favorable to the teacher and there was no showing that the refusal of induction had any adverse impact upon the effective operation of the schools. A federal court concluded that the denial of a certificate violated his due process rights, stating:

[U]nder the particular facts and circumstances of this case where the Board appoints a hearing examiner who considers the information provided (which information is all favorable to plaintiff) which shows that his refusal to be inducted has no adverse impact on the students, the school, or the community and which is not repudiated or challenged in any way, and where this hearing examiner recommends that the Board grant plaintiff a certificate, then the Board cannot arbitrarily reverse this recommendation and deny the certificate without some reasonable factual basis.[528]

In a case involving a highly evaluated teacher who was dismissed because he was convicted of buying a stolen motorcycle, the Washington Supreme Court held that the dismissal violated the teacher's right to substantive due process. The court held that in order to discharge the teacher, the school district had to show sufficient cause, which "has been interpreted to mean a showing of conduct which materially and substantially affects the teacher's performance. . . . Without an actual showing of impairment to teaching, simply labeling an instructor as a convicted felon will not justify a discharge."[529] Indeed, the court said that a teacher who committed an indiscretion might be more committed to persuading students to adhere to high moral standards than would other teachers.[530]

Similarly, a federal district court in New Orleans overturned, on substantive due process grounds, the ruling of a U.S. Civil Service Commission Board of Appeals and Review which upheld the dismissal of an Internal Revenue Service agent on the ground that the actions of the agent in renting and using an apartment, together with three other males, in the city's French Quarter, for the purpose of extramarital sexual relationships with consenting females during off-duty hours tended to discredit himself and the service. Concluding that the agent's acts were "circumspect, indeed clandestine," and citing New Orleans' boast that it was "the city that care forgot," the court determined that there was "no evidence that his actions were calculated to arouse, or did in fact arouse, odium for the employee or the IRS. The record demonstrates no rational basis for the conclusion reached by the Appeals Board. Its conclusion is a moral judgment, not a finding supported by evidence, that the disapproved conduct incurred discredit."[531] The court concluded that the substantive aspect of the due process clause prohibits "actions that do not bear at least a rational relationship to a valid governmental objective,"[532] and that "[t]he Constitution prevents the discharge of an employee merely because his conduct during off-duty hours incurs the disapproval of his supervisor.[533] Consistent with Fifth Circuit precedent,[534] the court did not inquire into whether the employee's discharge deprived him of a liberty or property interest.

It has been argued that "moonlighting" regulations limiting a teacher's outside employment violate substantive due process, but the courts have rejected such challenges, at least where the regulation is evenhandedly applied. A Tennessee federal district court held that the due process clause did not confer upon professors of medicine at an institution of higher learning a right to engage in the unlimited private practice of medicine outside of their teaching positions, and accordingly upheld their dismissals from their teaching and administrative posts for refusing to sign income-limiting agreements as required of all full-time faculty members. The court held that the agreements were rationally related to the legitimate goal of fostering full-time devotion to teaching duties.[535] Similarly, the Fifth Circuit, holding that a school district policy against moonlighting had been applied so as to bar only substantial outside involvement, held that the policy did not violate a teacher's substantive due process rights because it was "reasonably related to the legitimate state interest in assuring that public school employees devote their professional energies to the education of children . . . on the rational basis that persons engaged in outside businesses will tend to have less time and interest and to be less responsive to the demands of their jobs than they would were school teaching or administration their sole occupation."[536] The court held for the discharged plaintiff on equal protection grounds because the policy was discriminatorily applied to him but not to other teachers similarly situated.[537]

Where reasonable minds could differ as to whether a school board's reasons for terminating a teacher's employment are substantially related to the educational process or to working relationships within the educational institution, a court may be tempted to defer to the board and reject a due process challenge. Thus, where "fair minded men could reasonably dispute" this question, the First Circuit will not overturn the board's decision on constitutional grounds. That court refused to disturb the dismissal of an elementary-school teacher whose personality disorder resulted in out-of-school conduct "sufficiently bizarre and threatening so that, in the minds of many, it would destroy his ability to serve as a role-model for young children."[538] Nevertheless, it can be argued that the issue of whether board conduct is rational is one for the court to decide, and that deference to the board on this issue is inappropriate.

A Decision Made for Trivial Reasons

In *Johnson v. Branch*,[539] a case decided before the Supreme Court's rulings in *Roth* and *Sindermann*, the Fourth Circuit held that the termination of a teacher's employment could be arbitrary and capricious and violate the due process clause if the supporting reasons were trivial. In that case a school board had refused to renew a non-tenured teacher's contract allegedly because of multiple infractions of school rules. Although the Fourth Circuit determined that the actual reason for non-renewal was the teacher's civil rights activity, it also ruled that the infractions, ranging from coming to school a few minutes late to arriving 15 minutes late to supervise an evening athletic contest, were too insignificant to warrant the sanction of non-renewal. The court held that while a school board has discretion in determining whether to renew the contract of a non-tenured teacher, "[d]iscretion means the exercise of judgment, not bias or capriciousness. Thus it must be based on fact and supported by reasoned analysis."[540]

In another opinion handed down before the *Roth* and *Sindermann* decisions, the First Circuit, citing *Johnson*, agreed with the Fourth Circuit's view that the non-renewal of a teacher's contract would be arbitrary and capricious, and violate the due process clause, if the reasons were "simply too insignificant to justify the ultimate sanction of non-renewal," although the court thought this would be a "delicate judgment" and that a "court would be loath to interfere except in egregious cases."[541]

Although neither the First nor the Fourth Circuit considered the issue of whether deprivation of a property interest or an independent liberty interest was necessary to entitle a teacher to substantive due process protection, the opinions are nevertheless helpful in identifying the parameters of irrationality in those cases in which, under the law of the circuit, due process proscribes the irrational termination of a teacher's employment.

A Decision Based on Failure to Comply With an Unreasonable Directive

A teacher entitled to substantive due process protection arguably cannot be penalized for failing to comply with an unreasonable order, even if it is related to the educational process, e.g., an administrative directive to be in two places at once or to teach his class while standing on his head.

A Decision Based on the Teacher's Exercise of a Legal Right

It is arguably irrational to punish a teacher for exercising a legal right. A Delaware federal court, in a decision handed down before *Roth* and *Sindermann*, concluded that if the real reason for the refusal to renew a teacher's contract was the exercise of her lawful right to seek a transfer, "then a serious legal question arises whether defendants' action was not so arbitrary, unreasonable and discriminatory as to violate substantive due process."[542]

A Decision Based on an Unreasonably Discriminatory Criterion

As the Delaware case suggests, school authorities may violate the substantive due process rights of a teacher entitled to such protection if their decision is based on an unreasonably discriminatory criterion.

The Supreme Court has held that "discrimination may be so unjustifiable as to be violative of due process."[543] This was why, even though the Constitution contains no "equal protection" clause applicable to the federal government, the Supreme Court held racial segregation in the District of Columbia schools unconstitutional as a violation of the due process clause of the Fifth Amendment.[544]

Thus, a decision of a school board terminating a teacher's employment may violate his 14th Amendment due process rights where the decision rests upon an unreasonable classification, even though the same vice may also require invalidation of the decision under the Amendment's equal protection clause.

A Decision Based on an Act or Omission Without Prior Warning That It Would Constitute a Basis for Discharge or Discipline

A firm body of Supreme Court decisions recognizes "the fair-warning requirement embodied in the Due Process Clause."[545] The government must "give the person of ordinary intelligence a reasonable opportunity to know what is prohibited, so that he may act accordingly."[546]

This principle has been recognized in teacher cases. The Second Circuit, while rejecting a teacher's claims that a statute authorizing his dismissal was unconstitutionally vague as applied to him, recognized that "[t]he notion of due process requires that sanctions be imposed on individuals only if they could reasonably have known in advance that their questioned behavior had been proscribed. . . . Due process requires *prior* notice of what constitutes forbidden behavior."[547] The Seventh Circuit applied this principle in ruling that a discharged college president, "as a public employee," was "entitled to be protected from retaliation for actions which he had every reason to believe were a part of his assigned duties."[548] His complaint had alleged that he was discharged for circulating among his administrative staff a confidential memorandum, which somehow became public, requesting the staff to consider certain proposed changes in the college's ethnic studies program. The court concluded that "[t]he facts alleged in his complaint indicate that he has a cause of action resulting from the deprivation of substantive due process."[549] In a Delaware case a federal district court, noting that "the record . . . indicates that the plaintiff [a director of residence halls for women at a state college] had no notice or warning that she would be terminated for deciding to bear an illegitimate child," stated that "the lack of notice of prohibited conduct may . . . constitute a violation of substantive due process."[550]

To the extent that fair warning is a requirement of the due process clause, the requirement would seem applicable not merely to a teacher's acts but also to his omissions. In a Nebraska case a federal court ruled that a teacher could not be dismissed for failing to satisfy the superintendent's concept of "professional growth" when the teacher had fulfilled the requirement as defined in the personnel handbook published by the board of education.[551] The court said: "To set forth one definition and then apply another certainly runs contrary to the definition of the Board's attorney of due process, namely 'basic fairness.' "[552]

The fair-warning concept embodied in the due process clause arguably requires not only prior notice of what is forbidden or required, but also notice that punishment can be imposed for non-compliance and notice of the magnitude of the possible sanction. In an Arkansas case a teacher who was also a football coach violated a regulation governing off-season practice promulgated by an interscholastic athletic association consisting of public and parochial schools. The association then sought his dismissal from the position of teacher-coach. The Eighth Circuit ruled that he could not constitutionally be dismissed for violating the regulation, because even though it could be argued that he had fair notice that the off-season practice was prohibited and that it might subject the school to punitive sanctions, he did not have "fair notice that his employment contract could be coercively terminated" if he violated the regulation. Quoting from a Supreme Court decision, the court stated that "[o]ne of the fundamental requirements of fairness implicit within due process is 'warning . . . in language that the common world will understand, of what the law intends to do if a certain line is passed.' "553

A Decision Placing Responsibility upon a Teacher for the Conduct of Another

Presumably it would be irrational, as well as unfair, for a school system to terminate a teacher's employment, or otherwise discipline him, because of the conduct of another where the teacher bears no personal responsibility for the conduct.554 Cases may arise, for example, in which a school board imposes a sanction upon a teacher for the disruptive act of the teacher's spouse. A teacher may be disciplined because of conduct for which another teacher bears sole responsibility. Or a teacher may be unreasonably punished for the act of a parent or student.

In *St. Ann v. Palisi*555 two students had been suspended from one school and transferred to another because their mother had come into the first school and "struck [the assistant principal] on the face with her fist in which she was holding a key chain." The district court dismissed the students' claim that they had been denied substantive due process, but the Fifth Circuit reversed. The court relied upon the "fundamental" concept that guilt should be personal and the notion that "guilt by association" is alien to American liberty. This decision provides some support for the argument that it is irrational to subject a teacher to adverse action based solely upon the wrongdoing of others, and that a teacher who is entitled to invoke substantive due process may successfully challenge such action.556

The concept that it is irrational to evaluate a teacher based on matters for which he bears no personal responsibility may come into play where a teacher's employment is terminated based on test scores of his students. Where the test does not reflect the curriculum or the topics which the teacher was actually required to teach, such a termination may well be irrational, and thus vulnerable to challenge by a teacher entitled to invoke the substantive protections of the due process clause.[557]

NOTES

1. United States Constitution, 14th Amendment, § 1.
2. 408 U.S. 564, 569 (1972).
3. 408 U.S. 593, 600 (1972).
4. 408 U.S. at 576.
5. *Id*. at 577.
6. 408 U.S. at 602.
7. 408 U.S. at 577.
8. 408 U.S. 593 (1972).
9. *Id*. at 602 n.7. *Cf. Jago v. Van Curen*, 454 U.S. 14, 17–18 (1981).
10. 426 U.S. 341 (1976).
11. 279 N.C. 254, 182 S.E.2d 403 (1971).
12. 426 U.S. at 344–45.
13. *Id*. at 345–47.
14. 424 U.S. 693, 710 (1976).
15. *Confederation of Police v. City of Chicago*, 547 F.2d 375, 376 (7th Cir.), *cert. denied*, 431 U.S. 915 (1977).
16. *Id*.
17. *Stevens v. Joint School District No. 1*, 429 F.Supp. 477, 483 (W.D. Wis. 1977).
18. *Memphis Light, Gas & Water Division v. Craft*, 436 U.S. 1, 9 (1978). *See generally* Monaghan, *Of "Liberty" and "Property,"* 62 Cornell L.Rev. 405, 434–44 (1977).
19. *Quinn v. Syracuse Model Neighborhood Corp.*, 613 F.2d 438, 448 (2d Cir. 1980). *See also Logan v. Zimmerman Brush Co.*, 455 U.S. 422, 434 (1982) ("the State may not finally destroy a property interest without first giving the putative owner an opportunity to present his claim of entitlement").
20. *Quinn v. Syracuse Model Neighborhood Corp.*, *supra* note 19, at 448.
21. 350 U.S. 551 (1956).
22. *Id*. at 559.
23. 408 U.S. 564, 576 (1972). *See also Perry v. Sindermann*, 408 U.S. 593, 601 (1972) ("A written contract with an explicit tenure provi-

sion clearly is evidence of a formal understanding that supports a teacher's claim of entitlement to continued employment unless sufficient 'cause' is shown").

24. *See, e.g., Buck v. Board of Education,* 553 F.2d 315, 318 (2d Cir. 1977), *cert. denied,* 438 U.S. 904 (1978); *Wood v. Goodman,* 381 F.Supp. 413, 420 (D. Mass. 1974), *aff'd,* 516 F.2d 894 (1st Cir. 1975).

25. 408 U.S. 593, 602–03 (1972).

26. *Soni v. Board of Trustees,* 513 F.2d 347 (6th Cir. 1975), *cert. denied,* 426 U.S. 919 (1976).

27. *Zimmerer v. Spencer,* 485 F.2d 176, 178 (5th Cir. 1973). *See also Bignall v. North Idaho College,* 538 F.2d 243, 247 (9th Cir. 1976); *Decker v. North Idaho College,* 552 F.2d 872, 874 (9th Cir. 1977); *Ashton v. Civiletti,* 613 F.2d 923 (D.C. Cir. 1979) ("[A]ppellant's position was explicitly made probationary for one year. In the absence of any special definition of that word, appellant could only be expected to comprehend it in its normal meaning— that he was required to serve an initial proving period in which his performance could be tested and, if his employer was dissatisfied, in which he could be fired without ceremony. A probationary period, of course, would be unnecessary if the employer could dismiss a non-probationary employee at any time and for any reason").

28. *Lukac v. Acocks,* 466 F.2d 577 (6th Cir. 1972).

29. *Board of Regents v. Roth,* 408 U.S. at 576–77 (1972). *See also Stewart v. Bailey,* 556 F.2d 281, 285 (5th Cir. 1977); *Hostrop v. Board of Junior College District No. 515,* 471 F.2d 488, 494 (7th Cir. 1972), *cert. denied,* 411 U.S. 967 (1973); *Skehan v. Board of Trustees of Bloomsburg State College,* 501 F.2d 31, 38 (3d Cir. 1974), *cert. denied,* 429 U.S. 979 (1976); *Heins v. Beaumont Independent School District,* 525 F.Supp. 367, 371 (E.D. Tex. 1981); *Cochran v. Chidester School District,* 456 F.Supp. 390, 395 (W.D. Ark. 1978).

30. 426 U.S. 341, 345 n.8 (1976). *See also Ventetuolo v. Burke,* 596 F.2d 476, 481 (1st Cir. 1979) and cases cited; *United Steelworkers v. University of Alabama,* 599 F.2d 56, 60 (5th Cir. 1969).

31. *Peacock v. Board of Regents,* 510 F.2d 1324, 1326–27 (9th Cir.), *cert. denied,* 422 U.S. 1049 (1975).

32. 408 U.S. at 602.

33. 408 U.S. at 602.

34. *Soni v. Board of Trustees,* 513 F.2d 347, 351 (6th Cir. 1975), *cert. denied,* 426 U.S. 919 (1976).

35. *Eichman v. Indiana State University Board of Trustees,* 597 F.2d 1104, 1109 (7th Cir. 1979).

36. *See Steinberg v. Elkins,* 470 F.Supp. 1024, 1029 (D. Md. 1979).

37. *Id.* at 1026–29.

38. *Id.* at 1027, 1029–31.
39. *Needleman v. Bohlen*, 602 F.2d 1, 4 (1st Cir. 1979). *See also Beitzell v. Jeffrey*, 643 F.2d 870, 877 (1st Cir. 1981); *Willens v. University of Massachusetts*, 570 F.2d 403, 404 (1st Cir. 1978).
40. *Megill v. Board of Regents*, 541 F.2d 1073, 1078 (5th Cir. 1976). *See also Plummer v. Board of Regents*, 552 F.2d 716 (6th Cir. 1977); *Wells v. Board of Regents*, 545 F.2d 15 (6th Cir. 1976); *Ryan v. Board of Education*, 540 F.2d 222, 228 (6th Cir. 1976), *cert. denied*, 429 U.S. 1041 (1977); *Watts v. Board of Curators*, 363 F.Supp. 883, 888 (W.D. Mo. 1973), *aff 'd on other grounds*, 495 F.2d 384 (8th Cir. 1974).
41. *Haimowitz v. University of Nevada*, 579 F.2d 526, 528 (9th Cir. 1978). *See also Cotten v. Board of Regents*, 395 F.Supp. 388, 393 (S.D. Ga. 1974), *aff 'd*, 515 F.2d 1098 (5th Cir. 1975).
42. *Davis v. Oregon State University*, 591 F.2d 493, 496 (9th Cir. 1978); *Haimowitz v. University of Nevada*, 579 F.2d 526, 529 (9th Cir. 1978).
43. *Harris v. Arizona Board of Regents*, 528 F.Supp. 987, 996–97 (D. Ariz. 1981).
44. *Morris v. Board of Education*, 401 F.Supp. 188, 210 (D. Del. 1975). *See also Himmelbrand v. Harrison*, 484 F.Supp. 803, 808 (W.D. Va. 1980).
45. *Compare Sigmon v. Poe*, 564 F.2d 1093 (4th Cir. 1977) (rejecting argument that state statute conferred right upon probationary teacher not to have re-employment denied for "arbitrary, capricious, discriminatory, or for political or personal or political reasons," since statute was advisory only, and therefore created no property interest).
46. *Thomas v. Ward*, 529 F.2d 916, 918–19 (4th Cir. 1975) (emphasis in handbook).
47. *Lewis v. Delaware State College*, 455 F.Supp. 239, 246–47 (D. Del. 1978).
48. *Board of Regents v. Roth*, 408 U.S. 564, 577 (1972).
49. *See Lipp v. Board of Education*, 470 F.2d 802, 805 n.5 (7th Cir. 1972).
50. *Victor v. Brinkley*, 476 F.Supp. 888, 894 (E.D. Mich. 1979).
51. *Lake Michigan College Federation of Teachers v. Lake Michigan Community College*, 518 F.2d 1091, 1096 (6th Cir. 1975), *cert. denied*, 427 U.S. 904 (1976).
52. *Williams v. Day*, 553 F.2d 1160, 1163 (8th Cir. 1977) (Arkansas); *Cato v. Collins*, 539 F.2d 656, 660–61 (8th Cir. 1976) (Arkansas); *Brouillette v. Board of Directors*, 519 F.2d 126, 127 (8th Cir. 1975) (Iowa); *Buhr v. Buffalo Public School District*, 509 F.2d 1196, 1200 (8th Cir. 1974) (North Dakota).
53. *Haron v. Board of Education*, 411 F.Supp. 68, 71 (E.D. N.Y. 1976). *See also Summers v. Civis*, 420 F.Supp. 993, 995 (W.D. Okla. 1976). *Cf. Ring v. Schlesinger*, 502 F.2d 479, 487 (D.C. Cir. 1974).

54. *McElearney v. University of Illinois*, 612 F.2d 285, 291 (7th Cir. 1979).

55. *See Himmelbrand v. Harrison*, 484 F.Supp. 803, 808 (W.D. Va. 1980).

56. *E.g.*, *Prince v. Bridges*, 537 F.2d 1269, 1272 (4th Cir. 1976); *Himmelbrand v. Harrison*, 484 F.Supp. 803, 808 (W.D. Va. 1980); *Ely v. Honaker*, 451 F.Supp. 16, 19 (W.D. Va. 1977), *aff'd*, 558 F.2d 1348 (4th Cir. 1978). *But see Davis v. Oregon State University*, 591 F.2d 493, 497 (9th Cir. 1978) (rejecting former associate professor's argument that because Oregon statute requiring promulgation of regulations to give university employees access to confidential files was enacted to prevent arbitrary firings, failure of institution to establish or follow such regulations before terminating his employment gave him a property interest in continued employment to the extent that he was entitled to a pre-termination hearing).

57. *See, e.g.*, *Munro v. Elk Rapids Schools*, 385 Mich. 6181, 189 N.W.2d 224 (1971); *Zimmerman v. Minot State College*, 198 N.W. 2d 108 (N.Dak. 1972); *Hillis v. Meister*, 82 N.M. 474, 483 P.2d 1314 (1971); *Owens v. School District No: 8R of Umatilla County*, 3 Ore. App. 294, 473 P.2d 678, 680 (1970).

58. *Francis v. Ota*, 356 F.Supp. 1029, 1033–34 (D. Hawaii 1973). *But see Carr v. Board of Trustees*, 465 F.Supp. 886, 901 (N.D. Ohio 1979), *aff'd*, 663 F.2d 1070 (6th Cir. 1981).

59. *Francis v. Ota*, 356 F.Supp. 1029, 1034 (D. Hawaii 1973).

60. 416 U.S. 134 (1974).

61. *Id.* at 153–54 (opinion of Rehnquist, J.).

62. *Id.* at 166–67 (opinion of Powell, J., joined by Blackmun, J.); 185–86 (opinion of White, J.); 210–11 (opinion of Marshall, J., joined by Douglas, J., and Brennan, J.).

63. 408 U.S. 593 (1972).

64. *Id.* at 602.

65. *Roane v. Callisburg Independent School District*, 511 F.2d 633, 638–39 (5th Cir. 1975).

66. *Hermes v. Hein*, 511 F. Supp. 123, 125 (N.D. Ill. 1980).

67. *Soni v. Board of Trustees*, 513 F.2d 347, 350 (6th Cir. 1975), *cert. denied*, 426 U.S. 919 (1976). *See also Hawkins v. Board of Education*, 468 F.Supp. 201, 208 (D. Del. 1979) (school authorities, who admitted that it was "the practice, custom and usage of the Board [of Education] not to terminate employees in positions such as plaintiff [a Fireman Custodian] except for good cause shown" were "hardly in a position to argue that the plaintiff has not demonstrated any legitimate expectation that he would not be terminated except for good cause," and thus plaintiff had a property interest in continued employment sufficient to invoke the protections of the due process clause); *Terrien v. Metropolitan Milwaukee Criminal Justice Council*, 455 F.Supp 1375, 1382 (E.D. Wis. 1978).

68. *Soni v. Board of Trustees. supra.* at 350–51.

69. *E.g., McElearney v. University of Illinois*, 612 F.2d 285, 287 (7th Cir. 1979); *Haimowitz v. University of Nevada*, 579 F.2d 526, 529 (9th Cir. 1978).

70. *Ashton v. Civiletti*, 613 F.2d 923 (D.C. Cir. 1979).

71. *Carr v. Board of Trustees*, 465 F.Supp. 886, 901 (N.D. Ohio 1979), *aff'd*, 663 F.2d 1070 (6th Cir. 1981).

72. *Haimowitz v. University of Nevada*, 579 F.2d 526, 529 (9th Cir. 1978); *Bertot v. School District No. 1*, 522 F.2d 1171, 1177 (10th Cir. 1975).

73. *Stebbins v. Weaver*, 537 F.2d 939, 942 (7th Cir. 1976), *cert. denied*, 429 U.S. 1041 (1977).

74. *See Morris v. Board of Education*, 401 F.Supp. 188, 210 (D. Del. 1975).

75. *Stebbins v. Weaver*, 537 F.2d 939, 942 (7th Cir. 1976), *cert. denied*, 429 U.S. 1041 (1977).

76. *Beitzell v. Jeffrey*, 643 F.2d 870, 877 (1st Cir. 1981).

77. *Doyle v. University of Alabama*, 680 F.2d 1323 (11th Cir. 1982).

78. *Kramedas v. Board of Education*, 523 F.Supp. 1268, 1271–73 (D. Del. 1981).

79. *Id.* at 1273, *citing Bishop v. Wood*, 426 U.S. 341, 349 (1976), and *Clark v. Whiting*, 607 F.2d 634, 639–49 (4th Cir. 1979).

80. *Morris v. Board of Education*, 401 F.Supp. 188, 210 (D. Del. 1975); *Siler v. Brady Independent School District*, 553 F.2d 385, 388 (5th Cir. 1977); *Moore v. Knowles*, 377 F.Supp. 302, 309 (N.D. Tex. 1974), *aff'd*, 512 F.2d 72 (5th Cir. 1975); *Hix v. Tuloso-Midway Independent School District*, 489 S.W.2d 706 (Tex. Civ.App. 1972), *ref'd n.r.e.*

81. *Siler v. Brady Independent School District*, 553 F.2d 385, 388 (5th Cir. 1977). *See also Moore v. Knowles, supra; Hix v. Tuloso-Midway Independent School District, supra.*

82. *See Kohler v. Hirst*, 460 F.Supp. 412, 417 (E.D. Va. 1978).

83. *See Moore v. Knowles*, 377 F.Supp. 302, 308 (N.D. Tex. 1974), *aff'd on opinion of district court*, 512 F.2d 72 (5th Cir. 1975); *Mack v. Cape Elizabeth School Board*, 553 F.2d 720, 722 (1st Cir. 1977). *Cf. LaBorde v. Franklin Parish School Board*, 510 F.2d 590, 593 (5th Cir. 1975). *See also Ogletree v. Chester*, 682 F.2d 1366, 1370–71 (11th Cir. 1982) (representation to county employee); *Bollow v. Federal Reserve Bank*, 650 F.2d 1093, 1099–1100 (9th Cir. 1981), *cert. denied*, 455 U.S. 948 (1982).

84. *See Ventetuolo v. Burke*, 596 F.2d 476, 480–82 (1st Cir. 1979); *Davis v. Oregon State University*, 591 F.2d 493, 496 (9th Cir. 1978).

85. *Lee v. Conecuh County Board of Education*, 464 F.Supp. 333, 340 (S.D. Ala. 1979), *rev'd on other grounds*, 634 F.2d 959 (5th Cir. 1981).

86. *Davis v. Oregon State University*, 591 F.2d 493, 496 (9th Cir. 1978).

87. *Lake Michigan College Federation of Teachers v. Lake Michigan Community College,* 518 F.2d 1091, 1095–96 (6th Cir. 1975), *cert. denied,* 427 U.S. 904 (1976).

88. *Cf. Mathews v. Eldridge,* 424 U.S. 319, 332–33 (1976); *Wolff v. McDonnell,* 418 U.S. 539, 557–58 (1974).

89. *Thurston v. Dekle,* 531 F.2d 1264, 1271–72 (5th Cir. 1976), *vacated on other grounds,* 438 U.S. 901 (1978); *Muscare v. Quinn,* 520 F.2d 1212, 1215 (7th Cir. 1975), *cert. dismissed as improvidently granted,* 425 U.S. 560 (1976).

90. 419 U.S. 565, 576 (1975).

91. *Muscare v. Quinn,* 520 F.2d 1212 (7th Cir. 1975).

92. *Id.* at 1215.

93. *Id.* at 1215 n.3.

94. 425 F.2d 1252, 192 Ct. Cl. 1 (1970).

95. 425 F.2d at 1257 (Skelton, J., concurring).

96. *See Acanfora v. Board of Education,* 359 F.Supp. 843, 853 (D. Md. 1973), *aff'd on other grounds,* 491 F.2d 498 (4th Cir.), *cert. denied,* 419 U.S. 836 (1974) (teacher hired under formal contract with clearly implied promise of continued employment as a classroom teacher must be afforded a due process hearing in connection with transfer to department of curriculum, even though he suffers no loss of pay; *cf. Moore v. Gaston County Board of Education,* 357 F.Supp. 1037, 1041 (W.D. N.C. 1973) (where university and school system agreed that plaintiff would have a term of practice teaching at a particular school, she had a reasonable expectation that the opportunity for practice teaching would continue until the fall term as required by the university curriculum, and thus due process required a fair hearing in connection with her proposed discharge, even though her position was one without compensation). *Id.* at 1041.

97. *MacMurray v. Board of Trustees,* 428 F.Supp. 1171, 1176 (M.D. Pa. 1977). *See also James v. Board of School Commissioners,* 484 F.Supp. 705, 714 (S.D. Ala. 1979); *Peacock v. Board of Regents,* 380 F.Supp. 1081, 1087 (D. Ariz. 1974), *aff'd on other grounds,* 510 F.2d 1324 (9th Cir.), *cert. denied,* 422 U.S. 1049 (1975); *Lafferty v. Carter,* 310 F.Supp. 465, 470 (W.D. Wis. 1970).

98. *Sullivan v. Brown,* 544 F.2d 279, 282 (6th Cir. 1976). *See also Moore v. Otero,* 557 F.2d 435, 437 (5th Cir. 1977); *Kolz v. Board of Education,* 576 F.2d 747, 749 (7th Cir. 1978).

99. *Coe v. Bogart,* 519 F.2d 10, 12 (6th Cir. 1975). *See also Danno v. Peterson,* 421 F.Supp. 950 (N.D. Ill. 1976).

100. *Wooten v. Clifton Forge School Board,* 655 F.2d 552 (4th Cir. 1981).

101. *Childers v. Independent School District,* 676 F.2d 1338, 1341 (10th Cir. 1982).

102. *Acanfora v. Board of Education,* 359 F.Supp. 843, 853 (D. Md. 1973), *aff'd on other grounds,* 491 F.2d 498 (4th Cir.), *cert. denied,* 419 U.S. 836 (1974).

103. *Thomas v. Board of Trustees*, 515 F.Supp. 280, 287 (S.D. Tex. 1981).

104. *E.g.*, *Bignall v. North Idaho College*, 538 F.2d 243, 249 (9th Cir. 1976); *Collins v. Wolfson*, 498 F.2d 1100, 1104 (5th Cir. 1974). *See also Jimenez v. Almodovar*, 650 F.2d 363, 369–70 (1st Cir. 1981).

105. *E.g.*, *Mims v. Board of Education*, 523 F.2d 711, 715 (5th Cir. 1975); *Powell v. Jones*, 56 Ill. 2d 70, 81–82, 305 N.E.2d 166, 171–72 (1973); *Howell v. Woodlin School District R–104*, 198 Colo. 40, 46, 596 P.2d 56, 60 (1979).

106. *Klein v. Board of Higher Education*, 434 F.Supp. 1113 (S.D. N.Y. 1977); *Johnson v. Board of Regents*, 377 F.Supp. 227, 235 (W.D. Wis. 1974), *aff'd mem.*, 510 F.2d 975 (7th Cir. 1975); *Howell v. Woodlin School District R–104*, 198 Colo. 40, 46, 596 P.2d 56, 60 (1979).

107. *Bignall v. North Idaho College*, supra note 104.

108. *Klein v. Board of Higher Education*, 434 F.Supp. 1113 (S.D. N.Y. 1975); *Johnson v. Board of Regents*, 377 F.Supp. 227 (W.D. Wis. 1974), *aff'd mem.*, 510 F.2d 975 (7th Cir. 1975); *Howell v. Woodlin School District R–104*, 198 Colo. 40, 46, 598 P.2d 56, 60. (1979).

109. AAUP 1940 *Statement of Principles on Academic Freedom and Tenure.*

110. *Bignall v. North Idaho College*, supra.

111. *Collins v. Wolfson*, 498 F.2d 1100, 1104 (5th Cir. 1974).

112. *Howell v. Woodlin School District R–104*, 198 Colo. 40, 46, 596 P.2d 56, 60 (1979).

113. *Bignall v. North Idaho College*, 538 F.2d 243, 249 (9th Cir. 1976).

114. *See Klein v. Board of Higher Education*, 434 F.Supp. 1113 (S.D. N.Y. 1977); *Johnson v. Board of Regents*, 377 F.Supp. 227, 239 (W.D. Wis. 1974), *aff'd memo*. 510 F.2d 975 (7th Cir. 1975); *Howell v. Woodlin School District R–104*, 198 Colo. 40, 46, 598 P.2d 56, 60 (1979).

115. *Johnson v. Board of Regents*, 377 F.Supp. 227, 237 (W.D. Wis. 1974), *aff'd mem.*, 510 F.2d 975 (7th Cir. 1975).

116. *Id.* at 238. Accord *Klein v. Board of Higher Education of City of New York*, 434 F.Supp. 1113, 1118 (S.D. N.Y. 1977) (tenured faculty members "had no constitutional right to participate in the formulation of the retrenchment plans").

117. *Colm v. Vance*, 567 F.2d 1125, 1130 (D.C. Cir. 1977).

118. *Olson v. Trustees of California State Universities*, 351 F.Supp. 430, 433 (C.D. Cal. 1972).

119. *Colm v. Vance*, 567 F.2d 1125, 1130 (D.C. Cir. 1977). *Compare Burns v. Sullivan*, 619 F.2d 99, 104 (1st Cir.), *cert. denied*, 449 U.S. 893 (1980) (no property interest flowed from rank on eligibility list where under state law police chief and city manager could consider subjective factors in addition to written examination score).

120. *Colm v. Vance*, 567 F.2d 1125, 1130 (D.C. Cir. 1977); *see also Schwartz v. Thompson*, 497 F.2d 430, 433 (2d Cir. 1974). *Compare Johnson v. Cain*, 5 EPD ¶8509 (D. Del. 1973).

121. *Webster v. Redmond*, 599 F.2d 793, 801 (7th Cir. 1979), *cert. denied*, 444 U.S. 1039 (1980). *See also Kramedas v. Board of Education*, 523 F.Supp. 1268, 1271 (D. Del. 1981) (court rejects plaintiff's claim that he had entitlement to promotion to principal's position because of criteria adopted for selecting applicants for that position.)

122. *Colm v. Vance*, 567 F.2d 1125, 1132 (D.C. Cir. 1977).

123. *Needleman v. Bohlen*, 602 F.2d 1, 4 (1st Cir. 1979).

124. *Id. Cf. Doyle v. University of Alabama*, 680 F.2d 1323 (11th Cir. 1982) (fact that university employee was recommended for salary increase created no entitlement).

125. *Whitaker v. Board of Higher Education*, 461 F.Supp. 99, 105 (E.D. N.Y. 1978).

126. *State ex rel. McLendon v. Morton*, 249 S.E.2d 919 (1978). *See also Goldsmith v. United States Board of Tax Appeals*, 270 U.S. 117 (1926), *cited in Board of Regents v. Roth*, 408 U.S. 564, 576–77 n.15 (1972).

127. *Beitzell v. Jeffrey*, No. 75–57–B slip. op. at 35 (D. Me. May 8, 1980), *aff'd*, 643 F.2d 870 (1st Cir. 1981). *But see Marwil v. Baker*, 499 F.Supp. 560, 578 (E.D. Mich. 1980) (no property right to formal tenure review).

128. *Board of Regents v. Roth*, 408 U.S. 564, 573 (1972).

129. *Id.*

130. *Id.*

131. *McNeill v. Butz*, 480 F.2d 314, 319–20 (4th Cir. 1973).

132. *Hostrop v. Board of Junior College District*, 523 F.2d 569, 573 (7th Cir. 1975), *cert. denied*, 425 U.S. 963 (1976).

133. *Francis v. Ota*, 356 F.Supp. 1029, 1031–32 (D. Hawaii 1973). *See also Pederson v. South Williamsport Area School District*, 677 F.2d 312, 316 (3d Cir. 1982).

134. *See Lafferty v. Carter*, 310 F.Supp. 465, 470 (E.D. Wis. 1970).

135. *Vanelli v. Reynolds School District*, 667 F.2d 773, 777–78 (9th Cir. 1982) (teacher discharged for staring at female students' physical attributes and making statements with sexual overtones); *Huff v. County of Butler*, 524 F.Supp. 751, 754–55 (W.D. Pa. 1981).

136. *McGhee v. Draper*, 564 F.2d 902, 910 n.10 (10th Cir. 1977); *Austin v. Board of Education*, 562 F.2d 446, 450–51 (7th Cir. 1977). *See also Vanelli v. Reynolds School District*, 667 F.2d 773, 777–78 (9th Cir. 1982).

137. *Fisher v. Snyder*, 476 F.2d 375 (8th Cir. 1973), as interpreted in *Buhr v. Buffalo School District*, 509 F.2d 1196, 1203 (8th Cir. 1974). *See Berry v. Hamblin*, 356 F.Supp. 306, 308 (M.D. Pa. 1973) (*dictum*) (discharge based upon charge of "debauchery" may

be "badge of infamy" requiring a hearing to permit teacher to controvert charges).

138. *Cf. Acanfora v. Board of Education*, 359 F.Supp. 843, 853 (D. Md. 1973), *aff'd on other grounds*, 491 F.2d 498 (4th Cir.), *cert. denied*, 419 U.S. 836 (1974).

139. See *Wieman v. Updegraff*, 344 U.S. 183, 190–91 (1952), *cited in Board of Regents v. Roth*, 408 U.S. 564, 573 (1972).

140. *Kyles v. Eastern Nebraska Human Services*, 632 F.2d 57, 61 (8th Cir. 1980); *Bomhoff v. White*, 526 F.Supp. 488, 491 (D. Ariz. 1981). *But see Clemons v. Dougherty County*, 684 F.2d 1365, 1371–73 (11th Cir. 1982).

141. See *Wisconsin v. Constantineau*, 400 U.S. 433, 437 (1971); *cited in Board of Regents v. Roth, supra.*

142. *Dennis v. S&S Consolidated Rural High School District*, 577 F.2d 338, 343 (5th Cir. 1978). *Cf. Whitaker v. Board of Higher Education*, 461 F.Supp. 99, 105–06 (E.D. N.Y. 1978).

143. See *Colaizzi v. Walker*, 542 F.2d 969, 971–72 (7th Cir. 1976), *cert. denied*, 430 U.S. 960 (1977).

144. *Cf. Staton v. Mayes*, 552 F.2d 908, 911 (10th Cir.), *cert. denied*, 434 U.S. 907 (1977) (school superintendent discharged on public charges of willful neglect of duty and incompetence deprived of "liberty" in part because charges "might seriously damage" his "standing and associations in the community" and affect his good name and reputation).

145. *Phillips v. Puryear*, 403 F.Supp. 80, 85 (W.D. Va. 1975).

146. *An-Ti Chai v. Michigan Technological University*, 493 F.Supp. 1137, 1155 (W.D. Mich. 1980); *Wellner v. Minnesota State Junior College Board*, 487 F.2d 153, 156–57 (8th Cir. 1973).

147. *Ball v. Board of Trustees*, 584 F.2d 684, 685 (5th Cir. 1978), *cert. denied*, 440 U.S. 972 (1979).

148. 426 U.S. 341 (1976).

149. *Id.* at 347.

150. *Id.* at 348–49. See also *Fuller v. Laurens County School District No. 56*, 563 F.2d 137, 141 (4th Cir. 1977); *Austin v. Board of Education*, 562 F.2d 446, 450 (7th Cir. 1977).

151. *Burris v. Willis Independent School District*, 537 F.Supp. 801, 805 (S.D. Tex. 1982).

152. *Beitzell v. Jeffrey* 643 F.2d 870, 878 (1st Cir. 1981); *Harris v. Arizona Board of Regents*, 528 F.Supp. 987, 998 (D. Ariz. 1981); *Marwil v. Baker*, 499 F.Supp. 560, 579 (E.D. Mich. 1980); *Terrien v. Metropolitan Milwaukee Criminal Justice Council*, 455 F.Supp. 1375, 1378 (E.D. Wis. 1978).

153. *Burris v. Willis Independent School District*, 537 F.Supp. 801, 805 (S.D. Tex. 1982).

154. *Kyles v. Eastern Nebraska Human Services*, 632 F.2d 57, 61 (8th Cir. 1980).

155. *Quinn v. Syracuse Model Neighborhood Corp.*, 613 F.2d 438, 447 (2d Cir. 1980).

156. *Id.*, citing *Codd v. Velger*, 429 U.S. 624, 628 (1977). *See also McGhee v. Draper*, 564 F.2d 902, 910 (10th Cir. 1977); *Cox v. Northern Virginia Transportation Commission*, 551 F.2d 555, 558 (4th Cir. 1976); *Marcello v. Long Island Railroad*, 465 F.Supp. 54, 58–59 (S.D. N.Y. 1979).

157. *Owen v. City of Independence*, 445 U.S. 622, 633 (1980). *See Duggan v. Town of Ocean City*, 516 F.Supp. 1081, 1084 (D. Md. 1981); *Wilson v. Winstead*, 470 F.Supp. 271, 272 (E.D. Tenn. 1978). *Cf. Paul v. Davis*, 424 U.S. 693, 710 (1976).

158. *Board of Regents v. Roth*, 408 U.S. 564, 573–74 (1972). *See also Schware v. Board of Bar.Examiners*, 353 U.S. 232, 238 (1957), and other cases cited in *Roth, supra* at 574.

159. *Board of Regents v. Roth, supra* at 575 n.13.

160. 429 U.S. 624 (1977).

161. *Id.* at 629. *See also Johnson v. City Council of Green Forest*, 545 F.Supp. 43, 52 (W.D. Ark. 1982).

162. *Seal v. Pryor*, 670 F.2d 96, 99 (9th Cir. 1982). *See also Smith v. Lehman*, 533 F.Supp. 1015 (E.D. N.Y. 1982).

163. *Stevens v. Joint School District No. 1*, 429 F.Supp. 477, 485 (W.D. Wis. 1977).

164. *Austin v. Board of Education*, 562 F.2d 446, 449 (7th Cir. 1977).

165. *See Marcello v. Long Island Railroad*, 465 F.Supp. 54, 59 n.5 (S.D. N.Y. 1979).

166. *Cox v. Northern Virginia Transportation Commission*, 551 F.2d 555, 558 (4th Cir. 1976).

167. *Staton v. Mayes*, 552 F.2d 908, 911 (10th Cir.), *cert. denied*, 434 U.S. 907 (1977).

168. *Huntley v. Community School Board*, 543 F.2d 979, 985 (2d Cir. 1976), *cert. denied*, 430 U.S. 929 (1977).

169. *McGhee v. Draper*, 564 F.2d 902, 910 (10th Cir. 1977).

170. *Id.* at 908, 910 n.6.

171. *Id.* at 910 n.6.

172. *Id.* at 910.

173. *Snead v. Department of Social Services*, 355 F.Supp. 764, 771 (S.D. N.Y. 1973), *vacated on other grounds sub nom. Civil Service Commission of the State of New York v. Snead*, 416 U.S. 977 (1974); *see also* opinion of three-judge court on remand at 389 F.Supp. 935 (S.D. N.Y. 1974), *vacated for consideration of mootness*, 421 U.S. 982 (1975), and opinion on second remand at 409 F.Supp. 994 (S.D. N.Y. 1975). *See also Newman v. Board of Education*, 594 F.2d 299, 304 (2d Cir. 1979); *Lombard v. Board of Education*, 502 F.2d 631, 637 (2d Cir. 1974), *cert. denied*, 420 U.S. 976 (1975); *Velger v. Cawley*, 525 F.2d 334, 336–37 (2d Cir. 1975), *rev'd on other grounds sub nom. Codd v. Velger*, 429 U.S. 624 (1977);

Bomhoff v. White, 526 F.Supp. 488, 491 (D. Ariz. 1981); *Doe v. Anker*, 451 F.Supp. 241 250 (S.D. N.Y. 1978), *remanded*, 614 F.2d 1286 (2d Cir. 1979), *cert. denied*, 446 U.S. 986 (1980).

174. *Stevens v. Joint School District No. 1*, 429 F.Supp. 477, 486 (W.D. Wis. 1977). *See also Churchwell v. United States*, 545 F.2d 59, 62 (8th Cir. 1976).

175. *Goss v. Lopez*, 419 U.S. 565 (1975) (emphasis added). *See also Arnett v. Kennedy*, 416 U.S. 134, 157 (1974) (plurality opinion: liberty is offended "by a dismissal based on unsupported charges which *could* wrongfully injure the reputation of an employee") (emphasis added); *Suarez v. Weaver*, 484 F.2d 678, 680 (7th Cir. 1973); *Morris v. Board of Education*, 401 F.Supp. 188, 211 (D. Del. 1975).

176. *Cato v. Collins*, 539 F.2d 656, 660 (8th Cir. 1976); *Buhr v. Buffalo Public School District*, 509 F.2d 1196, 1199 (8th Cir. 1974); *Wellner v. Minnesota State Junior College Board*, 487 F.2d 153, 155–56 (8th Cir. 1973).

177. *Wellner v. Minnesota State Junior College Board, supra*. *See also Greenhill V. Bailey*, 519 F.2d 5, 8 (8th Cir. 1975) (information suggesting medical student's unfitness available to all accredited medical schools); *Walker v. Alexander*, 569 F.2d 291, 294–95 (5th Cir. 1978).

178. *Ortwein v. Mackey*, 511 F.2d 696, 699 (5th Cir. 1975); *Kaprelian v. Texas Woman's University*, 509 F.2d 133, 137 (5th Cir. 1975). *See also Sims v. Fox*, 505 F.2d 857 (5th Cir. 1974) (*en banc*), *cert. denied*, 421 U.S. 1011 (1975); *James v. Board of School Commissioners*, 484 F.Supp. 705, 718 (S.D. Ala. 1979).

179. *Swilley v. Alexander*, 629 F.2d 1018, 1022 (5th Cir. 1982) (emphasis in original).

180. *Velger v. Cawley*, 525 F.2d 334, 336 (2d Cir. 1975), *rev'd on other grounds sub nom. Codd v. Velger*, 429 U.S. 624 (1977). *See also Giordano v. Roudebush*, 448 F.Supp. 899, 909 (S.D. Iowa 1977); *Rew v. Ward*, 402 F.Supp. 331, 340–41 (D. N.M. 1975).

181. *Morris v. Board of Education*, 401 F.Supp. 188, 211 (D. Del. 1975).

182. *Simmonds v. Government Employees' Service Commission*, 375 F.Supp. 934, 937–38 (D. V.I. 1974).

183. *Morris v. Board of Education*, 401 F.Supp. 188, 211 (D. Del. 1975).

184. *McGhee v. Draper*, 564 F.2d 902, 908 (10th Cir. 1977).

185. *Id.*

186. *Schell v. Board of Trustees*, (D. Del. Jul. 31, 1973) at p. 45, *cited in Morris v. Board of Education*, 401 F.Supp. 188, 211 (D. Del. 1975); *See also Clemons v. Dougherty County*, 684 F.2d 1365, 1371–73 (11th Cir. 1982). *But see Gray v. Union County Intermediate Education District*, 520 F.2d 803, 806 (9th Cir. 1975); *Simard v. Board of Education*, 473 F.2d 988, 992 n.6 (2d Cir. 1973).

187. *Simmonds v. Government Employees' Service Commission, supra* note 182.

188. *McKnight v. Southeastern Pennsylvania Transportation Authority*, 583 F.2d 1229 (3d Cir. 1979).

189. *Victor v. Brickley*, 476 F.Supp. 888 (E.D. Mich. 1979).

190. *Francis v. Ota*, 356 F.Supp. 1029, 1031 (D. Hawaii 1973).

191. *E.g., Robertson v. Rogers*, 679 F.2d 1090, 1091 (4th Cir. 1982); *Beitzel v. Jeffrey*, 643 F.2d 870, 878 (1st Cir. 1981); *Stretten v. Wadsworth Veterans Hospital*, 537 F.2d 361, 365–66 (9th Cir. 1976). *See also Gray v. Union County Intermediate Education District*, 520 F.2d 803, 806 (9th Cir. 1975); *Blair v. Board of Regents*, 496 F.2d 322, 324 (6th Cir. 1974). (non-retention of untenured professor for "failure to meet minimum standards in his professional relationships with individual students" did not impose a stigma within meaning of *Roth* rule); *Jablon v. Trustees of California State Colleges*, 482 F.2d 997, 1000 (9th Cir. 1973), *cert. denied*, 414 U.S. 1163 (1974) (determination not to retain untenured state college teacher because he was not deemed "good enough overall teacher and scholar to merit retention" did not impose stigma within contemplation of *Roth*); *Perkins v. Board of Directors*, 528 F.Supp. 1313, 1321 (D. Me. 1981); *Haron v. Board of Education*, 411 F.Supp. 68, 72–73 (E.D. N.Y. 1976) (probationary teacher not entitled to due process hearing where termination was based on unsatisfactory rating).

192. *Willens v. University of Massachusetts*, 570 F.2d 403, 406 (1st Cir. 1978) (emphasis added). *See also Arnett v. Kennedy*, 416 U.S. 134, 214 (1974) (dissenting opinion) ("Dismissal from public employment for cause may . . . implicate liberty interests in imposing on the discharged employee a stigma of *incompetence* or wrongdoing that forecloses 'his freedom to take advantage of other employment opportunities' ") (emphasis added); *Huntley v. Community School Board*, 543 F.2d 979, 985 (2d Cir. 1976), *cert. denied*, 430 U.S. 929 (1977) (charges going "to the very heart" of [a principal's] professional competence" and made part of his employment record deprived him of liberty by seriously impairing his ability to take advantage of other employment opportunities). *Cf. Mulcahy v. Deitrick*, 39 Ohio App. 65, 176 N.E. 481 (Ohio 1931) (utterances that plaintiff "not fit to teach [and] no good as a teacher" "impute to him want of capacity as school teacher [and] are actionable [as slander] *per se*").

193. *Russell v. Hodges*, 470 F.2d 212, 217 (2d Cir. 1972) (emphasis added).

194. *Greenhill v. Bailey*, 519 F.2d 5, 8 (8th Cir. 1975).

195. *See Giordano v. Roudebush*, 448 F.Supp. 899, 906 (S.D. Iowa 1977).

196. 390 F.Supp. 103 (W.D. Mich. 1974).

197. *Id.* at 131.

198. *Lake Michigan College Federation of Teachers v. Lake Michigan Community College*, 518 F.2d 1091, 1097–98 (6th Cir. 1975), *cert. denied*, 427 U.S. 904 (1976).

199. *Hortonville Education Association v. Joint School District No. 1*, 66 Wis. 2d 469, 490–91, 225 N.W.2d 658, 669 (1975), *rev'd on other grounds*, 426 U.S. 482 (1976). *See also Stevens v. Joint School District No. 1*, 429 F.Supp. 477, 485 (W.D. Wis. 1977).

200. *Whitaker v. Board of Higher Education*, 461 F.Supp. 99, 106 n.5 (E.D. N.Y. 1978).

201. *Carpenter v. City of Greenfield School District No. 6*, 358 F.Supp. 220, 225 (E.D. Wis. 1973).

202. *Cochran v. Chidester School District*, 456 F.Supp. 390, 395 (W.D. Ark. 1978).

203. 424 U.S. 693 (1976).

204. *Id.* at 712.

205. *Id.* at 711.

206. *Id.* at 709–10. *See Zaccagnini v. Morris*, 478 F.Supp. 1199, 1201–02 (D. Mass. 1979).

207. *Id.* at 710.

208. *See Blank v. Swan*, 487 F.Supp. 452, 456 (N.D. Ill. 1980) and cases cited.

209. *See Harris v. Harvey*, 436 F.Supp. 143 (E.D. Wis. 1977); *Gruenburg v. Kavanaugh*, 413 F.Supp. 1132 (E.D. Mich. 1976).

210. *Moore v. Otero*, 557 F.2d 435, 438 (5th Cir. 1977).

211. *Danno v. Peterson*, 421 F. Supp. 950, 953–54 (N.D. Ill. 1976).

212. *Moore v. Otero*, *supra* note 210, at 438 n.11.

213. *Dennis v. S&S Consolidated Rural High School District*, 577 F.2d 338 (5th Cir. 1978).

214. *Gentile v. Wallen*, 562 F.2d 193, 198 (2d Cir. 1977), *citing Paul v. Davis*, 424 U.S. 693, 701–10 (1976).

215. *Duggan v. Town of Ocean City*, 516 F.Supp. 1081 (D. Md. 1981). *See also Cook v. Town of Davidson*, 534 F.Supp. 808 (W.D. N.C. 1982) (stigmatizing statements made 16 months after discharge).

216. *Duggan v. Town of Ocean City*, *supra*, 516 F.Supp. at 1085.

217. *Goss v. Lopez*, 419 U.S. 565, 577 (1975), *quoting Morrissey v. Brewer*, 408 U.S. 471, 481 (1972).

218. *Cafeteria Workers v. McElroy*, 367 U.S. 886, 895 (1961).

219. *Hannah v. Larche*, 363 U.S. 420, 442 (1960); *Morrissey v. Brewer*, 408 U.S. 471, 481 (1972).

220. 424 U.S. 319 (1976).

221. *Id.* at 335.

222. *Grannis v. Ordean*, 234 U.S. 385, 394 (1914). *See also Logan v. Zimmerman Brush Co.*, 455 U.S. 422, 434 (1982); 102 S. Ct. 1148, 1157; *Mullane v. Central Hanover Bank & Trust Co.*, 339 U.S. 306, 314 (1950).

223. *Mullane v. Central Hanover Bank & Trust Co.*, *supra; Armstrong*

Manzo, 380 U.S. 545, 550 (1965). *See also Goss v. Lopez*, 419 U.S. 565 (1975); *Goldberg v. Kelly*, 397 U.S. 254, 267–68 (1970).

224. *McGhee v. Draper*, 564 F.2d 902, 911 (10th Cir. 1977); *see also Willner v. Committee on Character and Fitness*, 373 U.S. 96, 105 (1963). *But see Branch v. School District No. 7*, 432 F.Supp. 608, 611 (D. Mont. 1977).

225. *McGhee v. Draper*, 564 F.2d 902, 911 (10th Cir. 1977). *See also Moore v. Board of Education*, 448 F.2d 709, 714 (8th Cir. 1971).

226. *In re Gault*, 387 U.S. 1, 34 n.54 (1967). *See Hawkins v. Board of Public Education*, 468 F.Supp. 201, 208, 209 (D. Del. 1979).

227. *See Hawkins v. Board of Public Education*, 468 F.Supp. 201, 208, 209 (D. Del. 1979); *Anapol v. University of Delaware*, 412 F.Supp. 675, 678 n.8 (1976). *See also Clemons v. Dougherty County*, 684 F.2d 1365, 1374 (11th Cir. 1982) ("vague and conclusory letter" informing employee that he was being fired for creating dissension and disturbance, for an obstinate attitude, and for a general lack of respect failed to provide him with adequate notice for hearing because it did not advise him "of the charges against him in sufficient detail fairly to enable him to show any error that might exist").

228. *Staton v. Mayes*, 552 F.2d 908, 912 (10th Cir.), *cert. denied*, 434 U.S. 907 (1977).

229. *Blackburn v. Board of Education*, 564 S.W. 2d 35, 36–37 (Ky. Ct. App. 1978). *See also Whitney v. Board of Regents*, 355 F.Supp. 321, 324 (E.D. Wis. 1973); *Board of Trustees v. Spiegel*, 549 P.2d 1161, 1171–72 (Wyo. 1976); *Sorin v. Board of Education*, 39 Ohio Misc. 108, 315 N.E.2d 848 (1974); *but see Wagner v. Little Rock School District*, 373 F.Supp. 876 (E.D. Ark. 1973). *See also DiLuigi v. Kafkalis*, 437 F.Supp. 868, 871 (M.D. Pa. 1977), *vacated on other grounds*, 584 F.2d 22 (3d Cir. 1978) (notices to federal employee that (1) his "conduct and general character traits were such that his retention in the Federal Service was not recommended" and (2) he was being terminated "because his demonstrated ability to cope with certain responsibilities inherent in his position was unacceptable and his ability to grasp and maintain basic fundamentals required of his position did not meet required standards" constituted "bureaucratic gobbledegook" and gave him only the vaguest idea of the reasons for his discharge, and accordingly violated the due process clause of the Fifth Amendment). *With Glenn v. Newman*, 614 F.2d 467, 473 (5th Cir. 1980) (rejecting 14th Amendment due process claim of inadequate notice on theory that employee had not been misled about the meaning of the notice).

230. *Bignall v. North Idaho College*, 538 F.2d 243, 247 (9th Cir. 1976).

231. *Cf. Bates v. Hinds*, 334 F.Supp. 528, 532–33 (N.D. Tex. 1971) (teacher discharge proceeding containing multiple deficiencies, among them lack of written notice of the charges, violated procedural due process). *Compare Wolff v. McDonnell*, 418 U.S. 539, 564 (1974) (due process requires written notice in prison disciplinary proceedings)

with Goss v. Lopez, 419 U.S. 729, 740 (1975) (oral notice suffices to meet due process requirements in context of student suspension for ten days or less).

232. *James v. Board of Education*, 484 F.Supp. 705, 715 (S.D. Ala. 1979).

233. *Vance v. Chester County Board of Education*, 504 F.2d 820, 824 n.2 (4th Cir. 1974); *Grimes v. Nottoway County School Board*, 462 F.2d 650, 653 (4th Cir.), *cert. denied*, 409 U.S. 1008 (1972).

234. *Ferguson v. Thomas*, 430 F.2d 852, 856 (5th Cir. 1970).

235. *Brouillette v. Board of Directors*, 519 F.2d 126, 128 (8th Cir. 1975). *See also Lindsay v. Kissinger*, 367 F.Supp. 949, 953 (D. D.C. 1973).

236. *Glenn v. Newman*, 614 F.2d 467, 473 (5th Cir. 1980).

237. *Whitney v. Board of Regents*, 355 F.Supp. 321, 324 (E.D. Wis. 1973). *See also Schreffler v. Board of Education*, 506 F.Supp. 1300, 1307–08 (D. Del. 1981).

238. *Carpenter v. City of Greenfield School District No. 6,* 358 F.Supp. 220, 226–27 (E.D. Wis. 1973). *See also Clemons v. Dougherty County*, 684 F.2d 1365, 1374 (11th Cir. 1982); *Johnson v. Angle*, 341 F.Supp. 1043, 1053 (D. Neb. 1971).

239. *Wagner v. Little Rock School District*, 373 F.Supp. 876, 881 (E.D. Ark. 1973).

240. *Bowling v. Mathews*, No. 73–M–138 (N.D. Ala. Feb. 18, 1974) at 10. For subsequent history, *see* 512 F.2d 112 (5th Cir. 1975), 587 F.2d 229 (5th Cir. 1979).

241. *Id*.

242. *Brown v. Bathke*, 416 F.Supp. 1194, 1201 (D. Neb. 1976), *rev'd on other grounds*, 566 F.2d 588 (8th Cir. 1977).

243. *Ferguson v. Thomas*, 430 F.2d 852, 856 (5th Cir. 1970) (emphasis added).

244. *See Wolff v. McDonnell*, 418 U.S. 539, 564 (1974) (prison inmate); *Bates v. Hinds*, 334 F.Supp. 528, 532 (N.D. Tex. 1971).

245. *Hawkins v. Board of Public Education*, 468 F.Supp. 201, 209 (D. Del. 1979).

246. *Id*. at n.14.

247. *Schreffler v. Board of Education*, 506 F.Supp. 1300, 1307 (D. Del. 1981). *See also Corrigan v. Donilan*, 639 F.2d 834, 837 (1st Cir. 1981) (violation of due process not to give notice of reasons within reasonable time).

248. *Hostrop v. Board of Junior College District No. 515*, 471 F.2d 488, 495 (7th Cir. 1972), *cert. denied*, 411 U.S. 967 (1973). *See also Sindermann v. Perry*, 430 F.2d 939, 944 (5th Cir. 1970), *aff'd on other grounds*, 408 U.S. 593 (1972); *Doe v. Anker*, 451 F.Supp. 241, 253 (S.D. N.Y. 1978), *remanded*, 614 F.2d 1286 (2d Cir. 1979), *cert. denied*, 446 U.S. 986 (1980).

249. *McGhee v. Draper*, 564 F.2d 902, 911 (10th Cir. 1977); *Thomas v. Ward*, 529 F.2d 916, 919 (4th Cir. 1975); *Lombard v. Board of*

Education, 502 F.2d 631, 637–38 (2d Cir. 1974), *cert. denied,* 420 U.S. 976 (1975); *McNeill v. Butz,* 480 F.2d 314, 322 (4th Cir. 1973); *Hostrop v. Board of Junior College District No. 515,* 471 F.2d 488, 495 (7th Cir. 1972), *cert. denied,* 411 U.S. 967 (1973); *Sindermann v. Perry,* 430 F.2d 939, 944 (5th Cir. 1970), *aff'd on other grounds,* 408 U.S. 593 (1972); *Cochran v. Chidester School District,* 456 F.Supp. 390, 397 (W.D. Ark. 1978); *Doe v. Anker,* 451 F.Supp. 241, 253 (S.D. N.Y. 1978), *remanded,* 614 F.2d 1286 (2d. Cir. 1979), *cert. denied,* 446 U.S. 986 (1980); *Snead v. Department of Social Services,* 355 F.Supp. 764, 772 (S.D. N.Y. 1973) (three-judge court), *vacated on other grounds,* 416 U.S. 977 (1974).

250. *See McNeill v. Butz,* 480 F.2d 314, 326 (4th Cir. 1973). *Cf. Codd v. Velger,* 429 U.S. 624, 627–28 (1977) (public employee deprived of liberty interest not entitled to procedural due process hearing unless he alleges that the charges are false).

251. *Cf. Thomas v. Ward,* 529 F.2d 916, 919 n.1 (4th Cir. 1975). *See also Board of Curators v. Horowitz.* 435 U.S. 78, 89–90 (1978); *Clark v. Whiting,* 607 F.2d 634, 644 (4th Cir. 1979); *Stretten v. Wadsworth Veterans Hospital,* 537 F.2d 361, 368–69 (9th Cir. 1976).

252. *Thomas v. Ward,* 529 F.2d 916, 919 (4th Cir. 1975).

253. *Nevels v. Hanlon,* 656 F.2d 372, 376 (8th Cir. 1981), *but see Koster v. United States,* 685 F.2d 407, 412 (Ct. Cl. 1982).

254. *McClelland v. Andrus,* 606 F.2d 1278, 1286 (D.C. Cir. 1979).

255. *Id.* at 1291.

256. *Newman v. Board of Education.* 594 F.2d 299, 305 (2d Cir. 1979).

257. *Christhilf v. Annapolis Emergency Hospital Assn., Inc.,* 496 F.2d 174, 179 (4th Cir. 1974).

258. *Lindsay v. Kissinger,* 367 F.Supp. 949, 953 (D. D.C. 1973).

259. *Goldberg v. Kelly,* 397 U.S. 254, 270 (1970), *quoting from Powell v. Alabama,* 287 U.S. 45, 68–69 (1932).

260. *Compare Goldberg v. Kelly,* 397 U.S. 254, 270 (1970) (while government is not constitutionally compelled to provide welfare recipients with publicly financed counsel at termination hearings, it cannot deny recipients the right to retain and be represented by counsel at their own expense) *with Wolff v. McDonnell,* 418 U.S. 539, 570 (1974) (prison inmates do not "have a right to either retained or appointed counsel in disciplinary hearings," in part because insertion of counsel into the disciplinary process "would inevitably give the proceedings a more adversary cast and tend to reduce their utility as a means to further correctional goals"), *Baxter v. Palmigiano,* 425 U.S. 308, 314–15 (1976), and *Gagnon v. Scarpelli,* 411 U.S. 778, 790 (1973) (requests for appointment of counsel in probation and parole revocation proceedings should be considered on a case-by-case basis, with presumptive entitlement where the probationer or parolee makes a request "based on a timely and colorable claim (i) that he has not committed the alleged violation of the conditions

upon which he is at liberty; or (ii) that even if the violation is a matter of public record or is uncontested, there are substantial reasons which justified or mitigated the violation and make revocation inappropriate, and that the reasons are complex or otherwise difficult to develop or present").

261. 397 U.S. 254 (1970).
262. *Cochran v. Chidester School District*, 456 F.Supp. 390 (W.D. Ark. 1978); *Doe v. Anker*, 451 F.Supp. 241, 253 (S.D. N.Y. 1978), remanded, 614 F.2d 1286 (2d Cir. 1979), *cert. denied*, 446 U.S. 986 (1980); *Aster v. Board of Education*, 72 Misc. 2d 953, 339 N.Y.S.2d 903 (Sup. Ct. 1972); *see also Ahern v. Board of Education*, 456 F.2d 399, 403 n.2 (8th Cir. 1972). *C.F. Lindsay v. Kissinger*, 367 F.Supp. 949, 953 (D. D.C. 1973) (foreign service or USIA officer with property interest in continued employment has constitutional right to retain counsel at his own expense in "selection-out" review hearing). *But see State ex rel. McLendon v. Morton*, 249 S.E.2d 919 (W. Va. 1978).
263. *Ortwein v. Mackey*, 358 F.Supp. 705, 715 (M.D. Fla. 1973).
264. 511 F.2d 696 (5th Cir. 1975).
265. *Frumkin v. Board of Trustees*, 626 F.2d 19 (6th Cir. 1980).
266. *Id*. at 21.
267. *Toney v. Reagan*, 467 F.2d 953, 958 (9th Cir. 1972), *cert. denied*, 409 U.S. 1130 (1973).
268. *Downing v. LeBritton*, 550 F.2d 689 (1st Cir. 1977).
269. *Id*. at 693.
270. *Id*.
271. *Id*. at 692.
272. *Id*. at 691.
273. *Id*.
274. *Compare Baker v. Wainwright*, 527 F.2d 372, 377 (5th Cir. 1976).
275. *Downing v. LeBritton*, 550 F.2d 689, 692 (1st Cir. 1977).
276. *Id*.
277. *United States v. Weller*, 309 F.Supp. 50, 51 (N.D. Cal. 1969), appeal dismissed, 466 F.2d 1279 (9th Cir. 1972). *Cf. Gagnon v. Scarpelli*, 411 U.S. 778, 786 (1973).
278. *Wilson v. Swing*, 463 F.Supp. 555, 561 (M.D. N.C. 1978).
279. *But see Marcello v. Long Island Railroad*, 465 F.Supp. 54, 59–60 (S.D. N.Y. 1979) and cases cited.
280. *See Goldberg v. Kelly*, 397 U.S. 254, 271 (1970) (an "elementary" requirement of due process is that "the decisionmaker's conclusion . . . must rest solely on the legal rules and evidence adduced at the hearing"); *Kiepura v. Local 1091, Steelworkers*, 358 F.Supp. 987, 990 (N.D. Ill. 1973).
281. *See Gonzales v. United States of America*, 348 U.S. 407, 416 (1955).
282. *Kinsella v. Board of Education*, 378 F.Supp. 54, 60 (W.D. N.Y. 1974). *See also Hall v. Ambach*, 50 A.D.2d 1015, 377 N.Y.S.2d 301 (1976).

283. *Doe v. Anker*, 451 F.Supp. 241, 253 (S.D. N.Y. 1978), *remanded*, 614 F.2d 1280 (2d Cir. 1979), *cert. denied*, 446 U.S. 986 (1980).

284. *Morgan v. United States*, 298 U.S. 468, 482 (1936).

285. 2 *Davis Administrative Law* § 11.03 at 44–45 (1958) (footnotes omitted). *See also Service v. Dulles*, 354 U.S. 363, 387 n.40 (1957); *Bates v. Sponberg*, 547 F.2d 325, 332 (6th Cir. 1976) and cases cited.

286. *Bates v. Sponberg*, 547 F.2d 325, 329 (6th Cir. 1976).

287. *Hawkins v. Board of Public Education*, 468 F.Supp. 201, 210 (D. Del. 1979).

288. *McGhee v. Draper*, 546 F.2d 902, 912 (10th Cir. 1977); *Staton v. Mayes*, 552 F.2d 908, 916 (10th Cir.), *cert. denied*, 434 U.S. 907 (1977); *Kinsella v. Board of Education*, 378 F.Supp. 54, 60 (W.D. N.Y. 1974); *Morrissey v. Brewer*, 408 U.S. 471, 489 (1972); *Goldberg v. Kelly*, 397 U.S. 254, 271 (1970). *But see Satterfield v. Edenton-Chowan Board of Education*, 530 F.2d 567, 576 (4th Cir. 1975); *Gilbertson v. McAlister*, 383 F.Supp. 1107, 1110 (D. Conn. 1974).

289. *See* text accompanying note 288, *supra*.

290. *McGhee v. Draper*, 564 F.2d 902, 912 (10th Cir. 1977).

291. *Kinsella v. Board of Education*, 378 F.Supp. 54, 60 (W.D. N.Y. 1974).

292. *Bogart v. Unified School District No. 298*, 432 F.Supp. 895, 904 (D. Kan. 1977) (emphasis added).

293. *Sindermann v. Perry*, 430 F.2d 939, 944 (5th Cir. 1970), *aff'd on other grounds*, 408 U.S. 593 (1972).

294. *Doe v. Anker*, 451 F.Supp. 241 (S.D. N.Y. 1978), *remanded*, 614 1286 (2d Cir. 1979), *cert. denied*, 446 U.S. 986 (1980). *See also* Friendly, *Some Kind of a Hearing*, 123 U.Pa. L.Rev. 1267, 1277–92 (1975).

295. *Appler v. Mountain Pine School District*, 342 F.Supp. 1131, 1138 (W.D. Ark. 1972). *See also Cochran v. Chidester School District*, 456 F.Supp. 390, 394 (W.D. Ark. 1978).

296. *Board of Regents v. Roth*, 408 U.S. 564, 569–70 (1972).

297. *Id.* at 570.

298. *Id.* at 570 n.8 (emphasis in original).

299. 416 U.S. 134 (1974).

300. *Cochran v. Chidester School District*, 456 F.Supp. 390, 395 (W.D. Ark. 1978).

301. *Anapol v. University of Delaware*, 412 F.Supp. 675, 678 n.8 (D. Del. 1976).

302. *Cantrell v. Vickers*, 495 F.Supp. 195, 200 (N.D. Miss. 1980).

303. *Mackey v. Montrym*, 443 U.S. 1, 13 (1979); *Dixon v. Love*, 431 U.S. 105 (1977); *Mathews v. Eldridge*, 424 U.S. 319, 343 (1976).

304. *Mathews v. Eldridge*, 424 U.S. 319, 334–35 (1976). *See also Dixon v. Love*, 431 U.S. 105, 113 (1977).

305. *Ricucci v. United States*, 425 F.2d 1252, 1257, 192 Ct. Cl. 1 (1970). *See also Muscare v. Quinn*, 520 F.2d 1212, 1215 n.3 (7th Cir. 1975), *cert. dismissed as improvidently granted*, 425 U.S. 560 (1976).

306. *Carpenter v. City of Greenfield School District*, 358 F.Supp. 220, 225 (E.D. Wis. 1973); *Cochran v. Chidester School District*, 456 F.Supp. 390, 395 (W.D. Ark. 1978); *Wertz v. Southern Cloud Unified School District*, 218 Kan. 25, 29, 542 P.2d 339, 344 (1975). *See also Vanelli v. Reynolds School District*, 667 F.2d 773 (9th Cir. 1982).

307. *See Mathews v. Eldridge*, 424 U.S. 319, 334–35 (1976).

308. *Withrow v. Larkin*, 421 U.S. 35, 58 n.25 (1975). *See also Gagnon v. Scarpelli*, 411 U.S. 778, 785–86 (1973); *Morrissey v. Brewer*, 408 U.S. 471, 485–86 (1972); *Goldberg v. Kelly*, 397 U.S. 254, 271 (1970).

309. *Skehan v. Board of Trustees*, 501 F.2d 31, 38 (3d Cir. 1974), *vacated on other grounds*, 538 F.2d 53 (3d Cir.), *cert. denied*, 429 U.S. 979 (1976). *Cf. Bell v. Board of School Commissioners*, 450 F.Supp. 162, 166 (S.D. Ala. 1978) ("The summary suspension of an employee from the payroll without notice or opportunity to be heard may also hamper that individual's ability to pursue even a post-termination hearing, due to the economic repercussions of suspension without pay").

310. *Mathews v. Eldridge*, 424 U.S. 319, 335 (1976).

311. *Stretten v. Wadsworth Veterans Hospital*, 537 F.2d 361, 369 (9th Cir. 1976)

312. *See Newman v. Board of Education*, 594 F.2d 299, 304 (2d Cir. 1979).

313. *Vanelli v. Reynolds School District*, 667 F.2d 773 (9th Cir. 1982).

314. *Id.* at 779.

315. *E.g., Glenn v. Newman*, 614 F.2d 467, 472 (5th Cir. 1980); *Kennedy v. Robb*, 547 F.2d 408, 413–15 (8th Cir. 1976), *cert. denied*, 431 U.S. 959 (1977); *Thurston v. Dekle*, 531 F.2d 1264 (5th Cir. 1976); *Knotts v. Bewick*, 467 F.Supp. 931, 935–36 (D. Del. 1979); *MacMurray v. Board of Trustees*, 428 F.Supp. 1171 (M.D. Pa. 1977); *Anapol v. University of Delaware*, 412 F.Supp. 675 (D. Del. 1976); *Eley v. Morris*, 390 F.Supp. 913 (N.D. Ga. 1975) (three-judge court); *Skelly v. State Personnel Board*, 15 Cal.3d 194, 539 P.2d 950, 124 Cal. Rptr. 14 (1975); *Gensolley v. Bushley*, 19 Or. App. 884, 529 P.2d 950 (1974). *But see Barrett v. Smith*, 530 F.2d 829 (9th Cir. 1975), *cert. denied*, 425 U.S. 977 (1976).

316. *Glenn v. Newman*, 614 F.2d 467, 472 (5th Cir. 1980); *Blair v. Robstown Independent School District*, 556 F.2d 1331, 1334–35 (5th Cir. 1977).

317. *Withrow v. Larkin*, 421 U.S. 35, 58 n.25 (1975). *See also Gagnon v. Scarpelli*, 411 U.S. 778, 785–86 (1973); *Morrissey v. Brewer*, 408 U.S. 471, 485–86 (1972); *Goldberg v. Kelly*, 397 U.S. 254, 271 (1970).

318. *Needleman v. Bohlen*, 602 F.2d 1, 5–6 (1st Cir. 1979).

319. *See Armstrong v. Manzo*, 380 U.S. 545, 552 (1965); *Huntley v.*

North Carolina State Board of Education, 493 F.2d 1016, 1020 (4th Cir. 1974).

320. *Corrigan v. Donilon,* 639 F.2d 834, 837 (1st Cir. 1981) (when board failed to provide hearing within one year of discharge to tenured teachers laid off due to alleged budget crisis, "This shilly-shallying clearly does not meet . . . due process standards").

321. *Armstrong v. Manzo,* 380 U.S. 545, 552 (1965). *See also Barry v. Barchi,* 443 U.S. 55 (1979) (delay in affording post-suspension evidentiary hearing violated due process).

322. *Brown v. Bathke,* 566 F.2d 588, 592 (8th Cir. 1977). *See also Hayes v. City of Wilmington,* 451 F.Supp. 696, 712 (D. Del. 1978); *Aiello v. City of Wilmington,* 426 F.Supp. 1272, 1290 (D. Del. 1976).

323. *Compare Skehan v. Board of Trustees,* 501 F.2d 31, 40 (3d Cir. 1974), *vacated and remanded on other grounds,* 421 U.S. 983 (1975), *vacated on other grounds,* 538 F.2d 53 (3d Cir.), *cert. denied,* 429 U.S. 979 (1976), *with Decker v. North Idaho College,* 538 F.2d 243, 248 (9th Cir. 1976), and *Kota v. Little,* 473 F.2d 1, 3 (4th Cir. 1973). *Cf. Corrigan v. Donilon,* 639 F.2d 834, 838 (1st Cir. 1981) (wait for post-deprivation hearing was so long that court orders back pay and injunctive relief without considering merits).

324. 435 U.S. 747 (1978).

325. *Skehan v. Board of Trustees,* 501 F.2d 31, 40 (3d Cir. 1974), *vacated and remanded on other grounds,* 421 U.S. 983 (1975), *vacated on other grounds,* 538 F.2d 53 (3d Cir. 1976), *cert. denied,* 429 U.S. 979 (1976).

326. 419 U.S. 565 (1975).

327. *Id.* at 582–83.

328. 520 F.2d 1212, 1215 (7th Cir.), *cert. dismissed as improvidently granted,* 425 U.S. 560 (1975). *See also Bell v. Board of School Commissioners,* 450 F.Supp. 162 (S.D. Ala. 1978) (summary suspension of teacher without pay, and resolution allowing for immediate suspension of any teacher without pay upon the principal's recommendation, violate due process).

329. *Muscare v. Quinn, supra,* 520 F.2d at 1215.

330. *Bell v. Board of School Commissioners,* 450 F.Supp. 162, 166 (S.D. Ala. 1978).

331. *Barry v. Barchi,* 443 U.S. 55 (1979). *See also Aiello v. City of Wilmington,* 426 F.Supp. 1272, 1290–91 (D. Del. 1976).

332. *Barry v. Barchi, supra* note 331, at 64.

333. *Id.*

334. *Id.*

335. *Id.* at 65.

336. *Id. See also Mackey v. Montrym,* 443 U.S. 1, 13 (1979) ("when prompt post-deprivation review is available for correction of administrative error, we have generally required no more than that the pre-deprivation procedures used be designed to provide a reasonably reliable basis for concluding that the facts justifying the official

action are as a responsible governmental official warrants them
to be").

337. *Barry v. Barchi, supra* note 331, at 65.

338. *Id.*

339. *Id.* at 66.

340. *Id.*

341. *Id.*

342. *Id. Cf. Victor v. Brickley,* 476 F.Supp. 888, 896 (E.D. Mich.
1979) ("In view of the promptness with which Plaintiff obtained
notice of the charges against him and ultimately a plenary trial-type
hearing at which he cleared his name and secured reinstatement
with back pay, I conclude he was not denied due process of law").

343. *Barry v. Barchi, supra* note 331, at 65.

344. *Victor v. Brickley,* 476 F.Supp. 888, 896 (E.D. Mich. 1979).

345. *Newman v. Board of Education,* 594 F.2d 299, 304 (2d Cir. 1979).
Cf. Dusanek v. Hannon, 677 F.2d 538, 542 (7th Cir. 1982)
(teacher's refusal to take medical leave following mandatory mental
health exam triggers right to hearing).

346. 443 U.S. at 64.

347. *Id.* at 65.

348. *See* cases cited in note 315, *supra.*

349. *Jacobs v. Kunes,* 541 F.2d 222, 225 (9th Cir. 1976), *cert. denied,*
429 U.S. 1094 (1977)

350. *Thurston v. Dekle,* 531 F.2d 1264, 1273 (5th Cir. 1976). *Accord
Baker v. School Board of Marion County,* 487 F.Supp. 380, 382–83
(M.D. Fla. 1980). *But see Jones v. Jefferson Parish School Board,*
533 F.Supp. 816, 822 (E.D. La 1982) (school board may suspend
teachers without pay pursuant to Louisiana law).

351. *See Peacock v. Board of Regents,* 510 F.2d 1324, 1329 (9th Cir.),
cert. denied, 422 U.S. 1049 (1975); *Lafferty v. Carter,* 310 F.Supp.
465 (W.D. Wis. 1970).

352. *Peacock v. Board of Regents, supra.*

353. *Cf. Goss v. Lopez,* 419 U.S. 565, 582–83 (1975).

354. *Id.*

355. *See* 11 Wright and Miller, *Federal Practice and Procedure* §2948
at 440 (1973).

356. *Sampson v. Murray,* 415 U.S. 61, 90–91 (1974).

357. *But see Baker v. School Board of Marion County,* 487 F.Supp. 380,
384–85 (M.D. Fla. 1980).

358. *See Johnson v. University of Pittsburgh,* 359 F.Supp. 1002, 1009
(W.D. Pa. 1973); *Roumani v. Leestamper,* 330 F.Supp. 1248, 1251–52
(D. Mass. 1971); *Newcomer v. Coleman,* 323 F.Supp. 1363, 1369
(D. Conn. 1970); *Hunter v. City of Ann Arbor,* 325 F.Supp. 847,
854 (E.D. Mich. 1971).

359. *Sigmon v. Poe,* 381 F.Supp. 387, 393 (W.D. N.C. 1974), *vacated,*
391 F.Supp. 430, *aff'd,* 528 F.2d 311 (4th Cir. 1975).

360. *See McConnell v. Anderson*, 316 F.Supp. 809, 815 (D. Minn. 1970), *rev'd on other grounds*, 451 F.2d 193 (8th Cir. 1971), *cert. denied*, 405 U.S. 1046 (1972).

361. *Peacock v. Board of Regents*, 510 F.2d 1324, 1329 (9th Cir.), *cert. denied*, 422 U.S. 1049 (1975) (trial court's order, which failed to grant all the relief requested on plaintiff's motion for preliminary injunction seeking restoration to his position as Department Head at College of Medicine, affirmed: "[W]hile the record indicates that the administrative position was important to him, its deprivation did not remove him from the 'mainstream of his occupation' . . . as a teacher and surgeon"); *Seaman v. Spring Lake Park Independent School District*, 363 F.Supp. 944, 945–46 (D. Minn. 1973) (preliminary injunction granted restraining defendants from requiring a pregnant teacher to take leave of absence: "[A] forced leave of a semester's duration would impose on plaintiff . . . separation from the team teaching situation through which she was advancing her career . . . . The harm . . . is thus of such a nature that it could not be repaired by any future monetary reimbursement"); *Duke v. North Texas State University*, 338 F.Supp. 990, 999 (E.D. Tex. 1971), *rev'd on other grounds*, 469 F.2d 829 (5th Cir. 1972), *cert. denied*, 412 U.S. 932 (1973) ("Money damages would be a poor substitute to afford plaintiff in lieu of allowing her to reenter into the life of the University clothed with her former rights, privileges, duties and expectations"); *Lafferty v. Carter*, 310 F.Supp. 465, 470 (W.D. Wis. 1970) (to totally separate a professor from the mainstream of his occupation as a teacher and significantly to separate him from the mainstream of his occupation as a scholar and researcher constitutes irreparable injury).

362. *Board of Regents v. Roth*, 408 U.S. 564, 574 (1972). *See also Codd v. Velger*, 429 U.S. 624, 633 n.3 (Stevens, J., dissenting).

363. *Huntley v. Community School Board*, 543 F.2d 979, 985 (2d Cir. 1976), *cert. denied*, 430 U.S. 929 (1977). *See also Terrien v. Metropolitan Milwaukee Criminal Justice Council*, 455 F.Supp. 1375, 1378 (E.D. Wis. 1978) ("A person whose Fourteenth Amendment liberty interests are implicated by the manner of his termination from employment is entitled to a procedurally adequate pretermination hearing").

364. *Board of Regents v. Roth*, 408 U.S. 564, 573 n.12 (1972).

365. *See Codd v. Velger*, 429 U.S. 624, 633 n.3 (Stevens, J., dissenting).

366. *See Victor v. Brickley*, 476 F.Supp. 888, 896 (E.D. Mich. 1979).

367. *Withrow v. Larkin*, 421 U.S. 35, 46–47 (1975); *Gibson v. Berryhill*, 411 U.S. 564, 579 (1973); *In re Murchison*, 349 U.S. 133, 136 (1955).

368. *Gibson v. Berryhill*, 411 U.S. 564, 579 (1973); *Tumey v. Ohio*, 273 U.S. 510 (1927).

369. 273 U.S. 510 (1927).

370. *Gibson v. Berryhill*, 411 U.S. 564, 579 (1973).

371. *Id.* at 571, 578–79.

372. 409 U.S. 57 (1972).

373. *Id.* at 58.

374. *Id.* at 60.

375. 426 U.S. 482, 491 (1976).

376. *See Kornit v. Board of Education*, 542 F.2d 593 (2d Cir. 1976), *vacated on other grounds*, 438 U.S. 902 (1978). The probability of bias may be too attenuated where the challenged members of the tribunal do not themselves have any responsibility for the budget of the institution. *See Aiello v. City of Wilmington*, 426 F.Supp. 1272, 1292 (D. Del. 1976).

377. *See Byrd v. Mullins School District No. 2*, No. 76–CP–33–170 (C.P.S.C. May 1, 1976) at 3.

378. 426 U.S. at 497. *See also Wolkenstein v. Reville*, 694 F.2d 35, 41–42 (2d Cir. 1982).

379. *Barndt v. Wissahickon School District*, 475 F.Supp. 503, 506 (E.D. Pa. 1979), *aff'd*, 615 F.2d 1352 (3d Cir.), *cert. denied*, 449 U.S. 831 (1980).

380. *Fuentes v. Roher*, 519 F.2d 379, 389 (2d Cir. 1975).

381. *Byrd v. Mullins School District No. 2*, No. 76–CP–33–170 (C.P.S.C. May 1, 1976) at 3. *Cf. Tincher v. Piasecki*, 520 F.2d 851, 855 (7th Cir. 1975) ("as a matter of fundamental due process, it is inherently improper for a person who has been charged by an accused in a collateral proceeding to participate as a committee member in the accused's disciplinary hearing").

382. *Gonzales v. McEuen*, 435 F.Supp. 460, 464–65 (D.C. Cal. 1977).

383. *Offut v. United States*, 348 U.S. 11, 14 (1954).

384. *Withrow v. Larkin*, 421 U.S. 35, 47 (1975).

385. 400 U.S. 455, 465–66 (1971).

386. 418 U.S. 488, 501–02 (1974).

387. 426 U.S. 482, 491–92 (1976).

388. 416 U.S. 134 (1974).

389. *Id.* at 196–97.

390. *Id.* at 170.

391. *Fuentes v. Roher*, 519 F.2d 379, 388–89 (2d Cir. 1975).

392. *Id.* at 390.

393. *Id.* at 389.

394. *Id.*

395. *Duke v. North Texas State University*, 469 F.2d 829, 840 (5th Cir. 1972), *cert. denied*, 412 U.S. 932 (1973).

396. *Id.*

397. *Id.* at 841.

398. *Id.* at 840.

399. *Vanelli v. Reynolds School District*, 667 F.2d 773, 780 (9th Cir. 1982).

400. *Simard v. Board of Education*, 473 F.2d 988, 993 (2d Cir. 1973).
401. *Id*.
402. 421 U.S. 35 (1975).
403. *Id*. at 58,
404. 421 U.S. at 58 n.25, *citing Gagnon v. Scarpelli*, 411 U.S. 778, 785–86 (1973); *Morrissey v. Brewer*, 408 U.S. 471, 485–86 (1972); and *Goldberg v. Kelly*, 497 U.S. 254, 271 (1970).
405. *Parkhurst v. D'Amico*, No. 750215, slip. op. at 27 (D.R.I. Feb. 5, 1976). *See also Cantrell v. Vickers*, 495 F.Supp. 195, (N.D. Miss. Aug. 7, 1980) ("The evidence shows without contradiction that the board of trustees decided [plaintiff's] future as a school teacher in the school district before she was advised that she might have a hearing. The board argues that if there should be a question as to the impartial and unbiased tribunal for the hearing of the charges against [plaintiff] the statute . . . provides for a trial or hearing before a hearing officer. . . . The ultimate judgment or determination, in any event, is that of the board. Since the decision had already been made by the individual members of the board in their directive of March 20, 1979 to [the superintendent], when the removal was made, [plaintiff] could not have been afforded an impartial forum in which to present her case"). *But see Glenn v. Newman*, 614 F.2d 467, 573 (5th Cir. 1980); *Thomas v. Board of Trustees*, 515 F.Supp. 280, 289–90 (S.D. Tex. 1981) (board's initial approval of reassignment did not vitiate its role as impartial fact finder); *Barber v. Exeter-West Greenwich School Committee*, 413 A.2d 13 (R.I. 1980).
406. *Armstrong v. Manzo*, 380 U.S. 545, 552 (1965).
407. *Huntley v. North Carolina State Board of Education*, 493 F.2d 1016, 1020 (4th Cir. 1974).
408. *King v. Caesar Rodney School District*, 380 F.Supp. 1112, 1119 (D. Del. 1974).
409. *Staton v. Mayes*, 552 F.2d 908, 914 (10th Cir.), *cert. denied*, 434 U.S. 907 (1977). *See also Clemons v. Dougherty County*, 684 F.2d 1365, 1374–75 (11th Cir. 1982); *Cinderella Career and Finishing Schools, Inc. v. FTC*, 425 F.2d 583, 589–92 (D.C. Cir. 1970). *But see Welch v. Barham*, 635 F.2d 1322 (8th Cir. 1980), *cert. denied*, 451 U.S. 971 (1981).
410. 426 U.S. 482 (1976).
411. *Id*. at 493, *citing United States v. Morgan*, 313 U.S. 409, 421 (1941). *See also FTC v. Cement Institute*, 333 U.S. 683, 701 (1948). *Cf. Wolkenstein v. Reville*, 694 F.2d 35, 41–42 (2d Cir. 1982) ("administrators serving as adjudicators are presumed to be unbiased", but presumption can be rebutted by showing of pecuniary or institutional interest).
412. 425 U.S. at 493. *See also Welch v. Barham*, 635 F.2d 1322, 1326–27 (8th Cir. 1980), *cert. denied*, 451 U.S. 971 (1981); *Hibbs v. Board of Education*, 392 F.Supp. 1202, 1205 (N.D. Iowa 1975).

413. *Withrow v. Larkin*, 421 U.S. 35, 55 (1975). *Accord Serafin v. City of Lexington*, 547 F.Supp. 1118, 1126–27 (D. Neb. 1982).
414. *Withrow v. Larkin*, *supra* at 55–56.
415. *Id.* at 47.
416. *Id.* at 57–58.
417. *See Miller v. Dean*, 430 F.Supp. 26, 28 n.2 (D. Neb. 1976), *aff'd on opinion of district court*, 552 F.2d 266 (8th Cir. 1977).
418. *Welch v. Barham*, 635 F.2d 1322, 1326 (8th Cir. 1980) (footnotes and citations omitted), *cert. denied*, 451 U.S. 971 (1981).
419. *Id.* at 1327–28.
420. *Id.* at 1329 (Heaney, J., dissenting).
421. *Withrow v. Larkin*, *supra*, 421 U.S. at 54–55.
422. *See Id.* at 53 n.20, 56 n.24; *In re Murchison*, 349 U.S. 133, 138 (1955). *But see Barszcz v. Board of Trustees*, 400 F.Supp. 675, 679 (N.D. Ill. 1975), *aff'd*, 539 F.2d 715 (7th Cir. 1976), *cert. dismissed*, 429 u.S. 1080 (1977).
423. 349 U.S. 133 (1955).
424. 421 U.S. 35, 53 (1975).
425. *In re Murchison*, 349 U.S. 133, 138 (1955).
426. *Withrow v. Larkin*, *supra*, 421 U.S. at 58.
427. *Phillips v. Puryear*, 403 F.Supp. 80, 87 (W.D. Va. 1975).
428. *Dixon v. Anderson*, No. 75–2730 (Super. Ct. Mass. Jan. 19, 1976) at 12.
429. *Commonwealth Department of Education v. Oxford Area School District*, 24 Pa. Commw. 421; 356 A.2d 857 (1976).
430. *White v. Board of Education*, 54 Hawaii 10, 16, 501 P.2d 358, 363 (1972).
431. *Gonzales v. McEuen*, 435 F.Supp. 460, 465 (C.D. Cal. 1977).
432. *Broady v. Hart County Board of Education*, No. 4503 (Cir. Ct. Ky. Apr. 4, 1978).
433. *Potemra v. Ping*, 462 F.Supp. 328, 333 (S.D. Ohio 1978).
434. *Niemi v. Board of Education*, 103 Mich. App. 818, 303 N.W.2d 905 (Mich. App. 1981).
435. *White v. Board of Education*, 54 Hawaii 10, 16, 501 P.2d 358, 363 (1972).
436. *Monahan v. Board of Trustees*, 486 P.2d 235, 238 (Wyo. 1971).
437. *Camero v. United States*, 179 Ct. Cl. 520, 527, 375 F.2d 777, 781 (1967).
438. *Id.*
439. 304 U.S. 1 (1938).
440. *Id.* at 19.
441. *Id.* 19–20. *See also Environmental Defense Fund, Inc. v. Environmental Protection Agency*, 510 F.2d 1292, 1305 (1975) (suggesting that ex parte communications between a "prosecutor" and an agency head regarding a final decision would be improper).
442. *Stein v. Mutuel Clerks Guild of Massachusetts, Inc.*, 384 F.Supp. 444, 448–49 (D. Mass. 1974), *aff'd*, 560 F.2d 486 (1st Cir. 1977).

443. *Id.* at 449.

444. *Gonzales v. McEuen*, 435 F.Supp. 460, 464–65 (C.D. Cal. 1977).

445. *English v. North East Board of Education*, 385 F.Supp. 1174, 1178 (W.D. Pa. 1974); *Kinsella v. Board of Education*, 378 F.Supp. 54, 60 (W.D. N.Y. 1974) (three-judge court), *aff'd*, 542 F.2d 1165 (2d Cir. 1976).

446. *Miller v. Board of Education*, 51 Ill. App. 2d 20, 200 N.E.2d 838 (1964) (emphasis added).

447. *English v. North East Board of Education*, 22 Pa. Commw. 240, 348 A.2d 494, 496 (1975). *See also Horn v. Township of Hilltown*, 461 Pa. 745, 337 A.2d 858 (1975).

448. 421 U.S. 35 (1975).

449. *Cinderella Career and Finishing Schools, Inc., v. FTC*, 425 F.2d 583, 592 (D.C. Cir. 1970) (unanimous decision of administrative agency reversed even though only one of its members shown to be biased); *American Cynamid Company v. FTC*, 363 F.2d 757, 767–68 (6th Cir. 1966); *Berkshire Employees Association of Berkshire Knitting Mills v. NLRB*, 121 F.2d 235, 239 (3d Cir. 1941).

450. *Berkshire Employees Association of Berkshire Knitting Mills v. NLRB*, 121 F.2d 235 (3d Cir. 1941).

451. *Bell v. Board of Education*, 450 S.W.2d 229 (Ky. 1970); *Osborne v. Bullitt County Board of Education*, 415 S.W.2d 607, 610 (Ky. 1967). *See also Board of Education v. Shockley*, 52 Del. 237, 246, 155 A.2d 323, 329 (1959).

452. *Board of Trustees v. Spiegel*, 549 P.2d 1161, 1165 (Wyo. 1976).

453. *Rea v. Board of Trustees*, No. 7839 (3d Judicial Dist., Idaho, Oct. 9, 1979) at 20. *See also Henderson v. Board of Trustees*, No. 7859 (3d Judicial Dist., Idaho, Oct. 9, 1979) at 9.

454. 429 U.S. 274 (1977).

455. *Id.* at 285–86.

456. *Id.* at 287. *See also NLRB v. Remington Rand, Inc.*, 94 F.2d 862, 872 (2d Cir.), *cert. denied*, 304 U.S. 576 (1938) (L. Hand, J.) ("It rests upon the [wrongdoer] to disentangle the consequences for which it is chargeable from those for which it is immune").

457. 435 U.S. 247 (1978).

458. *Id.* at 260.

459. *Id.* at 258.

460. *See Newman v. Board of Education*, 594 F.2d 299, 306 (2d Cir. 1979); *D'Iorio v. County of Delaware*, 592 F.2d 681, 690 n.16 (3d Cir. 1978); *Hawkins v. Board of Public Education*, 468 F.Supp. 201, 212–14 (D. Del. 1979); *Knotts v. Bewick*, 467 F.Supp. 931 (D. Del. 1979).

461. *See generally Bell v. Hood*, 327 U.S. 678, 684 (1946) ("it is . . . well settled that where legal rights have been invaded, and a federal statute provides for a general right to sue for such invasion, federal courts may use any available remedy to make good the wrong done"); *Wicker v. Hoppock*, 73 U.S. 94, 99 (6 Wall.) (1867)

("When a wrong has been done, and the law gives a remedy, the compensation shall be equal to the injury . . . . The injured party is to be placed, as near as may be, in the situation he would have occupied if the wrong had not been committed").

462. 435 U.S. 247, 258 (1978).

463. *Glenn v. Newman*, 614 F.2d 467, 473 (5th Cir. 1980). *See also Vanelli v. Reynolds School Board*, 667 F.2d 773, 780–81 (9th Cir. 1982).

464. *Board of Regents v. Roth*, 408 U.S. 564, 573 (1972).

465. *See Cochran v. Chidester School District*, 456 F.Supp. 390, 396 (W.D. Ark. 1978).

466. *Davis v. Oregon State University*, 591 F.2d 493, 496 (9th Cir. 1978); *Graves v. Duganne*, 581 F.2d 222 (9th Cir. 1978); *Dennis v. S&S Consolidated Rural High School District*, 577 F.2d 338 (5th Cir. 1978).

467. 408 U.S. 564 (1972).

468. 429 U.S. 624 (1977).

469. *Id.* at 627, *quoting Board of Regents v. Roth*, 408 U.S. 564, 573 (1972).

470. *Codd v. Velger*, 429 U.S. 624, 627 (1977); *Board of Regents v. Roth*, 408 U.S. 564, 573 (1972).

471. 408 U.S. 564, 573 n.12 (1972).

472. 429 U.S. 624, 627 (1977).

473. *Black's Law Dictionary* (4th ed. 1968).

474. *Codd v. Velger*, 429 U.S. 624, 627 (1977).

475. *See Austin v. Board of Education*, 562 F.2d 446, 452 (7th Cir. 1977).

476. *Rodriguez de Quinonez v. Perez*, 596 F.2d 486, 491 (1st Cir.), *cert. denied*, 444 U.S. 840 (1979). *Accord Corrigan v. Donilon*, 639 F.2d 834 (1st Cir. 1981).

477. *Carey v. Piphus*, 435 U.S. 247, 263–64 (1978).

478. *James v. Board of School Commissioners*, 484 F.Supp. 705, 715 (S.D. Ala. 1979) (teacher awarded damages for mental distress caused by denial of procedural due process).

479. *Carey v. Piphus, supra*, 435 U.S. at 266–67.

480. *See Harrah Independent School District v. Martin*, 440 U.S. 194, 197 (1979); *Kelley v. Johnson*, 425 U.S. 238, 244, 247–48 (1976).

481. *See Savodnik v. Korvettes, Inc.*, 488 F.Supp. 822, 825 n.3 (E.D. N.Y. 1980); *Protecting At Will Employees Against Wrongful Discharge: The Duty to Terminate Only in Good Faith*, 93 Harv.L.Rev. 1816 (1980).

482. *See Savodnik v. Korvettes, Inc., supra; Fortune v. National Cash Register Co.*, 373 Mass. 96, 364 N.2d 1251 (1977); *Monge v. Beebe Rubber Co.*, 114 N.H. 130, 316 A.2d 549 (1974); *Kelsay v. Motorola, Inc.*, 74 Ill. 2d 172, 384 N.E.2d 353 (1978); *Protecting At Will Employees Against Wrongful Discharge, supra*, 93 Harv.L.Rev. 1816 (1980).

483. *See James v. Board of Education*, 37 N.Y.2d 891, 340 N.E.2d 735, 378 N.Y.S.2d 371 (1975); *Savodnik v. Korvettes, Inc.*, *supra*.

484. *Jeffries v. Turkey Run Consolidated School District*, 492 F.2d 1, 3–5 (7th Cir. 1974).

485. *Eichman v. Indiana State University Board of Trustees*, 597 F.2d 1104, 1109 (7th Cir. 1979); *McGhee v. Draper*, 564 F.2d 902, 912–13 n.8a (10th Cir. 1977); *Stebbins v. Weaver*, 537 F.2d 939, 943 (7th Cir. 1976), *cert. denied*, 429 U.S. 1041 (1977); *Weathers v. West Yuma County School District*, 530 F.2d 1335, 1340–42 (10th Cir. 1976); *Buhr v. Buffalo Public School District*, 509 F.2d 1196, 1202 (8th Cir. 1974). *Compare Arceneaux v. Treen*, 671 F.2d 128, 134 (5th Cir. 1982); *Thompson v. Gallagher*, 489 F.2d 443, 447 (5th Cir. 1974).

486. *Harrah Independent School District v. Martin*, 440 U.S. 194, 197 (1979); *Kelley v. Johnson*, 425 U.S. 238, 244 (1976).

487. *Jeffries v. Turkey Run Consolidated School District*, 492 F.2d 1, 4 n.8 (7th Cir. 1974).

488. *Protecting At Will Employees Against Wrongful Discharge: The Duty to Terminate Only in Good Faith*, 93 Harv.L.Rev. 1816 (1980).

489. 414 U.S. 632 (1974).

490. *Id.* at 640.

491. *Id.* at 644.

492. *Id.* at 649–50.

493. *Gurmankin v. Costanzo*, 556 F.2d 184, 186 (3d Cir. 1977).

494. 425 U.S. 238 (1976).

495. *Id.* at 244.

496. *Id.* at 247.

497. *Id.* at 248.

498. *Ball v. Board of Trustees*, 584 F.2d 684, 686 n.2 (5th Cir. 1978) (Godbold, J., concurring), *cert. denied*, 440 U.S. 972 (1979).

499. *East Hartford Education Association v. Board of Education*, 562 F.2d 838, 859 (2d Cir. 1977) (*en banc*).

500. *Miller v. School District No. 167*. 495 F.2d 658, 667 (7th Cir. 1974).

501. *East Hartford Education Association v. Board of Education*, 562 F.2d 838, 859 (2d Cir. 1977); *Miller v. School District No. 167*, 495 F.2d 658, 667 (7th Cir. 1974). *See also Tardif v. Quinn*, 545 F.2d 761, 763 (1st Cir. 1976) (upholding the dismissal of a teacher for wearing short skirts).

502. *Pence v. Rosenquist*, 573 F.2d 395, 399–400 (7th Cir. 1978).

503. *See Hander v. San Jacinto Junior College*, 519 F.2d 273, 277 (5th Cir. 1975).

504. *See Braxton v. Board of Public Instruction*, 303 F.Supp. 958, 959 (M.D. Fla. 1969).

505. *East Hartford Education Association v. Board of Education*, 562 F.2d 838, 857 (2d Cir. 1977) (*en banc*).

506. *Id.* at 858.
507. *Finot v. Pasadena City Board of Education,* 250 Cal. App. 2d 189,
     58 Cal. Rptr. 520 (1968). Generally, claims that teacher hair or
     dress regulations violate the Constitution have not fared well in the
     state courts. *See Morrison v. Hamilton County Board of Education,*
     220 So. 2d 534 (La. App.), *writ denied,* 254 La. 17, 220 So. 2d 68
     (1969).
508. *See Richards v. Thurston,* 424 F.2d 1281, 1284–85 (1st Cir. 1970).
509. *West Virginia State Board of Education v. Barnette,* 319 U.S. 624,
     642 (1943). *See* L. Tribe, *American Constitutional Law* 961
     1978).
510. *Karr v. Schmidt,* 460 F.2d 609, 621 (5th Cir.) *(en banc), cert.
     denied,* 409 U.S. 989 (1972) (dissenting opinion of Wisdom, J.,
     joined by Brown, C.J., and Thornberry, Goldberg, and Simpson,
     J.J.).
511. *United States ex rel. Vajtauer v. Commissioner of Immigration at
     Port of New York,* 273 U.S. 103, 106 (1927).
512. 353 U.S. 232, 239 (1957).
513. *Id.* at 262 (1957).
514. 362 U.S. 199 (1960).
515. *Id.* at 206. *See also Vachon v. New Hampshire,* 414 U.S. 478 (1974);
     Johnson v. Florida, 391 U.S. 596 (1968); *Adderley v. Florida,* 385
     U.S. 39, 44 (1966).
516. *Fisher v. Snyder,* 476 F.2d 375, 377–78 (8th Cir. 1973). *See also
     Drown v. Portsmouth School District,* 451 F.2d 1106, 1108 (1st Cir.
     1971); *McEnteggart v. Cataldo,* 451 F.2d 1109, 1111 (1st Cir. 1971),
     cert. denied, 408 U.S. 943 (1972).
517. *Chase v. Fall Mountain Regional School District,* 330 F.Supp. 388,
     399 (D. N.H. 1971).
518. *Bogart v. Unified School District,* 432 F.Supp. 895, 905 (D. Kan.
     1977).
519. *Id.* at 906. *See also Morris v. Board of Education,* 401 F. Supp.
     188, 211 (D. Del. 1975) (termination for persistent insubordination
     where the charge was without any basis in fact violated teacher's
     substantive due process rights); *Sterzing v. Fort Bend Independent
     School District,* 376 F.Supp. 657, 661–62, (S.D. Tex. 1972), *vacated
     on other grounds,* 496 F.2d 92 (5th Cir. 1974).
520. 451 F.2d 1106 (1st Cir. 1971).
521. *Id.* at 1108. *See also McEnteggart v. Cataldo,* 451 F.2d 1109, 1111
     (1st Cir. 1971), *cert. denied,* 408 U.S. 943 (1972).
522. 451 F.2d at 1108.
523. *Martinez v. Brown,* 449 F.Supp. 207, 212 (N.D. Cal. 1978). *See
     also Society for Individual Rights v. Hampton,* 63 F.R.D. 399,
     400–01 (N.D. Cal. 1973), *aff'd in part,* 528 F.2d 905 (9th Cir.
     1975).
524. *Cf. Cord v. Gibb, Virginia,* 219 Va. 1019, 1022, 254 S.E.2d 71, 73

(1979) (unconstitutional to deny a female applicant admission to bar based on her out-of-wedlock living arrangements with a male since her conduct "bears no rational connection to her fitness to practice law").

525. *Sullivan v. Meade Independent School District*, 530 F.2d 799, 803–04 (8th Cir. 1976).

526. *DeLuca v. Sullivan*, 450 F.Supp. 736, 740 (D. Mass. 1977).

527. *Id.*

528. *Lodgwick v. Hendricks*, No. 74–1529A, slip. op. at 6–7 (N.D. Ga. Sept. 10, 1975). *But see Logan v. Warren County Board of Education*, 549 F.Supp. 145 (S.D. Ga. 1982) (after board dismissed principal who was convicted of submitting false documents to the U.S. government, court upholds dismissal as not violating principal's substantive due process rights because discharge was related to fitness in that it involved crime of moral turpitude).

529. *Hoagland v. Mount Vernon School District*, 95 Wash. 2d 424, 428, 623 P.2d 1156, 1159 (1981).

530. *Id.* at 429, 623 P.2d at 1159.

531. *Major v. Hampton*, 413 F.Supp. 66, 71 (E.D. La. 1976).

532. *Id.* at 69.

533. *Id.* at 70.

534. *See Thompson v. Gallagher*, 489 F.2d 443, 446 (5th Cir. 1974).

535. *Gross v. University of Tennessee*, 448 F.Supp. 245, 248 (W.D. Tenn. 1978). *See also Orr v. Koefoot*, 377 F.Supp. 673, 687 (D. Neb. 1974).

536. *Gosney v. Sonora Independent School District*, 603 F.2d 522, 526 (5th Cir. 1979).

537. *Id.* at 527.

538. *Wishart v. McDonald*, 500 F.2d 1110, 1115 (1st Cir. 1974).

539. 364 F.2d 177 (4th Cir. 1966), *cert. denied*, 385 U.S. 1003 (1967).

540. *Id.* at 181.

541. *Drown v. Portsmouth School District*, 451 F.2d 1106, 1108 (1st Cir. 1971). *See also McEnteggart v. Cataldo*, 451 F.2d 1109, 1111 (1st Cir. 1971), *cert. denied*, 408 U.S. 943 (1972).

542. *Conway v. Alfred I. DuPont School District*, 333 F.Supp. 1217, 1220 (D. Del. 1971).

543. *Bolling v. Sharpe*, 347 U.S. 497, 499 (1954).

544. *Id.* 499–500. In a case brought by students who had failed a state-mandated examination that they had to pass to graduate from high school, the Fifth Circuit stated that if the students proved that the examination covered material outside the curriculum, its lack of fairness and discriminatory effects would violate the due process clause. *Debra P. v. Turlington*, 644 F.2d 397 (5th Cir. 1981).

545. *Rose v. Locke*, 423 U.S. 48, 49 (1975); *Smith v. Goguen*, 415 U.S. 566, 572, 574 (1974); *Grayned v. City of Rockford*, 408 U.S. 104, 108 (1972); *Papachristou v. City of Jacksonville*, 405 U.S. 156, 162

(1972); *Bouie v. City of Columbia*, 378 U.S. 347, 350–52, 355 (1964).

546. *Grayned, supra* at 108.

547. *diLeo v. Greenfield*, 541 F.2d 949, 953 (2d Cir. 1976) (emphasis in original).

548. *Hostrop v. Board of Junior College District No. 515*, 471 F.2d 488, 493 (7th Cir. 1972), *cert. denied*, 411 U.S. 967 (1973). *See also Thomas v. Board of Education*, 607 F.2d 1043, 1054 (2d Cir. 1979), *cert. denied*, 444 U.S. 1081 (1980). (Newman, J., concurring) ("Whatever notice requirements the Due Process Clause mandates before student discipline may be imposed . . . there can be no doubt that discipline imposed exactly contrary to the announced standards of school authorities is constitutionally impermissible").

549. *Hostrup v. Board of Junior College District No. 515, supra*. In a later case, the Seventh Circuit made it clear that, in its view, a teacher can only invoke substantive due process if he is deprived of a property interest or an independent liberty interest. *Jeffries v. Turkey Run Consolidated School District*, 492 F.2d 1, 4 (7th Cir. 1974). *See also Stebbins v. Weaver*, 537 F.2d 939, 943 (7th Cir. 1976), *cert. denied*, 429 U.S. 1041 (1977).

550. *Lewis v. Delaware State College*, 455 F.Supp. 239, 248 (D. Del. 1978).

551. *Johnson v. Angle*, 341 F.Supp. 1043, 1047–48 (D. Neb. 1971).

552. *Id.* at 1048.

553. *Wright v. Arkansas Activities Association*, 501 F.2d 25, 28–29 (8th Cir. 1974).

554. *See* Hofstadter, *Protecting State Procedural Rights in Federal Court: A New Role for Substantive Due Process*, 30 Stan.L.Rev. 1019, 1033–34, 1042 (1978).

555. 495 F.2d 423 (5th Cir. 1974).

556. *See also Tyson v. New York City Housing Authority*, 369 F.Supp. 513, 518–19 (S.D. N.Y. 1974).

557. The termination may also be irrational on the ground that the test maker, as may be the case, has warned that it is inappropriate to use student test scores for the purpose of evaluating a teacher's performance. *But see Scheelhaase v. Woodbury Central Community School District*, 488 F.2d 237. (8th Cir. 1973), *cert. denied*, 417 U.S. 969 (1974). *See especially id.* at 245 (Bright, J., concurring).

VI

The Right to Equal Protection and Related Federal Statutory Rights

The equal protection clause of the 14th Amendment to the United States Constitution provides that no state shall "deny to any person within its jurisdiction the equal protection of the laws." This prohibition has been held applicable to state and local governmental bodies and to state and local officials. Basically, the mandate of the equal protection clause is that persons similarly situated be treated in like manner.

Equal protection claims frequently are coupled with claims under one or more federal (or state) statutes prohibiting a particular type of discrimination or under a state constitution's equal protection clause or analogous provision. Often a teacher will have broader rights under such a statute or state constitutional provision than under the equal protection clause of the Federal Constitution.

What standard of review will a court employ in determining whether a governmental classification making distinctions among teachers violates the equal protection clause of the 14th Amendment?

In determining whether the government has unconstitutionally differentiated between similarly situated individuals, a court ordinarily will uphold the classification if it is rationally related to a legitimate governmental interest.[1] In one case, for example, a school board adopted a prospective rule establishing contract non-renewal as the penalty for a teacher's violation of a continuing education requirement. Non-compliance previously had been penalized only by denying a salary raise, an option no longer available because the legislature had passed a law making such raises mandatory. Sustaining the new rule against an equal protection challenge, the Supreme Court concluded that "the only inquiry is whether the State's classification is 'rationally related to the State's objective.' "[2]

Will a governmental classification of teachers be more strictly scrutinized if it is based on race?

Yes. Certain classifications in themselves "supply a reason to infer antipathy,"[3] and accordingly are suspect. When the government makes a racial classification disadvantaging a minority group the classification, regardless of purported motivation, presumptively violates the equal protection clause and can be upheld only upon an "extraordinary" justification.[4] This rule applies as well to a classification that is ostensibly neutral but is an obvious pretext for racial discrimination.[5]

From two Supreme Court decisons—*Fullilove v. Klutznick* and *University of California Regents v. Bakke*—it has become clear that there is no consensus on the Supreme Court with respect to the standard of review that should be applied under the equal protection clause to a governmental racial or ethnic classification benefitting members of a minority group to compensate for past disadvantages. Justices Stewart and Rehnquist have taken the position that "any official action that treats a person differently on account of his race or ethnic origin is inherently suspect and presumptively invalid."[6] Justice Powell has expressed the view that the equal protection clause prohibits a remedial racial or ethnic classification by the government unless it is a necessary means of advancing a compelling governmental interest.[7] Justice Stevens, in a dissenting opinion dealing with an Act of Congress giving preference to particular minorities, has stated that in his view the remedial measure had to be "narrowly tailored," and that "[i]t [was] up to Congress to demonstrate that its unique statutory preference [was] justified by a relevant characteristic that [was] shared by the members of the preferred class."[8] Justices Brennan, White, Marshall, and Blackmun, apparently applying to remedial racial classifications an intermediate standard of review similar to the standard employed by the Court in cases involving challenges to sex-based classifications, have expressed the view that the test should be whether the classification serves important governmental objectives and is substantially related to the achievement of those objectives. [9]

In *United Steelworkers v. Weber* the Supreme Court ruled that Title VII of the Civil Rights Act of 1964 does not prohibit all voluntary, remedial race-conscious affirmative action plans in the private sector. The plan before the Court was collectively bargained by an employer and a union and reserved for black employees 50 percent of the openings in an in-plant craft training program until the percentage of black craft workers in the plant was commensurate with the percentage of blacks in the local labor force. The Court held that the plan did not violate Title VII. [10] Without defining in detail the line of demarcation between permissible and impermissible affirmative action plans, the Court held that the challenged plan fell on the permissible side of the line. The Court noted that the purposes of the plan "mirror those of the statute"; that both "were designed to break down old patterns of racial segregation and hierarchy"; and "[b]oth were structured to open employment opportunities for Negroes in occupations which have traditionally been closed to them." At the same time, the Court said, "the plan does not unnecessarily trammel the interests of the white employees. The plan does not require the discharge of white workers and their replacement with new black hires. . . . Nor does the plan create an absolute bar to the advancement of white employees; half of those trained in the program will be white. Moreover, the plan is a temporary measure; it is not intended to maintain racial balance, but simply to eliminate a manifest racial imbalance. Preferential selection of craft trainees at the . . . plant will end as soon as the percentage of black skilled craft workers in the . . . plant approximates the percentage of blacks in the local labor force." The Court concluded, therefore, that the adoption of the plan "falls within the area of discretion left by Title VII to the private sector voluntarily to adopt affirmative action plans designed to eliminate conspicuous racial imbalance in traditionally segregated job categories."[11]

Because of the lack of any definitive decision by the Court in *Bakke* on the constitutional issue and the unwillingness of the Court in *Weber* to attempt a detailed line of demarcation between those affirmative action plans which violate Title VII and those which do not, it is, as the California Supreme Court has noted, "somewhat hazardous to speculate on the

Court's ultimate resolution" of the constitutional and statutory issues presented by a voluntary affirmative action plan adopted by a public employer.[12] It seems reasonably certain that there will be litigation in the area of public education as well as public employment generally, fleshing out the governing standards.[13]

Does the equal protection clause prevent a court from ordering a school district to reassign black and white teachers to schools in a particular ratio in order to eliminate segregation imposed by law?

No, at least where the court's order is a "reasonable" step toward desegregation of the school system. Thus, the Supreme Court upheld an order of Frank Johnson—then a federal district court judge—which required an Alabama school system that was segregated by law and had a ratio of white to black teachers of three to two to have in each school with fewer than 12 teachers at least one full-time teacher whose race was different from the race of the majority of the teachers at that school. His order also required that in schools with 12 or more teachers the race of at least one of every six faculty and staff members be different from the race of a majority of such persons at that school.[14]

Similarly, in *Swann v. Charlotte-Mecklenburg Board of Education*—also involving a dual system of schools racially segregated by law—the Court rejected the contention that "the Constitution requires that teachers be assigned on a 'color blind' basis" and "prohibits district courts from using their equity power to order assignment of teachers to achieve a particular degree of faculty desegregation."[15]

In cases involving desegregation of dual school systems in which racial segregation has been imposed by law, some courts of appeals frequently have required integration plans to have the ratio of racial and ethnic minorities and non-minorities in faculties at each school be approximately the same as the district-wide ratio.[16]

The principle that a court may order reassignment of faculty as a remedy for de jure segregation in a school system is not limited to systems which are racially segregated by law, but extends to a school system which is "dual" by virtue of de jure acts of segregation.[17] And the federal courts have rejected the claim that the lack of de jure segregation in faculty assignment, as distinguished from pupil assignment, precludes a remedial order reassigning faculty.[18] Finally, a faculty reassignment remedy is not unconstitutional merely because it affects an otherwise lawful seniority system.[19] In the Detroit desegregation case, however, a federal district court, while reaching that conclusion, articulated this caveat: "Although we would not permit the [Detroit Federation of Teachers'] collective bargaining agreement to stand in the way of providing plaintiff's class with an adequate remedy, neither will we unnecessarily enter a court order providing for the wholesale eradication of a provision in its collective bargaining agreement." The court proceeded to reject a faculty reassignment proposal of the Detroit school board which would have effectively obliterated all seniority rights of DFT members.[20]

Does the equal protection clause bar a school district from taking voluntary action to obtain a better racial balance in its teaching faculty?

No. The Supreme Court has observed that school authorities have wide discretion in formulating school policy, and that as a matter of educational policy school authorities might well conclude that some kind of racial balance in the schools is desirable quite apart from any constitutional requirements.[21] Thus a school board may voluntarily adopt a plan to obtain a better racial balance in its faculty. Such a plan was upheld by the Ninth Circuit in the Los Angeles school desegregation case.[22]

Are sex-based classifications "suspect"?

Yes. The Supreme Court has said that any state law "overtly or covertly designed to prefer males over females in public employment would require an exceedingly persuasive justification" to withstand an equal protection challenge[23] Under the Court's decisions there is a federal constitutional right to be free from gender discrimination unless a gender classification serves important governmental objectives and is substantially related to the achievement of those objectives.[24]

Sex-based classifications also may violate Title VII of the Civil Rights Act of 1964, which prohibits most school employers from discriminating against employees on the basis of sex.[25] In addition, section 901(a) of Title IX of the Education Amendments of 1972 provides that with certain enumerated exceptions, "[n]o person . . . shall, on the basis of sex, be excluded from participation in, be denied the benefits of, or be subjected to discrimination under any education program or activity receiving Federal financial assistance."[26]

To implement section 901(a), the former Department of Health, Education, and Welfare issued regulations that, among other things, prohibit sex discrimination in all employment practices of recipients of federal education aid.[27] The Supreme Court recently upheld HEW's authority to issue such regulations under Title IX.[28] The Court said, however, that such regulations are not to apply to all the programs of an educational institution just because the institution receives federal aid; instead they are to apply only to the specific programs that receive federal financial assistance.[29]

While HEW has been empowered to reach employment discrimination prohibited by the Title IX regulations, this does not necessarily mean that the employee has a private right of action under the title.[30] The Supreme Court, however, has held that the Civil Rights Act (42 U.S.C. § 1983) authorizes a suit, in federal or state court, for the violation of a right under a federal statute.[31] Thus, section 1983 may authorize a teacher to bring such a suit to challenge any employment discrimination which HEW has prohibited, and is empowered to regulate, under Title IX.

Where a disparity in pay is involved, the Equal Pay Act may be implicated. In general, it bars an employer from discriminating in pay on the basis of sex by paying disparate wages for equal work on jobs the performance of which requires equal skill, effort, and responsibility, and which are performed under similar working conditions.[32] One of the areas in which the Equal Pay Act plays a significant role is sex discrimination in coaching pay. An excellent discussion of sex discrimination in coaching generally, including the relevant portions of the Equal Pay Act among other provisions of law, is contained in the article cited in the footnote.[33] Since publication of the article on coaching, the Supreme Court has held that while the Equal Pay Act gives one a right to sue only when one's compensation is discriminatorily lower than that of someone in an equal or substantially equal job, Title VII furnishes a right to sue for wage discrimination even when the plaintiff asserts that he or she is being discriminated against vis-a-vis employees who are not doing substantially equal work.[34]

This decision provides a potentially significant addition to a teacher's arsenal of weapons for use in fighting differentials in coaching pay.

A discussion of how the Equal Pay Act is enforced and the relationship between private enforcement and enforcement by the federal government is contained in the publication cited in the footnote.[35] Responsibility for federal government enforcement of the Equal Pay Act was transferred by President Carter's reorganization plan from the Department of Labor to the EEOC on July 1, 1979.[36]

Does a classification or selection process that has a disproportionate adverse impact upon one race or sex automatically violate the equal protection clause?

No. The 14th Amendment "guarantees equal laws, not equal results."[37] Thus the Supreme Court in *Washington v. Davis*[38] upheld a job-related employment test that white people passed in proportionately greater numbers than blacks because there had been no showing that racial discrimination entered into the establishment or formulation of the test.[39] When a neutral law has a disparate impact upon a group that historically has been the victim of discrimination, an unconstitutional purpose may still be at work.[40] Although such impact provides an "important starting point," purposeful discrimination is "the condition that offends the Constitution."[41] The Court has applied these same principles to determine whether a law or policy which has a disproportionate adverse effect on women violates the equal protection clause.[42]

It is important to bear in mind that Title VII of the Civil Rights Act of 1964 may afford minorities and women, as well as other historically disadvantaged groups,[43] greater protection than the equal protection clause. Title VII, which prohibits discrimination by covered employers against employees or applicants for employment on the basis of race, sex, or national origin, was amended in 1972 to bring state and local governing bodies, including school boards, within the definition of a covered employer.[44] The Court has distinguished between the requirements for proving discrimination under the Constitution and the requirements for proving discrimination in a Title VII case. The Court has held unlawful under Title VII employment practices, neutral on their face, which have a disproportionately harsh impact on members of a racial minority or on women, and which neither "have a manifest relationship to the job in question" nor "fulfill a genuine business need."[45]

In addition to the equal protection clause and Title VII, other provisions of law may be implicated by actions of school authorities adversely affecting teachers and having a racially discriminatory purpose or effect: among them Title VI of the Civil Rights Act of 1964, which prohibits certain discrimination by recipients of federal funds, and section 706 (d) (1) (B) of the Emergency School Aid Act. In *Board of Education v. Harris,* the Supreme Court held that "discriminatory impact is the standard by which ineligibility under ESAA is to be measured, irrespective of whether the discrimination relates to 'demotion or dismissal of instructional personnel' or to 'the hiring, promotion, or assignment of employees'; that a *prima facie* case of discriminatory impact may be made by a proper statistical study and that the burden of rebutting that case was on the board.[46] Thus the standard under the Emergency School Aid Act exceeds the constitutional equal protection standard and apparently the Title VI standard as well. In a 1983 decision, the Supreme Court finally addressed what the Title VI standard is, and it splintered over the question. Only two Justices held that Title VI sets forth a disparate impact standard, but they were joined by three other Justices who stated that while Title VI itself requires proof of discriminatory intent, it was permissible for the federal agency issuing regulations under the act to set forth a disparate impact standard.[47]

What kind of evidence is relevant to the issue of whether the defendant discriminated on the basis of race or sex in violation of the equal protection clause?

The Supreme Court has recognized that a defendant is unlikely to admit that he intended to discriminate, and that accordingly intent ordinarily will have to be found by a "sensitive inquiry into such circumstantial and direct evidence of intent as may be available," including the impact of the challenged official action; the historical background of the decision; the specific sequence of events leading up to the challenged decision; departures from the normal procedural sequence; substantive departures from other decisions, and the legislative or administrative history.[48]

Does a teacher who shows that race or sex was a factor in the challenged employment decision establish a constitutional violation warranting relief?

Not necessarily. The Supreme Court has indicated that when a plaintiff makes the requisite "threshold" showing of purposeful discrimination by the defendants, sufficient to make out a *"prima facie* case" of a violation of the equal protection clause, the burden shifts to the defendants to establish "that the same decision would have resulted even had the impermissible purpose not been considered."[49]

The conduct that the defendant claims would have resulted in the same decision even in the absence of an impermissible purpose may not always have resulted in such a decision in similar circumstances. Then the school authorities may be unable to prove their "same decision anyway" defense. In an Arkansas case, for example, school authorities attempted to justify their failure to hire a black teaching applicant by showing that she was not certified in a field in which there were vacancies, and thus would not have been hired even if race had not been considered. The Eighth Circuit concluded that "the defendants could not escape liability on that basis since there was also evidence in the record that certification was not uniformly required by the school district and that several white uncertified teachers were employed by the school district in the years she sought a faculty position.[50]

One factor that makes it especially difficult to ascertain whether discriminatory intent motivated hiring or promotion decisions in the teaching area is the subjectivity that surrounds so many of these decisions. This has caused one court to write:

> Although not illegal *per se,* subjective promotion procedures are to be closely scrutinized because of their susceptibility to discriminatory abuse. The mere fact that the subjective process is intended to recognize merit does not necessarily alleviate its susceptibility to discriminatory abuse. When the evaluation is in any degree subjective and when the evaluators themselves are not members of the protected minority, the legitimacy and undiscriminatory basis of the articulated reason for the decision should be subject to particularly close scrutiny by the trial judge [and on appeal].[51]

Where a school system with a history of racial segregation dismisses a disproportionate number of black teachers incident to the desegregation of its schools, is there a presumption that a black teacher's dismissal was racially motivated?

Yes. The Fourth Circuit, in decisions cited with approval by the Supreme Court,[52] has ruled that in such circumstances the burden shifts to the school system to show by clear and convincing evidence that a plaintiff was not dismissed for racial reasons in violation of the Constitution.[53] Other circuits have adopted similar rules.[54] Subjective standards carry little weight in meeting the school board's burden in such cases.[55]

Have any other rules been developed by the courts to protect black educators against job loss incident to school desegregation?

Yes. The courts have fashioned special rules designed to insure that black educators are not disadvantaged when school systems become unitary. For example, the Fifth Circuit has adopted a rule requiring that where there is a reduction in force attributable to school desegregation, no teacher can be dismissed or demoted unless previously promulgated, objective, non-racial criteria have been applied to determine which teachers are to be dismissed or demoted.[56] A vacancy must be filled with a displaced former teacher if one is minimally qualified.[57] The Fourth Circuit has ruled that where a formerly black school is closed and fewer teachers are needed as a result, teachers displaced from that school must be judged by definite, objective standards in comparison with all teachers in the system to determine who shall continue to be employed.[58] The Eighth Circuit has adopted the rule that a board of education is required to use objective, non-discriminatory standards in the employment, assignment, and dismissal of teachers, and that subjective factors may be used in making such decisions only if "nondiscriminatory," "established," and "previously announced."[59]

Is a classification distinguishing between pregnancy-related disabilities and other disabilities a classification based on sex for purposes of determining what type of scrutiny to apply to the classification under the equal protection clause?

No. The Supreme Court has held that a state's disability insurance program which excluded benefits for disability resulting from normal pregnancy created a classification based on pregnancy, not on "gender as such." Applying a "rational basis" test, the Court upheld the classification.[60]

While such a classification is not "suspect" for purposes of equal protection analysis, Congress has amended Title VII of the Civil Rights Act of 1964 to specifically include discrimination based on pregnancy, childbirth, or related medical conditions in Title VII's prohibition against sex discrimination in employment.[61] Excerpts from the EEOC's interpretive guidelines on the Act and on sex discrimination in general are reproduced in the Appendix.

May an employer offer teachers a retirement plan which requires male and female teachers to make the same contributions, but which pays women lower monthly retirement benefits than men because women tend to live longer?

No. In a 1983 decision, the Supreme Court held that this practice violates Title VII. The Court decided to apply this rule prospectively, stating that "all retirement benefits derived from contributions made after the decision today must be calculated without regard to the sex of the beneficiary [and] that benefits derived from contributions made prior to this decision may be calculated as provided by the [plan's] existing terms."[61a]

When a teacher believes that he or she has been the victim of a discriminatory employment practice, how much time does that teacher have to file a Title VII complaint?

The general rule is that a complaint of unlawful employment discrimination must be filed with the EEOC within 180 days of the alleged discriminatory act.[62] In *Delaware State College v. Ricks,*[63] a recent Supreme Court case, the board of trustees voted to deny tenure to Ricks on June 26, 1974. The board immediately informed Ricks of this decision and told him they would offer him a one-year terminal contract that would expire June 30, 1975. Ricks filed a grievance, claiming that the tenure denial was discriminatory, and on September 12, 1974, the board of trustees notified Ricks that it had denied his grievance.

The Court held that the alleged discriminatory practice occurred at the time the tenure decision was made and communicated to Ricks and that he had to file his employment discrimination complaint within 180 days of that event.[64] "That is so," the Court wrote, "even though one of the *effects* of the denial of tenure—the eventual loss of a teaching position—did not occur until later."[65] The Court concluded that it would be improper to start counting 180 days from either the time the board rejected his grievance or the time his terminal contract ended.[66] In addition, the court stated that "[t]he proper focus is upon the time of the *discriminatory acts,* not upon the time at which the *consequences* of the acts become most painful."[67] One court has interpreted the *Ricks* decision to mean that the 180-day period to file a complaint "begins to run from the time that the complainant knows or reasonably should know that the challenged act has occurred."[68] In another case, at the time the negative employment decision was made, the employee did not know about a discriminatory evaluation in his file and therefore did not have reason to know that the decision was discriminatory in nature. Thus, the court found that the 180-day period in which to file a complaint began, not when the alleged discriminatory employment decision was made, but when the employee learned years later of the discriminatory evaluation.[69]

Is a classification based on homosexuality a suspect classification for equal protection purposes?

Arguably such a classification fulfills the requirement for a suspect classification, since homosexuals historically have been a disfavored class and thus, it may be argued, the classification "supplies a reason to infer antipathy."

Whether or not it accepts this argument, a court might well conclude that it is irrational, and therefore a violation of the equal protection clause, to deny qualified homosexuals employment opportunities afforded other individuals.[70]

Is a citizenship requirement applicable to teaching in the public schools a suspect classification?

No. While classifications based on alienage generally are subject to "close judicial scrutiny" under the equal protection clause,[71] the Supreme Court has held that an exception exists where a governmental function is involved. In *Ambach v. Norwick* the Court ruled that public school teachers fall within the "governmental function" exception. Accordingly, it concluded, the Constitution requires only that a citizenship requirement applicable to teaching in the public schools bear a rational relationship to a legitimate state interest. The Court held that a New York statute forbidding certification as a public school teacher of any person who was not a citizen of the United States, unless that person had manifested an intention to apply for citizenship, satisfied this test and was thus constitutional.[72]

May classifications other than those based on race or sex also be regarded by a court as "suspect"?

Yes. In an Illinois case policemen had engaged in a "uniform protest" by failing to report for work in proper uniform. Hearings were scheduled on disciplinary charges, and all who appeared with an attorney were discharged and all who appeared without an attorney were merely suspended. The Seventh Circuit held that this constituted a suspect classification for which no compelling need was shown, in violation of the equal protection clause of the 14th Amendment.[73]

What level of scrutiny will the courts apply to classifications based on age?

In *Massachusetts Board of Retirement v. Murgia*,[74] the Supreme Court, employing a "rational basis" test, rejected an equal protection challenge to a state statute providing for compulsory retirement of uniformed state police officers at age 50. In *Murgia* there had been a trial, and there was evidence to support the conclusion that physical preparedness for police work was rationally related to age.

In *Gault v. Garrison*,[75] a case decided after the Supreme Court's decision in *Murgia*, the Seventh Circuit reversed an order dismissing a complaint by a teacher attacking the constitutionality of a mandatory retirement law for teachers. The court assumed that the strongest justification for such a law would be to remove those teachers who are unfit. Based on that premise, the court held that, absent an evidentiary showing, there was no reason to assume that there is any relationship between advancing age and fitness to teach. *Gault* distinguished *Murgia* as involving a question of whether physical fitness declines with age, noted that there was evidence in the record in *Murgia* to support the conclusion that it does, and contrasted this with the question whether teaching ability, which involves predominantly mental skills, similarly declines with age. Absent an evidentiary showing, the court saw no reason to assume that it does; in fact, it speculated that the knowledge and experience necessary for teaching increases with age.[76]

In *Palmer v. Ticcione,* however, the Second Circuit concluded that "*Gault* too narrowly conceives the possible rational bases for a compulsory retirement statute. Unrelated to any notion of physical fitness, a state might prescribe mandatory retirement for teachers to open up employment opportunities for young teachers—particularly in the last decade when supply has outpaced demand, or to open up more places for minorities, or to bring young people with fresh ideas and techniques in contact with school children, or to assure predictability and ease in establishing and administering pension plans. A compulsory retirement system is rationally related to the fulfillment of any or all of these legitimate state objectives."[77] Accordingly, the court affirmed the dismissal of a complaint attacking the constitutionality of the New York State compulsory retirement system for teachers.[78]

Teachers may be protected against compelled retirement before age 70, however, by the Age Discrimination in Employment Act of 1978. The footnote cites publications explaining these rights and how they may be enforced, i.e., the relationship between enforcement through private civil actions and federal administrative enforcement.[79] Administrative enforcement of the Act was transferred from the Department of Labor to the EEOC on July 1, 1979.[80]

In a case involving the Act that may prove significant nationwide, the Second Circuit has held that a school district policy of not hiring teachers with more than five years' experience violated the Act because of its disparate impact on older teachers.[81] The school district sought to justify its policy as a cost-cutting measure, but the court rejected that rationale as an insufficient justification for discriminating against older teachers.[82]

Is a classification based on physical handicap a suspect classification?

No. Unlike distinctions based on race, classifications based on physical handicap often can be justified by the differing abilities of those classified. Thus, the rational basis test is the applicable standard in such a case.[83]

Handicapped teachers also may have certain rights under section 504 of the Rehabilitation Act of 1973, which provides in pertinent part:

No *otherwise qualified* handicapped individual in the United States . . . shall, solely by reason of his handicap, be excluded from the participation in, be denied the benefits of, or be subjected to discrimination under any program or activity receiving Federal financial assistance.[84]

In *Southeastern Community College v. Davis* the Supreme Court concluded that "[a]n otherwise qualified person is one who is able to meet all of a program's requirements in spite of his handicap."[85] The Court ruled in *Davis* that "Section 504 imposes no requirement upon an educational institution to lower or to effect substantial modifications of standards to accommodate a handicapped person."[86]

The question whether section 504 affords a private right of action was left unresolved in the *Davis* case. The courst are divided over the question whether an employee has standing to bring a suit under section 504 for discrimination in employment on the basis of handicap. Some courts have held that private judicial enforcement of section 504 is limited to persons who are intended beneficiaries of federal assistance, and that therefore an employee can bring such a suit only where one of the purposes of the federal financial assistance is to provide employment.[87] Other courts have taken a broader view, holding that employees can bring private suits under section 504 against employers receiving federal financial assistance even though providing employment was not one of the principal purposes of the federal aid.[88] While the Supreme Court has ruled that the Civil Rights Act (42 U.S.C. § 1983) creates a cause of action for violation of a federal statutory right,[89] it remains to be determined whether a handicapped employee who was not an intended beneficiary of federal aid has a federal statutory right not to be discriminated against on the basis of handicap, and therefore a cause of action under section 1983.

Are there any circumstances in which a governmental classification, other than a "suspect" classification, will be strictly scrutinized?

Yes. Strict scrutiny will be applied to a classification which tends to penalize a right independently protected by the Constitution. Thus in *Shapiro v. Thompson*[90] the Supreme Court held unconstitutional statutory provisions of two states and the District of Columbia which imposed a one-year residence requirement on applicants for welfare assistance. Observing that the effect of such statutes was to discourage the influx of poor families who might wish "to migrate, resettle, find a new job, and start a new life,"[91] the Court stated that "the nature of our Federal Union and our constitutional concepts of personal liberty unite to require that all citizens be free to travel throughout the length and breadth of our land uninhibited by statutes, rules, or regulations which unreasonably burden or restrict this movement."[92] Since the plaintiffs, in "moving from State to State or to the District of Columbia . . . were exercising a constitutional right," the Court held that "any classification which serves to penalize the exercise of that right, unless shown to be necessary to promote a *compelling* governmental interest, is unconstitutional."[93] After considering the reasons advanced in support of the one-year residence requirement, the Court concluded that no such compelling interest existed.

A similarly strict standard of review will be applied to a classification which unequally distributes access to a right independently protected by the Constitution. An example is a classification under which the government treats two speakers unequally, triggering the "compelling interest" standard of review.[94]

Does a requirement that a teacher live within the jurisdiction in which he is employed serve to penalize the exercise of a "fundamental right," so as to require a showing that the classification is necessary to promote a compelling governmental interest?

A requirement that a teacher live within the jurisdiction in which he is employed, it has been argued, violates the equal protection clause because it serves to penalize the exercise of the constitutional right of all citizens freely to migrate and settle where they choose, and is not necessary to promote a compelling governmental interest. On this theory, the Supreme Court struck down requirements that a person reside in the jurisdiction for a specified period of time in order to be eligible for certain public benefits.[95] In *McCarthy v. Philadelphia Civil Service Commission*, however, the Supreme Court seemed to hold, for reasons which are not clear, that this constitutional standard was inapplicable to requirements that public employees reside, during their employment, within the jurisdiction in which they are employed.[96]

Where the constitutionality of a continuing residency requirement for public employees is evaluated under the "rational basis" test, the court is apt to find, as did the Supreme Court in *McCarthy*, that the requirement is rationally based. In a decision cited favorably in *McCarthy*, the Sixth Circuit upheld a residency requirement for teachers adopted by the Cincinnati School Board. The court found rational bases for the policy in the school superintendent's testimony that promulgation of the rule was based on the following conclusions: "(1) such a requirement aids in hiring teachers who are highly motivated and deeply committed to an urban educational system, (2) teachers who live in the district are more likely to vote for district taxes, less likely to engage in illegal strikes, and more likely to help obtain passage of school tax levies, (3) teachers living in the district are more likely to be involved in school and community activities bringing them in contact with parents and community leaders and more likely to be committed to the future of the district and its schools; (4) teachers who live in the district are more likely to gain sympathy and understanding for the racial, social, economic, and urban problems of the children they teach and are thus less likely to be considered isolated from the communities in which they teach, and (5) the requirement is in keeping with the goal of encouraging integration in society and in the schools."[97]

It is important to bear in mind that there may be state courts which, as they are free to do, interpret their own state constitutions to bar or limit residency requirements for teachers.[98] State legislatures may also decide to outlaw or restrict such requirements as a matter of policy.[99] It may be an unfair labor practice, moreover, for a school board to impose a residency requirement unilaterally without negotiating the question with the teachers' collective bargaining representative.[100]

Are there circumstances in which a court, employing the minimum rationality standard, has concluded that a chal-

lenged governmental classification affecting teachers was not rationally related to a legitimate governmental objective?

Yes. The California Supreme Court held repugnant to the equal protection clause a statute which in effect provided that a person convicted of a *felony* sex crime who applied for a certificate of rehabilitation and was otherwise fit could obtain certification to teach in the community college system, but that an otherwise fit person, convicted of a *misdemeanor* sex crime, was forever barred.[101] And the Fifth Circuit ruled that where all other teachers charged with immoral conduct were entitled to a public hearing, a policy denying such a hearing to those teachers whose alleged immorality consisted of un-wed parenthood violated the equal protection clause.[102]

In *Trister v. University of Mississippi* two members of the university's law school faculty were told to stop participating in an OEO program designed to provide legal services to the poor in northern Mississippi. The only reason for the university's decision was that the two faculty members wished to continue to represent clients who tended to be unpopular. The Fifth Circuit held that while the university could decide not to employ any part-time professors, or to forbid the practice of law by every member of its faculty, it could not, consistently with the equal protection clause, "arbitrarily discriminate against professors in respect to the category of clients they may represent."[103] And the Supreme Court of Arkansas concluded that it was irrational and a violation of the equal protection clause of the 14th Amendment for a state statute to forbid professors and associate professors at a state-funded school to practice law, but to exempt assistant professors from the ban.[104]

Can differences between the treatment of tenured teachers and the treatment of non-tenured teachers be so irrational as to violate the equal protection clause?

Yes. A federal court in Georgia struck down as violative of the equal protection clause a school board policy granting maternity leave to tenured teachers but denying it to non-tenured teachers. Noting that board regulations drew no distinction between the two categories of teachers with respect to leave for professional study, bereavement, personal illness, emergency, or military service, the court held that the policy was arbitrary and without rational basis.[105] Relying upon this decision, an Ohio federal court invalidated as a violation of the equal protection clause a policy which granted a maternity leave of absence to untenured pregnant teachers who had served three or more years in the system, but denied it to those with fewer than three years of service.[106]

May a state, consistently with the equal protection clause, discriminate between teachers in one county and teachers in another county?

Such discrimination would violate the equal protection clause if it lacked a rational basis. For example, acts of the Alabama legislature denied the benefits of the state teacher tenure law to teachers in 8 counties which, with one exception, were among the 12 counties of the state with a majority black population. An Alabama federal court held that the statutes classified on the basis of race and therefore violated the equal protection clause. But the court also ruled that the classification violated the equal protection clause because it was irrational. In making this determination, the court noted that the purposes of the tenure laws were to guarantee "freedom to teach" by protecting teachers from removal on unfounded charges or for political reasons and to benefit the public by assuring a more competent and efficient teaching force. The court found no rational basis for the creation of a "second class" in an area "where the rights involved are of paramount importance and the greatest sensitivity."[107]

One possible reading of this decision is that it is irrational to create rights of such importance as tenure rights in order to protect vital interests of teachers and the public, yet withhold those rights from teachers in particular locations within the state, even if geographical discrimination with respect to the provision of less important privileges or benefits might be rationally based, e.g., on a desire not to overburden small rural school districts by the imposition of procedural requirements which may be difficult for them to satisfy.[108]

Another example of a decision holding a statute repugnant to the equal protection clause by discriminating between teachers in one county and teachers in another county is a federal district court ruling invalidating a Florida law forbidding all administrators and supervisors in the Palm Beach County school system to participate or become a member in any organization which engaged in collective representation of teachers with respect to terms and conditions of employment. Although the court's conclusion that the law violated the First Amendment is questionable,[109] the court also held, in a ruling which may be sound, that the Florida law violated the equal protection clause. The court relied in part upon the fact that the defendants had "made no effort to demonstrate that Palm Beach County is in any way unique so as to justify placing its educational employees in a class apart from those of other Florida counties."[110]

Do school authorities violate the equal protection clause where they enforce a valid rule or policy against some teachers but not others?

Yes, at least where there is no rational basis for such differential treatment.

In one case, the employment of a teacher in Alabama was terminated for violation of a principal's "rule" forbidding male teachers to wear mustaches. The decision invalidating the termination was based partly on the ground that the only teacher other than the plaintiff who sported a mustache had not been asked to shave it off. The court concluded that this unequal treatment denied the plaintiff equal protection of the laws.[111] In a Delaware case a state college refused to renew the employment contract of the director of residence halls for women on the ground that she had borne a child out of wedlock. Because the college authorities had taken no action against other staff members similarly situated, a federal court held the non-renewal repugnant to the equal protection clause.[112]

NOTES

1. *Vance v. Bradley*, 440 U.S. 93, 97, 111 (1979); *New York Transit Authority v. Beazer*, 440 U.S. 568, 592 & n.39 (1979); *Massachusetts Board of Retirement v. Murgia*, 427 U.S. 307, 314–15 (1976).
2. *Harrah Independent School District v. Martin*, 440 U.S. 194, 199 (1979).
3. *Personnel Administrator of Massachusetts v. Feeney*, 442 U.S. 256, 272 (1979). *See also Vance v. Bradley*, 440 U.S. 93, 97 (1979).
4. *McLaughlin v. Florida*, 379 U.S. 184, 191 (1964); *Brown v. Board of Education*, 347 U.S. 483 (1954).
5. *Yick Wo v. Hopkins*, 118 U.S. 356 (1886); *Guinn v. United States*,

238 U.S. 347 (1915). *See Personnel Administrator of Massachusetts v. Feeney*, 442 U.S. 256, 272 (1979).

6. *Fullilove v. Klutznick*, 448 U.S. 448, 523 (1980) (Stewart, J., dissenting).

7. *Id.* at 496 (Powell, J., concurring).

8. *Id.* at 554 (Stevens, J., dissenting).

9. *Id.* at 518 (Marshall, J., concurring in the judgment); *University of California Regents v. Bakke*, 438 U.S. 265, 359 (1978) (Brennan, J., concurring in the judgment in part and disgussing in part).

10. 443 U.S. 208–09 (1979).

11. *Id.*

12. *See Price v. Civil Service Commission*, 26 Cal. 3d 257, 604 P.2d 1365, 1380, 161 Cal. Rptr. 475, *cert. dismissed as moot*, 449 U.S. 811 (1980).

13. For lower-court decisions construing *Bakke* and *Weber* in the area of public education, *see Cohen v. Community College of Philadelphia*, 484 F.Supp. 411 (E.D. Pa. 1980) (rejecting Title VII challenge to voluntary affirmative action plan, without quotas and with no expiration date, adopted by community college to increase minority representation on faculty); *Jackson Education Association v. Board of Education*, No. 77–911484CZ (Circuit Ct., County of Jackson, Mich. Aug. 31, 1979) (rejecting constitutional and Title VII challenges to a "seniority override" provision of voluntary affirmative action agreement between teacher association and school board giving minority and female teachers protection from layoff as long as their representation in the teaching force fell short of specified goals); *cf. Tangren v. Wackenhut Services, Inc.*, 658 F.2d 705 (9th Cir. 1981), *cert. denied*, 456 U.S. 916 (1982) (similar "seniority override" provision in agreement between employer and union in private sector upheld).

14. *United States v. Montgomery County Board of Education*, 395 U.S. 225 (1969).

15. 402 U.S. 1, 19 (1971).

16. *See Singleton v. Jackson Municipal Separate School District*, 419 F.2d 1211, 1217–18 (5th Cir. 1969), *cert. denied*, 396 U.S. 1032 (1970); *Nesbit v. Statesville City Board of Education*, 418 F.2d 1040, 1042 (4th Cir. 1969).

17. *Bradley v. Milliken*, 460 F.Supp. 299 (E.D. Mich. 1978), *remanded* 620 F.2d 1143 (6th Cir.), *cert. denied*, 449 U.S. 870 (1980.)

18. *Id.* at 318.

19. *Id. See also Arthur v. Nyquist*, 520 F.Supp. 961 (W.D. N.Y. 1981) (court order requiring hiring and promotion of one minority for each non-minority until minority composition attains 21 percent overcomes seniority provisions of collective bargaining agreement).

20. *Bradley v. Milliken, supra* note 17, at 316–17.

21. *North Carolina State Board of Education v. Swann*, 402 U.S. 43, 45 (1971).

22. *Zaslawsky v. Board of Education,* 610 F.2d 661, 664 (9th Cir. 1979). *See also Caulfield v. Board of Education,* 583 F.2d 605, 614–15 (2d Cir. 1978), *on remand,* 486 F.Supp. 862, 924 (E.D. N.Y. 1979), *aff'd,* 632 F.2d 999 (2d Cir. 1980), *cert. denied,* 450 U.S. 1030 (1981) (voluntary agreement between New York City Board of Education and HEW, acting through office of civil rights, to remedy discriminatory practices in school system and obligating board to alter certain teacher and supervisor employment and assignment practices did not violate statutory or constitutional rights of plaintiff teachers).

23. *Personnel Administrator of Massachusetts v. Feeney,* 442 U.S. 256, 273 (1979).

24. *Id; Kirchberg v. Feenstra,* 450 U.S. 455, 461 (1981); *Califano v. Westcott,* 443 U.S. 76, 89 (1979); *Davis v. Passman,* 442 U.S. 223 (1979); *Craig v. Boren,* 429 U.S. 190, 197 (1976); *but see Rostker v. Goldberg,* 453 U.S. 57 (1981) (upholding Congress's decision to require men and not women to register for the draft on the ground that women were not similarly situated to men in this case because women were generally not allowed to engage in combat. Because the purpose of the registration requirement was to speed combat readiness, Congress's decision not to require women to register was found to further the important government objective of military efficiency).

25. 42 U.S.C. §2000e-2(a).

26. 20 U.S.C. §1681 *et seq*.

27. 45 C.F.R. §86.51 *et seq*. (1982). Jurisdiction over educational matters was transferred to the U.S. Department of Education on May 4, 1980. The relevant Title VI regulations have been transferred by operation of law to the Department of Education and will ultimately be redesignated and recodified in Title 34 of the Code of Federal Regulations. *See* 34 C.F.R. Part 106, Subpart E (1982).

28. *North Haven Board of Education v. Bell,* 456 U.S. 512 (1982), aff'g, 629 F.2d 773 (2d. Cir. 1980).

29. *Id.* at 535–38; 102 S.Ct. at 1926–27. The Third Circuit has held that Title IX applies to private educational institutions even when the only federal assistance they receive is indirect, i.e., through federal grants to students. *Grove City College v. Bell,* 687 F.2d 684 (3d Cir. 1982), *cert. granted,* ——U.S.——, 103 S.Ct. 1181 (Feb. 22, 1983). The Third Circuit also held that the college itself was the relevant recipient program and that Title IX applied to all phases of that program.

30. *Compare Cannon v. University of Chicago,* 441 U.S. 677 (1979), *with Sobel v. Yeshiva University,* 477 F.Supp. 1161, 1167–68 (S.D.N.Y. 1979).

31. *Maine v. Thiboutot,* 448 U.S. 1 (1980).

32. 29 U.S.C. §206(d) (1). *See Corning Glass Works v. Brennan,* 417

U.S. 188, 196 (1974); *Hodgson v. American Bank of Commerce*, 447 F.2d 416 (5th Cir. 1971); *Brennan v. Woodbridge School District*, 8 EPD ¶9640 (D. Del. 1974).

33. L. Dessem, *Sex Discrimination in Coaching*, 3 Harv. Women's L.J. 97 (1980). Compare *Coble v. Hot Springs School District No. 6*, 682 F.2d 721 (8th Cir. 1982) (female coaches who show male coaches receive more pay and longer contracts have prima facie case of sex discrimination), *and Burkey v. Marshall City Board of Education*, 513 F.Supp. 1084, (N.D. W. Va. 1981) (paying female coach half as much as male coach violates Title VII), with *Jacobs v. College of William and Mary*, 517 F.Supp. 791 (E.D. Va. 1980) (pay differential between male and female coaches does not violate Title VII because male coach's job requires greater skill and more work). *See also* B. Schlei & P. Grossman, *Employment Discrimination Law* (BNA 1976) at 370–92, Supp. 1979 at 102–08.

34. *County of Washington v. Gunther*, 452 U.S. 161 (1981).

35. B. Schlei & P. Grossman, *Employment Discrimination Law* (BNA 1976), at 370–83, Supp. 1979 at 102–04.

36. B. Schlei & P. Grossman, *Employment Discrimination Law* (BNA 1976), Supp. 1979 at 103.

37. *Personnel Administrator of Massachusetts v. Feeney*, 442 U.S. 256, 273 (1979).

38. 426 U.S. 229 (1976).

39. *See also Village of Arlington Heights v. Metropolitan Housing Development Corp.*, 429 U.S. 252 (1977).

40. *Personnel Administrator of Massachusetts v. Feeney*, 442 U.S. 256, 273 (1979).

41. *Id.; Swann v. Board of Education*, 402 U.S. 1, 16 (1971).

42. *Personnel Administrator of Massachusetts v. Feeney*, 442 U.S. 256, 274–80 (1979).

43. Title VII prohibits discrimination on the basis of "race, color, religion, sex, or national origin." 42 U.S.C. §2000e-2(a).

44. P.L. 92–261, Sec. 3, March 24, 1972, 42 U.S.C. §2000e.

45. *Griggs v. Duke Power Co.*, 401 U.S. 424, 432 (1971); *Dothard v. Rawlinson*, 433 U.S. 321, 329 (1977). The *Griggs* decision has been applied by lower federal courts in holding invalid the use of the National Teacher Examination in the hiring or retention of teachers where the examination has a disparate impact on blacks and has not been validated for those uses. *Walston v. County School Board*, 492 F.2d 919 (4th Cir. 1974); *United States v. Chesterfield County School District*, 484 F.2d 70 (4th Cir. 1973); *Baker v. Columbus Municipal Separate School District*, 329 F.Supp. 706 (N.D. Miss. 1971), *aff'd*, 462 F.2d 1112 (5th Cir. 1972). Where the National Teachers Examination was found to have been properly validated for certification and pay purposes in South Carolina, however, a three-judge federal district court held such use consis-

tent with Title VII and the decision was summarily affirmed by the Supreme Court. *NEA v. South Carolina*, 434 U.S. 1026 (1978); *See also Newman v. Crews*, 651 F.2d 222 (4th Cir. 1981). In applying the "business necessity" standard articulated in *Griggs*, the Supreme Court seems to be requiring of the employer only a showing "that any given requirement [has] a manifest relationship to the job in question." If the plaintiff then shows that some other criterion or selection procedure would serve the employer's interests as well, with less impact on blacks, the challenged criterion or procedure will be invalidated under Title VII. *Scott v. University of Delaware*, 455 F.Supp. 1102, 1123 (D. Del. 1978), *aff'd in part and vacated in part*, 601 F.2d 76 (3d Cir.), *cert. denied*, 444 U.S. 931 (1979). Applying these concepts, a Delaware federal district court held that while a university's Ph.D. requirement or its equivalent for appointment or promotion to most of the professor, associate professor, and assistant professor positions had a disparate impact on blacks, it was justified by the university's legitimate interest in hiring and advancing persons likely to be successful in adding to the fund of knowledge in their chosen disciplines, and that the plaintiff had suggested no alternative criterion or selection procedure which would serve that interest as well with less potential for adverse effect on blacks. *Id.* at 1126; *see also Campbell v. Ramsay*, 631 F.2d 597 (8th Cir. 1980) (plaintiff established prima facie case of sex discrimination, but university's decision not to rehire her was upheld because she had only a master's degree and university policy requiring a doctorate was a legitimate, non-discriminatory selection criterion even though it had an adverse impact on women). For an excellent discussion of disparate treatment, disparate impact and their differences, see *Williams v. Colorado Springs School District*, 641 F.2d 835, 839–42 (10th Cir. 1981).

46. 444 U.S. 130, 151–52 (1979).

47. *Guardians Association v. Civil Service Commission*, 51 U.S.L.W. 5105 (July 1, 1983). Justice White, writing the opinion for the badly divided Court, stated that proof of disparate impact alone can make out a violation of Title VI, *id.* at 5106, a view shared by Justice Marshall. *Id.* at 5114. Justice Stevens, joined by Justices Brennan and Blackmun, stated that Title VI provided for an intent standard, but found that the act nevertheless empowered the federal agency issuing regulations under the act to set forth a disparate impact standard. *Id.* at 5120. Justice White said, however, that if there were just a showing of disparate impact, he would only allow injunctive, non-compensatory relief.

48. *Village of Arlington Heights v. Metropolitan Housing Development Corp.*, 429 U.S. 252, 266–68 (1977); *Personnel Administrator of Massachusetts v. Feeney*, 442 U.S. 256, 279 n.24 (1979). *See also Lynn v. University of California Regents*, 656 F.2d 1337 (9th Cir.

1981). In an individual Title VII case in which a claim of "disparate treatment," i.e., purposeful discrimination, is made, the plaintiff must establish a "prima facie case" of discrimination. This then requires the defendant to "articulate" a legitimate, non-discriminatory reason for its adverse action regarding the plaintiff. If the defendant "articulates" such a reason, the plaintiff must prove that the reason given is a pretext for discrimination. *Texas Department of Community Affairs v. Burdine,* 450 U.S. 248 (1981); *McDonnell-Douglas Corp. v. Green,* 411 U.S. 792 (1973); *Furnco Construction Corp. v. Waters,* 438 U.S. 567 (1978); *International Brotherhood of Teamsters v. United States,* 431 U.S. 324 (1977). For the application of the rules laid down in these cases to hiring, promotion, and tenure decisions involving teachers, see *Coble v. Hot Springs School District No. 6,* 682 F.2d 721 (8th Cir. 1982); *Banerjee v. Board of Trustees of Smith College,* 648 F.2d 61 (1st Cir.), *cert. denied,* 454 U.S. 1098 (1981). *Jepsen v. Florida Board of Regents,* 610 F.2d 1379 (5th Cir. 1980); *Kunda v. Muhlenberg College,* 621 F.2d 532 (3d Cir. 1980); *Sweeney v. Board of Trustees,* 604 F.2d 106 (1st Cir. 1979), *cert. denied,* 444 U.S. 1045 (1980). Before the *Sweeney* decision some courts had expressed an attitude of deference to the decisions of universities in personnel matters, even in Title VII suits. *See, e.g., Faro v. New York University,* 502 F.2d 1229 (2d Cir. 1974). *Since Sweeney,* the Second Circuit has restated its position, agreeing that *McDonnell-Douglas* is the appropriate standard. *Powell v. Syracuse University,* 580 F.2d 1150, 1154 (2d Cir.), *cert. denied,* 439 U.S. 984 (1978). *See Jepsen v. Florida Board of Regents,* 610 F.2d 1379, 1382 n.2 (5th Cir. 1980).

49. *See Village of Arlington Heights v. Metropolitan Housing Development Corp.,* 429 U.S. 252, 270 n.21 (1977); *Williams v. Anderson,* 562 F.2d 1081, 1087 (8th Cir. 1977). *See also Lulac v. City of Salinas Fire Department,* 654 F.2d 557 (9th Cir. 1981).

50. *Williams v. Anderson,* 562 F.2d 1081, 1094 (8th Cir. 1977).

51. *Coble v. Hot Springs School District No. 6,* 682 F.2d 721, 726–27 (8th Cir. 1982), *quoting Royal v. Missouri Highway and Transportation Commission,* 655 F.2d 159, 164 (8th Cir. 1981).

52. *Keyes v. School District No. 1,* 413 U.S. 189, 209–10 (1973).

53. *Chambers v. Hendersonville City Board of Education,* 364 F.2d 189, 192 (4th Cir. 1966) *(en banc); North Carolina Teachers Association v. Asheboro City Board of Education,* 393 F.2d 736, 743 (4th Cir. 1968) *(en banc).*

54. *See, e.g., Barnes v. Jones County School District,* 544 F.2d 804, 807 (5th Cir. 1977); *Roper v. Effingham County Board of Education,* 528 F.2d 1024, 1025 (5th Cir. 1976); *McFerren v. County Board of Education,* 455 F.2d 199, 201 (6th Cir. 1972); *Moore v. Board of Education,* 448 F.2d 709, 711 (8th Cir. 1971); *Lee v. Macon County Board of Education,* 453 F.2d 1104, 1108–09 n.6 (5th Cir. 1971);

United States v. Jefferson County Board of Education, 380 F.2d 385 (5th Cir. 1967).

55. *E.g.*, *Moore v. Board of Education*, 448 F.2d 709, 713 (8th Cir. 1971); *Cochran v. Chidester School District*, 456 F.Supp. 390, 393 (W.D. Ark. 1978).

56. *Singleton v. Jackson Municipal Separate School District*, 419 F.2d 1211 (5th Cir. 1969). *See also Moore v. Tangipahoa Parish School Board*, 594 F.2d 489 (5th Cir. 1979); *Campbell v. Gadsden County School Board*, 534 F.2d 650, 657 (5th Cir. 1976); *Adams v. Rankin County Board of Education*, 485 F.2d 324, 327 n.2 (5th Cir. 1973).

57. *E.g.*, *Adams v. Rankin County Board of Education*, 485 F.2d 324, 326 (5th Cir. 1973); *Lee v. Macon County Board of Education*, 453 F.2d 1104, 1111 (5th Cir. 1971). *See also Reynolds v. Abbeville County School District*, 554 F.2d 638, 643 (4th Cir. 1977).

58. *Wall v. Stanly County Board of Education*, 378 F.2d 275, 276 (4th Cir. 1967).

59. *Moore v. Board of Education*, 448 F.2d 709, 713 (8th Cir. 1971).

60. *Geduldig v. Aiello*, 417 U.S. 484, 496, 497 n.20 (1974).

61. Pregnancy Discrimination Act, Pub.L. 95–555, 92 Stat. 2076, Oct. 31, 1978, codified at 42 U.S.C. § 2000e. Before this amendment the extent to which Title VII reached discrimination based on pregnancy was unclear. *Compare General Electric v. Gilbert*, 429 U.S. 125 (1976), *with Nashville Gas Company v. Satty*, 434 U.S. 136 (1977).

61a. *Arizona Governing Committee for Tax Deferred Annuity Plans v. Norris*, 51 U.S.L.W. 5243 (July 6, 1983). Nor may an employer require female employees to make larger contributions to a pension fund than males in order to receive the same benefits upon retirement. *Los Angeles Department of Water & Power v. Manhart*, 435 U.S. 702 (1978).

62. 42 U.S.C. § 2000e–5(e). This section provides, however, that if the employee first files a grievance with a state or local employment discrimination agency, the employee has to file within 300 days of the alleged unlawful employment practice or within 30 days of the date that the state or local agency notifies the employee that it has terminated its proceedings, whichever is earlier.

63. 449 U.S. 250 (1980).

64. *Id.* at 258.

65. *Id.*

66. *Id.* at 259–61. *Accord Stafford v. Muscogee County Board of Education*, 688 F.2d 1383, 1388 (11th Cir. 1982).

67. *Delaware State College v. Ricks*, *supra* note 63 at 258, *quoting Abramson v. University of Hawaii*, 594 F.2d 202, 209 (1979).

68. *Allen v. United States Steel Corp.*, 665 F.2d 689, 692 (5th Cir. 1982); *see also Stafford v. Muscogee County Board of Education*, 688 F.2d 1383, 1387 (11th Cir. 1982); *Carpenter v. Board of*

Regents of the University of Wisconsin, 529 F.Supp. 525 (W.D. Wis. 1982).

69. *Stoller v. Marsh*, 682 F.2d 971, 974, 978 (D.C. Cir. 1982). This decision cited and was consistent with *Zipes v. Trans World Airlines, Inc.*, 455 U.S. 385 (1982), which stated that filing a timely complaint with the EEOC is not a jurisdictional prerequisite to filing suit, but a requirement which, like a statute of limitations, is subject to waiver, estoppel, and equitable tolling.

70. See *Gay Law Students v. Pacific Telephone*, 24 Cal. 3d 458, 595 P.2d 592, 602, 156 Cal. Rptr. 14 (1979). *See also Baker v. Wade*, 553 F. Supp. 1121 (N.D. Tex. 1982). (statute prohibiting private consensual sodomy denies equal protection); *New York v. Onofre*, 51 N.Y.2d 476, 434 N.E.2d 936, 434 N.Y.S.2d 947, 948 (1980), *cert. denied*, 451 U.S. 987 (1981) (anti-sodomy statute violates equal protection). *Compare benShalom v. Secretary of Army*, 489 F.Supp. 964 (E.D. Wis. 1980) (plaintiff discharged from army reserves because of her sexual preferences, and court orders reinstatement, writing: "The court is satisfied from the record that her sexual preferences had as much relevance to her military skills as did her gender and the color of her skin"), *with Childers v. Dallas Police Department*, 513 F.Supp. 134 (N.D. Tex 1981) (court upholds refusal to hire gay activist, asserting that he would create a material interference within the department). *See generally B. Schlei and P. Grossman, Employment Discrimination Law* 365–68 (BNA 1976).

71. *Graham v. Richardson*, 403 U.S. 365, 372 (1971).

72. 441 U.S. 68 (1979).

73. *Olshock v. Village of Skokie*, 541 F.2d 1254 (7th Cir. 1976).

74. 427 U.S. 158 (1976).

75. 569 F.2d 993 (7th Cir. 1977), *cert. denied*, 440 U.S. 945 (1979)

76. *Id.* at 996.

77. 576 F.2d 459, 462 (2d Cir. 1978).

78. *Id.* at 465. *See also Klain v. Pennsylvania State University*, 434 F.Supp. 571, 575–79 (M.D. Pa. 1977), *aff'd*, 577 F.2d 726 (3d Cir. 1978). Cases explaining what is necessary to demonstrate a prima facie case of age discrimination include *Lovelace v. Sherwin-Williams Co.*, 681 F.2d 230 (4th Cir. 1982); *Loeb v. Textron, Inc.*, 600 F.2d 1003 (1st Cir. 1979); and *Pace v. Southern Railway System*, 530 F.Supp. 381 (N.D. Ga. 1981).

79. B. Schlei and P. Grossman, *Employment Discrimination Law* (BNA 1976) at 393–415, Supp. 1979 at 109–20.

80. *Id.* at Supp. at 113.

81. *Geller v. Markham*, 635 F.2d 1027 (2d Cir. 1980), *cert. denied*, 451 U.S. 945 (1981).

82. *Id.* at 1034.

83. *Upshur v. Love*, 474 F.Supp. 332, 337 (N.D. Cal. 1979).

84. 29 U.S.C. § 794 (1978) (emphasis added).

85. 442 U.S. 397, 406 (1979).
86. *Id.* at 413. *See generally* K. Hull, *The Rights of Physically Handicapped People* (An American Civil Liberties Handbook) (Discus/Avon 1979).
87. *See, e.g., Carmi v. Metropolitan St. Louis Sewer District,* 620 F.2d 672, 675 (8th Cir.), *cert. denied,* 449 U.S. 892 (1980); *Trageser v. Libbie Rehabilitation Center, Inc.,* 590 F.2d 87, 89 (4th Cir. 1978), *cert. denied,* 442 U.S. 947 (1979).
88. *Jones v. Metropolitan Atlanta Rapid Transit Authority,* 681 F.2d 1376 (5th Cir. 1982); *Hart v. County of Alameda,* 485 F.Supp. 66 (N.D. Cal. 1979).
89. *Maine v. Thiboutot,* 448 U.S. 1 (1980).
90. 394 U.S. 618 (1969).
91. *Id.* at 629.
92. *Id.*
93. *Id.* at 634 (emphasis the Court's). *See also Dunn v. Blumstein,* 405 U.S. 330 (1972) (applying *Shapiro* rationale to invalidate Tennessee law requiring one year's residence in the state and three months' residence in the county as a condition for voting); *Memorial Hospital v. Maricopa County,* 415 U.S. 250, 261–62 (1974) (holding unconstitutional an Arizona statute requiring one year of residence in a county as a condition of receiving certain medical care at county expense).
94. *Police Department of Chicago v. Mosely,* 408 U.S. 92, 96 (1972).
95. *Shapiro v. Thompson,* 394 U.S. 618, 629, 634 (1969).
96. 424 U.S. 645 (1976). *See also Andre v. Board of Trustees,* 561 F.2d 48 (7th Cir. 1977), *cert. denied,* 434 U.S. 1013 (1978); *Mogle v. Sevier County School District,* 540 F.2d 478 (10th Cir. 1976), *cert. denied,* 429 U.S. 1121 (1977).
97. *Wardwell v. Board of Education,* 529 F.2d 625, 628 (6th Cir. 1976). *See also Lorenz v. Logue,* 611 F.2d 421 (2d Cir. 1979).
98. *E.g., Angwin v. City of Manchester,* 118 N.H. 336, 386 A.2d 1272 (1978); *Donnelly v. Manchester,* 111 N.H. 50, 274 A.2d 789 (1971).
99. *E.g.,* R.I. Rev. Stats., 16–12–9 ("*Residency within municipality not required.*—No city or town shall require that an individual reside within the city or town as a condition for appointment or continued employment as a school teacher"); Cal. Rev. Stats. §4859 ("No school district may adopt or maintain any rule or regulation which requires a candidate for a position requiring certification qualifications to be a resident of the district, or which requires that an employee maintain residency within the district. Nor may a district grant any preferential treatment to candidates or employees because they are residents of the district").
100. *See, e.g., School Committee of Boston v. Massachusetts Labor Relations Commission,* School Law News, June 24, 1977, at 3.
101. *Newland v. Board of Governors of the California Community Colleges,* 19 Cal.3d 705, 566 p.2d 254, 139 Cal. Rpts. 620 (1977).

102. *Andrews v. Drew Municipal Separate School District*, 507 F.2d 611, 616 (5th Cir. 1975), *cert. dismissed as improvidently granted*, 425 U.S. 559 (1976).
103. *Trister v. University of Mississippi*, 420 F.2d 499, 504 (5th Cir. 1969). *Compare Debra P. v. Turlington*, 644 F.2d 397 (5th Cir. 1981) (students who failed state examination that they had to pass to graduate from public high school would have their equal protection rights violated if it was proved that the examination covered material outside the curriculum because the examination would then discriminate against the "failers" without there being a rational basis for the test).
104. *Atkinson v. Board of Trustees*, 262 Ark. 552, 559 S.W.2d 473 (1977).
105. *Jinks v. Mays*, 332 F.Supp. 254 (N.D. Ga. 1971).
106. *Heath v. Westerville Board of Education*, 345 F.Supp. 501 (S.D. Ohio 1972).
107. *Alabama State Teachers Association v. Lowndes County Board of Education*, 289 F.Supp. 300, 303, 305 (M.D. Ala. 1968).
108. *Id.* at 303.
109. *York County Fire Fighters v. York County*, 589 F.2d 775, 778 (4th Cir. 1978) (rule prohibiting supervisors from belonging to union of rank-and-file employees constituted valid limitation of supervisors' First Amendment right of association).
110. *Orr v. Thorp*, 308 F.Supp. 1369, 1372 (S.D. Fla. 1969).
111. *Ramsey v. Hopkins*, 320 F.Supp. 477 (N.D. Ala. 1970), *modified on other grounds*, 447 F.2d 128 (5th Cir. 1971).
112. *Lewis v. Delaware State College*, 455 F.Supp. 239 (D. Del. 1978). *See also Ciechon v. City of Chicago*, 686 F.2d 511, 522–24 (7th Cir. 1982); *Ziegler v. Jackson*, 638 F.2d 776 (5th Cir. 1981) (violation of police officer's equal protection rights found when he was discharged after being convicted of criminal provocation, while three other police officers who had been convicted of more serious crimes were not discharged).

VII

The Privilege Against Self-Incrimination

The Fifth Amendment confers a privilege against compulsory self-incrimination. If a person's answers to official questions might be used as evidence, or might lead to evidence, in a future criminal prosecution of that person, the Fifth Amendment, made applicable to the states through the 14th, creates a privilege to remain silent. Exercise of the privilege cannot be equated with guilt nor can it form the basis for a sanction by the government. Once the person has been promised immunity from prosecution based on compelled answers or their "fruit," however, refusal to answer questions closely related to a legitimate governmental interest may be punished. It is important to remember that this principle does not entitle the government to launch a fishing expedition into beliefs or associations, which are independently protected by the First Amendment.[1]

What is the privilege against self-incrimination?

The Fifth Amendment provides that no person "shall be compelled in any criminal case to be a witness against himself." The Amendment, which applies to state proceedings by virtue of its incorporation into the 14th, not only protects the individual against being involuntarily called as a witness against himself in a criminal prosecution but also privileges him not to answer official questions put to him in any other proceeding, civil or criminal, formal or informal, where the answers might incriminate him in future criminal proceedings.[2]

Do public employees, like citizens generally, have the benefit of the privilege against self-incrimination?

Yes. The Supreme Court has stated that "public employees are entitled, like all other persons, to the benefit of the Constitution, including the privilege against self-incrimination."[3]

May a public employee constitutionally be discharged because he has exercised his privilege against self-incrimination?

No. In *Slochower v. Board of Higher Education*, for example, the Supreme Court held that a public employee could not constitutionally be discharged because he had exercised his privilege against self-incrimination before a legislative committee.[4] Nor may a state constitutionally compel testimony from a public employee by threatening him with loss of employment.[5]

Can a public employee be discharged because he has refused to sign a waiver surrendering his Fifth Amendment immunity from prosecution in return for his testimony before a grand jury?

No. The Supreme Court has held that a public employee cannot constitutionally be terminated for refusing to waive the constitutional privilege.[6]

May a teacher constitutionally be discharged for refusing to answer his employer's questions pertinent to the faithful performance of his duties?

Yes, at least where he refuses to answer questions "specifically, directly, and narrowly relating to the performance of his official duties."[7] The teacher's answers, however, cannot be used against him in subsequent criminal prosecutions,[8] and he must be so advised in clear terms.[9]

NOTES

1. *See* L. Tribe, *American Constitutional Law* (Foundation Press 1978) at 709–10 and cases cited.
2. *Lefkowitz v. Turley*, 414 U.S. 70, 76 (1973).
3. *Uniformed Sanitation Men Association v. Commissioner of Sanitation*, 392 U.S. 280, 284–85 (1968).
4. 350 U.S. 551 (1956).

5. *Lefkowitz v. Turley*, 414 U.S. 70 (1973); *Garrity v. New Jersey*, 385 U.S. 493 (1967).
6. *Uniformed Sanitation Men Association v. Commissioner of Sanitation*, 392 U.S. 280 (1968); *Gardner v. Broderick*, 392 U.S. 273, 279 (1968).
7. *Uniformed Sanitation Men Associaton v. Commissioner of Sanitation*, 392 U.S. 280, 284 (1968); *Gardner v. Broderick*, 392 U.S. 273, 278 (1968).
8. *Gardner v. Broderick*, 392 U.S. 273, 278 (1968); *Uniformed Sanitation Men Association v. Commissioner of Sanitation*, 392 U.S. 280, 283–84 (1968).
9. *Kalkines v. United States*, 473 F.2d 1391 (Ct. Cl. 1973).

Appendix

Rights Against Discrimination Based on Sex and Pregnancy

What follows are excerpts of the text of the Equal Employment Opportunity Commission's guidelines on discrimination based on sex and pregnancy, codified in 29 C.F.R. §1604 (1982), and excerpts of the EEOC's Questions and Answers on the Pregnancy Discrimination Act, which appear as an appendix to section 1604.10.

Equal Employment Opportunity: Sex Discrimination. Part 1604—Guidelines on Discrimination Because of Sex.

Sec. 1604.1: General Principles

(a) References to "employer" or "employers" in Part 1604 state principles that are applicable not only to employers but also to labor organizations and to employment agencies insofar as their action or inaction may adversely affect employment opportunities.

(b) To the extent that the views expressed in prior Commission pronouncements are inconsistent with the views expressed herein, such prior views are hereby overruled.

(c) The Commission will continue to consider particular problems relating to sex discrimination on a case-by-case basis.

Sec. 1604.2: Sex as a Bona Fide Occupational Qualification

(a) The Commission believes that the bona fide occupational exception as to sex should be interpreted narrowly. Labels—"Men's jobs" and "Women's jobs"—tend to deny employment opportunities unnecessarily to one sex or the other.

(1) The Commission will find that the following situations do not warrant the application of the bona fide occupational qualification exception:

(i) The refusal to hire a woman because of her sex based on assumptions of the comparative employment characteristics of women in general. For example, the assumption that the turnover rate among women is higher than among men.

(ii) The refusal to hire an individual based on stereotyped characterizations of the sexes. Such stereotypes include, for example, that men are less capable of assembling intricate equipment; that women are less capable of aggressive salesmanship. The principle of non-discrimination requires that individuals be considered on the basis of individual capacities and not on the basis of any characteristics generally attributed to the group.

(iii) The refusal to hire an individual because of the preferences of coworkers, the employer, clients or customers except as covered specifically in paragraph (a) (2) of this section.

(2) Where it is necessary for the purpose of authenticity or genuineness, the Commission will consider sex to be a bona fide occupational qualification, e.g., an actor or actress.

(b) Effect of sex-oriented state employment legislation.

(1) Many States have enacted laws or promulgated administrative regulations with respect to the employment of females. Among these laws are those which prohibit or limit the employment of females, e.g., the employment of females in certain occupations, in jobs requiring the lifting or carrying of weights exceeding certain prescribed limits, during certain hours of the night, for more than a specified number of hours per day

or per week, and for certain periods of time before and after childbirth. The Commission has found that such laws and regulations do not take into account the capacities, preferences, and abilities of individual females and, therefore, discriminate on the basis of sex. The Commission has concluded that such laws and regulations conflict with and are superseded by Title VII of the Civil Rights Act of 1964. Accordingly, such laws will not be considered a defense to an otherwise established unlawful employment practice or as a basis for the application of the bona fide occupational qualification exception.

Sec. 1604.3: Separate Lines of Progression and Seniority Systems

(a) It is an unlawful employment practice to classify a job as "male" or "female" or to maintain separate lines of progression or separate seniority lists based on sex where this would adversely affect any employee unless sex is a bona fide occupational qualification for that job. Accordingly, employment practices are unlawful which arbitrarily classify jobs so that:

(1) A female is prohibited from applying for a job labeled "male," or for a job in a "male" line of progression; and vice versa.

(2) A male scheduled for layoff is prohibited from displacing a less senior female on a "female" seniority list and vice versa.

(b) A seniority system or line of progression which distinguishes between "light" and "heavy" jobs constitutes an unlawful employment practice if it operates as a disguised form of classification by sex, or creates unreasonable obstacles to the advancement by members of either sex into jobs which members of that sex would reasonably be expected to perform.

Sec. 1604.4: Discrimination Against Married Women

(a) The Commission has determined that an employer's rule which forbids or restricts the employment of married women and which is not applicable to married men is a discrimination based on sex prohibited by Title VII of the Civil Rights Act. It does not seem to us relevant that the rule is not directed against all females, but only against married females, for so long as sex is a factor in the application of the rule, such application involves a discrimination based on sex.

(b) It may be that under certain circumstances, such a rule could be justified within the meaning of Section 703(e)(1) of Title VII. We express no opinion on this question at this time except to point out that sex as a bona fide occupational qualification must be justified in terms of the peculiar requirements of the particular job and not on the basis of a general principle such as the desirability of spreading work.

* * *

Sec. 1604.8: Relationship of Title VII to the Equal Pay Act

(a) The employee coverage of the prohibitions against discrimination based on sex contained in Title VII is co-extensive with that of the other prohibitions contained in Title VII and is not limited by Section 703(h) to those employees covered by the Fair Labor Standards Act.

(b) By virtue of Section 703(h), a defense based on the Equal Pay Act may be raised in a proceeding under Title VII.

(c) Where such a defense is raised the Commission will give appropriate consideration to the interpretations of the Administrator, Wage and Hour Division, Department of Labor, but will not be bound thereby.

Sec. 1604.9: Fringe Benefits

(a) "Fringe benefits," as used herein includes medical, hospital, accident, life insurance and retirement benefits, profit-sharing and bonus plans; leave; and other terms, conditions, and privileges of employment.

(b) It shall be an unlawful employment practice for an employer to discriminate between men and women with regard to fringe benefits.

(c) Where an employer conditions benefits available to employees and their spouses and families on whether the employee is the "head of the household" or "principal wage earner" in the family unit, the benefits tend to be available only to male employees and their families. Due to the fact that such conditioning discriminatorily affects the rights of women employees, and that "head of household" or "principal wage earner" status bears no relationship to job performance, benefits which are so conditioned will be found a prima facie violation of the prohibitions against sex discrimination contained in the Act.

(d) It shall be an unlawful employment practice for an employer to make available benefits for the wives and families of male employees where the same benefits are not made available for the husbands and families of female employees or to make available benefits for the wives of male employees which are not made available for female employees; or to make available benefits to the husbands of female employees which are not made available for male employees. An example of such an unlawful employment practice is a situation in which wives of male employees receive maternity benefits while female employees receive no such benefits.

(e) It shall not be a defense under Title VII to a charge of sex discrimination in benefits that the cost of such benefits is greater with respect to one sex than the other.

(f) It shall be an unlawful employment practice for an employer to have a pension or retirement plan which establishes different optional or compulsory retirement ages based on sex, or which differentiates in benefits on the basis of sex. A statement of the General Counsel of

September 13, 1968, providing for a phasing out of differentials with regard to optional retirement age for certain incumbent employees is hereby withdrawn.

Sec. 1604.10: Employment Policies Relating to Pregnancy and Childbirth

(a) A written or unwritten employment policy or practice which excludes from employment opportunities applicants or employees because of pregnancy, childbirth, or related medical conditions is in prima facie violation of Title VII.

(b) Disabilities caused or contributed to by pregnancy, childbirth, or related medical conditions, for all job-related purposes, shall be treated the same as disabilities caused or contributed to by other medical conditions, under any health or disability insurance or sick leave plan available in connection with employment. Written or unwritten employment policies and practices involving matters such as the commencement and duration of leave, the availability of extensions, the accrual of seniority and other benefits and privileges, reinstatement, and payment under any health or disability insurance or sick leave plan, formal or informal, shall be applied to disability due to pregnancy, childbirth or related medical conditions on the same terms and conditions as they are applied to other disabilities. Health insurance benefits for abortion, except where the life of the mother would be endangered if the fetus were carried to term or where medical complications have arisen from an abortion, are not required to be paid by an employer; nothing herein, however, precludes an employer from providing abortion benefits or otherwise affects bargaining agreements in regard to abortion.

(c) Where the termination of an employee who is temporarily disabled is caused by an employment policy under which insufficient or no leave is available, such a termination violates the Act if it has a disparate impact on employees of one sex and is not justified by business necessity.

Sec. 1604.11: Sexual Harassment

(a) Harassment on the basis of sex is a violation of Sec. 703 of Title VII.* Unwelcome sexual advances, requests for sexual favors, and other verbal or physical conduct of a sexual nature constitute sexual harassment when (1) submission to such conduct is made either explicitly or implicitly a term or condition of an individual's employment, (2) submission to or rejection of such conduct by an individual is used as the basis for employment decisions affecting such individual, or (3) such conduct has the purpose or effect of substantially interfering with an individual's work performance or creating an intimidating, hostile, or offensive working environment.

(b) In determining whether alleged conduct constitutes sexual harassment, the Commission will look at the record as a whole and the totality of the circumstances, such as the nature of the sexual advances and the context in which the alleged incidents occurred. The determination of the legality of a particular action will be made from the facts, on a case by case basis.

(c) Applying general Title VII principles, an employer, employment agency, joint apprenticeship committee or labor organization (hereinafter collectively referred to as "employer") is responsible for its acts and those of its agents and supervisory employees with respect to sexual harassment regardless of whether the specific acts complained of were authorized or even forbidden by the employer and regardless of whether the employer knew or should have known of their occurrence. The Commission will examine the circumstances of the particular employment relationship and the job functions performed by the individual in determining whether an individual acts in either a supervisory or agency capacity.

(d) With respect to conduct between fellow employees, an employer is responsible for acts of sexual harassment in the workplace where the employer (or its agents or supervisory employees) knows or should have known of

---

*The principles involved here continue to apply to race, color, religion or national origin.

the conduct, unless it can show that it took immediate and appropriate corrective action.

(e) An employer may also be responsible for the acts of non-employees, with respect to sexual harassment of employees in the workplace, where the employer (or its agents or supervisory employees) knows or should have known of the conduct and fails to take immediate and appropriate corrective action. In reviewing these cases the Commission will consider the extent of the employer's control and any other legal responsibility which the employer may have with respect to the conduct of such non-employees.

(f) Prevention is the best tool for the elimination of sexual harassment. An employer should take all steps necessary to prevent sexual harassment from occurring, such as affirmatively raising the subject, expressing strong disapproval, developing appropriate sanctions, informing employees of their right to raise and how to raise the issue of harassment under Title VII, and developing methods to sensitize all concerned.

(g) Other related practices: Where employment opportunities or benefits are granted because of an individual's submission to the employer's sexual advances or requests for sexual favors, the employer may be held liable for unlawful sex discrimination against other persons who were qualified for but denied that employment opportunity or benefit.

B. Questions and Answers on the Pregnancy Discrimination Act

Introduction

On October 31, 1978, President Carter signed into law the *Pregnancy Discrimination Act* (Pub. L. 95–955). The Act is an amendment to Title VII of the Civil Rights Act of 1964 which prohibits, among other things, discrimination in employment on the basis of sex.

The basic principle of the Act is that women affected

by pregnancy and related conditions must be treated the same as other applicants and employees on the basis of their ability or inability to work. A woman is therefore protected against such practices as being fired, or refused a job or promotion, merely because she is pregnant or has had an abortion. She usually cannot be forced to go on leave as long as she can still work. If other employees who take disability leave are entitled to get their jobs back when they are able to work again, so are women who have been unable to work because of pregnancy.

In the area of fringe benefits, such as disability benefits, sick leave and health insurance, the same principle applies. A woman unable to work for pregnancy-related reasons is entitled to disability benefits or sick leave on the same basis as employees unable to work for other medical reasons. Also, any health insurance provided must cover expenses for pregnancy-related conditions on the same basis as expenses for other medical conditions. However, health insurance for expenses arising from abortion is not required except where the life of the mother would be endangered if the fetus were carried to term, or where medical complications have arisen from an abortion.

Some questions and answers about the *Pregnancy Discrimination Act* follow.

Q. What procedures may an employer use to determine whether to place on leave as unable to work a pregnant employee who claims she is able to work or deny leave to a pregnant employee who claims that she is disabled from work?

A. An employer may not single out pregnancy-related conditions for special procedures for determining an employee's ability to work. However, an employer may use any procedure used to determine the ability of all employees to work. For example, if an employer requires its employees to submit a doctor's statement concerning their inability to work before granting leave or paying sick benefits, the employer may require employees affected by pregnancy-related conditions to submit such statement. Similarly, if an employer allows its employees to obtain doctor's statements from their personal physicians for absences due to other disabilities or return dates from other disabilities, it must accept doctor's statements from personal physicians for absences and return dates connected with pregnancy-related disabilities.

Q. Can an employer have a rule which prohibits an employee from returning to work for a predetermined length of time after childbirth?

A. No.

Q. If an employee has been absent from work as a result of a pregnancy-related condition and recovers, may her employer require her to remain on leave until after her baby is born?

A. No. An employee must be permitted to work at all times during pregnancy when she is able to perform her job.

Q. Must an employer hold open the job of an employee who is absent on leave because she is temporarily disabled by pregnancy-related conditions?

A. Unless the employee on leave has informed the employer that she does not intend to return to work, her job must be held open for her return on the same basis as jobs are held open for employees on sick or disability leave for other reasons.

Q. May an employer's policy concerning the accrual and crediting of seniority during absences for medical conditions be different for employees affected by pregnancy-related conditions than for other employees?

A. No. An employer's seniority policy must be the same for employees absent for pregnancy-related reasons as for those absent for other medical reasons.

Q. For purposes of calculating such matters as vacations and pay increases, may an employer credit time spent on leave for pregnancy-related reasons differently than time spent on leave for other reasons?

A. No. An employer's policy with respect to crediting time for the purpose of calculating such matters as vacations and pay increases cannot treat employees on leave for pregnancy-related reasons less favorably than employees on leave for other reasons. For example, if employees on leave for medical reasons are credited with the time spent on leave when computing entitlement to vacation or pay raises, an employee on leave for pregnancy-related disability is entitled to the same kind of time credit.

Q. Must an employer hire a woman who is medically unable, because of a pregnancy-related condition, to perform a necessary function of a job?

A. An employer cannot refuse to hire a woman because of her pregnancy-related condition so long as she is able to perform the major functions necessary to the job. Nor can an employer refuse to hire her because of his preferences against pregnant workers or the preferences of co-workers, clients, or customers.

Q. May an employer limit disability benefits for pregnancy-related conditions to married employees?

A. No.

Q. If an employer has an all female workforce or job classification, must benefits be provided for pregnancy-related conditions?

A. Yes. If benefits are provided for other conditions, they must also be provided for pregnancy-related conditions.

Q. For what length of time must an employer who provides income maintenance benefits for temporary disabilities provide such benefits for pregnancy-related disabilities?

A. Benefits should be provided for as long as the employee is unable to work for medical reasons unless some other limitation is set for all other temporary disabilities, in which case pregnancy-related disabilities should be treated the same as other temporary disabilities.

Q. Must an employer who provides benefits for long-term or permanent disabilities provide such benefits for pregnancy-related conditions?

A. Yes. Benefits for long-term or permanent disabilities resulting from pregnancy-related conditions must be provided to the same extent that such benefits are provided for other conditions which result in long-term or permanent disability.

Q. If an employer provides benefits to employees on leave, such as installment purchase disability insurance, payment of premiums for health, life or other insurance, continued payments into pension, saving or profit sharing plans, must the same benefits be provided for those on leave for pregnancy-related conditions?

A. Yes, the employer must provide the same benefits for those on leave for pregnancy-related conditions as for those on leave for other reasons.

Q. Can an employee who is absent due to a pregnancy-related disability be required to exhaust vacation benefits before receiving sick leave pay or disability benefits?

A. No. If employees who are absent because of other disabling causes receive sick leave pay or disability benefits without any requirement that they first exhaust vacation benefits, the employer cannot impose this requirement on an employee absent for a pregnancy-related cause.

Q. Must an employer grant leave to a female employee for childcare purposes after she is medically able to return to work following leave necessitated by pregnancy, childbirth, or related medical conditions?

A. While leave for childcare purposes is not covered by the *Pregnancy Discrimination Act*, ordinary Title VII principles would require that leave for childcare purposes be granted on the same basis as leave which is granted to employees for other non-medical reasons. For example, if an employer allows its employees to take leave without pay or accrued annual leave for travel or education which is not job related, the same type of leave must be granted to those who wish to remain on leave for infant care, even though they are medically able to return to work.

Q. If state law requires an employer to provide disability insurance for a specified period before and after childbirth, does compliance with the state law fulfill the employer's obligation under the Pregnancy Discrimination Act?

A. Not necessarily. It is an employer's obligation to treat employees temporarily disabled by pregnancy in the same manner as employees affected by other temporary disabilities. Therefore, any restrictions imposed by state law on benefits for pregnancy-related disabilities, but not for other disabilities, do not excuse the employer from treating the individuals in both groups of employees the same. If, for example, a state law requires an employer to pay a maximum of 26 weeks benefits for disabilities other than pregnancy-related ones but only six weeks for pregnancy-related disabilities, the employer must provide benefits for the additional weeks to an employee disabled by pregnancy-related conditions, up to the maximum provided other disabled employees.

Q. If a State or local government provides its own employees income maintenance benefits for disabilities, may it provide different benefits for disabilities arising from pregnancy-related conditions than for disabilities arising from other conditions?

A. No. State and local governments, as employers, are subject to the Pregnancy Discrimination Act in the same way as private employers and must bring their employment practices and programs into compliance with the Act, including disability and health insurance programs.

Q. Must an employer provide health insurance coverage for the medical expenses of pregnancy-related conditions of the spouses of male employees? Of the dependents of all employees?

A. Where an employer provides no coverage for dependents, the employer is not required to institute such coverage. However, if an employer's insurance program covers the medical expenses of spouses of female employees, then it must equally cover the medical expenses of spouses of male employees, including those arising from pregnancy-related conditions.

But the insurance does not have to cover the pregnancy-related conditions of non-spouse dependents as long as it excludes the pregnancy-related conditions of such non-spouse dependents of male and female employees equally.

Q. Must an employer provide the same level of health insurance coverage for the pregnancy-related medical conditions of the spouses of male employees as it provides for its female employees?

A. No. It is not necessary to provide the same level of coverage for the pregnancy-related medical conditions of spouses of male employees as for female employees. However, where the employer provides coverage for the medical conditions of the spouses of its employees, then the level of coverage for pregnancy-related medical conditions of the spouses of male employees must be the same as the level of coverage for all other medical conditions of the spouses of female employees.

Q. May an employer offer optional dependent coverage which excludes pregnancy-related medical conditions or offers less coverage for pregnancy-related medical conditions where the total premium for the optional coverage is paid by the employee?

A. No. Pregnancy-related medical conditions must be treated the same as other medical conditions under any health or disability insurance or sick leave plan *available in connection with employment,* regardless of who pays the premiums.

Q. Where an employer provides its employees a choice among several health insurance plans, must coverage for pregnancy-related conditions be offered in all of the plans?

A. Yes. Each of the plans must cover pregnancy-related conditions. For example, an employee with a single coverage policy cannot be forced to purchase a more expensive family coverage policy in order to receive coverage for her own pregnancy-related condition.

Q. On what basis should an employee be reimbursed for medical expenses arising from pregnancy, childbirth, or related conditions?

A. Pregnancy-related expenses should be reimbursed in the same manner as are expenses incurred for other medical conditions. Therefore, whether a plan reimburses the employees on a fixed basis, or a percentage of reasonable and customary charge basis, the same basis should be used for reimbursement of expenses incurred for pregnancy-related conditions.

Coverage provided by a health insurance program for other conditions must be provided for pregnancy-related conditions. For example, if a plan provides major medical coverage, pregnancy-related conditions must be so covered. Similarly, if a plan covers the cost of a private room for other conditions, the plan must cover the cost of a private room for pregnancy-related conditions. Finally, where a health insurance plan covers office visits to physicians, pre-natal and post-natal visits must be included in such coverage.

Q. May an employer limit payment of costs for pregnancy-related medical conditions to a specified dollar amount set forth in an insurance policy, collective bargaining agreement or other statement of benefits to which an employee is entitled?

A. The amounts payable for the costs incurred for pregnancy-related conditions can be limited only to the same extent as are costs for other conditions. Maximum recoverable dollar amounts may be specified for pregnancy-related conditions if such amounts are similarly specified for other conditions, and so long as the specified amounts in all instances cover the same proportion of actual costs. If, in addition to the scheduled amount for other procedures, additional costs are paid for, either directly or indirectly, by the employer, such additional payments must also be paid for pregnancy-related procedures.

Q. May an employer impose a different deductible for payment of costs for pregnancy-related medical conditions than for costs of other medical conditions?

A. No. Neither an additional deductible, an increase in the usual deductible, nor a larger deductible can be imposed for coverage for pregnancy-related medical costs.

Q. If a health insurance plan excludes the payment of benefits for any conditions existing at the time the insured's coverage becomes effective (pre-existing condition clause), can benefits be denied for medical costs arising from a pregnancy existing at the time the coverage became effective?

A. Yes. However, such benefits cannot be denied unless the pre-existing condition clause also excludes benefits for other pre-existing conditions in the same way.

Q. Can an employer self-insure benefits for pregnancy-related conditions if it does not self-insure benefits for other medical conditions?

A. Yes, so long as the benefits are the same. In measuring whether benefits are the same, factors other than the dollar coverage paid should be considered. Such factors include the range of choice of physicians and hospitals, and the processing and promptness of payment of claims.

Q. Can an employer discharge, refuse to hire or otherwise discriminate against a woman because she has had or is contemplating having an abortion?

A. No. An employer cannot discriminate in its employment practices against a woman who has had or is contemplating having an abortion.

Q. Is an employer required to provide fringe benefits for abortions if fringe benefits are provided for other medical conditions?

A. All fringe benefits other than health insurance, such as sick leave, which are provided for other medical conditions, must be provided for abortions. Health insurance, however, need be provided for abortions only where the life of the woman would be endangered if the fetus were carried to term or where medical complications arise from an abortion.

Q. If complications arise during the course of an abortion, as for instance excessive hemorrhaging, must an employer's health insurance plan cover the additional cost due to the complications of the abortion?

A. Yes. The plan is required to pay those additional costs attributable to the complications of the abortion. However, the employer is not required to pay for the abortion itself, except where the life of the mother would be endangered if the fetus were carried to term.

Q. May an employer elect to provide insurance coverage for abortions?

A. Yes. The Act specifically provides that an employer is not precluded from providing benefits for abortions whether directly or through a collective bargaining agreement, but if an employer decides to cover the costs of abortion, the employer must do so in the same manner and to the same degree as it covers other medical conditions.

Selected Bibliography

L. Dessem, *Sex Discrimination in Coaching*, 3 Harv. Women's Law Journal, 97 (1980).

K. Hull, *The Rights of Physically Handicapped People*, an American Civil Liberties Union Handbook (Discus/Avon 1979).

B. Schlei and P. Grossman, *Employment Discrimination Law* (BNA 1976) and Supp. 1979.

L. Tribe, *American Constitutional Law* (Foundation Press 1978) and Supp. 1979.

Protecting At Will Employees Against Wrongful Discharge: The Duty to Terminate Only in Good Faith, 93 Harv. L.Rev. 1816 (1980).

ADDITIONAL TITLES IN ACLU HANDBOOK SERIES

THE RIGHTS OF ALIENS by David Carliner

THE RIGHTS OF CANDIDATES AND VOTERS by Burt Neuborne and Arthur Eisenberg

THE RIGHTS OF DOCTORS, NURSES & ALLIED HEALTH PROFESSIONALS by George J. Annas, Leonard H. Glantz and Barbara F. Katz

THE RIGHTS OF EX-OFFENDERS by David Rudenstine

THE RIGHTS OF GOVERNMENT EMPLOYEES by Robert O'Neil

THE RIGHTS OF LAWYERS & CLIENTS by Stephen Gillers

THE RIGHTS OF MENTAL PATIENTS by Bruce J. Ennis & Richard D. Emery

THE RIGHTS OF MENTALLY RETARDED PERSONS by Paul R. Friedman

THE RIGHTS OF MILITARY PERSONNEL by Robert S. Rivkin and Barton F. Stichman

THE RIGHTS OF OLDER PERSONS by Robert N. Brown

THE RIGHTS OF PARENTS by Alan Sussman and Martin Guggenheim

THE RIGHTS OF PHYSICALLY HANDICAPPED PEOPLE by Kent Hull

THE RIGHTS OF POLICE OFFICERS by Gilda Brancato and Elliot E. Polebaum

THE RIGHTS OF THE POOR by Sylvia A. Law

THE RIGHTS OF RACIAL MINORITIES by Richard Larson and Laughlin McDonald

THE RIGHTS OF REPORTERS by Joel A. Gora

THE RIGHTS OF STUDENTS by Alan H. Levine and Eve Cary

THE RIGHTS OF SUSPECTS by Oliver Rosengart

THE RIGHTS OF TENANTS by Richard E. Blumberg and James R. Grow

THE RIGHTS OF UNION MEMBERS by Clyde W. Summers and Robert J. Rabin

THE RIGHTS OF VETERANS by David F. Addlestone, Susan H. Hewman & Frederic J. Gross

YOUR RIGHTS TO PRIVACY by Trudy Hayden and Jack Novik

The books are available from the
ACLU, 132 W. 43 St.,
New York, N.Y. 10036

AMERICAN CIVIL LIBERTIES UNION HANDBOOKS

We Deliver!
And So Do These Bestsellers.